BYZANTIUM
The Apogee

BYZANTIUM

The Apogee

JOHN JULIUS NORWICH

Alfred A. Knopf   *New York*   1992

Contents

List of Illustrations

Maps

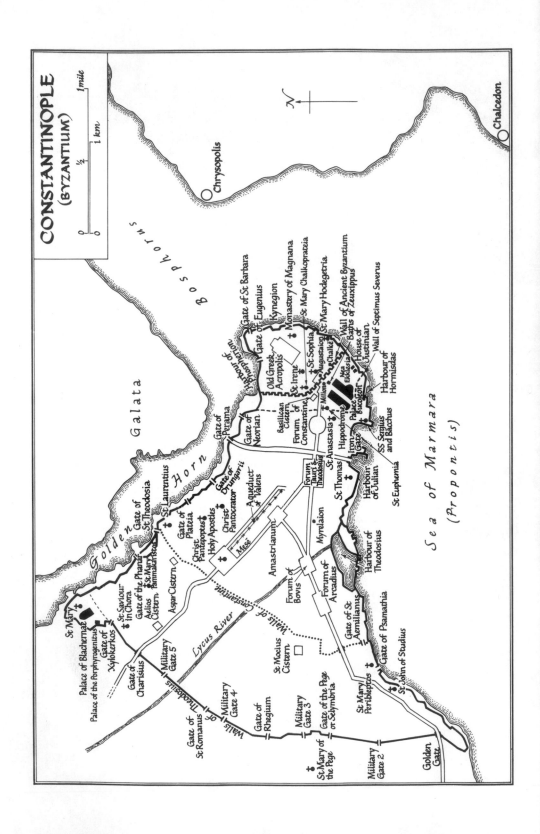

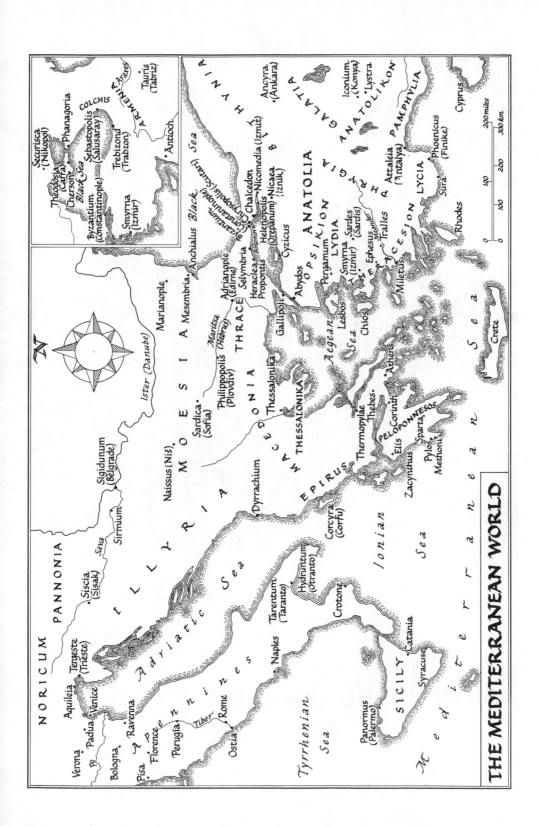

THE MEDITERRANEAN WORLD

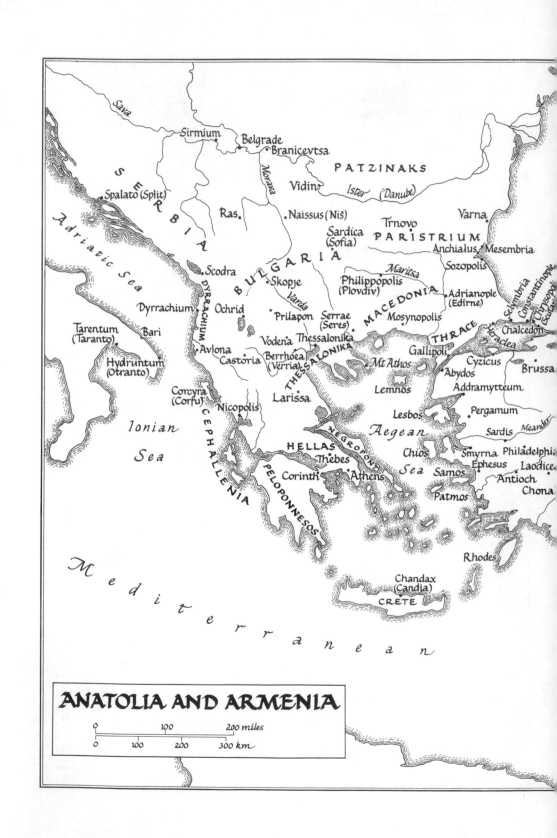

Sava

Sirmium
Belgrade
Branicevtsa

PATZINAKS

S E R B I A

Spalato (Split)

Morava

Vidin

Ister (Danube)

Varna

Ras.

Naissus (Niš)

Sardica
(Sofia)

Trnovo

PARISTRIUM

Anchialus.•Mesembria

Adriatic Sea

Scodra

B U L G A R I A

Maritsa

Sozopolis

Scymbria
Constantinople
Chrysopolis
(Scutari)

Skopje

Philippopolis
(Plovdiv)

Adrianople
(Edirne)

Dyrrachium

DYRRACHIUM

Ochrid

Varda

Prilapon

Serrae
(Seres)

MACEDONIA

Mosynopolis

THRACE

Heraclea

Chalcedon

Tarentum
(Taranto)

Bari

Vodena

Thessalonika

Gallipoli

Cyzicus

Brussa

Avlona

Castoria

Berrhoea
(Verria)

THESSALONIKA

•Mt Athos

Abydos

Hydruntum
(Otranto)

Addramytteum

Corcyra
(Corfu)

Nicopolis

Larissa

Lemnos

Pergamum

Ionian

Sea

CEPHALLENIA

Aegean

Lesbos

Sardis

Meander

HELLAS

NEGROPONT

Sea

Chios

Smyrna

Philadelphia

Thebes

Ephesus

Laodice

Corinth

Athens

Samos

Antioch

PELOPONNESOS

Patmos

Chona

Rhodes

M
e
d
i
t
e
r
r
a
n
e
a
n

Chandax
(Candia)

CRETE

ANATOLIA AND ARMENIA

0   100   200 miles

0   100   200   300 km

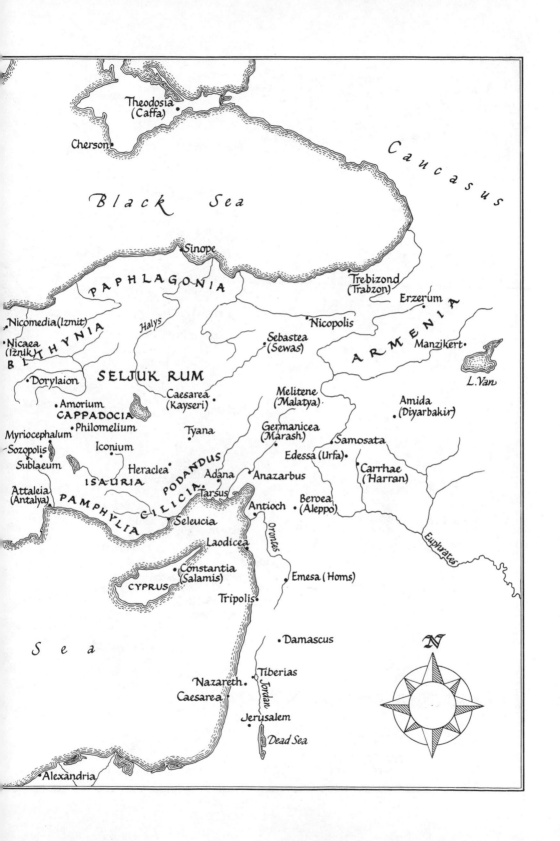

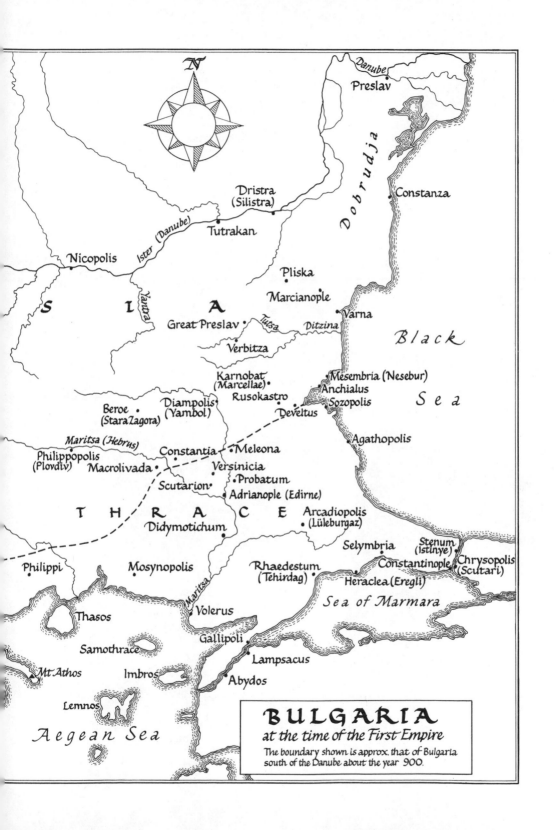

N

Danube
Preslav

Dristra
(Silistra)

Tutrakan

Constanza

Dobrudja

Ister (Danube)

Nicopolis

Yantra

Pliska

S · L · A

Marcianople

Black

Great Preslav

Tutsa

Varna

Ditzina

Verbitza

Sea

Karnobat
(Marcellae)

Mesembria (Nesebur)

Diampolis
(Yambol)

Rusokastro

Anchialus

Beroe
(Stara Zagora)

Develtus

Sozopolis

Maritsa (Hebrus)

Constantia

Meleona

Agathopolis

Philippopolis
(Plovdiv)

Macrolivada

Versinicia

Scutarion

Probatum

T · H · R · A · C · E

Adrianople (Edirne)

Didymotichum

Arcadiopolis
(Lüleburgaz)

Selymbria

Stenum
(Istinye)

Philippi

Mosynopolis

Rhaedestum
(Tehirdag)

Constantinople

Chrysopolis
(Scutari)

Heraclea (Eregli)

Maritsa

Sea of Marmara

Thasos

Volerus

Samothrace

Gallipoli

Lampsacus

Mt Athos

Imbros

Abydos

Lemnos

Aegean Sea

BULGARIA
at the time of the First Empire
The boundary shown is approx. that of Bulgaria
south of the Danube about the year 900.

Family Trees

THE AMORIAN DYNASTY

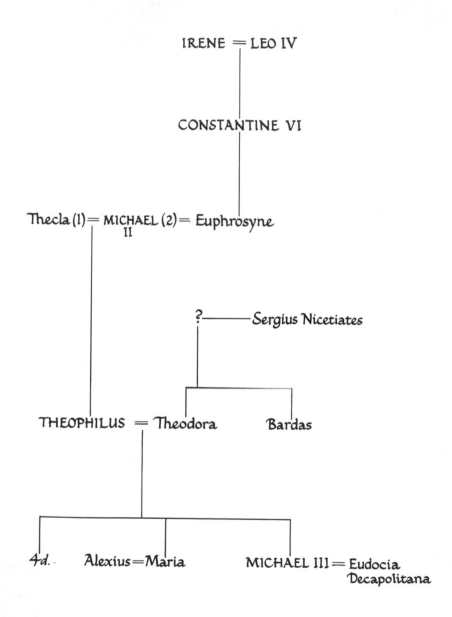

IRENE = LEO IV

CONSTANTINE VI

Thecla (1) = MICHAEL (2) = Euphrosyne
II

? —————— Sergius Nicetiates

THEOPHILUS = Theodora   Bardas

4 d.   Alexius = Maria   MICHAEL III = Eudocia
                                              Decapolitana

THE MACEDONIAN DYNASTY

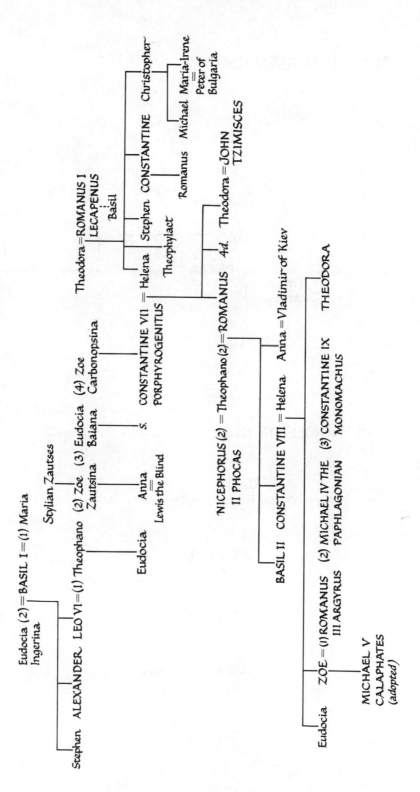

THE BULGARIAN KHANS

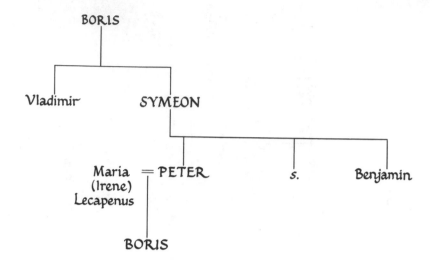

BORIS

Vladimir   SYMEON

Maria = PETER   s.   Benjamin
(Irene)
Lecapenus

BORIS

THE PRINCES OF KIEV

Rurik
Grand Prince of Kiev

Igor = Olga

Svyatoslav

Vladimir = Anna

Introduction

There is little to be said by way of introduction to this book, whose purpose is simply to continue the story which I began three years ago with its predecessor. In *Byzantium: The Early Centuries* I tried first to set the scene for Constantine the Great's tremendous decision to establish a new capital for the Roman Empire on the banks of the Bosphorus, and then to trace the fortunes of Constantine and his successors up to that memorable Christmas Day of AD 800 when Pope Leo III invested Charlemagne with the imperial crown and the title of Emperor of the Romans, thus – in effect if not in theory – calling into question the supposed unity of Christendom and giving Europe two Emperors instead of one.

The present volume covers a shorter period than the first: rather less than three centuries as opposed to rather more than five. This is partly because, as always throughout history, there is an acceleration in the march of events: ever greater numbers of characters make their appearance on the scene and the whole canvas of the Eastern Mediterranean becomes, in consequence, increasingly crowded. The principal reason, however, lies in the fact that the contemporary authorities for this second period are a good deal more informative. For the first centuries of the Byzantine era the surviving records are – as I pointed out in my earlier introduction – quite pitifully thin, and, moreover, as likely as not to contradict each other. As to their entertainment value, only Procopius affords any real enjoyment – although he, it must be said, makes up for a lot. Now, as the pace increases and the story builds up its own momentum, the chroniclers begin to proliferate and to enliven their accounts more and more frequently with portraits, descriptions and anecdotes. There are still isolated periods – the early eleventh century is a case in point – for which our sources are infuriatingly inadequate; but such periods are henceforth the exception rather than the rule. For the rest, thanks to such writers as Liudprand of Cremona, St Theophanes and his continuators, George Cedrenus, John Scylitzes and above all the odious but ever-fascinating Michael Psellus, we can enjoy an incomparably more colourful picture of life in the Imperial Palace of Byzantium in the early middle ages than we can of any other court in Europe. I have seized upon these writers with gratitude, and have quoted them, both directly and indirectly, with liberal – some may think too liberal – abandon; and if this has resulted in a reduction of the time spanned by the pages that follow, I can only say that it has seemed to me a price worth paying.

It has enabled me, too, to end this second volume, as I ended the first, with one of the most important events in all Byzantine history. But whereas the accession of Charlemagne, traumatic as it was, proved a good deal less prejudicial to the Empire of the East than was generally believed at the time, the battle of Manzikert was an unmitigated catastrophe, the full significance of which was revealed with the gradual realization that the Empire had effectively lost, in the space of a few nightmare hours, three-quarters of Asia Minor – the territory on which it most relied and the most valuable that it possessed. And that loss, as it turned out, was only the beginning: once the Turks had overrun part of the Anatolian heartland it would be only a question of time before they occupied it all. The Balkan peninsula would follow; and then, finally, Constantinople itself. The Oriental conquerors were not inclined to hurry; the whole process would take them the best part of four centuries. But there can be no question that the advance that ended on Tuesday, 29 May 1453, when Sultan Mehmet II touched his turban to the floor of St Sophia in prayer and thanksgiving, had its origin on the distant field of Manzikert, 382 years before.

In the decade immediately following that most shattering and shameful defeat, while more and more of Asia Minor was engulfed in the Seljuk tide and the governments of Michael VII and Nicephorus III watched in helpless paralysis while the Empire descended further and further into anarchy, few intelligent Byzantines could have doubted that its days were numbered. But then, as happens so often in Byzantine history – for was not Constantinople known to enjoy divine protection? – came last-minute salvation. After a dozen near-grotesque occupants of the throne in little more than half a century, the figure of Alexius Comnenus takes on positively heroic proportions. The present book, of which the last page records his coronation on Easter Sunday 1081, thus ends on a note of hope; the story of how that hope was realized, however, must await the third volume – which will, I trust, bring the long story to a close.

It remains only for me to add my usual *caveat*: that although I have done everything I can do to make it as accurate as the existing sources permit, this book, like its predecessor, makes no claim to academic rigour. I knew little about Byzantium when I began writing about it, and shall doubtless have forgotten a good deal of what I have written soon after I come to the close. If I tend to give economic considerations less than their due, this is because I am not an economist and a three-volume work is quite long enough already. Similarly, if I concentrate on the personalities of Emperors and Empresses rather than on sociological developments, I can only plead that I prefer people to trends. Similarly, I have made no great efforts at consistency where the spelling of proper names is concerned. I have usually preferred the Latin version of the name, merely because it will probably be more familiar to English readers. On the other hand, where the Greek has seemed more suitable I have not hesitated to use it.

Those who wish to sink their teeth into something more challenging need look no further than the Bibliography, where they will find the titles of many books of formidable scholarship; this one is not for them. From the outset my only object has been to provide the interested non-specialist with the sort of bird's-eye view of Byzantine history that I myself wanted when I first fell under the spell of the Eastern Mediterranean. The measure of my success must remain an open question: even in this relatively modest undertaking there is still the best part of four centuries to go. But we have now comfortably passed the point of no return; I, at least, am enjoying myself; and if I can persuade other kindred spirits to share my enjoyment I shall be happy indeed.

John Julius Norwich
London, Christmas 1990

I

Krum

[800–14]

Even were we birds, we could not hope to escape.

The Emperor Nicephorus I,
just before his death

When, on Christmas Day, AD 800, Pope Leo III lowered the imperial crown on to the head of Charles, son of Pepin the Frank, and prostrated himself before him as Emperor of Rome, the Empire of Byzantium had been in existence for 470 years. Founded in 330 by Constantine the Great, in the city to which he had officially given the name of New Rome but which we know as Constantinople, it had had to fight hard for its survival: in the West against the barbarian tribes – Goths and Huns, Vandals and Avars; in the East against the Persians and, all too soon after the destruction of the Sassanid Empire, the still more formidable menace of Islam. Over the centuries it had lost much. The Saracens had snatched away Palestine and Syria, North Africa and Egypt; much of Italy, reconquered by Justinian, had been forfeited to the Lombards, who in their turn had voluntarily surrendered it to the Pope. To past losses were added present anxieties: the Caliph Harun al-Rashid was exerting ever greater pressure on the Anatolian frontier; nearer home, in the Balkans, the Bulgars posed a continual threat; while the Empire itself was still torn asunder by the violent controversy which, after three-quarters of a century, still showed no signs of solution: was it, or was it not, a sin to venerate icons and holy images of Jesus Christ, the Holy Virgin and the Saints?

This question had come to the fore as early as 726, when the Emperor Leo III,[1] 'the Isaurian', had ordered the destruction of the great golden icon of Christ which stood above the bronze doors of the Chalkē, the

---

1 Not, of course, to be confused with the Pope of the same name, who was to succeed to the throne of St Peter some seventy years later.

main entrance to the Imperial Palace in Constantinople. Four years later he had issued a more general edict, directed against all images throughout the Empire; and the iconoclasm that he had set in train was pursued with still greater fanaticism by his son, Constantine V. Only after Constantine's death in 775 did the pendulum swing back in favour of the iconodules – the worshippers, or at least the venerators, of images – thanks to the machinations of his deeply unpleasant daughter-in-law, the Empress Irene.

Though Irene's husband, the weak and feckless Leo IV, was temperamentally an iconoclast like his father, he was completely dominated by his wife; in any case he died at thirty-one, leaving her as Regent for their ten-year-old son Constantine VI. And when that son, having grown to manhood, attempted to take over the authority that was rightfully his, his mother unhesitatingly had him blinded, in a particularly barbarous manner which caused his death soon afterwards – as she had known perfectly well that it would. She thus became the first woman to reign, not just as a regent but in her own right, over the Byzantine Empire. Always a passionate iconodule, she had no difficulty in restoring the cult of images and even succeeded in getting it formally defined and approved at the second Council of Nicaea in 787; but in all other respects she proved a disaster. By the end of the century she had reduced the Empire to penury and brought it to the brink of revolution.

It was at this moment of universal dissatisfaction and plunging morale that a new threat presented itself: a threat that was neither economic nor even military and was indeed unlike any that Byzantium had ever faced before, directed as it was against the very cornerstone on which the Empire had been founded – the union of the Roman Empire with the Christian faith. This union was, in Byzantine eyes, symbolized and personified by the Emperor himself, at once the successor of Augustus and God's Vice-Gerent, the Elect of Christ, Equal of the Apostles. It followed that, just as there was but a single Ruler in heaven, so – although he might choose to share his throne for purely administrative reasons – there could be but a single Emperor on earth, any challenge to whose divinely ordained authority was not only treason but blasphemy. The fact that there had been many such challenges over the centuries is immaterial: consciousness of sin seldom serves to prevent it. The important point to remember is that this concept – of an Emperor occupying a higher spiritual plane than his subjects and standing, as it were, half-way to heaven – was no abstruse doctrine; on the contrary, it was a firm conviction, consciously held by virtually every Byzantine from the *basileus* himself to the meanest peasant: an article of faith at least as universal as, let us say, Christianity in Victorian England. No wonder that the reaction to the news of the coronation in Rome, when it reached Constantinople at the beginning of 801, was one of incredulity and horror.

How much of the Byzantine theory of Empire was understood by Charlemagne, as he rose from his knees before the high altar of St Peter's that Christmas morning, we shall never know. To him, however, the question would have been largely academic; for in his eyes the imperial throne of Byzantium was not tottering but vacant. According to the old Salic tradition in which he had been raised, no woman might wear a crown except as consort of her husband; and Pope Leo, we may assume, fully shared his views. Thus – despite the fateful ceremony just completed – the Roman Empire remained, so far as either of them was concerned, one and indivisible, with Charles as its Emperor. All that had happened was that the Pope had arrogated to himself the right to appoint and invest the Emperor of the Romans – a right which for nearly five centuries had been exercised by Byzantium.

At the same time there was no denying that Irene claimed for herself every inch of imperial territory, and little doubt that the coronation, with all that it implied, would be furiously contested in Constantinople; and it was with this thought uppermost in his mind that in 802 Charlemagne sent ambassadors to the Empress to seek her hand in marriage. For him, the advantages were self-evident: with all the imperial domains of East and West united under a single crown the Empire would once again be a single entity, just as Constantine had conceived it. Nor, even, would there be any members of Irene's family to contest the succession after her death; she herself had most efficiently seen to that.

The Empress too – unlike any of her subjects – was inclined to look favourably on the idea. Marriage to Charles would mean an opportunity to refill her empty treasury and, more important still, might even avert the insurrection that she was aware could not long be delayed. It would also offer a chance of escape from the suffocating and intrigue-ridden atmosphere of Constantinople. Her advisers, on the other hand, when they had recovered from their astonishment – for, as an imaginative German historian once pointed out, the effect on them of such a proposal must have been roughly equivalent to the effect on an eighteenth-century Viennese of a suggested match between the Empress Maria Theresa and the Negus of Abyssinia – would have none of it: how

3

could they possibly sanction the surrender of the Roman Empire to an uncouth and illiterate barbarian? Before the year was out a group of senior officials, led by Irene's long-suffering Logothete of the Treasury (effectively her Minister of Finance) declared her deposed and sent her off – to her own scarcely disguised relief – into exile on the not entirely appropriate island of Lesbos, where she died soon afterwards.

The story of Charlemagne's coronation and of his marriage *manqué* has been told in rather more detail, and its significance more thoroughly discussed, in the first volume of this history; it has seemed worthwhile to summarize it here merely to remind the reader of the point at which that volume ended and to set the scene for the events to follow. And the first of those events is the accession to the throne of Byzantium of the leader of the palace revolt which deposed Irene: the former Logothete of the Treasury, who now assumed the name and title of Nicephorus I.

The new Emperor is said to have been of Arab extraction, a descendant of King Jaballah of Ghassan.[1] A man of vigour and determination, he was firmly resolved to set the Empire to rights after the damage done by his predecessor, and not perhaps unduly concerned about the methods by which this object was to be achieved. No one, certainly, better understood the gravity of the imperial condition. Irene's determination to purge the army of all traces of iconoclasm had resulted in a disastrous weakening of its strength, of which the enemies of the Empire were swift to take advantage. Unable to restrain them by force of arms, she had been obliged to offer vast annual tributes to both the Bulgar Khan and the Caliph Harun al-Rashid; and, to make matters worse, the constant irruptions of the Caliph's armies into Asia Minor had wrought havoc among the immense numbers of peasant small-holders with military obligations on whom, since the days of Justinian II in the late seventh century, the defence of the Empire had been based. Many of these, driven from their homes, had drifted to the capital; thus, instead of swelling the exchequer with their regular taxes, they were now a further drain on it with their unceasing demands for food and maintenance. Their farms meanwhile fell prey to the rapacity of the big land-owners – and, in particular, to the monasteries, which Irene had most irresponsibly exempted from all taxation. Having also seen fit to remit the residence tax payable by all free citizens of Constantinople, the tax

---

1 A Christian-Arab enclave in Syria.

on receipts[1] and half the customs duties levied on imports at Abydos and in the straits, she had succeeded in the space of a very few years in bringing the Empire perilously close to financial and fiscal suicide. The *coup* which led to her downfall had been launched not a moment too soon.

It was Nicephorus's misfortune to have aroused the fury and intense hatred of the monkish chronicler Theophanes, our only full – and generally reliable – contemporary source for the period, for whom the Emperor ranks only a little above Antichrist. For many centuries, in consequence, he suffered an extremely bad press. There were in fact few men more experienced, or better qualified, to set Byzantium back on its financial feet. Irene's tax exemptions were countermanded; other levies were massively increased. Destitute small-holders were drafted into the regular army, the cost of their equipment – valued at 18½ gold pieces – being compulsorily met by their more prosperous neighbours. Private loans to merchants were forbidden; shipowners were permitted to raise money only from the State, which charged exorbitant interest at the rate of almost 17 per cent. Nor did the Emperor hesitate, as had so many of his predecessors, to move against the Church; he instructed his provincial officials to treat bishops and clergy 'like slaves', giving them full authority to sequestrate gold and silver plate as necessary. The monasteries he treated with even more contempt (a fact which does much to explain the wrath of Theophanes), quartering troops upon them, authorizing the imperial land commission to confiscate certain of their properties without according them corresponding fiscal relief and levying poll-tax on the families of their tenants and employees. None of this, obviously, was a recipe for popularity; but under his direction the economy was soon on a sounder footing than it had been for years.

It needed to be; for one of Nicephorus's first actions on his accession had been to write to the Caliph, informing him that he intended to pay no further tribute and even demanding the restitution of the immense sums disbursed by his predecessor. Harun's only reply was to launch an immediate attack, which proved the more damaging when in 803 the Byzantine commander, an Armenian named Bardanes Turcus, suddenly

1 It must be said in Irene's favour that the tax on receipts was, by its very nature, particularly liable to abuse. Theodore of the Studium – one of the Empress's few admirers – describes (*Epistolae*, i, 6) the sufferings of tradesmen of every kind, and the positive infestation of fiscal officers on every road and along every coast. 'When a traveller came to some narrow defile, he would be startled by the sudden appearance of a tax-gatherer, sitting aloft like a thing uncanny' (*A History of the Later Roman Empire*, Bury, p. 3).

rebelled and proclaimed himself Emperor.[1] The revolt was almost immediately crushed, but not before the Saracens had made considerable territorial gains – which they were to increase substantially in the years that followed. In 806 a Muslim army of 135,000, led by the Caliph in person, drove deep into Cappadocia, capturing Tyana – now an insignificant village called Kalesihisar but then an important city and a bishopric – and withdrawing only after a payment of 50,000 gold pieces as a ransom.

Fortunately for the Empire, Harun died three years later; but by that time Nicephorus was occupied on two other fronts. The first was the area which we now know as Greece, in particular the Theme of Hellas – roughly comprising Attica, Boeotia and Phocis – and the Peloponnese. In the sixth century, Slav settlers had overrun this whole region, thus seriously weakening Byzantine influence: in the Peloponnese there had not been a single imperial garrison since 747, and the Emperor's writ had long ceased to run. Fortunately the immigrants had shown themselves a mild and peace-loving people, who asked nothing more than to be left to cultivate their land unmolested; but after the rise of the Bulgars and their large-scale incursions into Macedonia there had been a grave danger that the situation might change, swiftly and for the worse. One huge Slavonic bloc, united and belligerent, extending from the Danube to Cape Matapan, was not a possibility that the Byzantines cared to contemplate.

The Emperor's fears were confirmed when in 805 a considerable force of Slavs attacked the city of Patras on the Gulf of Corinth. They were repulsed, but not without some difficulty; and the incident encouraged Nicephorus to embark on a wholesale resettlement of the Peloponnese, to which he brought vast numbers of his Greek-speaking subjects from all over the Empire – including substantial colonies from Calabria and Sicily. With them of course came the Christian religion, to which the Slavs had not yet been converted and which since their arrival had been very largely forgotten. As with most resettlement programmes, the majority of those who were obliged to abandon their homelands for a

---

1 The story goes that soon after his revolt Bardanes, accompanied by three of his closest associates, decided to consult a hermit of Philomelion, near Antioch, who was widely believed to possess the gift of prophecy. The hermit fixed the general with a piercing eye and shook his head: there was no hope for him. Then, turning his gaze towards the others, he foretold that two of them would wear the imperial crown and that the third would come near to doing so. The first two proved to be the future Leo V and Michael II; the third was Thomas the Slav. (See p. 32.)

terra incognita peopled, so far as they knew, by hostile barbarians did so only through fear of the consequences of refusal; but without Nicephorus's wise and far-sighted policy the later history of the Balkan peninsula might have been different indeed.

This argument acquires additional force when we remember that the first decade of the ninth century saw the rise of the most formidable leader that the Bulgar nation had ever produced. His name was Krum. Of his origins we know nothing. All that can be said for certain is that in the first years of the century he utterly annihilated the Avars, who now disappear from history never to return; and that in 807 he somehow rose to supremacy, uniting the Bulgars of the Danube basin with those who lived across the Carpathians in Pannonia and Transylvania and welding them together to form a military force unprecedented in Bulgar history. In that same year the Emperor, taking advantage of the dearly-bought truce on his eastern frontier, decided to lead an expedition against them; but he had got no further than Adrianople when he uncovered a conspiracy among his officers and abruptly abandoned the campaign. Now it was Krum's turn to take the initiative. In the late autumn of 808 he surprised a large Byzantine army encamped near the mouth of the river Strymon and totally destroyed it, and in the spring of 809 he tricked his way into Serdica – the modern Sofia – razing the fortress and slaughtering the entire garrison, 6,000 strong.

Unpopular as he was, Nicephorus had never been so openly reviled by his subjects in the streets of his capital as when the news of the massacre reached Constantinople on the Thursday before Easter. He had proved, they grumbled, not only rapacious and grasping but a woefully incompetent leader in the field. Of the two campaigns that he had launched against Krum one had been still-born, abandoned before a single arrow had been loosed, while the other had ended in an annihilating defeat. This time, however, their Emperor gave them no cause for complaint. His blood, too, was up. Leaving the capital at once with the army, by dint of forced marches he had reached the Bulgar capital, Pliska, by Easter Sunday – finding it, to his delight, virtually undefended. His men fell on it like locusts – burning, pillaging, reducing the Khan's wooden palace to ashes. Passing on to Serdica, he paused to rebuild the fortress; then, well pleased with his achievement, he returned in triumph to Constantinople.

But Krum was not defeated, and Nicephorus knew it. All the next year was spent in preparing what he was determined would be his last

7

great offensive against the Bulgar Khan – an offensive that would eliminate him and his loathsome tribe as effectively as Krum himself had eliminated the Avars less than a decade before. Since the death of Harun the eastern frontier had been quiet, the Caliph's sons being too busy quarrelling among themselves to pay any attention to Byzantium. The armies of the Asian Themes were accordingly summoned to join their European colleagues; and in May 811 an immense host marched out through the Golden Gate, the Emperor himself and his son Stauracius at its head.

To begin with, all went well. Before so massive a force the Bulgars could only retreat. Once again Pliska was devastated, Nicephorus – who, if we are to believe Theophanes, seems to have suffered some sort of breakdown – sparing neither women nor children: there is a terrible story of babies being hurled into threshing machines. The palace of the Khan, so recently rebuilt, was razed a second time to the ground. Desperate now, Krum sued for peace; but the Emperor was determined to finish the work that he had begun and marched on in search of the Bulgar army, which had fled into the mountains.

He was soon to regret his inflexibility. On Thursday, 24 July, still in pursuit of his prey, he led the bulk of his army through a rocky defile – probably the Pass of Verbitza, some thirty miles south of the modern Turgovishte in Bulgaria[1] – without first having ordered an adequate reconnaissance. The Bulgars, who had been secretly watching the invaders' every move, saw their chance: under cover of night they blockaded the gorge at each end with heavy wooden palisades. As dawn broke, Nicephorus realized that he had been drawn into a trap. Escape was impossible; he and his men were doomed. All that day they awaited the attack; but the Bulgars, still working on their fortifications, were in no hurry. Only in the early morning of Saturday the 26th did they strike.

The ensuing massacre continued all night and for much of the next day. The majority of the army was cut to pieces; of the remainder, many were burnt to death when the Bulgars fired the palisades, while others were crushed by artificially-induced landslides. A few managed to escape, chiefly cavalry; but these, hotly pursued by the Bulgar horsemen, plunged in their panic headlong into a nearby river in which many were

---

1 The exact site of the battle is still disputed; but the Pass of Verbitza – which was locally known as the 'Greek Hollow' until well into the present century – seems the most likely candidate. The question is more fully discussed by Sir Steven Runciman, *A History of the First Bulgarian Empire*, p. 57n.

drowned. Among the handful of survivors was the Emperor's son-in-law, Michael Rhangabe. His son Stauracius was less fortunate: paralysed by an appalling wound in the neck which had severed his spinal cord, he was carried back to Constantinople where he was to die, still in unspeakable agony, six months later.

As for Nicephorus himself, his body was retrieved where it fell and carried triumphantly back to the Bulgar camp. There the head was cut off, impaled on a stake and exposed for several days to public mockery. And even then the indignity was not complete: Krum had the skull mounted in silver, and for the rest of his life used it as his drinking cup.

On the Bosphorus, the news of the Emperor's death was received with horror. The Byzantines had to cast their minds back over more than four centuries to recall a comparable disaster: the last of their Emperors to have been killed in battle was Valens, at Adrianople in 378. Though they had never liked Nicephorus, they were acutely conscious of the humiliation that he – and they – had suffered at the hands of the Bulgar Khan. They knew, too, that although he had left the Empire financially sound, from the military point of view its situation could hardly have been worse. What was now needed above all was another strong leader, capable of rebuilding the army and of negotiating, from a position of at least some strength, with Charlemagne – whose demands for the recognition of his imperial claims were growing ever more insistent. Nothing of the kind, clearly, could be hoped for from the pitiable figure of Stauracius, whom his father had made co-Emperor as early as 803 but who now lay bedridden, paralysed and in constant pain, and for whom a merciful death could not be long delayed. Since he was childless, the obvious course was for him to abdicate in favour of the only other male member of the family of Nicephorus – the husband of his daughter Procopia, Michael Rhangabe, whose almost miraculous escape from the fatal battle suggested to many that he must enjoy some special divine favour. For reasons which are unclear Stauracius detested him, and made a feeble attempt to name as his successor his wife Theophano;[1] but he was in no condition to enforce a plan which, in the circumstances then

---

1 Theophano was an Athenian, whose apparent (though probably only distant) kinship with Irene had not debarred her from being placed on a short list, drawn up by command of Nicephorus, of dazzlingly beautiful virgins who might be possible brides for his son. She herself, we are given to understand, did not prove entirely satisfactory on either count; she was eventually selected only because Nicephorus decided to keep both her rivals for himself.

9

prevailing, might well have been catastrophic. Accordingly on 2 October 811, without the dying Emperor's consent or even his knowledge, Michael was crowned and acclaimed as *basileus* – the first in Byzantine history to bear a name that was neither Greek nor Roman, but Hebrew. Stauracius, meanwhile, was tonsured and hastily dispatched to a monastery, where three months later the death he had so longed for came to him at last.

The Emperor Michael I was now in the prime of his manhood. His round face, we are told, was framed by curls of thick black hair and a full beard. It soon became clear, however, that such gifts as heaven had been pleased to bestow upon him included neither intelligence nor firmness of character. He proved weak-willed and easily led, a natural puppet who would allow himself to be manipulated by anyone who managed to seize the strings; and since he was also profoundly religious, it was hardly surprising that the principal manipulators during his brief reign should have been the two leading churchmen of the day: Nicephorus, Patriarch of Constantinople and Theodore, Abbot of the Studium. Nicephorus had been appointed by his imperial namesake to succeed Patriarch Tarasius on the latter's death in 806. Like Tarasius, he had been up to that time a civil servant and a layman: his enthronement in the patriarchal chair had occurred exactly a week after his first receiving the tonsure.[1] A man of considerable ability and utter integrity, he was also the author of one of the few trustworthy sources for the period of history extending from the reign of Heraclius to that of Constantine V; we can only regret that he did not continue it into his own day. But although he proved a devout churchman and a staunch supporter of the holy images, he was from the moment of his appointment looked on by the extremist monastic party – led by Theodore of the Studium – with hatred and mistrust.

The reason for this attitude is not far to seek: Theodore and his followers understandably considered Nicephorus an impostor: a tool of the Emperor who was an ecclesiastic only in name and whose very ordination had made a mockery of one of the most solemn sacraments of the Church. They had taken precisely the same view of his predecessor Tarasius – a view for which they had found ample confirmation when in 795 Tarasius had permitted the young Constantine VI to pack off his wife, Mary of Amnia, to a nunnery and go through a form of marriage

---

1 In the Orthodox Church, bishops were – and still are – always chosen from the monasteries rather than from the parish priesthood.

with one of the ladies of his court, Theodotē. Their anger at such conduct – despite the mildly embarrassing fact that the lady in question was a cousin of Abbot Theodore's – had been to some extent appeased when the celebrant at the marriage ceremony, an unfortunate cleric by the name of Joseph, was subsequently excommunicated; but a decade later, in 806, the Emperor had called a synod which rehabilitated him. The decision was endorsed by the new Patriarch and the whole affair blew up again, Theodore being sent away – for the second time – into exile.

For as long as the Emperor Nicephorus lived, there could be no hope of reconciliation between the moderates and the extremists. Constantine VI was long since in his grave, and insofar as the question of his marriage was not by this time entirely academic it is probably safe to say that the *basileus* disapproved of it almost as much as Theodore himself; but that was not the point. The vital necessity, so far as the Emperor was concerned, was to establish the principle that – if he desired it and a synod of the Church decreed it – dispensation could be granted, even on a matter of canon law. And to attain that object, what became known as the Moechian dispute (*moicheia* being the Greek word for adultery) provided a test case as valid as any other.

But now Nicephorus was dead too, and his gutless son-in-law was as unable as he was unwilling to prolong the quarrel. The Patriarch himself felt much the same way, and in any case realized that in the new circumstances prevailing the two factions must be reconciled. Having made it a condition of Michael's coronation that he should sign an undertaking to uphold the Orthodox faith and to grant to monks and clergy alike immunity from corporal punishment or physical constraint, he encouraged the Emperor to recall Abbot Theodore and his fellow-exiles, and even to reimpose the sentence of excommunication on poor Joseph. In doing so, he may have obtained rather more than he bargained for: Theodore, who was for all his bigotry a man of formidable energy and personal magnetism, quickly acquired immense influence over the Emperor – who consulted him on everything, whether or not Church affairs were involved, and invariably followed his advice.

There has been something of a fashion among more recent historians to credit Michael I – and through him Theodore of the Studium – with the dramatic reversal in the Byzantine attitude towards the West that took place about this time. Nicephorus I had for most of his reign simply ignored Charlemagne's imperial claims – a policy which had not been rewarded with any striking success, having resulted in a somewhat desultory naval war with the Franks and having led, indirectly, to the defection of the young Republic of Venice.[1] What easier explanation could there be for the sudden change of heart in Constantinople than the fact that, after the disaster of 811, the Empire was no longer capable of pursuing the war, and that the death of the ever-inflexible Nicephorus enabled his easy-going successor to open peace negotiations?

None: but for the fact that imperial ambassadors are known to have passed through Venice on their way to Charlemagne's court at Aachen in the late autumn of 810, and that agreement was almost certainly reached on all major issues some time in the spring of 811 – several weeks, at the very least, before the annihilation of the Byzantine army. True, it was another year before new envoys – now representing Michael – went to acclaim Charlemagne as Emperor, and another three before the treaty was finally ratified; but there can be no doubt that the initial olive branch, such as it was, was extended by Nicephorus; and to him, more than to his successor or to Theodore, must be given the credit for the ensuing peace. It was not to be known as the *Pax Nicephori* for nothing.

Perhaps, on reflection, he had found himself wondering whether an Emperor of the West was, after all, such a very bad idea. Constantinople might be the New Rome, the heir to Roman civilization, law and traditions; but Constantinople was by now Greek through and through. It had nothing – not even language, not even religion – in common with the new Europe that was beginning to emerge beyond the Adriatic; nor did it any longer wield any effective power in those regions. It was Aachen, not Byzantium, that had re-established the *Pax Romana* in the West. The Roman Empire must remain indivisible, of that there could be no question; but would two Emperors necessarily divide it? So long as they remained on good terms with each other might they not, on the contrary, give it new strength?

Charlemagne, for his part, was prepared to offer excellent terms. He would relinquish all claims to Venice and to the entire province of Venetia, together with the cities of Istria and the Dalmatian coast; all he

---

1 Although Venice had been effectively autonomous since 727, she had heretofore remained politically as well as culturally within the Byzantine sphere of influence; it had certainly caused a *frisson* of dismay in Greek hearts when, on Christmas Day 805, Doge Obelerio degli Antenori did homage to Charlemagne as Emperor of the West, returning to the lagoons with a Frankish bride – the first *dogaressa* known to history.

asked in return was the recognition of his imperial status and, in particular, the right to style himself *basileus* in official documents. In theory this meant that he would henceforth be the equal of the Byzantine Emperor, and that he and his heirs would enjoy the acknowledged right of succession to the throne of Constantinople; though whether such an interpretation was ever wholly accepted by the Byzantines even intellectually – they certainly never accepted it emotionally – is open to doubt.[1]

In the event, it hardly mattered. Charlemagne's Empire was to disintegrate within a few years of his death; not for a century and more – until the appearance of Otto the Great – would it regain its former stature, and neither then nor at any later time would there be any serious question of the succession of the Western Emperor as of right to the Byzantine throne. But the *Pax Nicephori* is no less important for that. It marked the acceptance, for the first time, of two simultaneous Roman Emperors: Emperors who were not sharing – even theoretically – a single throne for reasons of administrative convenience, according to the system attempted (with almost invariably disastrous results) by Diocletian and his successors, but who were genuinely independent of each other, each pursuing his own policies but at the same time fully recognizing and respecting the claims and titles of his counterpart. And, in doing so, it created the mould in which later medieval Europe was to be formed.

The dying Stauracius had been right in opposing the succession of Michael Rhangabe. Had it not been for the peace with Charlemagne over which he was fortunate enough to preside, the reign of that hapless monarch would have been one of almost unmitigated catastrophe. Again in marked contrast to his predecessor, he and his wife Procopia – whose coronation had taken place a mere ten days after his own – were almost insanely prodigal with money, lavishing huge sums on churches and monasteries and, it sometimes seemed, on anyone who asked for it. In one department only did Michael refuse to loosen his purse-strings – or indeed to take any interest at all: that which was concerned with the defence of his Empire.

And seldom had the Empire needed it more. In the spring of 812 Krum, encouraged by his triumph of the previous year, had seized Develtus, a fortified Byzantine town on the Black Sea commanding the

---

1 It is worth noting, too, that they were careful never to call Charlemagne Emperor *of the Romans* – a style which they reserved for their own ruler and were indeed to use with increasing frequency from this time forward.

coast road to the south, and forcibly carried off all its inhabitants – including the bishop – to his own territory. In June Michael set out to confront him; but the newly-recruited army, untried and virtually untrained, mutinied almost at once and he was obliged to return. Inevitably, the news of his withdrawal spread quickly through Thrace and Macedonia whose populations, realizing that they were now at Krum's mercy, fled in terror. Several of the smaller frontier fortresses were completely abandoned; abandoned too, in a large measure, were the important strong-points of Anchialus and Beroe – now the Bulgarian towns of Pomorie and Stara Zagora – whose defences had been only recently repaired by Irene. The infection spread even as far as Philip-popolis (Plovdiv), the chief city of western Thrace.

Such panic proved unfounded, at least for the time being. Krum, who saw no reason to fight for anything that he could get for nothing, proposed peace. In the circumstances, Michael should have leapt at the chance; but it so happened that the conditions offered by the Khan included the perfectly reasonable demand that all Bulgar prisoners and deserters in Byzantine hands should be returned to him. This was more than Abbot Theodore could stomach. Quoting – quite inappropriately – the words of Christ as recorded by St John, 'He that cometh to me I will in no wise cast out',[1] he easily persuaded the Emperor to reject the terms; and the war was resumed.

Krum's next target was Mesembria (Nesebur), one of the richest ports in the whole Balkan peninsula. Itself almost an island, it was joined to the mainland only by a narrow and heavily fortified isthmus some quarter of a mile long. Since the Bulgars had no ships, this was their only possible point of attack; in the old days a few vessels of the imperial navy would have been enough to maintain supplies of food and ammunition for an indefinite period. But the navy, after years of neglect, was now in the last stages of disrepair and Michael made no attempt to revictual the city.

As the siege began, Patriarch Nicephorus held a service of intercession in the Church of the Holy Apostles in Constantinople. Half-way through the ceremony there was a sudden commotion: a section of the congregation, including a large group of recently demobilized army veterans, surrounded the great marble tomb of Constantine V and besought the dead Emperor to burst his cerements and to lead them again, as so often

---

1 John 6:37.

in the past, to victory and salvation. Their prayers, it need hardly be said, went unanswered; but the point had been made, and the conclusion was not hard to draw. The victorious Constantine had been an iconoclast; under his three icon-loving successors the Empire had, time and time again, been humiliated and brought low. The pendulum, in short, was once again ready to swing: one more defeat, and it would surely do so.

That defeat was not long in coming. On 5 November 812 Mesembria fell. With it there passed into Krum's hands vast stores of gold and silver and, more precious still, canisters of liquid Greek fire – the Empire's most effective and most secret weapon – together with thirty-six bronze siphons with which to discharge it. To the Emperor in Constantinople, it was now clear that if he wished to retain his throne he would have to march once more against his adversary; and this time he would have to win. All that winter he spent gathering troops, from every corner of the Empire; and in May 813 he marched from his capital, Procopia accompanying him as far as Heraclea on the Marmara and waving him goodbye from the aqueduct.

The Bulgar army was always notoriously difficult to engage in battle until it was ready to fight; and Michael, doubtless remembering his hair's-breadth escape in 811, appears to have been unwilling to enter enemy territory. For over a month he dithered in Thrace, while the Asiatic troops – who were in the overwhelming majority – grew steadily more restive. Only in early June did Krum himself cross the frontier; and at last, on the field of Versinicia some twenty miles north-east of Adrianople, the armies came face to face. The imperial forces easily outnumbered the Bulgars; but Michael still seemed reluctant to take the initiative and for another sweltering fortnight he and Krum stood watching each other. It was not till 21 June that John Aplakes, commander of the Macedonian regiment on the left wing, sought his Emperor's permission to attack. On the next day he did so. The Bulgars fell back in confusion before his onslaught, and for a moment it looked as if the battle were over almost before it had begun. But then an astonishing thing happened: the Anatolian troops on the right, commanded by Leo the Armenian, suddenly turned tail and fled from the field.

At first, we are told, Krum stood speechless, refusing to believe the evidence of his own eyes; then, realizing their good fortune, he and his men fell on the luckless Macedonians – abandoned by their comrades and now, in their turn, hopelessly outnumbered – and slaughtered them wholesale. Their way was now clear: nothing more lay between them and Constantinople. On 17 July the Bulgar army pitched its camp beneath the walls of the city.

By this time, however, Michael Rhangabe was no longer Emperor. Escaping from the battle once again unscathed, he had returned at full speed to the capital and had immediately informed the Patriarch of his intention to abdicate. He could no longer struggle, he maintained, against the will of the Almighty, who had now conclusively demonstrated His hatred of the house of Nicephorus. The Patriarch may or may not have agreed with this last hypothesis, but he certainly approved of Michael's decision – in which, he very much feared, lay the only hope of the imperial family's survival. The Empress Procopia, on the other hand, took a very different view. She had no wish to give up the throne, the occupation of which she greatly enjoyed; and she clearly saw herself as another Theodora, encouraging her husband to hold firm. But her arguments were ignored. She, the ex-Emperor and their five children, all disguised in monastic habits, took refuge in the Church of the Virgin of Pharos, where they remained till they had received assurances of their safety. Their lives were spared, though their three sons were castrated to prevent their making any future bids for power;[1] Procopia and her daughters were immured in convents. As for Michael himself, he adopted the monastic name of Athanasius and passed the thirty-two years that remained to him in a monastery on one of the Princes' Islands in the Marmara, where he was eventually to die on the anniversary of the death of his predecessor Stauracius, 11 January 845. And Leo the Armenian, commander of those perfidious Anatolians who had betrayed their Emperor and thrown away the decisive victory that lay within their grasp, entered Constantinople by the Golden Gate, to be acclaimed as *basileus* at the Church of St John the Baptist in the Studium before riding in triumph through the streets to the Imperial Palace.

What, we may ask, had really happened? Leo's Anatolian troops were brave and experienced fighters – the last men in the world to lose their heads on the field of battle, least of all when facing an inferior force on open ground. The only remotely reasonable explanation for their action can be treachery. It follows that their apparent cowardice must have

1 One of them, Nicetas, we shall meet later in this story as Ignatius, Patriarch under Michael III and Basil I.

been deliberately feigned, as a means of instilling a genuine panic among the rest of the army. As for their commander, he played his cards with his usual cunning: by standing firm himself until the last possible moment and leaving the field only after all his men had fled, he was later able to claim that his own conduct had been blameless. Inevitably there were grave suspicions, but nothing could be conclusively proved. By then, in any case, he had achieved his object: the crown of Byzantium. And it is worth noting that, after what seemed on the face of it to be among the most humiliating defeats in the history of the Roman Empire, none of those who took flight was ever punished.

Not for the first time – for he had been deeply implicated in the insurrection of Bardanes Turcus some years before – Leo had betrayed his Emperor; and his troops had abetted him. Were he and they, however, the only parties to the plot? It may be that they were; but it seems probable that there was yet another, who also contributed largely to the success of the whole operation: Krum himself. Ever since the Bulgars had first become a threat to the Empire they had invariably avoided pitched battles on an open plain, preferring in every instance to keep to the mountain passes and defiles which were infinitely better suited to their fighting methods; why then should their wily and experienced Khan suddenly abandon the practice of a lifetime and draw up his men as he did before a vastly superior army? And was it really astonishment that kept him and his troops rooted to the spot as the Anatolians hurried from the field, allowing them to get clean away before he himself settled down to the massacre of the valiant Macedonians? How much more likely that Leo should have further assured the success of his plan by making an accomplice of the Bulgar leader – who would have found the idea irresistible, particularly since he would have been under no further obligations once his fellow-conspirators had made their escape.

As Krum watched his soldiers digging themselves in beneath the walls to each side of the Golden Gate, he could have looked back on six years of unbroken success. He had been responsible for the deaths of two Roman Emperors, and the downfall of a third; and he had overwhelmingly defeated two imperial armies, one of which had been utterly destroyed while the other – for whatever reason it may have been – had fled ignominiously from the field. For the moment, however, he had been brought to a halt: those mighty ramparts towering above him could never, he knew, be taken by storm. According to a curious and

unidentified fragment which has come down to us – its author is known
only as Scriptor Incertus – he covered his own uncertainty as to how best
to proceed by staging a whole series of weird ceremonies and demonstrations of strength. The defenders on the walls gazed down incredulously
on the elaborate sacrifices, both animal and human, with which the
pagan priests propitiated their gods; they even watched, fascinated,
while Krum himself – 'the new Sennacherib', as Theophanes calls him –
slowly advanced into the sea for the ritual washing of his feet, emerging
to sprinkle the water over his soldiers in benediction. On other occasions
he would parade in state through serried rows of his own ululating
concubines, while his warriors bellowed their approbation.

What precisely the Khan hoped to achieve by such manifestations
remains unclear. A few days later, however, in the absence of any
reaction from within the walls, he sent a message to the Emperor with a
demand that he be allowed, as a sign of his victory, to fix his lance on
the Golden Gate; and when this overture met – as he must have known
it would – with a curt refusal, he showed his displeasure by pillaging
and plundering the countryside around for several days before taking his
next initiative: a peace proposal in which he demanded, as the price of
his withdrawal, huge quantities of gold, chests full of sumptuous vestments and, finally, a selection of the most beautiful maidens that the
Empire could provide. Leo, it need hardly be said, had no more
intention of humouring Krum over the maidens than he had over the
lance; but the offer of terms, however unacceptable, suggested to his
ever-devious mind a possible way out of the impasse. He now proposed
a meeting between Krum and himself, to be held at the point where the
northern end of the walls ran down to the Golden Horn. He would
arrive by water, Krum by land; they would carry no weapons, and
would be accompanied only by a few similarly unarmed followers.

The Khan accepted the suggestion, and the very next morning rode
down with his treasurer, his Greek brother-in-law Constantine Patzikos
and his young nephew – the latter's son – to the appointed spot. Here he
was joined by the Emperor and a Byzantine court official named
Hexabulios. After the usual civilities the conversation began, Constantine
acting as interpreter. All seemed to be going smoothly enough when
Hexabulios suddenly covered his face with his hands. Krum, possibly
seeing the gesture as an insult – or, more probably (and correctly)
recognizing it as a prearranged signal – leapt on to his horse, which his
nephew was holding, saddled and bridled and ready for just such an

eventuality, immediately behind him. He was only just in time. At that
moment three armed men burst out of a nearby hiding-place. The
treasurer was killed outright, Patzikos and his son taken captive. As
Krum galloped away to safety, he was slightly wounded by darts fired
by the attackers; but they did him no serious harm – merely increasing
his fury at so shameless a betrayal of trust and his determination to take
his revenge.

That revenge began on the following day, and was dreadful to
behold. The Bulgars could not penetrate the city walls; but the suburbs
beyond the Golden Horn, with all their churches, their palaces and their
rich monasteries and convents, were consumed in one mighty conflagra-
tion. Among the buildings destroyed was the Imperial Palace of St
Mamas,[1] one of the most opulent of the Emperor's several residences in
the capital, from which all the elaborately carved marble columns and
rows of sculptured animals were carted off to Krum's own palace at
Pliska. Every living creature left unburnt was butchered. To the west of
the city, the countryside suffered a similar fate. The Palace of the
Hebdomon went the same way as St Mamas, and as the still-furious
Khan began his journey homeward he left behind him a nightmare trail
of slaughter and destruction. The city of Selymbria was reduced to a
smouldering heap of ashes, as were innumerable other towns and
villages; Heraclea was saved, thanks to the stoutness of its defences –
only one degree less impregnable than those of Constantinople itself –
but the avenging horde levelled the fortress of Rhaedestum (now
Tekirdağ) before moving up to the neighbouring hills, whither the
country people had fled for refuge. Family by family they were tracked
down; the men were put to the sword, the women and children sent off
into slavery. Then, after a quick punitive excursion to the Hellespont,
Krum turned north to Adrianople. For some weeks already the city had
been under attack by his brother, against whom the garrison had put up
a courageous resistance; but now food was running out, and the arrival
of the terrible Khan himself with the main body of his army finally
broke its morale. All 10,000 inhabitants were carried off beyond the
Danube, where many – including the archbishop – found martyrdom.

Now it was the turn of the Byzantines to sue for peace. But Krum
could not forget Leo's treachery, nor was his anger assuaged when
reports reached him in the autumn of a surprise attack on a Bulgar army

1 The building stood on the shore of the Bosphorus in the quarter now known as Beşiktaş, a
little beyond the Dolmabahçe Palace.

19

near Mesembria. It had been planned and carried out by the Emperor in person – who, by one of those devious stratagems for which he was famous, had taken his victims completely by surprise as they slept and massacred the lot of them. He had followed up this success by advancing deep into enemy territory where, while sparing the adult populations, he had seized all the children he could find and dashed their heads against the rocks. The Khan's mind was now made up: however formidable the walls of Constantinople might appear, he would smash them – and, with them, the Byzantine Empire.

By the early spring of 814 the capital was abuzz with rumours of his preparations: of towering siege-engines under construction; of gigantic catapults capable of hurling huge boulders against the walls or flaming firebrands over them; of scaling ladders and battering rams, of 1,000 oxen and 5,000 iron-bound wagons standing ready to haul these massive engines into position. The Emperor for his part worked furiously to strengthen the defences – especially around the quarter of Blachernae, where Krum had been so dishonourably set upon and where he was expected to launch the weight of his attack – simultaneously sending ambassadors to the court of Lewis the Pious, who had succeeded his father Charlemagne on the latter's death a few months before. That mission failed, Lewis understandably pointing out that he had enemies enough of his own; but by the time the envoys returned to the capital the danger was past. On Holy Thursday, 13 April 814, just as his new expeditionary force was ready to march, Krum suffered a sudden seizure. Blood streamed from his nose, mouth and ears, and within a few minutes he was dead.

There now occurred something rare indeed in Byzantine history: peace descended on the Empire. Krum's son Omortag was young and inexperienced, and the first year of his reign was further troubled by a revolt of the Bulgar aristocracy which kept him fully occupied at home. Similar upheavals in Baghdad pre-empted any aggression on the part of Harun al-Rashid's successor, the Caliph Mamun. In the West, the *Pax Nicephori* still held. Leo was free at last to turn his attention to home affairs – and to take the decisive step for which, more than any other, he is remembered.

2

The Return of Iconoclasm

[814–29]

Leave the Church to its pastors and masters; attend to your own province, the State and the army. If you refuse to do this, and are bent on destroying our faith, know that though an angel came from heaven itself to pervert us we would not obey him. Far less would we obey you.

Abbot Theodore of the Studium
to the Emperor Leo V, 815

Of the personal appearance of the Emperor Leo V we know little; the sole description that has come down to us reports only that he was short and bearded, with thick curly hair and an unusually loud voice. Of his character, on the other hand, we can deduce a good deal more. First of all there was his consuming ambition: unlike his predecessor Michael, who came of noble stock and had the additional advantage of being an Emperor's son-in-law, Leo had made his way from humble beginnings, rising to the supreme power entirely through his own efforts, assisted by boundless physical energy. If we accept the explanation of his conduct at Versinicia given in the previous chapter, we have no cause to question his powers of leadership, still less his courage; all accounts of his punitive expedition into Bulgar territory in the autumn of 813, however, point to a streak of bestial cruelty which was quick to burst forth when his anger was aroused. Nor must it ever be forgotten that he was an Armenian; as such, he possessed in full measure – indeed it was perhaps the salient feature of his unusually complex personality – that quality for which his countrymen have always been noted: a keen and subtle intelligence, shot through with resourcefulness and guile.

It was this intelligence that had probably first endeared him to his rebellious compatriot Bardanes Turcus. He had shown it a few years later at Versinicia, and again when he had carried out his nocturnal surprise attack on the Bulgar force in 813; and it was once more in evidence when, in the year following, he set about the reimposition of iconoclasm on the Empire. His reasons for taking so tremendous a step were very different from those which had impelled his namesake to do the same eighty-eight years before. Leo III had been a devout theologian, who had thought long and earnestly about the issues involved and had genuinely believed that he was obeying the will of God. As for Leo V, this was not a question to which he gave much thought: his approach to the question was a purely practical one. Already in the days of Irene the imperial government had had to contend with the problem posed by vast numbers of destitute peasant small-holders, dispossessed and driven from their homes by Saracen incursions into the eastern provinces. En-rolled by Nicephorus as regular soldiers, they had proved useful enough during the Bulgarian war as an emergency militia for the capital; with the coming of peace, however, they had been disbanded and were once again reduced to penury, begging at street corners for their daily bread. Being easterners, these men were nearly all iconoclasts by tradition and upbring-ing; moreover, since their misery had had its origins during the reign of Irene, they not unnaturally tended to associate it with her, and through her with the reaction against iconoclasm which she had brought about.

Thus, by the summer of 814, there was in Constantinople an ominous ground-swell of iconoclast opinion which, while not yet presenting any serious threat to the security of the State, might well have turned dangerous if ignored for too long. Nor was this opinion confined to the dissatisfied ex-soldiers; it was also widespread – as it had always been – among the upper classes of the capital, as well as in the senior ranks of the army. We have seen how a demonstration at the tomb of Constantine V two years before had recalled the military triumphs of the iconoclast Emperors, in marked contrast to the failures of their iconodule succes-sors: there must have been many men and women in the Empire not normally given to theological speculation who felt nevertheless that the Almighty had made His own point of view on the matter clear enough, and that the time had come for a change.

It was thus as a means of preserving domestic peace rather than as an expression of any deep religious conviction that Leo went ahead with his plan. His first step was to appoint, in June 814, a special commission with orders to examine the scriptures and all the writings of the early Fathers of the Church for evidence in favour of the iconoclastic persua-sion. As its chairman he nominated another of his countrymen: the brilliant young Armenian abbot of the monastery of SS. Sergius and

Bacchus – he was still in his early thirties – whose real name was John Morocharzamius but who is more conveniently known to posterity as John the Grammarian. As his deputy the Emperor rather surprisingly selected Antony, Bishop of Syllaeum in Pamphylia, an agreeable old reprobate who – according to the violently anti-iconoclast Scriptor Incertus – spent most of his time telling dubious stories to the two monks and two laymen who made up the rest of the commission. Throughout their six-month labour they were bound to the strictest secrecy, being lodged and fed – superbly, it appears – inside the Great Palace and encouraged to remain as far as possible within its walls.

The results of their endeavours were completed in early December and submitted to the Emperor, who immediately summoned Patriarch Nicephorus to the Palace. Still treading warily, he first proposed – as a compromise 'to please the soldiers' – the removal only of those holy pictures which were hanging low on the walls; the Patriarch, however, who knew the thin end of a wedge when he saw one, would have none of it. 'But why,' pursued Leo, 'do you venerate images, when there is no scriptural injunction to do so?' Nicephorus replied that the Church endorsed many beliefs and practices for which there was no written authority; further than that he refused to go. In such circumstances the Emperor had no option but to set the example himself – acting, however, with typical disingenuousness. The icon on which he had set his sights was the huge representation of Christ which stood above the main gate of the Palace known as the Chalkē – the very same that had been pulled down by Leo III in 726, only to be subsequently replaced by Irene; but whereas the Isaurian had simply ordered the military to get on with the job, the Armenian laid his plans with care. He too sent for a detachment of soldiers, but his orders to them were somewhat different. Their task would be to create a disturbance, apparently spontaneous, in the course of which they would hurl imprecations and abuse at the holy image, pelting it with mud and stones; this would be the cue for the arrival of the Emperor himself, who would order its removal to save it from any further desecration.

The operation went according to plan, whereupon the Patriarch on his own initiative summoned a meeting of all the local bishops and abbots, warning them of the approaching storm and calling upon them to stand firm on the principles laid down by the Seventh Ecumenical Council in 787.[1] Then, early on Christmas morning, he had another

1 This was the Council called by Irene to condemn iconoclasm. See *Byzantium: The Early Centuries*, pp. 369–72.

audience with Leo. He implored the Emperor to dismiss him if he so wished, but to make no radical change in Church doctrine; Leo smoothly assured him that he had no intention of doing either – in confirmation of which, at the Christmas Mass in St Sophia, he ostentatiously bowed down as usual before a representation of the Nativity. Less than two weeks later, on the other hand, during the service of Epiphany on 6 January 815, it was noted by all present that he made no such obeisance. Nicephorus could only stand by and await developments.

They were not long in coming. The Emperor now summoned a number of iconoclast churchmen to the capital – carefully giving them no opportunity to pay their customary respects to the Patriarch on their arrival – and handed them the collection of scriptural and patristic citations that the commission had prepared. Then, once again, he called Nicephorus to the Palace. The Patriarch obeyed the summons – but he did not come alone. With him there appeared a large body of the faithful, including Abbot Theodore of the Studium, formerly one of his bitterest enemies but now steadfast at his side. The ensuing meeting was a stormy one, in the course of which Theodore openly defied the Emperor in the words quoted at the head of this chapter; the assembled ecclesiastics were shortly afterwards dismissed. A few days later there was promulgated an edict forbidding the Patriarch and all members of the iconodule faction to hold meetings in public places or even private residences. Nicephorus himself was put under something closely resembling house arrest and thus effectively prevented from performing his official duties.

That Easter, what was called a General Synod – to which, however, a considerable number of iconodule bishops failed to receive their invitations – was held in St Sophia. By this time the Patriarch had fallen seriously ill: summoned to attend the assembly, he was not well enough to do so, and was accordingly deposed *in absentia*. When sufficiently recovered he was exiled to the monastery of St Theodore the Martyr, some distance up the Bosphorus on the Asiatic side. There he lived on for some years, but never returned to Constantinople. In his place the Emperor appointed – significantly – a relative of Constantine V named Theodotus Cassiteras. Iconoclast the new Patriarch undoubtedly was; like Constantine, however, he seems to have been far from puritanical in other respects. One of his first acts on his succession was to give a sumptuous luncheon party in the Patriarchal Palace, at which distinguished ecclesiastics and austere monks, many of whom had not

touched meat for years, were obliged by their host to make free of the
succulent dishes and superb wines that were set before them and, in the
words of Professor Bury, 'the dull solemnity of an archiepiscopal table was
now enlivened by frivolous conversation, amusing stories, and ribald wit'.

But the Patriarch's life was not all pleasure. It was also his duty to
preside at the Synod – an unenviable task and one which, as soon
became clear, lay well beyond his capabilities. Nicephorus, one feels – or
Tarasius before him – would somehow have managed to impose his
authority; but when certain Orthodox bishops were called in for examination and tempers became heated, Theodotus lost control. The
unfortunate prelates were physically attacked, thrown to the ground,
punched, kicked and spat upon. The prestige of the Synod – already
weakened by the obvious one-sidedness of its composition – was still
further diminished by this unedifying display; at last, however, the
delegates dusted themselves down, resumed their places – and did what
they were told. Their findings were consequently a foregone conclusion;
and their final decree, in an only slightly abridged form, ran as follows:

The Emperors Constantine [V] and Leo [III], considering the safety of the
Empire to depend on Orthodoxy, formerly gathered a numerous synod of
spiritual fathers and bishops and condemned the unprofitable practice, unwar-
ranted by tradition, of making and adoring icons, preferring worship in spirit
and in truth.

On this account, the Church of God remained tranquil for a number of years,
and the people enjoyed peace, until the government passed from men to a
woman, and the Church became the victim of feminine simplicity. This woman
followed the counsel of ignorant bishops; she convoked an injudicious assembly;
she laid down the doctrine of painting in a material medium the Son and Word
of God, and of representing the Mother of God and the Saints by dead images;
and she enacted that these representations should be adored, thus heedlessly
defying the proper doctrine of the Church. In such a way did she sully our
adoration which is due to God alone, declaring that what should be given only
to Him should be offered to lifeless icons. Furthermore she foolishly maintained
that they were full of divine grace, encouraging the lighting of candles and the
burning of incense before them. Thus did she cause the simple to err.

We do therefore now forbid throughout the Orthodox Church the
unauthorized manufacture of pseudonymous icons; we reject the adoration
defined by Tarasius;[1] we annul the decrees of his synod, on the ground that
they granted to images undue honour; and we condemn the lighting of candles
and the offering of incense.

---

1 Patriarch at the time of the Seventh Ecumenical Council of 787.

25

Gladly recognizing, however, the Holy Synod which met at Blachernae in the temple of the unspotted Virgin in the reigns of Constantine and Leo as firmly based on the doctrine of the Fathers, we decree that the manufacture of icons – we abstain from calling them *idols*, for there are degrees of evil – is neither worshipful nor of service.

With iconoclasm once again introduced throughout the Empire, the dangers of civil disruption removed – at least for the immediate future – and continued peace established on all his frontiers, Leo V could congratulate himself on an excellent start to his reign. Lacking any deep religious convictions of his own, he took no stringent measures against the general run of icon-worshippers who refused to submit to the new edict. A few of its most vociferous opponents – those who continued publicly to demonstrate against it and openly to defy the ban on images – were punished for form's sake: Abbot Theodore, for example, now the acknowledged leader of the iconodule camp, was thrown into three different prisons. His biographer recalls with relish his repeated floggings and the hideous extremes of heat and cold – to say nothing of the enthusiastic visitations of rats, fleas and lice – that he was called upon to endure. But then, as the Emperor would have been quick to point out, Theodore had asked for it: he had never minced words during his imperial audiences, and on the Palm Sunday before the Synod he had staged a procession in which the monks of the Studium had flagrantly paraded round the monastery, carrying all their most precious icons shoulder-high before them. More serious still, in 817, he was found to be in regular correspondence with the newly elected Pope Paschal I, not only informing him of the plight of the Orthodox faithful but on one occasion actually proposing an appeal for help to the Western Emperor. Such a proposal was obviously treasonable, and in the circumstances it was hardly surprising that Leo should have taken firm action against him. Most of those churchmen who shared his opinions found, on the other hand, that provided they kept a suitably low profile they were permitted to carry on as they always had, without molestation or interference. Leo's primary interests were State security and public order. So far as he was concerned, the doctrinal considerations so dear to Theodore and his followers were at most of secondary importance.

Inevitably, however, the edict of 815 unleashed a new wave of wholesale destruction. Any holy image, we are told, could be smashed or desecrated by any person at any time, without fear of punishment. Any vestment or piece of embroidery bearing representations of Jesus

Christ, the Virgin or the Saints was liable to be torn to shreds and trampled underfoot; painted wooden panels were smeared with ordure, attacked with axes or burnt in the public squares. The extent of the artistic loss, then and over the next twenty-eight years, may not have been as great as that sustained in the sixty-one years of iconoclasm during the previous century: the time-span of this second period was less than half that of the first, and in any case Leo and his successors possessed little of the blazing conviction that had driven Leo III and Constantine Copronymus. The fact remains that that loss must have been by any standards immense; and when we consider the breathtaking quality and pathetically small quantity of Byzantine art that has survived from before the middle of the ninth century, it is a loss that we can still feel today.

From an early stage in his career – perhaps even before the two of them had been involved in the ill-fated revolt of Bardanes Turcus in 803 – Leo had enjoyed the close friendship of a brother-officer named Michael, who came from the Phrygian city of Amorium.[1] The bond that existed between them is not immediately easy to understand – Michael was a bluff, unlettered provincial of humble origins with some sort of impediment in his speech[2] – but it was strong enough for Leo to have stood as godfather to his son, and there is evidence to suggest that Michael gave his friend invaluable support and encouragement at the time of the battle of Versinicia and the subsequent march on the capital. When Leo rode in triumph to the Imperial Palace, the Amorian had followed immediately behind; and although, when the two dismounted to enter the building, Michael had committed an unfortunate *faux pas* by treading on the Emperor's cloak and almost dragging it off, Leo nevertheless appointed him Commander of the Excubitors – one of the crack Palace regiments – and the incident was soon forgotten.

Some time in the summer or early autumn of the year 820, however, word came to the Emperor that Michael was speaking slanderously of him and spreading sedition. Unwilling to take precipitate action against his old friend, he first instructed another of his court officials, the

1 Once the capital of the province of Anatolia and an important bishopric, Amorium is now only a few sad-looking ruins near the village of Asarköy, some thirty-five miles south-west of Sivrihisar.

2 Most modern historians speak of it as a lisp, but it is more likely to have been a stammer – hence his nickname *Psellus*, 'the Stammerer'. (He is not of course to be confused with the later chronicler.)

Logothete of the Drome John Hexabulios – the same who had been
involved in the perfidious meeting with Krum seven years before – to
have a private word with him, pointing out the imprudence of his
behaviour and its potential consequences; but Michael took no notice.
As time went on he continued to speak more and more openly against
his sovereign until, on Christmas Eve, Hexabulios uncovered a
conspiracy in which several high-ranking military officers were believed
to be implicated, and of which Michael was unquestionably the
ringleader. He informed Leo, who at once had the Amorian brought
before him. Confronted by unassailable evidence, Michael had no choice
but to confess his guilt; and the Emperor, beside himself with rage at
the treachery of so trusted a friend and colleague, ordered him forthwith
to be hurled into the huge furnace that heated the baths of the Palace.

Although night had long since fallen, this terrible sentence would
have been immediately carried out had it not been for his wife, the
Empress Theodosia. Hearing the news from one of her ladies, she
jumped from her bed and rushed barefoot to her husband. It was now,
she pleaded, only an hour or two before Christmas; how could he
possibly accept the Sacrament on the day of Christ's Nativity with an act
of such unspeakable cruelty on his conscience? Moved by her words –
and also, perhaps, by her reminder that longer and more careful examination of Michael might yield further information about his fellow-conspirators – Leo agreed to defer the execution. He had the condemned man
put in irons and locked in a small room in a distant corner of the Palace,
where he was to be kept under constant guard. He himself took charge
of the keys, both to the room and to the fetters. Then, deeply troubled
in mind and spirit, he retired to bed.

But he could not sleep. Again and again, his thoughts returned to that
day in 813 when Michael had trodden on his cloak and had come near to
tearing the imperial insignia from his shoulders. Could the incident have
been an omen? And what about the illuminated book of divination that
he had recently been reading, in which he had found a representation of
a lion, its throat transfixed by a sword, between the Greek letters *Chi*
and *Phi*? If *Chi* stood for Christmas (χριστους ἡ γέννησις) and *Phi* for
Epiphany (φῶτα), was that not an unmistakable prediction of the death
of Leo some time between those two feasts? How much better if he had
refused to listen to his wife's entreaties and had had the sentence carried
out there and then – and besides, was his prisoner really safe? On a
sudden impulse he got up, seized a candle and set off down the

labyrinthine corridors of the Palace to the room in which Michael was confined, smashing down or bursting open – for despite his small stature he was a man of colossal physical strength – any door along his path which chanced to be locked. He then let himself silently into the cell – to find, to his fury, the gaoler sound asleep on the floor while the prisoner lay on a pallet bed, apparently in the same state. Unable to believe that anyone in such a situation could slumber so soundly, he laid his hand on Michael's chest to satisfy himself by the beating of his heart that his sleep was indeed genuine. Finding that it was, he quietly withdrew, pausing only to shake his fist at the two unconscious men.

What the Emperor did not know was that there was a third person in the room, very much awake. Somehow Michael had contrived to bring with him one of his personal servants, a young eunuch who on hearing footsteps had hastily concealed himself under the bed. From this hiding-place he could not see the face of the intruder; but the purple boots, which only the *basileus* could wear, were more than sufficient identification. The moment Leo had gone, he woke up his master and the gaoler and told them what he had seen; and the latter, realizing that his life too was now under threat, readily agreed to make common cause with his prisoner. On the pretext that Michael was anxious to confess his sins before sentence was carried out, he sent another of the Amorian's trusted servants into the city, ostensibly to find a priest but in fact to gather his fellow-conspirators for a last-minute rescue.

The servant moved fast, and the plan was soon made. It was the custom, on great feasts of the Church, for the choir of monks who sang the Matins in the Palace to assemble in the early hours by the Ivory Gate before making their way to the Chapel of St Stephen. And so, long before first light on that freezing Christmas morning, the conspirators shrouded themselves in monks' robes – the perfect concealment for the swords and poignards that they carried beneath them – and joined the choristers with whom, their faces hidden deep in their cowls, they proceeded into the Palace. Once inside the chapel, they lost themselves among the shadows and settled down to wait.

The beginning of the opening hymn was the accepted signal for the arrival of the Emperor, who took his seat as usual and at once joined in the anthem. There were varying opinions – of which his own was by far the most favourable – as to the quality of his voice, but all sources are agreed on its volume. The conspirators waited until the music reached a climax; then they struck. Strangely enough, both Leo and the officiating priest were wearing peaked fur caps to protect their heads from the bitter cold; and the first blows were directed against the priest, who managed only just in time to whip off his cap, revealing an egg-bald head and so convincing his assailants of their mistake. This momentary delay allowed the Emperor to seize from the altar a heavy cross with which to defend himself; but a moment later a tremendous sword stroke severed his right arm at the shoulder sending it, with the hand still clutching the cross, spinning across the floor. He fell to the ground, where another blow struck off his head. And so, soon after four o'clock in the morning of Christmas Day 820, the reign of the Emperor Leo V came to an end.

Once again, the murderers lost no time. Hurrying to the room in which Michael was still captive, they found to their dismay that they had no means of unlocking his fetters: the new Emperor of Byzantium was carried bodily to his throne and seated upon it with the heavy iron shackles still on his legs, while the hastily assembled officers of the imperial household prostrated themselves before him. Only around midday did a blacksmith arrive with a sledgehammer and chisel to set him free[1] – just in time for him to limp into St Sophia for his coronation by the Patriarch. The thoughts of Theodotus as he laid the crown on the usurper's shaggy head are not recorded; but he was an inveterate time-server and not the sort of man to raise objections.

Soon afterwards, what remained of Leo V was retrieved from the common privy into which it had been thrown and dragged naked to the Hippodrome, where it was exposed to the public gaze. Thence it was carried on muleback to the harbour where the Empress Theodosia and her four sons were waiting, and loaded with them on to the ship that was to take them to exile on the Princes' Islands in the Marmara. On their arrival, further grim news awaited them: to ensure that they should plan no retaliation, it was the wish of the new Emperor that the boys should all be immediately castrated.[2] Three of them survived the ordeal – one, Gregory, living on to become Archbishop of Syracuse in Sicily; the youngest, Theodosius, died under the knife and was buried with his father.

---

1 So at least we are assured by our principal source, the Continuator of Theophanes (see below). Other chroniclers claim that John Hexabulios suddenly remembered that Leo had put the key in his pocket, and had it recovered from the corpse.

2 So that they could not supplant him. The Emperor, in the Byzantine view, must be free from all physical imperfections.

The reader of these last two pages may perhaps have been struck by a note of theatricality, even sensationalism, making a sharp contrast with the austerity and restraint which has heretofore characterized our narrative. This is a reflection, not of any change of approach on the author's part, but of a new source who took over the chronicle of the monk Theophanes shortly before the latter's death in 814 on the island of Samothrace, whither he had been exiled for his religious opinions. This Continuator – as he is generally known, though in fact the later chapters of the work attributed to him are obviously by several different successors – has a penchant for drama and an eye for the telling detail which sets him apart from the vast majority of his fellows. We may suspect him of occasionally elaborating his account with more than a touch of artistic licence, and are probably right to do so – particularly since the later compilation dates from the middle of the tenth century, well over a hundred years after the events here described; but he certainly knows how to tell a story, and natural storytellers are all too rare in medieval history. In all essentials, we have no reason to doubt his reliability; and even for the rest, so long as we hold an occasional pinch of salt at the ready, there is no reason not to enjoy him.

To say that Michael II ascended the Byzantine throne with blood on his hands is an understatement. Many other Emperors, to be sure, had done the same; none, however, with the arguable exception of Phocas in 602,[1] had dispatched his predecessor quite so cold-bloodedly – or with less excuse. Leo had had his faults, cruelty and duplicity prominent among them; but he had been a wise and effective ruler who had done much to restore the imperial fortunes and who, given the opportunity, would doubtless have continued to guide the Empire with firmness and confidence. Michael could not attempt to justify his murder on the grounds of his incapacity any more than he could on those of religion, since he fully shared Leo's views on iconoclasm. His sole motivation, in short, was a compound of jealousy and naked ambition – together, perhaps, with just a touch of superstition: for he had never forgotten the words uttered by the hermit of Philomelion, seventeen years before.

The people of Constantinople were perfectly well aware of all this. They laughed at Michael for his boorishness and lack of education – in the time it took him to write the six Greek letters of his name, they used

---

1 See *Byzantium: The Early Centuries*, p. 277.

to say, another man could read a whole book – and from the moment of his accession they made him a popular target for political lampoons; but they feared him too. He had, after all, shown that in order to get what he wanted there was no conduct of which he was not capable. And yet, surprisingly, he was to prove a better ruler than anyone had expected – and one whose reign, troubled as it was, was to be characterized less by stupidity or cruelty than by moderation and sound common sense.

It was perhaps a manifestation of this latter virtue that led Michael, on Whit Sunday 821, to have his seventeen-year-old son Theophilus crowned co-Emperor. He was deeply conscious of the fact that he was the seventh occupant of the Byzantine throne in a quarter of a century, and that of his immediate predecessors two had been deposed, two killed in battle and two assassinated. Furthermore, the last three had all been unrelated to each other, and to himself. More than anything, it seemed, the Empire needed stability; and the coronation of Theophilus was the first step towards it. But Theophilus too must produce a son and heir: and the second step, which was taken very shortly afterwards – probably on the very same day – was to marry him to a Paphlagonian lady of high birth and startling beauty by the name of Theodora[1], of whom we shall be hearing a good deal more in the years to come.

But already by this time Michael had problems on his mind more immediate than that of the imperial succession; for the Empire was once again under threat – not, as so often in the past, from the Saracens or the Bulgars, but from a military adventurer known as Thomas of Gaziura or, more usually, as Thomas the Slav. He was the third of the three officers who had accompanied Bardanes Turcus to the hermit of Philomelion in 803; since his two comrades Leo and Michael had already ascended the throne, it must have been clear to him that, by the terms of the prophecy, his own attempt must be doomed to failure; he seems, however, to have been determined to prove the prophet wrong. Throughout the reigns of Nicephorus and Michael I he had remained in exile in Muslim lands; but he had returned on the accession of Leo who, rather surprisingly – since the Armenians were known to dislike the Slavs even more than the Greeks did – had entrusted him with a high military command. Until about the time of Leo's murder he had caused no trouble; but as soon as the throne passed to Michael – with

1 Like Theophano, the wife of Stauracius (see p. 9n.), she was almost certainly selected by means of a 'bride show' – a sort of beauty contest of eligible maidens, from whom the prospective bridegroom would make his choice.

whom he had maintained a long-standing rivalry – he began to stir up rebellion.

His success was remarkable, and for several reasons. In the eastern provinces he claimed to be the Emperor Constantine VI – who had somehow miraculously escaped the blinding ordered by his mother Irene twenty-three years before – and actually went through a ceremony of coronation in Muslim-held Antioch. In the West he took a violently anti-iconoclastic stand which was sure, he knew, to win him a large measure of support. Everywhere he set himself up as a champion of the poor, and of all those who were oppressed by high taxation and the widespread corruption of provincial government officials. Though relatively advanced in age – he was certainly well into his fifties, and may have been older – and afflicted with a pronounced limp, there seems to have been something almost irresistibly attractive about him: those who knew them both would always contrast his courtesy and charm with the incoherent coarseness of the Emperor. And he possessed another advantage too: the revulsion felt by all right-thinking men and women for the cold-blooded brutality of the crime by which the Amorian had seized the throne. We may wonder, none the less, whether his innumerable supporters would have felt quite the same had they known that Thomas was enjoying considerable financial support from Caliph Mamun – to whom he may well have promised, if successful, to hold the Empire as a fief of the Caliphate.

The army with which this twisted, resentful yet somehow charismatic figure invaded the Empire in the spring of 821 was immense: some 80,000, including Arabs and Persians, Georgians and Armenians, Alans and Goths, Huns and Slavs. So heterogeneous a collection was hardly likely, one would have thought, to rally much support inside the Greek-speaking Anatolian heartland; yet within a matter of months only two Themes in all Asia Minor – the Opsikion and the Armeniakon – remained loyal to Michael. And so, in the knowledge that he had virtually the entire Empire behind him from Ararat to the Aegean, Thomas crossed to Thrace in December 821 and laid siege to Constantinople.

It was not, as we know, the first time that the capital had faced a besieging army. True, on the most recent occasion – only eight years previously – Krum had made no serious attempt to breach the 400-year-old walls of Theodosius II, contenting himself with ravaging the outer suburbs and the district of Galata beyond the Golden Horn. But there had been full-blooded sieges too – by the Persians in 626, and by the

33

Saracens in 674 and again in 717–18 – when the people had had to contend with simultaneous onslaughts from both land and sea, and all the men and women of Constantinople had felt themselves – rightly – to be in the front line of the attack. Thanks in part to their courage and determination, but in still greater part to those magnificent defences which no other city could match, they had always prevailed; and so they did against Thomas the Slav, for the same reasons. Thomas directed his main offensive against the Blachernae quarter, where the northern end of the land walls ran down to the Golden Horn and the fortifications were believed to be somewhat weaker; he seems to have been unaware that this particular area had been greatly strengthened by Leo V in expectation of Krum's last expedition that had never happened. In the event, his siege-engines proved hopelessly ineffective, certainly no match for the huge catapults and mangonels that Michael had ranged along the ramparts. At sea, too, though Thomas had had no difficulty in winning over the provincial fleet in its bases around the Anatolian coast, together with all its armaments and even its stocks of Greek fire, the raging winter winds prevented his ships from advancing far enough inshore to do any appreciable damage.

In the spring of 822 he tried again, with no better success. This time the Emperor managed to address the besieging army from the top of one of the towers, ostensibly appealing to their loyalty but in fact subtly contriving to suggest that the defenders of the city were at their last gasp. His hearers, assuming that they would therefore meet with little serious resistance, advanced to the attack carelessly and in loose order; they were taken totally by surprise when several gates were suddenly thrown open to release an avalanche of imperial troops, who fell on them before they had time to recover themselves and slaughtered them by the score. After that, the assault on Blachernae was abandoned. A naval battle, apparently fought on the same day, ended in another reverse for the rebels; while their second fleet, arriving from Hellas and the Peloponnese in the early summer, had scarcely engaged the Emperor's navy before being totally destroyed by Greek fire.

By the second winter of the rebellion – which, in view of the numbers involved, might perhaps be more properly described as a civil war – Thomas had still not achieved a single major victory; both to him and to his close associates it must have been clear that his bid for the crown had failed. But he did not give up the struggle; and there is no telling how long the stalemate might have continued had it not been for the Bulgar

Khan Omortag, Krum's son, who soon after his accession had concluded a thirty-year treaty with the Empire and who now offered Michael armed assistance. The Emperor is said to have politely declined the offer, being reluctant to permit Christian blood – even that of traitors – to be shed by pagan swords; but he could not prevent the Khan, for whom the prospects of plunder were well-nigh irresistible, from acting on his own account and may even, for all we know, have given him covert encouragement. However that may be, in March 823 the Bulgar horde swept down from Mount Haemus in Thrace and a few weeks later, on the plain of Keduktos[1] near Heraclea, smashed the rebel army to pieces. The plunder proved fully up to expectations. Well satisfied with his work, Omortag returned home.

Thomas, now desperate, gathered up what was left of his shattered forces and led them some twenty miles west of Constantinople to another expanse of flat, open country known as the plain of Diabasis. Shortly afterwards – it must have been about the beginning of May – the Emperor rode out of the capital, at the head of his own army, to meet him; and there, where the two little rivers Melas (now the Karasu) and Athyras flowed down from the hill of Kushkaya near the Anastasian walls,[2] the issue was finally decided. Thomas adopted the time-honoured tactic of a pretended flight; but when the moment came to spin round and charge the enemy his remaining troops, dispirited and demoralized, could not bring themselves to do so and laid down their arms instead. Their erstwhile commander, escaping with a handful of followers, fled to Arcadiopolis – the modern Lüleburgaz – and barricaded himself in.

Now the roles were reversed: Michael was the besieger, Thomas the besieged. The latter, acutely conscious of the shortage of provisions, expelled from the city all the women, the children and the men who were too old or incapacitated to bear arms and so managed to hold out through the summer; but in October, by which time he and his men were reduced to eating the putrescent corpses of their own horses, it became clear that they could resist no longer. Many deserted, lowering themselves by ropes from the walls, and made straight for the imperial camp; the Emperor thereupon sent a message to the soldiers left in the city, promising them all a free pardon if they would deliver their leader

1 A corruption of *Aquaeductus*. Heraclea (now Ereğli) was famous for the great Roman aqueduct just outside the city.

2 The great outer defence of Constantinople, built in the early sixth century by Anastasius I across the thirty-odd miles from Selymbria (Silivri) on the Marmara to the Black Sea.

into his hands. They in turn, realizing that the alternative might well be a general massacre, agreed.

Thomas and Michael had been enemies for many years; only for the last two had their enmity flared up into open warfare, but during those two years the damage done to the Empire, morally as well as materially, had been beyond computation. Vast tracts of rich farming land had been laid waste; the resident small-holders, faced with savagely increased taxation and possessing no capital to fall back on, were ruined. Once again they flocked to Constantinople in search of sustenance. The old problem – the same that had plagued both Nicephorus and Leo V – was back again, in a more acute form than ever. As the sole cause of all the misery and devastation, the Slav knew that he could expect no mercy. Brought in chains into the Emperor's presence, he was pushed roughly to the ground before him; and Michael made no attempt to conceal his satisfaction. Resting one purple-booted foot on the neck of his victim, he pronounced his fate: the hands and feet to be cut off, the body then to be impaled on a stake. The sentence was carried out on the spot, before the walls of Arcadiopolis.

Mopping-up operations continued for a few more months. Thomas's adopted son, a somewhat feckless former monk named Anastasius, suffered the same punishment as his father; other rebel leaders in the Asiatic provinces were hanged. The overwhelming majority of their followers, however, having given themselves up to the Emperor's representatives, were pardoned and allowed to return to their homes. By the beginning of 824 the rebellion – perhaps the greatest and most widespread in all Byzantine history – was at an end.

The same could not be said, however, for the tribulations of Michael II. His Empire had scarcely begun to recover from the havoc wrought by Thomas the Slav when two further disasters befell: disasters curiously similar in both cause and effect, which were to deprive him of two of his most important strategic bases in the Mediterranean. There has long been a tendency among historians of the period to hold Thomas responsible for these losses also, on the grounds that his rebellion had weakened the Empire to the point where it no longer had the power to resist; in fact, it was itself largely to blame. In former days the Emperors had maintained a strong navy, as a necessary defence against the formidable sea power of the Omayyad Caliphs of Damascus; after 750, however, with the transfer of the Caliphate to the Abbasids of Baghdad, that power had rapidly declined and the Byzantine fleet had been in its turn increasingly neglected. When, therefore, in 825 some 10,000 Arabs from Spain sailed with a fleet of forty ships into imperial waters, Michael could do little to prevent them.

These Arabs had been expelled from Andalusia in 816 after an unsuccessful insurrection of their own against their local Emir, and had set off eastward across the Middle Sea in a determined attempt to restore their shattered forces. Their first target had been Egypt, where in 818 they had captured Alexandria; seven years later, forcibly expelled by the Caliph Mamun, they headed for Crete. According to a venerable tradition – supported by both Byzantine and Arabic sources – their leader Abu Hafs gave them twelve days to plunder the island, after which they were to return to the harbour; on doing so, they found to their horror that he had ordered the destruction of all their ships. In vain did they remind him of the wives and children that they had left behind in Egypt; he told them brusquely that they must content themselves with the women of Crete. This, with what we must assume to be varying degrees of reluctance, they did – simultaneously founding the city of Candia (now Heraklion) which has ever since been the island's capital. From it they marched out to take twenty-nine other towns, forcibly imposing the Islamic faith and reducing the inhabitants to slavery. One community only was spared – unfortunately we are not given its name – in which Christianity might still be openly professed.

Crete henceforth became a nest of pirates, from whom no island in the Eastern Mediterranean or the Aegean, no harbour on the coast of Greece or Asia Minor, could consider itself safe. Over the next century Aegina, Paros and the Cyclades were devastated again and again; the monks of Mount Athos were driven from their monasteries; and similar stories could doubtless be told, had more written records survived, of innumerable other islands, towns and monastic communities pillaged and plundered by the Arab corsairs. Soon, too, Candia became the busiest slave market of its time. The Empire sought repeatedly to bring its inhabitants to heel; Michael II alone launched three separate expeditions between 827 and 829, and there were to be several more attempts by his successors before control was finally reimposed by the Byzantine general – and future Emperor – Nicephorus Phocas in 961.

Within only two years of the capture of Crete another, unrelated, company of Arabs invaded the island of Sicily. This time, however, they came by invitation – to support the cause of a former Byzantine admiral,

Euphemius by name, who had been dismissed from his post after an unseemly elopement with a local nun. Realizing that surrender would almost certainly mean death – or, at the very least, hideous mutilation – he had risen in revolt, killing the Imperial Governor and proclaiming himself Emperor. Even then, however, it was clear that he would never be able to maintain the position unaided. He therefore crossed to North Africa to seek the armed assistance of the Emir of Kairouan, undertaking to pay him an annual tribute once he was firmly established in power.

To the Emir, such an invitation was irresistible; and on 14 June 827 a fleet of between seventy and a hundred ships sailed northward to Sicily, carrying 700 cavalry and 10,000 foot-soldiers under the command, somewhat surprisingly, of one of the leading judges in the religious court of Kairouan, Asad Ibn al-Furat. Although his force was imposing enough at first sight, Asad soon found that he was not to have things entirely his own way. He himself was to die during an outbreak of plague the following year, and Euphemius was shortly afterwards killed by members of the imperial garrison at Enna; but the contest between Christian and Saracen – still fought, amid much clattering of toy swords on biscuit-tin breastplates and lopping of turbanned heads, in the traditional puppet-shows of Palermo – was to continue for another half-century until the fall of Syracuse in 878 marked the effective triumph of Muslim power in the island.[1] Long before then, however, Sicily had proved itself, for a people bent on piracy and conquest, an even better springboard than Crete: the armies of the Prophet had crossed the Straits of Messina, overrun Calabria and much of Apulia, and had even passed thence over the Adriatic to the southern Dalmatian coast. Michael and his successors did all they could to hold them in check, but the Byzantine navy in the middle of the ninth century was simply not large enough to tackle the problems of Crete and Sicily at the same time. It tended to concentrate more on the former, as being a closer and more immediate danger – with the result that the Saracens of Sicily found that they could do very much as they liked. As the centuries passed, the island was to suffer further invasions – by Normans and Germans, Angevins and Aragonese; inevitably, perhaps, the Arabic element became smaller and was gradually Christianized. But it was never entirely driven out, and the descendants of those first Islamic invaders are still there, to this day.

*

1 Even then, a few heroic communities continued to resist. Taormina, thanks to its superbly defensible position, managed to hold out till 902.

Nothing that we know of Michael the Amorian leads us to suppose that he would have bothered his head unduly with theological speculation. Insofar as he gave any thought to the question at all, he was an iconoclast; as he himself pointed out, he had never in his life worshipped a holy image, and he was furthermore resolved to leave the Church as he found it. But he possessed none of the fanaticism of his iconoclast predecessors, or even of his own son Theophilus. Already at the time of his accession he had freed or recalled all those whom his predecessor had condemned to imprisonment or exile – including of course Theodore of the Studium, who had immediately renewed his campaign for the general restitution of the images; and though Michael was to remain firm on basic principles, he was perfectly prepared – even more than Leo V had been – to allow his subjects to practise whatever form of worship they liked, so long as they did so in private and refrained from preaching or proselytizing one way or the other. Nor did he ever make any sustained effort to enforce iconoclast doctrines outside the capital. Even in Leo's reign, professional icon-painters or fervent image-worshippers had been able to retire to Greece, or to the coast and islands of Asia Minor, with a reasonable chance of being left to pursue their chosen activities undisturbed; under Michael their prospects were better still. What he mistrusted above all about the iconodules was not so much their religious habits as their insistence on the ultimate supremacy of the Pope in matters of dogma; and when one of his own subjects, an Orthodox monk named Methodius, returned from Rome with a letter from Paschal I calling upon him to restore the True Faith, he became almost apoplectic with anger: Methodius was first scourged and then imprisoned in a tomb on the tiny island of St Andreas in the Gulf of Nicomedia, where he was to remain for nearly nine years.

Michael's reaction to Paschal's letter did not however prevent his considering the dispatch of a reply, describing the excesses to which the cult of images had led its more enthusiastic adherents and urging the Pope to withdraw his active support; but before doing so he decided to seek the advice of the Western Emperor Lewis the Pious, to whom he rehearsed the principal arguments:

Lights were set in front of the images and incense burnt, and they were held in the same honour as the life-giving Cross. Prayers were addressed to them, and their intercession was sought. There were even those who would cover them with cloths and appoint them godparents at the baptisms of their children. Some priests would scrape the paint from the pictures and mix it in the bread and wine which they dispensed at Holy Communion; others would place the body of the Lord in the hands of the images, from whom the communicants would receive it.

His letter was carried to Lewis by a mixed delegation of priests and laymen, who were received with elaborate courtesy at the imperial court in Rouen. Then they passed on to Rome, only to find that Paschal was dead, and that he had been succeeded by Eugenius II in the chair of St Peter. How they fared with the new Pope is not recorded; all we know is that Eugenius gave his permission for Lewis to summon a synod of Frankish bishops, which met in Paris in 825. This body ruled, with admirable common sense, that images should be displayed in churches as ornaments or memorials, but that they should not be worshipped; unfortunately it could claim no ecumenical status, and the Byzantines simply ignored it.

All in all, if we except the hostility of a few extremists, Michael's moderation in matters of doctrine won him general popularity in ecclesiastical circles. His only serious differences with the Church concerned not the worship of icons but his own remarriage, probably in 824, after the death of his beloved first wife Thecla. Among theologians of the strictest Orthodoxy second marriages, especially by Emperors, were to be deplored; what made things still more difficult on this occasion was the fact that the lady concerned – Euphrosyne, daughter of Constantine VI and granddaughter of the unspeakable Irene – had been for many years a nun in an island convent in the Marmara. By precisely what means Michael managed to obtain her release from her vows we shall never know; but he did so at last, and this second marriage proved, so far as we know, as happy as the first had been – Euphrosyne keeping vigil at her husband's bedside throughout his last illness (a disease of the kidneys) and, in October 829, finally closing his eyes in death. He was the first Emperor for half a century to expire, while still a reigning monarch, in his bed; the first, too, to leave a strong and healthy son, still in the prime of life, to succeed him.

3
Theophilus
[829–42]

Miracle, bird or golden handiwork,
More miracle than bird or handiwork,
Planted on the star-lit golden bough,
Can like the cocks of Hades crow
Or, by the moon embittered, scorn aloud
In glory of changeless metal
Common bird or petal
And all complexities of mire or blood.

W. B. Yeats, *Byzantium*

At the time of his father's death, Theophilus had already been co-Emperor for eight years, during which time the chroniclers barely mention him. There is one brief and tantalizing moment in 821, at the very beginning of the joint reign, when we are given a glimpse of the seventeen-year-old prince, bearing the Empire's most precious relics – the fragments[1] of the True Cross and the robe of the Virgin Mary – in solemn procession along the land walls while the army of Thomas the Slav was encamped below; but in general he seems to have been content to remain in his father's shadow, performing various ceremonial functions as necessary but otherwise avoiding the limelight. Now, with his assumption of the effective power at the age of twenty-five, he comes into his own – and at last reveals himself as being magnificently qualified to take on the responsibilities of Empire.

In marked contrast to the barely literate Michael, Theophilus was an intellectual, with all the characteristically Byzantine passion for theology; but he had also acquired a thorough military training, so that even if he

---

1 Fragments only: the main body of the Cross, after two periods in Constantinople and fourteen years in Persian hands, having been personally returned to Jerusalem by the Emperor Heraclius in 629. (See *Byzantium: The Early Centuries*, p. 305.) The Virgin's robe had been discovered in 629 in a coffin at Blachernae.

41

could never be described as an inspired leader in the field he was at least a highly competent one. Finally, he was an aesthete and a patron of the arts, with a particular love and understanding – despite almost continual warfare with the Caliphate throughout his reign – for the culture of the Islamic world. Far more than any Christian Emperor, he took as his exemplar an Abbasid Caliph: the great Harun al-Rashid, who had died in 809 when Theophilus was five years old. Like Harun, he early adopted the habit of dressing as a poor man and wandering incognito through the streets and markets of Constantinople, listening to the grievances and grumbles of the people and endlessly investigating prices – especially of food. Once a week, too, he would ride from the Great Palace to the Church of the Virgin (Theotokos) at Blachernae – a journey that would take him on a long diagonal from one end of the city to the other, in the course of which he encouraged any of his subjects with complaints of unfair treatment to lay their case before him. On one occasion, we read, he was approached by an elderly widow who claimed that the Emperor's own brother-in-law, his wife's brother Petronas, was enlarging his palace in such a way as to block out all the light from her own house nearby. Theophilus ordered an immediate inquiry, and on learning that the old lady was justified in her accusation, had the offending buildings torn down and his brother-in-law publicly flogged.

The story, it must be admitted, lacks the ring of absolute truth; yet there is no quality in a ruler more certain than a passion for justice to earn him the love and respect of his subjects, and the fact that this and many other similar tales enjoyed such wide currency during his reign is a clear indication that Theophilus became something of a legend in his own lifetime – in a way, perhaps, that none of his predecessors had done since the days of Heraclius, two centuries before. It suggests, too, that he made a genuine effort to communicate directly with his people: a rare phenomenon indeed in an Empire whose sovereign, Equal of the Apostles and standing half-way to heaven, was set on so lofty a pedestal and imprisoned in so tight a cocoon of protocol and ceremonial as to be normally inaccessible to all but his family and a few close advisers.

And yet, for all his love of justice and his comparative approachability, Theophilus had his own firmly-held ideas of Empire. However often he might attempt to descend from his pedestal, he never doubted that that pedestal must be of the finest gold. Here again he modelled himself on Harun: in a love of opulence and splendour for which we have to go back still further into the past to find an equal – as far, indeed, as Justinian himself. Already in 830, after only a few months on the throne, he sent a diplomatic mission to Baghdad, led by John the Grammarian. Its ostensible object was to give the Caliph Mamun formal intimation of his succession, but the Emperor seems to have been above all determined to impress his Arab neighbours by his wealth and generosity. John took with him, as presents to Mamun, works of art as sumptuous as any ever wrought by the jewellers and craftsmen of Constantinople. In his own baggage he carried two huge salvers of solid gold, encrusted with precious stones; one of these, in the course of a banquet, he deliberately arranged to have 'stolen'. His Arab guests, horrified at this apparent breach of the laws of hospitality, were all the more astonished when John showed no concern but simply called for an identical replacement, which was immediately brought in. Apart from such treasures, he had also been given 36,000 gold pieces to distribute as he liked, which he is said to have scattered 'like the sand of the sea'.

Where all this wealth came from remains a mystery. The reign of Michael II had seen a serious depletion of the imperial coffers: Thomas's insurrection and the constant – if largely ineffectual – campaigns against the Saracens of Crete and Sicily had all taken their toll. True, Michael hated spending money and always practised a rigid economy; but he could never have saved a quarter of the amount that his son dispensed with such largesse. What makes the enigma more baffling still is the fact that Theophilus did not spend beyond his means, still less run into debt; on the contrary, he was to leave his treasury a good deal fuller than he found it. It follows, therefore, that some time towards the end of Michael's reign the Empire must suddenly have had access to a new and seemingly inexhaustible source of wealth. One recent historian[1] attributes this to the opening or reopening of certain gold mines, probably in Armenia – adducing in support of this theory some evidence which suggests that the economy at this time suffered an acute bout of inflation. In the absence of any explanation by our contemporary chroniclers and of any other more likely hypothesis, we may assume him to be right; but we shall never know.

In any case, the new *basileus* was fortunate: he enjoyed both expensive tastes and the means by which to indulge them. At once he initiated a huge construction programme in the capital, understandably concentrating on the Great Palace. This was not so much one large

1 Romilly Jenkins, *Byzantium: The Imperial Centuries*, p. 147.

building as a collection of small ones – much as is the Ottoman Palace of Topkapi today – standing together in a vast enclosure to the south-east of the Hippodrome and extending all the way down to the Marmara shore. Originally established by Constantine the Great at the time of his foundation of the city, it had been largely rebuilt by Justinian; but that was nearly three hundred years before, and Theophilus was probably well justified in deciding that alterations and improvements were long overdue. Few other Emperors, however, would have tackled the programme with such panache.

His principal creation was the Triconchos, or Triple Shell, whose three apses, supported on pillars of porphyry and revetted with immense slabs of polychrome marble, gave the building a distinctively Oriental appearance. To the west, silver doors opened into a semi-circular hall, known as the Sigma and also lined with marble, while to the north rose the Hall of the Pearl – its white marble floor richly ornamented with mosaic, its roof resting on eight rose-pink marble columns. Off the main space was a smaller bedchamber, where the Emperor slept during the hot summer months. Opposite this lay the Karianos, designed for his daughters and so called for the broad staircase of milk-white Carian marble that led up to it; while a short distance to the south stood the Kamiles, in which six columns of green Thessalian marble led the eye up to a field of mosaics depicting a fruit harvest and on to a roof glittering with gold.

To the north-east of the Great Palace, next to the Church of St Sophia, was the Palace of The Magnaura, another of Constantine's foundations; it was here that Theophilus installed his most celebrated mechanical toy. An ambassador received here in audience would be astonished to find the imperial throne overshadowed by a golden plane tree, its branches full of jewelled birds – some of which appeared to have hopped off the tree and on to the throne itself. Around the trunk were lions and gryphons couchant, also of gold. Still greater would be the visitor's wonderment when, at a given signal, the animals would rise up, the lions would roar and all the birds would burst simultaneously into song. After a while the chorus would be interrupted by a peal of music from a golden organ, after which there would be silence to permit the Emperor and his guest to talk. Then, the moment the ambassador rose to leave, the whole chorus would start up again and continue till he had left the chamber.

This barely credible contrivance seems to have been inspired by a similar marvel in the possession of the Caliph – as was the splendid palace that Theophilus built for himself in the Oriental style at Bryas, on the Bithynian coast across the Marmara. It is only fair to add, however, that he also spent much time and money on the strengthening of the defences of Constantinople. The land walls needed little attention; but those along the shore of the Golden Horn had given rise to some anxiety during Thomas's siege, when it was realized that they might well prove insufficiently high to hold back a determined enemy. An ambitious plan to heighten them along their entire length, though initiated by Michael II, was almost wholly carried out by Theophilus, whose name appears more frequently on inscriptions along the walls and towers than does that of any other Emperor. Extravagant and self-indulgent he may have been; but he was well aware of his responsibilities too, and he never shirked them.

It was a sad stroke of irony – felt, we may be sure, by no one more than Theophilus himself – that decreed that this most instinctively pro-Arab of all the Emperors of Byzantium should have had to pass almost the whole of his reign in warfare against the forces of Islam. For the past sixteen years the eastern frontier had been quiet. There had been no formal treaty of peace; but the Caliphate, struggling for its life against a widespread insurrection on the part of a sect known as the Hurramites, had been obliged to call a halt to the annual invasions that had previously been the norm. Then, in 829, hostilities flared up again. To some extent this seems to have been the fault of Theophilus. He would infinitely have preferred to maintain friendly relations with his Arab neighbours, with plenty of cultural and intellectual exchange; but when, soon after his accession, an army of Hurramites crossed into the territory of the Empire and demanded to enlist under the imperial standards he decided that the opportunity was too good to miss and settled them on his north-eastern border, in a newly-established Theme which he called Chaldia. This was seen by the Caliph Mamun as a hostile act, and within a matter of months a Saracen army was again on the march.

In the first campaigns fortune favoured Theophilus. He led a successful expedition into enemy territory in 830, sacking the city of Zapetra, and in the following year took the initiative by invading Muslim-held Cilicia – with such gratifying results that, on returning with his victorious army to Constantinople, he awarded himself a triumph. The celebrations were impressive enough for the chroniclers to have left us detailed descriptions.

We read how the Empress Theodora, accompanied by the chief ministers and members of the Senate, sailed across the Bosphorus to welcome her husband at the Palace of Hieria, and how the party remained in Asia another ten days until the arrival of a sufficient quantity of prisoners to swell the procession to a proper size. Only when all were present and the necessary preparations had been made did the Emperor cross the straits and continue up the Golden Horn to Blachernae. Thence, after a short pause, he rode through the open country outside the walls to a point some few hundred yards west of the Golden Gate, where a brilliantly-coloured pavilion had been set up for his reception.

From this pavilion the triumphal procession started off towards the city. It was led by the seemingly endless train of prisoners, together with the principal trophies and spoils of war. These were followed by the Emperor himself, mounted on a white charger with jewelled harness. The diadem was on his head, in his hand the imperial sceptre. Over his breastplate he wore a loose gold tunic, embroidered with a design of roses and clusters of grapes. Beside him – also riding a white horse and wearing golden armour – was his adopted son-in-law the Caesar Alexius, whom he had recently married to his daughter Maria.[1] When the two reached the gate, they dismounted and bowed three times towards the east; the three senior civic officers – praepositus, magister and prefect – then advanced to meet the Emperor and presented him with a crown of gold. Having thus ceremonially resumed authority in the capital he continued his procession down the broad central thoroughfare, the Mesē, to St Sophia.

Constantinople, we are told, had been 'decked like a bridal chamber'. Carpets hung from the windows, the streets were adorned with festoons of purple and silver, the Mesē strewn with flowers. On reaching the Great Church, the Emperor attended a brief service of thanksgiving; then he walked across the Augusteum to the Bronze Gate of the Imperial Palace, the Chalkē, where a golden throne had been set up. On one side of it was a cross, also of gold, and on the other the great golden organ – one of several that he had ordered for the city, since he could never resist ingenious machinery – which was known as the *protothauma*,

---

1 After a run of five daughters Theodora had finally borne her husband a son, Constantine, who had however died in infancy. The Emperor had consequently chosen Alexius as his successor. The Caesar was to remain as heir apparent until the unexpected birth in 840, after twenty years of marriage, of the future Michael III.

the Prime Miracle. Seated on his throne, Theophilus next acknowledged the plaudits of the Greens and the Blues and received a further present from the citizenry in the shape of a pair of golden armlets; he then rode on past the Baths of Zeuxippus to the Hippodrome, whence he finally entered the Palace and was lost to view. On the day following he held an investiture – at which honours were conferred on all those who had distinguished themselves in battle – before taking his seat in the imperial box and giving the signal for the start of the games.

Alas, the festivities were premature. In the autumn of the same year the imperial army sustained a crushing defeat, and Theophilus was obliged to write Mamun two letters – the first having been rejected on the grounds that he had begun it with his own name rather than with that of its addressee – offering 100,000 gold dinars and 7,000 prisoners in return for the restitution of a number of captured fortresses and an agreement to a five-year peace. Even after the required redrafting, however, the offer was rejected; and a third overture early the next year, following the fall to the Saracens of the key stronghold of Lulon – which commanded the northern approach to the Cilician Gates – met with no greater success, the Caliph making clear that he would never agree to peace until Emperor and Empire alike forswore Christianity for Islam. Mamun's death on campaign in August 833 afforded a few years' respite, while his brother and successor Mutasim overcame the usual difficulties in confirming and consolidating his authority; but in 837 hostilities flared up again. Once more Theophilus, who had done much in the interim to strengthen his army, started off well; expeditions into Mesopotamia and western Armenia were successful enough – at least in his eyes – to justify another triumph, and in the games that followed he even went so far as to enter the lists himself, driving a white chariot in the uniform of the Blues and winning – to nobody's surprise – by a comfortable margin, while the crowd hailed his victory with cries of 'Welcome, Champion Incomparable!'

Once again he had celebrated too soon. In April 838 Mutasim rode out of his palace at Samarra at the head of an army estimated by one of our most reliable sources, Michael the Syrian, at 50,000, with an equal number of camels and 20,000 mules. On his banner was inscribed the single word AMORIUM – home of the Emperor's family and by now the second city of the Empire – which he made no secret of his intention of reducing to rubble. A week or two later, probably as soon as he had heard the news of the Caliph's departure, Theophilus set out from

Constantinople determined to block his path; his army met one wing of the Saracen host at Dazimon, the modern Tokat. At first all went well; then, suddenly, the sky darkened and the rain began to fall in torrents. At this point the Emperor saw that his opposite wing was in difficulties and led 2,000 men round behind his centre to reinforce it; unfortunately he omitted to tell his junior commanders what he was doing, and his unexpected disappearance immediately gave rise to a rumour that he had been killed. Panic broke out, followed – as always – by flight; and when the rain stopped and the light returned Theophilus realized that he and his men were surrounded. Somehow – largely because the bowstrings of the enemy archers had been rendered useless by the rain – they fought their way out, though with frightful casualties; but the battle was lost, the surviving soldiers were dispersed in all directions and the Caliph was already marching on Ancyra (Ankara), which surrendered a few days later without a struggle.

From the moment that Mutasim drew up his triumphant army before Amorium, however, it seemed that the capture of that huge and mightily-walled city was going to be a very different matter; and so, doubtless, it would have been had there not been a weak section of the bastion which, despite the Emperor's express orders that it should be properly strengthened, had been only roughly filled in with rubble and the surface hurriedly made good. This vulnerable spot was revealed to the besiegers by a converted Muslim resident; the Caliph directed all his available siege-engines against it and within a few days a breach was made. Even then the garrison fought on courageously; but at last its commander sent out three of his officers with the local bishop, offering to deliver up the city in return for the promise of safe conduct to all who wished to leave. Mutasim refused, insisting on unconditional surrender; but then one of the officers, Boiditzes by name, took an Arab general aside and promised his cooperation. What he actually did is uncertain: perhaps he stood down his soldiers at that particular point, or ordered them to hold their fire until he gave the order. At all events the Saracens were able to pour unchecked into the breach. Amorium was theirs.

Many of the inhabitants took refuge in a large church, in which they were promptly burnt alive by the conquerors; others, taken captive and led off into slavery, were slaughtered when the army's water supplies threatened to run low, or were left to die of thirst in the desert. Only forty-two survived the journey back to Samarra; these, after seven years' captivity during which they had steadfastly refused to renounce their religion, were finally offered the choice: conversion or death. All of them chose without hesitation to die, and on 6 March 845 were decapitated on the banks of the Tigris – to go down in the history of the Greek Orthodox Church as the Forty-Two Martyrs of Amorium.[1]

The news of the destruction of the city – for Caliph Mutasim was as good as his word – was received with horror in Constantinople, where the disaster was seen not only as a damaging blow to the very heart of the Empire but also as a personal affront to the Emperor and his line. Theophilus himself, now seriously alarmed by the growing power of Islam, immediately sent an impassioned appeal for aid to the Emperor Lewis, proposing a joint offensive. His original idea was, so far as we can gather, for the Eastern Empire to launch a major attack on Crete while the Western moved simultaneously against Sicily and south Italy; but there may well have been a still more ambitious plan – a combined attack on Saracen North Africa and even Egypt. It was also agreed that the alliance between the two Empires should be sealed by the marriage of one of the daughters of Theophilus to Lewis's grandson, the future Lewis II.

The Byzantine envoys were warmly received at the imperial court at Ingelheim in June 839, and the talks which were then initiated continued spasmodically for another four years, despite the deaths of both Emperors during that time. Had those talks proved fruitful, the age of the Crusades might have been brought forward by some two and a half centuries; but they came to nothing, and a similar appeal to Venice – one of the first occasions on which we find the young republic being addressed respectfully as an independent state – proved equally abortive. In the event, the Caliph made no immediate attempt to follow up his victory until 842, when a huge fleet sailed against Constantinople from the Syrian ports. Victim of a sudden storm, all but seven of the 400 *dromonds*[2] were smashed to pieces. But Mutasim never heard of this catastrophe. Already on 5 January he had died in Samarra; and just fifteen days later Theophilus followed him to the grave.

---

1 There is an old tradition that their headless bodies, when flung into the river, all obstinately refused to sink. Only the corpse of the traitor Boiditzes – who, despite having become a Muslim, had shared their fate – went plummeting to the bottom.

2 The *dromond* was the smallest type of Byzantine warship, designed for lightness and speed. It carried a crew of some twenty rowers at a single bank of oars, and was roofed over to protect them from enemy missiles.

With his known admiration for Arabic art and learning, it is hardly surprising that Theophilus should have shared the iconoclast convictions of his immediate predecessors; some writers, indeed, have accused him of fanaticism. In fact, his reputation in this regard rests on only a few known instances of ill-treatment, all of them in one way or another special cases. Thus Lazarus, the leading icon-painter of the day, was eventually – after repeated warnings – scourged and branded on the palms of his hands with red-hot nails; but after his release (at the intercession of the Empress) he is known to have completed at least two more important commissions, including a new gigantic figure of Christ to replace the one removed by Leo V from the Chalkē, so his injuries cannot have been too severe.

Lazarus was probably singled out for such punishment because of his prominence in the icon-loving community and his open defiance of the imperial decree; in the circumstances, the Emperor had little choice but to make an example of him. Similar considerations explain his actions in another case, still more fully documented: that of two brothers from Palestine, the writer Theodore and the hymnographer Theophanes, who had together assumed the mantle of Theodore of the Studium, after the latter's death in 826, as principal champions of the iconodules. According to their own account, they were summoned to Constantinople, kept for a week in prison and then brought before the Emperor. When he asked them why they had entered the Empire in the first place, they refused to answer, whereupon they were beaten severely about the head. On the next day they were flogged, but still refused to renounce their views. Four days later still, Theophilus offered them their last chance: if they would consent to take communion just once with the iconoclasts, they would hear no more of the matter. But they only shook their heads. And so, by the imperial command, they were laid across a bench while an abusive lampoon was tattooed across their faces. It was not, Theophilus admitted, a very good lampoon; but it was good enough for them. A free translation, thoughtfully provided by Professor Bury[1] – complete with its majestic mixed metaphor in the second line – confirms the Emperor's opinion:

> In that fair town whose sacred streets were trod
> Once by the pure feet of the Word of God –

---

1 'Some admiration,' observes the Professor, 'is due to the dexterity and delicacy of touch of the tormentor who succeeded in branding twelve iambic lines on a human face.'

The city all men's hearts desire to see –
These evil vessels of perversity
Were driven forth to this our City where,
Persisting in their wicked, lawless ways,
They are condemned and, branded in the face,
As scoundrels, hunted to their native place.

The tenor of the Emperor's questions – as well as that of this deplorable doggerel – suggests that not the least of the two brothers' offences was the fact that they were foreign immigrants who had, in Theophilus's eyes, entered the Empire deliberately to stir up trouble. They were not, however, returned to Palestine as the last line claims, but were imprisoned in the small Bithynian town of Apamea. Here Theodore died; his brother survived to become, in happier times, Bishop of Nicaea.

This unedifying story demonstrates clearly enough the cruelty and brutality of which Theophilus was capable when his authority was openly defied; there can be little doubt, on the other hand, that his motives on such occasions were more political than religious. Where he drew the line was at the public profession of the cult of icons in Constantinople. Elsewhere in the Empire, or within the privacy of their own homes in the capital, his subjects might do as they pleased. Even in the Imperial Palace, although he must have been perfectly well aware – for all their transparent subterfuges – that both his pious Paphlagonian wife Theodora and her mother Theoktistē were enthusiastic iconodules, he made no serious attempt to stop them.

Perhaps he himself subconsciously understood that the forces of iconoclasm were almost spent. The second period of its enforcement had after all been but a pale reflection of the first. Leo the Isaurian and Constantine Copronymus had changed the face of the Empire, subordinating all other issues to the single, simple belief that dictated and dominated their lives; Leo the Armenian, Michael and Theophilus shared their views, but possessed little of their inward fire. The times, too, were changing. The mystical, metaphysical attitude to religion that had originally given birth to iconoclasm was becoming less fashionable every day. Of the eastern lands in which it had first taken root, some had already been lost to the Saracens; and the populations of those that remained, beleaguered and nervous, had developed an instinctive mistrust of a doctrine that bore such obvious affinities with those of Islam. There was a new humanism in the air, a revived awareness of the old classical spirit that stood for reason and clarity, and had no truck with the tortuous, introspective spiritualizings of the Oriental mind. At the same time a naturally artistic people, so long starved of visual beauty, were beginning to crave the old, familiar images that spoke to them of safer and more confident days. And when, on 20 January 842, the Emperor Theophilus died of dysentery at thirty-eight, the age of iconoclasm died with him.

4
The Images Restored

[842–56]

All worship whatsoever must proceed by symbols, by idols: we may say, all
idolatry is comparative, and the worst idolatry is only more idolatrous.

Thomas Carlyle,
Heroes and Hero-Worship, IV

The story is told of how, one day during Theophilus's reign, his wife
Theodora was suddenly surprised by Denderis, the court jester, in the
act of kissing certain sacred images that she had concealed in her
bedchamber. Hiding her confusion as best she could, she told him that
she had merely been playing with a few dolls that she had preserved
from her childhood. It seems unlikely that Denderis believed her; at all
events he reported the conversation to the Emperor, who flew into a
towering rage and furiously accused her of idolatry. This time Theodora
had another explanation: there were no dolls – Denderis had been
deceived by the reflections in a mirror of herself and some of her ladies.
Theophilus seems to have accepted the story – mirrors were rarities in
the ninth century, and it might then have sounded a little less far-fetched
than it does today – but doubts clearly lingered in his mind, for some
time later he asked the jester whether he had noticed any repetition of
his wife's strange behaviour. 'Hush,' replied Denderis, putting one hand
to his lips and using the other to give himself a resounding slap on the
behind, 'hush, Emperor – not a word about the dolls!'

It is a silly little story, and probably apocryphal to boot; but it
illustrates clearly enough why Theodora, finding herself on her husband's
death Regent on behalf of her two-year-old son, should have made her
first concern the eradication of iconoclasm throughout the Empire. She
moved, perforce, with caution: John the Grammarian, a fervent
iconoclast, had for the past five years been firmly ensconced upon the
patriarchal throne, and there must have been plenty of old men still

living in Constantinople who could remember the fiasco of 786, when the last woman to wield the supreme power had had the same purpose in mind and, by acting prematurely, had nearly started a riot. But Theodora was a good deal more intelligent than Irene had been; moreover she was lucky to have as her chief advisers three men of quite exceptional ability – her uncle Sergius Nicetiates, her brother Bardas and Theoctistus, Logothete of the Course. The first two shared her views: Theoctistus had formerly been a professed iconoclast, but he was above all a statesman and he realized that times had changed: if the new regime did not act decisively over the iconoclast issue, the image-worshippers might well take the law into their own hands. The four laid their plans with care, and then gave notice that a Council would be summoned early in March 843 – fourteen months after the Emperor's death. Meanwhile a commission was set up under the chairmanship of old Methodius – who, having suffered persecution under both Michael II and his son, had finally become reconciled with Theophilus and had been living for some years in quiet retirement in the Imperial Palace – to prepare the agenda and the necessary documentation.

On the whole, the Council passed off smoothly enough, the only major problem being presented by John the Grammarian, who refused to resign and whom it consequently proved necessary to depose. Even then, according to several normally reliable sources, he could not be induced to leave the Patriarchal Palace and, when Bardas went to reason with him, pulled up his robes and exhibited several unpleasant abdominal wounds which he claimed to be the work of a platoon of soldiers sent to evict him but which were subsequently revealed to have been self-inflicted. Finally however he agreed to go quietly, and retired to his villa on the Bosphorus – where, his enemies whispered, he abandoned himself to necromancy and the black arts. Methodius was elected in his place, and the decrees of the Seventh Ecumenical Council – that which had put an end to the first period of iconoclasm in 787 – were confirmed. At the Empress's insistence, however, her dead husband's name was omitted from the lists of those prominent iconoclasts who were now anathematized as heretics. The story, assiduously circulated, that he had repented on his deathbed and that Theodora had held an icon to his lips as he expired can safely be discounted, and probably gained little enough credence at the time; but it got everybody out of a potentially embarrassing position and no serious objections were raised.

The victory was won: a victory not of iconodule over iconoclast but of clarity over mysticism, of Greek thought over Oriental metaphysics, ultimately of West over East – a victory every bit as crucial for the cultural life of the Empire as were, for its political development, the triumph over the Persians and the continuing struggle against the Arabs. And, as with so many victories, it almost certainly owed its long-term success to the moderation and magnanimity shown by the victors. On 11 March – which chanced to be the first Sunday in Lent, a day still celebrated by the Eastern Church as the Feast of Orthodoxy – a service of thanksgiving was held in St Sophia, attended by the entire imperial family and by vast crowds of monks from all the neighbouring monasteries.[1] Icons by the hundred were carried shoulder-high, and thenceforth gradually reappeared on the walls of the churches; but there was no sudden or uncontrolled proliferation such as might have provoked indignant reaction from the diehards. Even the ever-controversial image of Christ from above the Chalkē had to wait some years before its eventual restoration, and it was almost a quarter of a century before the first figurative mosaic was unveiled in the Great Church itself[2] – that huge, haunting image of the Virgin and Child enthroned which, after more than eleven centuries, still gazes impassively down on us today.

Nor, despite his past sufferings, did Patriarch Methodius show any desire for vengeance. Anathematized the iconoclast leaders might be; they were never ill-treated, still less deprived of their liberty. Such expressions of indignation as there were came, on the contrary, from the iconodules – notably the fanatical monks of the Studium, whose vitriolic attacks on the Patriarch when he passed them over for promotion to vacant sees in favour of moderates like himself finally obliged him to excommunicate them *en masse*. By this time, we are told, they had even tried to force his resignation – by the singularly inept contrivance of bribing a young woman to accuse him of seduction. At the ensuing inquiry Methodius is said to have given visual proof of his innocence by producing for inspection those parts which might have been thought most directly responsible for the alleged offence, explaining the shrivelled remnants of his manhood with a story of how, years before in Rome, a

---

1 Genesius maintains that these included representatives from Mount Athos. If he is right, this is the earliest reference we have to the Mountain as a holy place – though its inhabitants at that period would have been individual hermits rather than members of any organized monastic community. (See Chapter 12.)

2 Had there been any such figurative mosaics in Justinian's church, they could not conceivably have survived the iconoclasts; in point of fact, however, it is virtually certain that none ever existed in his day. See *Byzantium: The Early Centuries*, p. 203.

prayer to St Peter for deliverance from lustful thoughts had been answered with distressing efficiency. Not surprisingly, he won his case; the girl confessed that the whole story had been a fabrication. But its instigators suffered no more severe punishment than to join every year, with torches in their hands, the ceremonial procession which passed on the Feast of Orthodoxy from Blachernae to St Sophia, there to hear the sentence of anathema repeated publicly upon them.

Meanwhile, the iconodule martyrs received their posthumous reward. The bodies of Theodore of the Studium and the Patriarch Nicephorus, both of whom had died in exile, were brought back to Constantinople where, in the presence of the Empress and the entire court, they were ceremonially reinterred in the Church of the Holy Apostles. A less edifying spectacle was the desecration of the tomb of the arch-iconoclast Constantine V, from whose green marble sarcophagus several slabs were cut away and used to adorn a room in the Great Palace.

For the defeated image-haters, one small consolation remained. In pre-iconoclast days, and even in the iconodule interval under Irene, her son and successors, religious painting and sculpture had been alike permitted; the Council of 843 had drawn no distinction between them. After this time, however, as if by some tacit agreement, Byzantine art restricted itself to two dimensions. Sculpture – whether in stone or marble, wood or plaster, gold, silver or bronze – was set aside. This should not, perhaps, occasion us too much astonishment: the second Commandment is after all quite clear enough on the matter, and we might a good deal more reasonably wonder why it has been so universally ignored in Western Europe – were it not for the fact that very little more respect has been shown for most of the other nine. It is, none the less, a very real cause for regret. If Byzantium had gone on to produce sculptors and woodcarvers as talented as its painters and mosaicists, the world would have been enriched indeed.

Soon after the restoration of the icons, the Logothete Theoctistus succeeded in ousting his two colleagues; and for the next thirteen years he was, with Theodora, the effective ruler of Byzantium. He was that most unusual of combinations, a Patrician and a eunuch; but he was also a man of considerable learning and wide culture, who devoted much time and effort to the improvement of educational standards in the capital – they were already far ahead of anything known in the West – and laid the foundations for the cultural renaissance of the later ninth and tenth centuries of which we shall have more to say later. His financial policy in particular yielded excellent results: gold continued to flow into the imperial coffers, just as it had in Theophilus's day – and for no clearer reason.

In the military sphere, too, Theoctistus was a good deal more successful than was formerly believed. For reasons which will shortly become clear, Michael III and his ministers have been the victims of a campaign of deliberate disparagement on the part both of near-contemporary sources and of later chroniclers – above all the Emperor Constantine Porphyrogenitus himself – who had no hesitation in falsifying the work of their predecessors. Only quite recently has it been realized how far even modern historians have been deceived. We now know, for example, that the expedition led personally by Theoctistus against the Saracens of Crete, far from collapsing after his own return to Constantinople, in fact resulted in the recovery of the island for a number of years; while a decade later, on 22 May 853 – in what was by far the most daringly aggressive naval or military operation since the beginning of the Muslim invasions – a Byzantine fleet under the command of the High Chamberlain of the Palace, the eunuch Damianus, suddenly appeared off Damietta at the eastern extremity of the Nile Delta, set fire to the city and to all the Saracen vessels lying in the harbour, destroyed a huge store of arms and returned with scores of prisoners. Arab records recently come to light report other operations, by no less than three more fleets numbering 300 vessels in all, around the Aegean and off the Syrian coast.

Where Theoctistus must stand condemned is in his undeniable association with the Empress in what Professor Bury describes as 'one of the greatest political disasters of the ninth century' – the persecution of the Paulicians. This widespread but fundamentally harmless Christian sect had arisen some 200 years before in Armenia and had existed in peace with the Empire until the days of Michael I, who had yielded – as he always did – to ecclesiastical pressure and ordered the first measures to be taken against them. The reasons were purely doctrinal. It was not that the Paulicians were iconoclasts – though they were; it was that they rejected not only holy images but also the institutions of baptism, marriage and the Eucharist, the sign of the cross, all the Old Testament and quite a lot of the New, and the entire hierarchy of the Church. Espousing as they did the Manichean belief in the two opposing principles of good and evil, they held the material world to be a creation of the devil; it followed that Christ's single nature – for they were also staunch monophysites[1] – owed nothing to that world; as for His Mother, she had served merely as a physical vessel for the divine essence, through which it had flowed 'as water through a pipe'.

With the return of the iconoclasts the Paulicians had had reason to hope that their troubles might be over, but they had been disappointed: both Leo the Armenian and Theophilus had actively pursued the policies of their predecessors. And now that the iconodules were back in power the persecutions continued with redoubled zeal. A new decree was promulgated, calling on all members of the sect to renounce their errors on pain of death; and a vast military expedition set out for the East to put the order into effect. The result – since the victims almost all remained true to their faith – was a massacre: 100,000 are reported to have perished – by hanging, drowning, the sword, even by crucifixion. All their property and lands were confiscated by the State. Fortunately a considerable number managed to escape, and sought refuge in the only place available – across the imperial frontier with Omar ibn Abdullah, the Emir of Melitene (now Malatya) and his fellow Saracens.

Never before had the Byzantine Empire deliberately set out to destroy an entire religious community in such a manner; never would it attempt to do so again. But the treatment of the Paulicians was not only brutal and barbaric, leaving an indelible stain on the memory of the Empress in whose name it was carried out; it was also almost unbelievably short-sighted. Left to themselves, these sober, devout, disciplined men and women would have constituted a formidable bulwark against Saracen attacks, earning the respect and gratitude of every right-thinking Byzantine; instead, they were driven despite themselves into the territory of the Caliphate, of which they soon proved themselves loyal and courageous allies against the Empire. Meanwhile, as always under persecution, their religion spread. We find it – or something very like it – professed by the Bogomils in Bulgaria and Bosnia in the tenth century and by the Cathars of the Languedoc in the eleventh and twelfth. It was not an attractive creed, and untold suffering would have been avoided if it could have been contained among the Armenian fastnesses from which it sprang. That it was not so contained was the fault, above all, of successive rulers of Byzantium.

*

1 For the belief in the single (and divine) nature of Christ, see *Byzantium: The Early Centuries*, pp. 155–6.

The Emperor Michael III, meanwhile, was growing up. We hear little of him during his long minority; his mother was a strong-willed, decisive woman who kept him firmly in the background, and he himself always remained, throughout his short life, almost childishly weak and easily led. In other respects, however, he seems to have been rather more mature: in 855 at the age of just fifteen he took as a mistress a certain Eudocia Ingerina, and might well have married her had not his mother – horrified at the prospect of a half-Swedish daughter-in-law who showed her, she considered, insufficient respect – forced him to cast her aside in favour of another Eudocia, surnamed Decapolitana, in whom he took no interest whatever. It was characteristic of Michael that he obeyed unquestioningly; perhaps he was already resolved to maintain the relationship with his first love which, we have reason to believe, was to continue until his death. It may well be, none the less, that his suppressed resentment at Theodora's high-handedness induced him to lend a sympathetic ear to the conspiracy which, only a few months later, was to bring about her downfall.

The leading spirit in this conspiracy was the Empress's own brother, Bardas. He had never forgiven Theoctistus for out-manoeuvring him in 843; and for twelve years he had waited patiently for his chance. That chance had now come. With the assistance of the High Chamberlain Damianus – hero of the Damietta raid two years before, who may well have felt that his services on that occasion had been insufficiently recognized – he easily persuaded Michael that he would never be allowed to exert his rightful authority for as long as his mother and Theoctistus remained supreme, and that if he were even to attempt to assert himself they would have no compunction in deposing him.

Once assured of the young Emperor's support, Bardas acted quickly. A day or two later, on 20 November 855, the Logothete was walking through the Palace on his way to Theodora's apartments when he suddenly found his path blocked by Michael himself and Damianus. The Emperor angrily pointed out that he was no longer a child, and that if there were any state business to be transacted it should be referred to himself rather than to his mother. An argument ensued, after which Theoctistus turned on his heel and went back the way he had come; but he had not gone far before Bardas, together with a group of disaffected army officers, suddenly leapt forward and struck him to the ground. Somehow he managed to draw his sword, but he was quickly overpowered and hustled, still struggling, to the Skyla – a small semi-circular antechamber which gave direct entrance into the Hippodrome. Bardas's original idea, so far as we can tell, was to send him to some distant place of banishment; it was the Emperor himself who gave his guards the order to kill him. At this point Theodora, informed by her ladies of what had happened, appeared at the doors of the Skyla and tried to remonstrate; but she was rudely turned away. The guards dragged Theoctistus out from the chair under which he had crawled, and held him fast while their captain ran him through.

With the death of the great Logothete, Theodora's power was ended – though for the moment she continued to live, bitter and unforgiving, in the Imperial Palace. Meanwhile in March 856, at a special session of the Senate, her son was proclaimed sole Emperor, in which capacity he was to reign for the next eleven years. To reign, however, is not necessarily to rule; and in view of Michael's weak character and general irresponsibility it was a good thing indeed for the Empire that the effective power should have passed into the hands of his uncle. Despite the unprincipled manner in which he had seized that power – and his reported intention of dealing with Theoctistus by exile rather than execution does little to mitigate his guilt, since he could almost certainly have persuaded the Emperor had he wished to do so – Bardas quickly proved more capable even than his predecessor. A brilliant administrator possessed both of farsighted statesmanship and boundless physical energy, he stamped his imprint indelibly on what was soon to become, in the opinion of many, the golden age of Byzantium; while as principal magistrate of the Empire and commander-in-chief of its armed forces he presided over a period of almost uninterrupted success. In the military sphere, for example, we learn – from Arab sources, rather than falsified Byzantine ones – that in 856 an army under the command of his brother Petronas crossed the Euphrates and penetrated deep into Muslim territory as far as Amida (the modern Diyarbakir), taking many prisoners. Another expedition three years later, led on this occasion by the Emperor himself, crossed the same river at a time when it was in flood and later passed into legend, becoming the theme of one of the most popular traditional Greek folk epics. Then in the summer of 859 there was another raid on Damietta, every bit as successful as the first; while in 863 imperial armies scored two crushing defeats over the Saracens within the space of some ten weeks.

The first of these battles was fought against Omar ibn Abdullah, Emir of Melitene. Always a dangerous enemy, he had now further strengthened his forces with detachments of embittered Paulician refugees. In the early summer he led his army, Christians and Muslims together, through the Armeniakon Theme on the southern shore of the Black Sea, sacking the important commercial centre of Amisus (Samsun). The Byzantine army of some 50,000 sent against him was commanded once again by Petronas, who divided his forces into three and, advancing simultaneously from north, south and west, contrived to surround the Emir at Poson, a spot no longer precisely identifiable between the River Halys and its tributary, the Lalakaon. In the desperate fighting that followed Omar himself was killed, as were almost all his men, Saracens and Paulicians alike. The Emperor – who, according to the Arab chroniclers, was present throughout – and Petronas then returned in triumph to Constantinople, bringing with them as their prisoner the Emir's own son, one of the few Arabs to have survived. They had not been long in the capital before news reached them of yet another decisive victory – at Mayyafariqin over the Saracen Governor of Armenia, Ali ibn Yahya, who had also fallen in the fray.

The disgrace of Amorium had been avenged. The tide was beginning to turn. Until this time, from the earliest days of the Arab invasions, the Byzantines had been obliged to fight a defensive war against them; more than once, indeed, they had had to struggle for their very survival. Henceforth, we find them increasingly on the attack. Not only are they stronger and better equipped; there is a new spirit, a new confidence, in the air.

5
Of Patriarchs and Plots
[857–66]

Not merely were they deluded into illegalities but, if there be any summit of error, to this they have raised themselves . . . Who has ever heard such claims, bursting from the mouths of even the most abandoned, up to now? What tortuous serpent has belched his poison into their hearts?

Patriarch Photius, in a letter to
the Eastern Patriarchs, summer 867

The combination of wise government at home and military successes abroad should – or so one might have thought – have been a recipe for a happy and harmonious state. But happiness and harmony were rare visitors to Byzantium, and among all the various creators of discord pride of place must go to the Christian Church. Diligent readers of this history will have no difficulty in citing occasions without number on which it was at least arguable that the Empire would have been better off had it remained pagan – had Julian the Apostate been right after all; and it is especially ironical that this time of spectacular upsurge in Byzantine fortunes should have coincided with the gravest crisis yet to arise in the unedifying story of relations between the Patriarch of Constantinople and the Pope of Rome.

The root of the trouble can be traced back to the death of the wise old Patriarch Methodius in 847 and his succession by Ignatius the eunuch, son of the deposed Emperor Michael I.[1] Ignatius had other assets besides his imperial blood: in the darkest days of iconoclasm he had never wavered in his support for the holy images, and had made the monastery that he had founded on the island of Terebinthos – now Tavşan – in the Marmara a popular refuge for all who shared his views and who no longer felt safe in the capital. But where Methodius had been moderate and conciliatory in all his dealings with the former

1 See p. 16n.

iconoclasts, Ignatius was a blinkered bigot who understood neither forgiveness nor compromise. He owed his promotion to the Empress alone, and did not even wait for the end of his own consecration in St Sophia before giving his colleagues a foretaste of what was in store. His victim on this occasion was Gregory Asbestas, Archbishop of Syracuse, leader of the moderate party and thus by definition the object of his vindictiveness. On some fabricated pretext he suddenly turned on Gregory in the middle of the service and ordered him out of the church. Nor was that the end of the affair: he continued his persecution of the unfortunate archbishop for the next six years, until finally in 853 Gregory was arraigned before a synod that had been overwhelmingly packed in the Patriarch's favour, deposed and excommunicated.

Gregory appealed to two successive Popes for reinstatement; but Ignatius, like all extreme iconodules, had always been a staunch upholder of papal supremacy and the Vatican had no wish to antagonize him. Meanwhile the former moderates had become most distinctly less so. United in their detestation of the Patriarch, they were determined somehow to get rid of him; and they were fortunate indeed to find, at the very moment that he was most needed, a stronger and more effective leader than Gregory could ever have been. His name was Photius. Though he could not, like his adversary, boast imperial descent, he too was an aristocrat and was connected to the Emperor – if somewhat tenuously – by marriage, his father's brother-in-law having married Theodora's sister. He could also claim to be the most learned scholar of his day, capable of running rings round Ignatius, whose mind was too narrow to encompass any but the simplest theological doctrines. In one particularly successful exercise in Patriarch-baiting he even went so far as to propound a new and deeply heretical theory that he had just thought up, according to which man possessed two separate souls, one liable to error, the other infallible. His own dazzling reputation as a scholar and intellectual ensured that he was taken seriously by many – including of course Ignatius – who should have known better, and after his doctrine had had its desired effect and made the Patriarch look thoroughly silly he cheerfully withdrew it. His friend Constantine – whose mission to the Slavs is soon to be described – is said to have reproached his old master for so deliberately corrupting the minds of the faithful; but Photius always maintained that he had done no serious harm. Nor had he: it is no bad thing for the pigeons to have the cat set among them from time to time. Photius was responsible for perhaps the only really satisfactory practical joke in the whole history of theology, and for that alone he deserves our gratitude.

For all his immense learning, however, he was not a churchman. He had chosen instead a political career in the imperial chancery, where his promotion had been predictably swift; and it was inevitable that when Bardas came to power Photius should soon become his closest friend and counsellor. To Patriarch Ignatius, few developments could have been more unwelcome. Any sensible man, however, wishing in such circumstances to protect his own position, would have kept a low profile and played his hand as discreetly as he could; it was entirely characteristic of Ignatius that he should have come out, fists flailing, to the attack. On the particular issue he chose he was, it must be admitted, on firm ground. Bardas had had the misfortune to fall in love with his own daughter-in-law, for whom he had abandoned his wife; and the ensuing scandal was, not surprisingly, the talk of Constantinople. Ignatius first administered a public rebuke; then, when Bardas took no notice, he excommunicated him and, on the Feast of the Epiphany 858, refused him the Sacrament.

It was a brave thing to do; but it was also disastrous. From that moment on, Bardas was watching for his opportunity to rid himself of the turbulent Patriarch once and for all. That opportunity came some months later when the Emperor – who had for some time been growing increasingly suspicious of his mother – finally decided to pack her off, together with his unmarried sisters, to the monastery of Karianos near Blachernae. To make doubly sure that they would remain there, he also resolved to have their heads shaved; but when he called upon Ignatius to perform the operation, he met with a point-blank refusal. Bardas had no difficulty in persuading Michael that this could mean only one thing: that Patriarch and Empress were in unholy alliance against him. Fortunately, too, an epileptic pretender named Gebeon made his appearance at about the same time, implausibly claiming to be the son of Theodora by a former marriage; it was the work of a moment to manufacture evidence that he also was receiving patriarchal support. On 23 November Ignatius was put under arrest and banished, without trial, to his monastery on Terebinthos.

There was no question in Bardas's mind as to who his successor should be: Photius was the obvious candidate. Two obstacles, however, remained to be overcome. The first was that he was a layman; but that problem was easily solved. On 20 December he was tonsured; on the

21st he was ordained lector; on the 22nd, subdeacon; on the 23rd, deacon; on the 24th, priest; and on Christmas Day he was consecrated bishop by his friend Gregory Asbestas. His enthronement as Patriarch followed at once. The process may have been a trifle undignified, but there were plenty of precedents: Patriarch Tarasius – who had been Photius's uncle – and his successor Nicephorus had both acquired their ecclesiastical eminence in the same way. The second obstacle was more serious. No amount of pressure – and it was, we may be sure, considerable – would induce Ignatius to resign. Since the only other way of legally getting rid of him – canonical deposition by a Council of the Church – was manifestly impossible, the law would have to be set aside. Photius would occupy the patriarchal throne *de facto*; he could not hope to do so *de jure*, unless or until Ignatius changed his mind.

With his rival at least temporarily out of the way, he settled down to consolidate his position. His first step was to write to the Pope in Rome, giving official notice of his elevation. Such letters were usually little more than a formality, and received a formal reply; Pope Nicholas I, however, unlike the vast majority of his predecessors, took an active interest in the Eastern Church, over which he was determined to assert his authority. As a long-time member of the papal Curia he may well have been involved in the earlier correspondence with the Archbishop of Syracuse, and he had almost certainly heard of the events leading up to Photius's enthronement. Moreover, although the new Patriarch's letter was a model of tactful diplomacy, containing not one word against his predecessor, it was accompanied by another, ostensibly from the Emperor himself, in which Ignatius was said to have neglected his flock and to have been properly and canonically deposed – both of which claims the Pope rightly suspected of being untrue. He received the Byzantine legates with all due ceremony in S. Maria Maggiore and graciously accepted the presents they had brought with them;[1] but he made it clear that he was not prepared to recognize Photius as Patriarch without further investigation. In his reply, therefore, he proposed a Council of inquiry, to be held the following year in Constantinople, to which he would send two commissioners who would report back personally to him. He also took the opportunity of reminding the Patriarch – and through him the Emperor himself – about the Sicilian

---

1 They included a golden paten set with precious stones, a golden chalice with jewels hanging from its rim by threads of gold, a gem-encrusted golden shield and a gold-embroidered robe, featuring scenes from the Bible surrounded by a design of trees and roses.

and Calabrian bishoprics, the vicariate of Thessalonica and various other Balkan dioceses which in 732 had been removed by Leo III from the jurisdiction of Rome and placed under that of Constantinople;[1] was it not time that they were returned to papal control? There was, of course, no overt suggestion of a *quid pro quo*; but the implication was clear enough.

In the high summer of the year 860, a year or so after Pope Nicholas had received the imperial envoys in Rome, the people of Constantinople underwent as terrifying an experience as any of them could ever remember. The Emperor and his uncle had recently set out with the army for another campaign against the Saracens when, suddenly and without warning on the afternoon of 18 June, a fleet of some 200 ships from the further reaches of the Black Sea appeared at the mouth of the Bosphorus and made its way slowly towards the city, plundering the wealthy monasteries that lined the banks, burning and pillaging every town and village it passed. Emerging at the southern end of the channel, some of the vessels continued into the Marmara to lay waste the Princes' Islands, while the majority cast anchor at the entrance to the Golden Horn. For the Byzantines it was their first true confrontation with a people whose future was over the centuries to be inextricably involved with their own: the Russians. Their leaders were, in all probability, not Slavs at all but Norsemen – warriors whose fathers had been part of that huge migration from Scandinavia which had begun towards the end of the eighth century and was to have a lasting impact on Europe, western Asia and even, ultimately, the New World. In about 830 they had established a principality or khaganate around the upper Volga; a quarter of a century later they were using that mighty river, together with the Dnieper and the Don, to carry their dreaded longships southward against the great trading cities of the Black Sea and the Caspian. With them came their Slav subjects, by whom they were soon to be completely absorbed: almost – but not quite – the last of the barbarian tribes to strike terror into the hearts of the citizens of Constantinople.

Individual Rus (as they called themselves) had been seen in the capital before – notably in 838–9, when a small group of them had arrived on an unspecified diplomatic mission to the court of Theophilus. There was, however, nothing diplomatic about the present occasion, and the

1 See *Byzantium: The Early Centuries*, p. 357.

situation was made more serious still by the absence in Asia of the Emperor, his commander-in-chief and the bulk of his army. What happened at this point is not altogether clear;[1] it seems virtually certain, however, that the Prefect Oryphas, who had been left in command of the capital, sent messengers after Michael to alert him to the emergency. He returned at once, but by the time he reached Constantinople the raiders had sailed back up the Bosphorus into the Black Sea and headed for their homes.

Why did they leave so soon? Photius, who preached two sermons on the raid – the first while it was still in progress, the second within a few days of the Russians' departure – paints a blood-curdling picture of the outrages and atrocities suffered by all who fell victim to the raiders, and ascribes the city's deliverance to the miraculous robe of the Virgin,[2] its holiest relic, which was carried shoulder-high around the walls and provoked their immediate retreat. Other sources[3] carry the supernatural element still further, claiming that the Patriarch dipped the robe in the sea, whereat there arose a dreadful tempest which dashed the Russian ships to pieces. This however seems highly unlikely, if only because had it been true Photius would surely have mentioned it. By far the most probable explanation is that the raiders, finding the city impregnable and having exhausted the possibilities of extra-mural plunder, simply decided to call it a day and return home.

Whatever the truth about the Russian withdrawal, there can be no doubt that the Patriarch emerged from the incident with his reputation if anything higher than before. His adversary Ignatius was less fortunate. Since his effective deposition he had suffered a degree of persecution that would have broken most men of his age. After some time on Terebinthos he had been removed to Hieria – site, ironically enough, of one of the most luxurious of imperial palaces – where he was lodged in a shed that had previously been occupied by goats. Sent back to the capital, he was then thrown into a prison in Promotos on the far side of the Golden Horn, where he was weighed down with heavy irons and subjected to such beatings that two of his teeth were knocked out. After a brief spell in another prison – that of the Numera, near the Palace – he

---

1 For the fullest discussion of the problems and probabilities, see C. Mango, *The Homilies of Photius, Patriarch of Constantinople:* English translation, introduction and commentary, Harvard, 1958.

2 See p. 41n.

3 The followers of Simeon Logothetes, including Leo Grammaticus, Theodosius Melitenus and others.

was transferred to the island of Lesbos (Mytilene) whence, six months later, he was allowed to return to his monastery. That, one might think, should have been enough; but now it was the turn of the Russians. Those of them who had sailed on to the Princes' Islands fell on Terebinthos with berserk fury, ravaging and plundering the monastic buildings and killing no less than twenty-two monks and domestic staff. Ignatius himself barely escaped with his life.

Predictably enough, the catastrophe was seen in Constantinople as a further sign of divine displeasure, and doubtless eliminated a number of Ignatius's remaining supporters. But it made no difference. The stubborn old eunuch held firm, resolved to accept whatever hardships, whatever ill-treatment his enemies might inflict upon him. His hour would come. Meanwhile he would bide his time – and would put his faith in Pope Nicholas, whose emissaries were confidently expected the following spring.

The papal commissioners, Zachary of Anagni and Rodoald of Porto, reached Constantinople in April 861. Whether or not they had been given firm instructions by the Pope, they can certainly have had no doubts where his sympathies lay. From the moment of their arrival, however, they found themselves under formidable pressure from Photius; indeed, the first of the many presents that they were to receive – embroidered robes of unexampled richness – were delivered to them *en route*, before they had even completed their journey. Immediately they were swept up into a ceaseless round of Church ceremonies, receptions, banquets and entertainments of every kind, while the Patriarch himself remained constantly at their side, dazzling them with his erudition, captivating them with his charm. Their audiences with the Emperor, on the other hand, were distinctly less pleasant. He too treated them with perfect courtesy; but they were more than once reminded that their return home depended entirely on his benevolence towards them, and that a prolonged period of residence in a place celebrated for the voraciousness of its insect life might prove a most disagreeable alternative. Thus, by a judicious combination of bribery, cajolery and veiled threats, it was quickly made clear to Zachary and Rodoald which side they should support; and well before the Council held its opening session – just before Easter, in the Church of the Holy Apostles – Photius had satisfied himself that they would give no trouble. As for Ignatius, they were not allowed so much as to clap eyes on him until he was led into the church to give his evidence. His attempt to appear in full patriarchal regalia was unsuccessful, and it was in a simple monk's habit that he was obliged to listen while seventy-two witnesses testified that his former appointment was invalid, being due to the personal favour of the Empress Theodora rather than to any canonical election. At the close of the fourth session his deposition was confirmed by a formal document at the foot of which, prominent among the signatories, were the names of Zachary of Anagni and Rodoald of Porto.

Pope Nicholas, as might have been expected, was furious, and when the unfortunate prelates returned to Rome in the autumn he left them in no doubt of his displeasure. Their task, he reminded them, had been to discover the facts; they had no authority to appoint themselves judges. By exceeding their instructions in so unwarrantable a fashion they had not only been guilty of grave insubordination; they had betrayed the interests of the entire Church and had succumbed to Byzantine blandishments in a manner more in keeping with the ways of innocent children than with those of senior ecclesiastics. Worse still, they had done so without obtaining a single concession in return. If, as seemed likely, the Bulgar Kingdom was shortly to adopt Christianity it was of vital importance that the Illyrian bishoprics should return to the Roman obedience as soon as possible, and this would have been the perfect opportunity of ensuring that they did so. Had the wretched envoys even mentioned such a possibility in their conversations with Photius? They had not. They had allowed themselves to be made his dupes, and in doing so had shown themselves utterly unworthy of their rank and position. He would consider their futures later. Meanwhile they could go.

Trembling, they withdrew. But the Pope's anger was given no chance to abate; for there now arrived in Rome another delegation from Constantinople, bringing a full report of the proceedings of the Council together with a letter from Photius calculated to inflame his wrath still further. While remaining suavely polite throughout, it contained none of the expressions of reverence and respect appropriate in such communications. On the contrary, the Patriarch addressed the Pope as an equal, and although at no point did he specifically assert the independence of the see of Constantinople, such an assertion was implicit in every line. As for the disputed bishoprics, he pointed out that he himself would have asked nothing better than to see them returned to the authority of Rome; unfortunately this was a matter for the Emperor, and the Emperor did not at present consider the time ripe for any further changes.

By now it was clear to Nicholas that firm action must be taken; and his determination was strengthened by the sudden and unexpected appearance of a certain Theognostus who, apart from various high ecclesiastical distinctions – he was an archimandrite of the Roman Church, abbot of the monastery of Pegae, *skeuophylax*[1] of St Sophia and Exarch of the monasteries of Constantinople – was also the senior and most vocal champion of the deposed Patriarch. Kept under close surveillance on the Emperor's orders, he had somehow managed to escape from the capital in disguise; and he now treated the Pope to a graphic account of the unfairness of the recent inquiry, the perfidy of the witnesses, the iniquity of Photius and his friends, the loyalty of Ignatius to Rome and, finally, all the tribulations that the old Patriarch had been called upon to endure. These, it appeared, had if anything increased in severity since the Council. In their efforts to force him into an abdication – not that this should have been any longer necessary – his tormentors had arrested him once again, subjected him to further repeated beatings, starved him for a fortnight and incarcerated him, naked except for a shirt, in the mortuary chapel of the Church of the Holy Apostles, where he had been stretched across what was left of the desecrated sarcophagus of the arch-iconoclast Constantine V, with heavy stones tied to his ankles. At last, when the poor man was barely conscious, a pen was thrust into his hand and guided to form a signature, above which Photius himself wrote an act of abdication.[2]

The Pope hesitated no longer. First he addressed an encyclical letter to the Patriarchs of Alexandria, Antioch and Jerusalem, informing them that Ignatius had been illegally deposed and his place usurped by a base scoundrel, and calling upon them to do everything in their power to restore him to his rightful throne. (Since the sees of all three Patriarchs were now in Saracen hands, their chances of intervention were slim.) He then wrote to the Emperor and to Photius, setting out in no uncertain terms his own view of the matter and emphasizing once again the supreme authority of the Roman Pontiff, without whose approval no Patriarch could assume or be deprived of office. When these letters remained unanswered he summoned a synod, which met at the Lateran in April 863. It divested Photius of all ecclesiastical status; declared him

---

1 Literally, Keeper of the Stores; but in fact a purely honorary title with no practical duties attached.

2 So, at least, avers the *Vita Ignatii*; but it is, like almost all works of hagiography, far too heavily biased in its subject's favour to be trustworthy.

The Western Emperor Lewis the Pious, depicted
on a manuscript poem: c.831–40

НІКНФОРЪ ЦРЬ ИДЕ НА БЛЪГАРЫ

nicephorus

ѡ ситѧ кеде макеdon

црь ѹмыслна въ хвати ннкнфора црь
нѡстѹ глвѧ его

Illuminations from the *Chronicle of Manasses, c.*1345

(*Opposite, top*) Krum leads his troops into battle, 811

(*Opposite, bottom*) Nicephorus I stands, hands bound, before Krum

(*Above*) The conversion of the Bulgars; Boris watches a baptism

The Virgin and Child, *c.*861, apse mosaic, St Sophia, Istanbul

The Archangel Gabriel, *c.*861, mosaic on arch of
north bema, St Sophia, Istanbul

(*Above*) Greek fire: thirteenth- or fourteenth-century
illumination from the Scylitzes Codex

(*Opposite*) The Crucifixion: eighth- or ninth-century
cloisonné-enamel cover of the reliquary of the True Cross

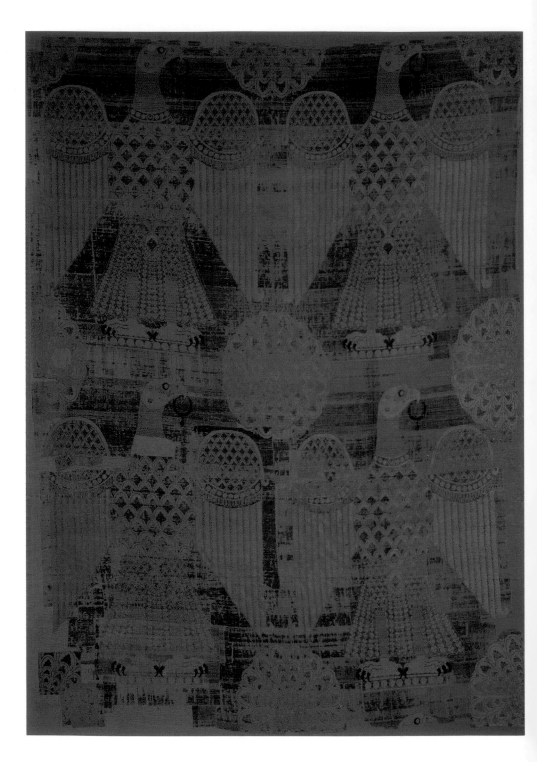

Byzantine silk shroud of St Germain l'Auxerrois:
ninth or tenth century

excommunicate unless he immediately renounced all claims to the Patriarchate; pronounced a similar sentence on all other churchmen who owed their advancement to him; and restored Ignatius and all who had lost office in his cause to their former ranks and positions. Zachary of Anagni was condemned for his conduct at Constantinople and dismissed from his see. Surprisingly, no immediate action was taken against Rodoald.[1]

The Emperor and his Patriarch were no doubt intensely annoyed at the Pope's obduracy, but they were not unduly concerned. Michael in particular was in a bullish mood. The year 863 had proved, as we have seen, something of an *annus mirabilis* for Byzantine arms; and even in the field of religion there had been developments in the Balkan peninsula compared with which the whole Photian dispute must have seemed insignificant indeed.

The Slavs had constituted an unpleasant and unwelcome element in the Roman Empire ever since their first irruption into imperial territory in the sixth century; and the Russian raid of 860 had done little to increase their popularity with the Byzantines. Within another two years, however – at the very height of the quarrel between Patriarch Photius and Pope Nicholas I – there arrived a group of envoys from Rostislav, Prince of Moravia, on a very different mission. Their master, they explained, wished with all his subjects to embrace Christianity, but such Christian teachers as had previously come among them had all expounded contradictory doctrines. Would the Emperor therefore agree to send them trustworthy missionaries from whom the truth, and nothing but the truth, could be learned?

So, at least, runs the legend. There can be no question that the Moravians did indeed send a mission to Constantinople; it is unlikely, however, that their motives in sending it were quite as ingenuous as they are traditionally made out to be. Mass conversions of whole nations and peoples almost invariably have political undertones, and this was no exception to the rule. Rostislav was under severe pressure from the Franks beyond his north-western border and when, early in 862, the Frankish King Lewis[2] concluded a treaty of alliance with the Bulgar

---

1 As it turned out, the Bishop of Porto was also to receive his come-uppance, but at a later synod held in November 864.

2 The Emperor Lewis I (the Pious) had divided the Western Empire between his three sons. The youngest was Lewis, surnamed 'the German', who had been made King of the Eastern Franks.

Khan Boris, he found himself in desperate need of a strong ally. It seems virtually certain, therefore, that the main object of his mission was to alert the Byzantine Emperor to the dangers facing the peninsula and to persuade him, before it was too late, to take up arms against his Bulgar neighbours. His proposed adoption of Christianity – and Orthodox Christianity at that – was merely an additional inducement, particularly since it seemed likely that Boris might at any moment announce a mass conversion of his own people, and in such an event would almost certainly lead them into the Roman fold.

Patriarch Photius was not the man to let slip so golden an opportunity. Here was the prospect not only of spreading the Gospel among the heathen, but of extending the influence of Orthodoxy to the far north-west. Here too – still more satisfactory in the present circumstances – was a chance of striking a major blow at the Papacy, for he was fully aware of Nicholas's anxiety that all newly-converted Balkan peoples should be subject to papal authority. He had, moreover, a perfect candidate for the job: a monk from Thessalonica whose baptismal name was Constantine, but who is generally known to posterity by the Slavonic name of Cyril that he was to adopt on his deathbed a few years later. This young man – he was still only thirty-five – had attracted attention from an early age by his erudition and saintly character, with which he combined a remarkable flair for languages. Brought by Theoctistus to Constantinople, he had pursued his studies under Photius himself, who had been so impressed by him that he had made him his librarian. Subsequently Cyril had undertaken a mission to the Khazars, to whom he had preached in their own tongue and among whom he had made a number of conversions, gaining such favour with their ruler as to obtain the release of some 2,000 Christian prisoners.

Where military intervention was concerned, the Emperor Michael was initially unenthusiastic. On the eastern front his armies were scoring one success after another, and he was reluctant to interrupt this unprecedented succession of victories in favour of a distinctly more problematical campaign in the West. But he saw too – or, if he did not, Photius would have been quick to persuade him – that to allow Lewis a free hand in the Balkans would be to invite disaster. Several regiments were summoned back to Constantinople; meanwhile the fleet, most of which had been lying idle during the eastern campaigns, made ready for war. In the summer of 863 it sailed up the Bosphorus into the Black Sea and dropped anchor off the Bulgarian coast. At the same time the Emperor advanced across the frontier at the head of his army.

He could not have chosen a better moment. The Bulgar forces were away in the north, drawn up along the Moravian border, while the south was in the grip of the most severe famine of the century. Boris saw at once that resistance was impossible, and sent envoys to Michael to ask his terms. They proved simple enough: the Khan must give up his alliance with the Franks and adopt Christianity according to the Orthodox rite. Boris agreed with almost unseemly haste. In September 865 he travelled to Constantinople, where he was baptized into the Christian faith by the Patriarch in St Sophia and took the name of Michael, the Emperor himself standing sponsor at the font.

Meanwhile, in the spring of the previous year, Cyril had set off on his Moravian mission – accompanied by his brother Methodius, almost as well qualified as himself for the task that lay ahead. During an early career in government service he had been posted to a province with a largely Slav population, and he too had learned their language. Later, deciding on a life of contemplation, he had retired to a monastery on the Bithynian Mount Olympus; but when his brother invited him to share the burden of his new mission he had readily agreed to join him. The pair left Constantinople – as nearly as we can deduce – in the early summer of 864, and remained in Moravia for over three years. According to an ancient tradition, Cyril now invented a new alphabet with which to transcribe the hitherto unwritten Slavonic speech, and then proceeded to translate the Bible and parts of the liturgy. Oddly enough, however, the language he chose was Macedonian Slavonic – only distantly related to the Slovakian dialect spoken by the Moravians, few of whom could have understood a word of it; it therefore seems a good deal more likely that he had devised his alphabet with the Bulgars rather than the Moravians in mind, and that he later simply made his translations into the only Slav language he knew.[1]

In such circumstances, it comes as no surprise to learn that the Moravian experiment was to have extremely disappointing results. It remains true none the less that by providing the Slav peoples with an alphabet tailor-made, as it were, to the phonetic peculiarities of their various tongues, Cyril laid the foundations for their literary development;

---

1 It was long believed that the alphabet invented by Cyril was not the modern Cyrillic – as used by the Russians, Serbs, Bulgars and various other races today embraced by the Soviet Union – but another, far more ungainly and long fallen into disuse, known as the Glagolitic. This theory, however, seems no longer tenable. See Appendix IX to Sir Steven Runciman's *A History of the First Bulgarian Empire*, and the article 'St Cyril Really Knew Hebrew' by E. H. Minns, in *Mélanges publiés en l'honneur de M. Paul Boyer*, Paris, 1925.

and it is perhaps for this benefaction, as much as for his and his brother's achievements in the missionary field, that the two scholar-saints are remembered and revered today.

In August 865 Pope Nicholas received a letter from the Byzantine Emperor. For three years the controversy had hung fire: three years during which Michael's successes in Bulgaria – political, military and religious – had made him more arrogant than ever. The two papal legates, he now pointed out, could consider themselves extremely fortunate to have been permitted even to attend a synod called to settle an internal problem which was no concern of theirs; but they were of no serious importance. The real responsibility for the quarrel lay with slanderers and trouble-makers like Theognostus, who were busy spreading their venom all over Rome. These men must be extradited forthwith and returned to Constantinople. If the Pope were to refuse, the Emperor himself would come to Rome and fetch them.

Nicholas, replying, gave as good as he got. He confined himself to a single major issue – the supremacy of Rome. There could be no question about this, and certainly no alternative: only twenty years before, had not both the Emperors and the Patriarchs of Constantinople been iconoclast heretics? Any council not authorized by the Pope was an illegal council, its actions automatically null and void. As for Theognostus and his friends, they were at liberty to remain at the papal court for as long as they wished. He himself would make one concession, and one only: if the two rival Patriarchs were to come to Rome and present themselves before him he would once more consider their respective claims. That was as far as he would go.

It is unlikely that Michael ever intended to carry out his threat, which was probably little more than a stylistic flourish to lend force to his arguments; but we shall never know for certain, owing to an unexpected development which put an entirely new complexion on the controversy, obliging Photius at least – for the Emperor, by now a hopeless alcoholic, was spending the greater part of the day in a drunken stupor – to take it far more seriously than he had done before. The Bulgar Khan, less than a year after his conversion, was growing dangerously restive. Suddenly he had found his Kingdom overrun with Greek and Armenian priests, more often than not at loggerheads with each other over abstruse points of doctrine incomprehensible to his bewildered subjects, most of whom had been perfectly happy in their former paganism and were far from pleased to discover that they were expected not only to take instruction from these unwelcome and discordant strangers but to feed and lodge them as well. And there was something else. The magnificent ceremony of his own baptism by Photius in St Sophia had impressed him deeply, and he now wished to have similar ceremonies performed among – and by – his own people. He had accordingly written to Constantinople asking for the appointment of a Bulgarian Patriarch.

It was at this point that Photius made perhaps the most disastrous miscalculation of his life. Determined to keep the Bulgarian Church firmly under his own control, he not only refused the request but dismissed it out of hand. Boris – in the interests of clarity he must keep his pagan name – had also mentioned various small points of Orthodox doctrine and social custom which in one way or another conflicted with local traditions, suggesting that if the latter could be permitted to continue much of the popular resistance to the new faith might be overcome; some of his proposals were rejected, the rest were simply ignored. The Khan was furious. He was happy to be the Emperor's godson, but he had no intention of being made his vassal. Fully aware of the state of affairs existing between Rome and Constantinople and the consequent possibility of playing one off against the other, in the summer of 866 he sent a delegation to Pope Nicholas with a list of all the points that Photius had so insultingly dismissed, adding a number of new ones for good measure and requesting the Pope's views on each.

For Nicholas, this was the chance he had been waiting for. At once he dispatched two more bishops – Paul of Populonia and Rodoald's successor Formosus of Porto – to the Bulgarian court as his own personal legates. They carried with them a remarkable document in which he gave thoughtful and meticulous answers to every one of the 106 items in Boris's questionnaire – showing consideration for all local susceptibilities, making all possible concessions that were not actually contrary to canon law and, where these could not be granted, explaining the reasons for his refusal. Trousers, he agreed, could certainly be worn, by men and women alike; turbans too, excepting only in church. When the Byzantines maintained that it was unlawful to wash on Wednesdays and Fridays, they were talking nonsense; nor was there any cause to abstain from milk or cheese during Lent. All pagan superstitions, on the other hand, must be strictly forbidden, as must the accepted Greek practice of divination by the random opening of the Bible. Bigamy, too, was out.

The Bulgars were disappointed about the bigamy, but on the whole more than satisfied with the Pope's answers and – perhaps equally important – by the obvious trouble that he had taken over them. Boris at once swore perpetual allegiance to St Peter and, with every sign of relief, expelled all Orthodox missionaries from his Kingdom; Paul and Formosus settled down to a year of almost constant preaching and baptizing, and were soon joined by a whole supplementary team of bishops and priests, by whom the good work was carried on.

6
Double Murder
[866–7]

I have got rid of the fox; but in his place I have put a lion who will end by devouring us all.

Bardas, after the dismissal
of the High Chamberlain Damianus

It has seemed worth telling in some detail the story of what was to become known as the Photian schism, not only for its own inherent interest but for its importance in the history of East–West relations within the Christian Church. Nor is that story altogether finished. The time has come, however, to look briefly at the secular scene during the reign of Michael III and at the men who loomed largest in it – beginning with the Emperor himself.

If Michael has so far appeared a somewhat shadowy figure in this account, it is because he himself was an unusually weak personality who allowed himself to be dominated first by his mother, then by his uncle Bardas and finally by his intimate friend, murderer and successor Basil the Macedonian. Although it was plain from the start that he would never make the sort of ruler the Empire needed, he was not entirely without qualities: by his early twenties he was already a seasoned campaigner, and his physical courage in the field was never in question. What he lacked above all was strength of will. Content to sit back and enjoy himself while others took on the responsibilities of government, he seemed unable and even unwilling to check his own moral decline: a decline which, in the last five years of his life until his violent death at the age of twenty-seven, finally reduced him to a level of drunkenness and debauchery that fully earned him his later sobriquet of 'the Sot'.

It was fortunate for the Empire that there were others – statesmen, moreover, of quite exceptional ability – ready to take up the reins of power and to govern in his name: first, in the days of his mother's

Regency, the eunuch Theoctistus; later, after her downfall, her brother
Bardas. Some time around the year 859 Bardas received the dignity of
curopalates, a rare distinction normally reserved for members of the
imperial family and giving its holder some claim to the succession
should the Emperor die without issue; but as his power and influence
increased even this was not enough and in April 862, on the Sunday
after Easter, he was created Caesar. By this time Michael had long since
put away his wife Eudocia Decapolitana, and his chances of legitimate
progeny were negligible. Bardas was universally accepted as the next
Emperor of Byzantium, and with the present one already far advanced in
alcoholism nobody believed that his succession could be long delayed.

Meanwhile he continued to act as *basileus* in all but name, and did so
supremely well. The ten years of his government saw the string of
victories over the Saracens in the East and the conversion of the
Bulgars, to say nothing of major advances in the long-drawn-out
struggle of the Byzantine Church for independence from Rome; he
himself followed the example of his brother-in-law Theophilus in the
personal and active interest he took in the administration of justice, and
that of Theoctistus in his encouragement of learning. The old University
of Constantinople, founded early in the fifth century in the reign of
Theodosius II, had been allowed to decline until, during the days of the
first iconoclasts, it had collapsed completely. Bardas it was who revived
it, establishing it this time in the Imperial Palace of The Magnaura under
the direction of Leo the Philosopher – or, as he is sometimes called, Leo
the Mathematician.

With Photius the Patriarch and Constantine-Cyril the missionary, Leo
was one of the three greatest scholars of his time. A cousin of John the
Grammarian, he had earned his living as a young man by teaching
philosophy and mathematics in Constantinople; but he had become
famous only after one of his pupils, captured by the Saracens and taken
off to Baghdad, had so impressed the Caliph Mamun by his knowledge
that the latter had inquired who his master had been. The Caliph –
himself an intellectual and a dedicated patron of the arts and sciences –
had then actually written to the Emperor Theophilus, offering 2,000
pounds of gold and a treaty of eternal peace in return for the loan of Leo
for a few months; but Theophilus had wisely preferred to set him up as
a public teacher in the capital, where he gave regular lectures in the
Church of the Forty Martyrs. Later he was appointed Archbishop of
Thessalonica, but on the Emperor's death Leo – a fervent iconoclast –

was deposed from his see and returned to academic life. Under his direction at Magnaura, Constantine-Cyril had briefly occupied the chair of philosophy, while others of his pupils held those of geometry, astronomy and philology. It is interesting to note that there was no chair of religious studies; the university concerned itself solely with secular learning – which accounted for the implacable hostility with which it was viewed by Ignatius and his followers.

Among the Emperor's many unattractive habits in these latter years was that of surrounding himself with favourites and cronies, who would don obscene fancy dress and accompany him in wild roisterings through the streets of the capital. One of these men, who makes his first appearance in 857 or thereabouts, was a rough and totally uneducated Armenian peasant by the name of Basil. His family, like so many of their country-men, had been settled in Thrace; but they had subsequently been taken prisoner by Krum and had been transported beyond the Danube to an area known as 'Macedonia' – probably because of the number of Macedonians who had suffered a similar fate. Here Basil had spent much of his childhood, and it is as 'the Macedonian' that he and his dynasty are most misleadingly known, despite the fact that he possessed not one drop of true Macedonian blood, spoke Armenian as his first language and Greek only with a heavy Armenian accent. Devoid of any intellectual accomplishments – he was entirely illiterate, and remained so all his life – he could boast only two obvious assets: Herculean physical strength and a remarkable way with horses. Either of these may have been responsible for his first attracting the Emperor's notice. Genesius tells of how he distinguished himself at a wrestling contest, in which he was pitted against a gigantic Bulgar who had defeated several previous champions. When Basil's turn came, he is said to have picked the fellow up bodily and hurled him across the room. The Continuator of Theophanes gives a similar account, but also tells another story, accord-ing to which Michael was presented with a magnificent but totally unmanageable horse. Neither he nor any of his friends could control it, but one of them suggested that his groom might succeed where all the others had failed. Basil – for it was he – approached the horse, took its bridle with one hand and stroked its ear with the other, whispering gently as he did so. Immediately the animal became quiet. So delighted was the Emperor by this performance that he there and then took the young Armenian into his service.

We can accept these trivial anecdotes or reject them; it hardly matters. There is, however, another story of Basil's youth which, although obviously belonging to legend, was sedulously fostered in his later years and proves rather more significant as an indication of his need to justify his later accession to the throne. In Book V of the Continuator – a most flattering biography of Basil now known to be the work of his putative grandson, the Emperor Constantine VII Porphyrogenitus – we read of how he first arrived in Constantinople one Sunday evening at dusk, and lay down to sleep in the porch of the Church of St Diomed near the Golden Gate. During the night, the abbot of the monastery to which the church belonged was awoken by a mysterious voice, commanding him to go and open the door to the Emperor. He rose, but seeing only a poor traveller in rags huddled on the floor, returned to his bed. A second time the summons came, with the same result; then a third, more insistent still and accompanied, we are told, by a hefty punch in the ribs. 'Rise,' ordered the voice, 'and bring in the man who lies before the door. He is the Emperor.' The abbot obeyed, took the youth into the monastery, fed him, washed him and gave him new clothes, asking only to be considered thenceforth his friend and brother.

We do not know whether this improbable tale came to the ears of the Emperor Michael or, if it did, what effect it had on him; but from the moment of Basil's admission to the imperial court his promotion was swift. He soon became more of a friend than a servant; and when the office of High Chamberlain[1] suddenly fell vacant – the eunuch Damianus having been discharged after losing his temper with Bardas – Michael immediately appointed him to the post. Thenceforth Emperor and Chamberlain lived together on terms of close intimacy – so close indeed that some historians have spoken darkly of a homosexual relationship. What makes such a theory improbable, however, is the somewhat unusual arrangement that Michael now made for their future domestic felicity. Basil was obliged to divorce his wife Maria, and to marry instead the Emperor's own first love and long-time mistress Eudocia Ingerina. It was a surprising step to say the least, and one for which there can be only one plausible explanation: it enabled Michael to

---

[1] The Greek word *parakoimomenos* literally means 'one who sleeps nearby' – i.e. the court dignitary required to sleep in the Emperor's bedchamber. As time went on, the office gradually increased in importance (cf. the Lord Chamberlain in England) while the duty itself was delegated to junior officials. Traditionally, it was always held by a eunuch – which made Basil's appointment more surprising still.

introduce the lady into the Palace without provoking the scandal that would have been inevitable had he done so by any other method. This, however, leads us to another still more remarkable conclusion: that he intended her to remain imperial property – in which case the baby boy, Leo, to whom she gave birth on 19 September 866 was in all probability not Basil's child but Michael's, and what we know today as the Macedonian dynasty was in fact simply a continuation of the Amorian.[1]

Now all this is clearly hypothetical, and several recent historians have been inclined to reject it. There is on the other hand a body of circumstantial evidence which seems difficult to dismiss. First of all, at least one of our sources – Simeon – states categorically that Leo was Michael's son, suggesting indeed that the fact was common knowledge in Constantinople. Second, Basil always hated Leo. The only one of his children, real or pretended, to whom he showed any real affection was Constantine, the son of his first wife Maria – a boy whom he idolized, and whose early death was to plunge him into a depression from which he never recovered. Third – and in many ways strangest of all – is the fact that if Eudocia had been living with Basil as his wife it is hardly likely that the Emperor would have gone to the trouble of providing his favourite with another bedfellow, in the unexpected and distinctly matronly shape of his sister Thecla, now in her middle forties, who had recently been freed from the monastic seclusion to which she was clearly unsuited and was now brought in to complete this improbable *ménage à quatre*. Basil's liaison with her, however, was to prove little more than a stop-gap: whether or not he shared Eudocia's bed while Michael was alive, he certainly did after the latter's death – for she was to bear two further sons, Alexander and Stephen, in 870 and 871 respectively.[2] As for Thecla, she soon formed an attachment with one of the noblemen at court, John Neatocomites; but this too was ill-fated. When Basil found out, the two were severely chastised; in addition John was tonsured and sent to a monastery while Thecla had all her property confiscated except her house at Blachernae – where she died, bedridden and in poverty, a few years later.

*

1 Correctly or not, the paternity of Basil will be assumed where necessary as the story continues.

2 Or so it appears. The sources as usual give conflicting dates, and it is possible – though the weight of the evidence is against it – that one at least of the baby princes may have been born during Michael's lifetime or within a few months of his death, thus once again raising the question of paternity.

As Basil's influence over Michael increased, so too did the mutual hostility between himself and Bardas. On the Caesar's side it had begun with contempt rather than suspicion. He believed that his nephew trusted him implicitly with the government of the Empire, and that as long as his pleasures were not interrupted or interfered with would continue to do so; as for the Armenian, Bardas probably looked upon him as a somewhat unsavoury companion in those pleasures and not very much more. But the alarming speed with which Basil tightened his hold on the feckless Emperor soon caused him to revise his former opinions. The man was becoming a serious threat to the State, and – if the words quoted at the head of this chapter are not entirely apocryphal – Bardas knew it.

As for Basil, his ambition was still far from satisfied. By now his eyes were fixed on the throne, which seemed almost within his grasp – were it not for the fact that a rival was blocking his path. And so – just as Bardas had poisoned the young Emperor's mind against the eunuch Theoctistus a dozen years before – now Basil, quietly and insidiously, aroused his suspicions of his uncle. It was not, he pointed out, simply that the Caesar despised his nephew; he wanted him out of the way, in order to make himself the sole and undisputed ruler of Byzantium. The only solution was for Michael to act first, while there was still time.

Despite all their recent successes against the Saracens in the East, there remained one theatre of war in which the Byzantines had achieved nothing. Crete, after its brief recovery by Theoctistus, was now once more in the hands of the infidel. This was a situation that Bardas was no longer willing to tolerate and he had set about preparations for a major expedition against the island in the spring of 866. Some time during the previous winter, however, word reached him that the coming campaign was to be the occasion for a plot against his life, in which the Emperor himself and his Chamberlain were both involved. His first reaction was to withdraw from the expedition altogether, and to remain in the capital where he could better protect himself; he seems, too, to have faced his nephew squarely with his suspicions, for on Lady Day, 25 March, at the Church of St Mary Chalcoprateia,[1] we find Michael and Basil putting their signatures – in the latter's case, presumably, a simple cross – to a

---

1 St Mary in the Copper-Market, so called because it had been built in the fifth century on the site of a synagogue formerly used by Jewish coppersmiths. The church was one of the most revered in the city, since it seems to have shared the robe of the Virgin with St Mary at Blachernae. All that remains of it today is a short stretch of crenellated wall, a hundred yards or so to the west of St Sophia.

formal declaration swearing that they had no hostile intentions towards him. So solemn was this oath – it is said to have been signed in the blood of Jesus Christ, a small and diminishing quantity of which was kept among the most precious of the sacred relics in St Sophia – that the Caesar relented; and he was in his accustomed place beside the Emperor when the expedition left Constantinople soon after Easter.

The chosen route took the army across the corner of Asia Minor to a point at the mouth of the river Meander, near the ancient city of Miletus, where the fleet lay at anchor. On the evening before the embarkation Bardas received a further warning. He laughed it aside; but that night he hardly slept, and early on the following day – it was 21 April – he confided his fears to his friend Philotheus, the General Logothete. Philotheus did his best to reassure him. 'Put on your peach-coloured gold cloak,' he advised, 'and face your enemies. They will scatter before you.' The Caesar did as he was bid and rode off, sumptu-ously arrayed, to the imperial pavilion, where he seated himself next to his nephew and listened with every show of attention while another of the Logothetes read out the morning report. When this was over, he turned to Michael and suggested that if there were no more business to transact the embarkation might now begin; but at that moment, out of the corner of his eye, he saw the Chamberlain make a surreptitious signal. His hand flew to his sword; but it was too late. With one tremendous blow Basil struck him to the ground, while other conspira-tors rushed forward to finish him off.

The Emperor himself made no move. He seemed not so much surprised as stunned by what had occurred, and opinion is still divided as to the extent to which he had been party to the plot. But there can be no doubt that he was aware, at least in general terms, of Basil's intention, and his own subsequent actions certainly argue some degree of complicity. He wrote at once – obviously on his Chamberlain's instructions – to Photius in Constantinople, informing him that his uncle had been found guilty of high treason and summarily executed. The Patriarch's reply was a masterpiece of sly innuendo. 'The virtue and clemency of Your Majesty,' he wrote, 'forbid me to suspect that the letter was fabricated or that the circumstances of the Caesar's death were other than it alleges' – a clear enough indication that he did indeed suspect precisely that. He concluded by imploring the Emperor, in the name of the Senate and the people, to return at once to the capital.

He was right to do so, and Michael and Basil both knew it. A few days later they were back in Constantinople. The Cretan expedition was over before it had begun.

On Whit Sunday, 866, early worshippers at the Church of St Sophia were intrigued to notice, not the single throne in its accustomed place, but two similar thrones, set side by side. They were still more surprised when the Emperor arrived in the usual procession from the Palace, but instead of moving directly to his seat climbed to the top level of the ambo, that great three-decker pulpit of polychrome marble normally used for the reading of the Gospel and the committal prayers. Basil, robed as High Chamberlain, then mounted to the middle level, while one of the secretaries took his place on the lowest and began to read in the Emperor's name:

The Caesar Bardas plotted against me to slay me, and for this reason induced me to leave the city. Had I not been informed of the conspiracy by Symbatius[1] and Basil, I should not be alive today. The Caesar was guilty, and brought his death upon himself.

It is my will that Basil, the High Chamberlain, who is loyal to me, who has delivered me from my enemy and who holds me in great affection, should be the guardian and manager of my Empire and should be proclaimed by all as *basileus*.

While Basil was being attired by the eunuchs in the purple buskins and the rest of the imperial regalia, Michael handed his diadem to the Patriarch, who blessed it and returned it to his head; then, removing it again, the Emperor himself performed the coronation of his new colleague. Basil's ambition had been fulfilled. The transition from stable-boy to *basileus* had taken him just nine years.

The shared monarchy, by contrast, was to last only sixteen months – a period during which the centre of the stage was once again occupied by religious affairs. As the Western missionaries poured into Bulgaria in ever greater numbers, Photius realized that he had lost the initiative: Boris and his subjects had been drawn, it seemed irrevocably, into the Roman camp. To make matters worse these missionaries were spreading dangerous heresies, at least one of which – that Constantinople was not, as the Byzantines maintained, the senior Patriarchate but the most recent and therefore the least venerable of the five[2] – was nothing short of an insult. Equally pernicious was the Latin insistence on the celibacy of the

---

1 The Logothete of the Course, another Armenian and one of Basil's closest confederates.

2 Rome, Alexandria, Antioch, Jerusalem, Constantinople.

clergy; if this were to gain general acceptance it could not fail to bring the Orthodox parish priests – who were actually required to be married – into disrepute.[1] Worst of all, however, to serious theologians like Photius, was a doctrine to which Pope Nicholas had now for the first time given official endorsement and which was to become the very cornerstone of the whole controversy between the Eastern and the Western Churches: that of the Double Procession of the Holy Ghost.

In the early days of Christian belief, the Third Person of the Trinity was held to proceed, directly and exclusively, from God the Father. Then, towards the end of the sixth century, the fatal word *Filioque* – 'and the Son' – began to appear; and soon after 800, when it became the practice in Charlemagne's Empire to recite the Nicene Creed during the course of the Mass, this insertion was generally adopted in the West. To the Eastern Church, on the other hand, it remained the vilest heresy; and to learn that accredited papal representatives were now disseminating this poison among the Bulgars was more than the Patriarch could bear. He resolved therefore to call a General Council, to meet in Constantinople in the late summer of 867, which would anathematize the Double Procession and the various other heresies of which the Roman missionaries were guilty and so snatch back the poor misguided Bulgars from the jaws of hell. Finally and most dramatically, it would depose the Pope.

But would this be more than an empty gesture where Rome was concerned? Photius believed that it would. He knew that Nicholas was now almost as unpopular in the West as he was in Byzantium. By refusing to allow King Lothair II of Lorraine to divorce his wife and marry his mistress, he had antagonized not only Lothair himself but his elder brother, the Western Emperor Lewis II; nothing would give the two brothers greater pleasure than to see him brought low and replaced by another, more amenable Pontiff. Imperial emissaries sped to Lewis's court, and – though there was no formal agreement – an understanding was quickly reached. Not only would the Council declare Pope Nicholas deposed; Lewis would send a military force to Rome to remove him physically. In return, the Byzantine government would grant its ally full imperial recognition and hail him as Emperor of the Franks.

This, it must be emphasized, was no small concession. Admittedly such recognition had been accorded to Lewis's great-grandfather in 812;

1 Though not of course the bishops and hierarchy, who were drawn exclusively from the monasteries and continued to be bound by the vow of chastity.

but circumstances then had been very different, and Charles had paid dearly for the privilege. Even so, many Byzantines had bitterly opposed the decision, and the act had never been repeated. Lewis, moreover, was no Charlemagne. Although he might call himself Emperor, he was in fact only a relatively insignificant princeling in Italy; was he really – by the decision of the Byzantines themselves – to be raised to the same level as God's Vice-Gerent on Earth, the Elect of Heaven, Equal of the Apostles? Michael himself, whose personal supremacy was at stake, might have been expected to protest; or, if he were too sodden with drink and debauch, his co-Emperor Basil. But Photius did his work well; and neither of them, so far as is known, breathed a word in opposition.

They did, however, preside jointly at the Council, which performed just as the Patriarch had intended that it should. Heresies were condemned, the Pope was deposed and, for good measure, anathematized. Lewis and his wife Engelbertha were acclaimed in their most sonorous imperial titles. Photius for his part was jubilant: this was his finest moment, the summit of his career. How could he tell that, in barely a single month, all his efforts would be set at naught and that he himself, so soon after his supreme triumph, would be humbled before his two oldest and most implacable enemies?

When Michael III and Basil I took their places side by side to inaugurate the Council of 867, few of those present could have guessed the true state of relations between them. Michael had raised his friend to the throne because he had no delusions about his own incapacity to rule and understood more than anyone the need of a strong hand at the helm; but as he grew more and more demoralized and sank ever lower into dissipation, his drunkenness, his desecrations and depredations of churches and his senseless acts of cruelty made him less an embarrassment than a dangerous liability. In his sober moments, he now seemed to think only of chariot racing. He had built himself a magnificent new stable whose marble walls made it look more like a palace, and a private race track at St Mamas where he would practise for the games in the Hippodrome, spending whole days together with the professional charioteers – always considered the dregs of Byzantine society – showering them with gold and gifts and regularly standing godfather to their children. On one infamous occasion while he was personally competing, it was whispered that he had even set up an image of the Virgin in the imperial box, to preside over the games in his stead and to applaud his safely predictable victory. Bardas had been able in some measure to control him; but for Basil, not unnaturally, Michael never had the same respect, and he bitterly resented any attempt on the part of his co-Emperor to remonstrate with him. The partnership had in short become unworkable. Once again, Basil the Macedonian made up his mind to act.

On 24 September 867, the two Emperors and Eudocia Ingerina were dining together in the Palace of St Mamas. Towards the end of the meal Basil made an excuse to leave the room and hurried to Michael's chamber, where he bent back the bolts of the door in such a way that it could not be locked. He then returned to the table until such time as his colleague, now as usual blind drunk, staggered off to bed and immediately fell into a deep alcoholic slumber. His fellow-conspirators had meanwhile gathered in a distant corner of the Palace. Basil joined them, and together they settled down to wait.

Byzantine Emperors never slept alone; on this particular night, however, the official who normally shared the imperial bedchamber was away on a mission, and his place had been taken by the Patrician Basiliscianus, one of Michael's old drinking companions.[1] He had noticed the condition of the bolt and was still lying anxiously awake some hours later when he heard footsteps: there on the threshold stood Basil, with eight of his friends. Basiliscianus tried to block his entrance, but was hurled aside; he was seriously wounded by a sword-thrust as he fell to the floor. Meanwhile one of the conspirators, John Chaldos, approached the sleeping Emperor, but apparently had not the courage to kill him outright; he hacked off both his hands, then fled from the room. It was left to Basil's cousin Asylaion to administer the *coup de grâce*.

Leaving Michael dead or dying in a pool of his own blood, the assassins hurried down to the Golden Horn – where a boat awaited them – and rowed across to the Great Palace. One of the guards was expecting them, and the doors were immediately opened. On the following morning Basil's first act was to instal Eudocia Ingerina – his own wife and his victim's mistress – in the imperial apartments. The news of the murder seems to have been received with little surprise, and still less regret, outside Michael's immediate family; but one of the court officials, sent the following morning to St Mamas to arrange for the funeral, found the horribly mutilated body wrapped in a horse-cloth and the

1 Some months previously, Michael had tried to raise Basiliscianus too to the purple; Basil had had the greatest difficulty in restraining him.

Empress Theodora with her daughters – all now released from their monastery – weeping uncontrollably over her son. He was buried with the minimum of ceremony at Chrysopolis, on the Asiatic shore.

7
Basil the Macedonian

[867–86]

I doubt whether any other family has ever been so much favoured by God as [that of the Macedonians] has been: which is strange when one considers the criminal manner of its coming to power, and how it was born of murder and bloodshed. And yet the plant took root, and sent out such mighty shoots, each bearing imperial fruit, that no other can be compared with it for beauty and splendour.

Michael Psellus

Relieved at last of the dead weight of his co-ruler, Basil lost no time in setting the Empire on a radically different course. Michael's body was hardly cold before Photius was dismissed from the Patriarchate. It was not an unpopular decision. Photius had not raised a finger in condemnation of the murder of Caesar Bardas, nor of the obscene and sacrilegious cavortings of the pitiable Emperor – whom, it was rumoured, he had once challenged to a drinking-bout and had beaten by sixty cups to fifty; distinguished churchmen who had stood next to him during Mass were ready to swear that he would murmur passages of secular Greek poetry instead of the liturgy; and the majority of thinking Byzantines had been deeply shocked by his cynical willingness to grant Lewis II imperial recognition in return for ephemeral advantage. For the Patriarch, none the less, it was a stab in the back, delivered at precisely the moment when his plans were coming to fruition and his long battle with Pope Nicholas almost won. His humiliation was further intensified by the reinstatement two months later of his old adversary Ignatius, whose bigotry he deplored and whose intellect he despised.

What were the reasons for this dramatic volte-face? Basil had presided, with his co-Emperor, over the Council at which the Pope had been anathematized and Photius had attained all his immediate objectives. Why, the moment he found himself his own master, did he initiate a policy that could be interpreted as an effective recognition of papal supremacy – one that ran, moreover, directly counter to everything on which he had set his seal less than two months before? Simply because for him, materialist and man of action that he was, there were issues more important than the right of patriarchal selection; and foremost among these issues was the recovery of the Empire's western provinces. For the first time since Justinian – we can discount the ineffectual and mildly ridiculous attempt of Constans II in the seventh century – the Byzantine throne was occupied by a ruler who had thought long and hard about reconquest and was determined to achieve it. That task, he knew, would be immeasurably helped by papal support, and for such support the reinstatement of Ignatius was a small enough price to pay. Already by the time Photius was informed of his dismissal, imperial legates were on their way to Rome.

Whether or not Pope Nicholas would have been prepared to accept the Emperor's sudden change of heart we cannot tell; he died on 13 November 867. His successor Hadrian II shared his views, but was of a milder, less tempestuous character; besides, he had not himself been the victim of any personal attack. He therefore interpreted Basil's friendly overtures as a sign of contrition and willingly accepted his invitation to send delegates to yet another Council at Constantinople, by which the schism so regrettably engineered by Photius would be healed at last. When, however, this new assembly held its opening session at the beginning of October 869, the papal delegates at once discovered that Basil was neither contrite nor particularly submissive. Their assumption that they would be invited to preside was firmly corrected; the *basileus* himself, or his accredited representative, would take the chair.[1] Later, when they finally reached the most important item on the agenda – the fate of Photius – Basil refused to accept their demand for his immediate condemnation unheard, insisting that the former Patriarch be permitted to stand before them and speak in his own defence. In fact, when Photius did appear, he wisely refused to say a word; and he continued silent when, on 5 November, sentence of anathema was pronounced upon him. But this hardly mattered. Where Basil was concerned, two important points of principle had been made: first, that the correct Byzantine – not Roman – legal procedure had been complied with in every detail, leaving the accused no grounds on which to appeal; second, that he himself – and not the papal legates – had delivered the verdict.

*

1 Of the ten sessions of the Council, the Emperor in fact attended only the sixth, seventh, eighth and last; during all the others his place was taken by the *praepositus* Baanes.

The Council continued to sit, sporadically, until February 870; shortly before it closed, however, two separate embassies arrived in Constantinople within a few days of each other. The first had been sent by Boris of Bulgaria. He was still dissatisfied. Converting his people to Christianity was proving a good deal more troublesome than he had imagined. In the four and a half years since his baptism he had been obliged to put down a rebellion of local boyars that had almost cost him his throne; he had quarrelled with Byzantium over Photius's high-handed and patronizing attitude and his refusal to grant him a Bulgar Patriarch; and although he had been initially delighted with Pope Nicholas's more generous response to his approaches, it was gradually becoming clear to him that his honeymoon with Rome was over. Bishop Formosus – his particular friend – and Paul of Populonia had been recalled; the Roman missionaries were rapidly making themselves every bit as disliked as their Orthodox predecessors. Worst of all, the new Pope, Hadrian, seemed even more determined than Nicholas not to allow him his Patriarch, or even an archbishop. Once already he had turned the Roman–Byzantine dispute to his advantage; despite the ostensible reconciliation, there might be a chance of doing so again. His envoys had one question only to ask the Council, but that question was the one which, more than any other, could be guaranteed to sow the maximum dissension among the delegates: if he were to have no Patriarch of his own, to which see did Bulgaria belong, Constantinople or Rome?

Basil himself forbore to reply. Instead, he referred the question to the theoretically neutral representatives of the other three Patriarchates: Alexandria, Antioch and Jerusalem. Neither he nor anyone else present had any doubt as to what the answer would be. The papal legates, in a minority of two, protested as forcibly as they could; but nobody took much notice. In the highest possible dudgeon they took ship for Rome; and their tempers could hardly have been improved when, as their vessel entered the Adriatic, they were seized by Dalmatian pirates who stripped them of all that they possessed and held them for nine months before allowing them to continue on their journey.

And so Bulgaria returned to the Orthodox fold, in which it has remained to the present day; and with Photius out of the way Boris had no difficulty in finally getting what he wanted. In St Sophia on 4 March, Ignatius consecrated a Bulgarian archbishop and several bishops. Technically they were to remain under the authority of Constantinople, but in the day-to-day running of their affairs they were to be autonomous. Basil had given his full approval; he was fully conscious, however, of the price he had had to pay – his recent *rapprochement* with Rome, for which Photius had been sacrificed in vain.

The second embassy to arrive on the Bosphorus that February carried a letter from Lewis II. Its tone was distinctly unpleasant. The Emperor of the West considered that he had been insulted, and was writing to express his indignation. Two years before, while he had been unsuccessfully laying siege to Muslim-held Bari, Basil had offered him the services of the Byzantine navy, proposing at the same time a marriage between his eldest son Constantine and Lewis's daughter Hermingarde. Lewis had sent a favourable reply, and in 869 the fleet had set sail for Bari. It had arrived, however, only after the Franks had gone into their winter quarters, and the Byzantine admiral Nicetas had been horrified to find his new allies not only far fewer in number than he had been led to expect but roaring drunk into the bargain. He had immediately sought out the Emperor and, scarcely bothering to conceal his contempt, had addressed him as *King* of the Franks. Lewis had protested and a furious argument had ensued, in consequence of which Nicetas and most of the fleet had returned at once to Constantinople, the Frankish envoys following shortly afterwards. Admitted to Basil's presence, they left him in no doubt of their master's wrath – simultaneously emphasizing his claim, not just to the title of Emperor of the Franks but to another, more resonant still, which the Byzantines had withheld even from Charlemagne: *Imperator Romanorum*, Emperor of the Romans.[1]

Thus, within a matter of weeks, Basil had antagonized both his prospective allies. Where the Pope was concerned, the recovery of Bulgaria had been a worthwhile *quid pro quo*; but the quarrel with Lewis brought no compensating advantage – only an acrimonious correspondence over his claim, in the course of which both parties became more and more deeply entrenched in the positions that they already held. Since both were also rivals for the possession of south Italy, their relations might easily have deteriorated still further, to the point of open war; fortunately, however, the Emperor fell foul of Adelchis, the Lombard Duke of Benevento, by whom in 871 he and his wife were both taken prisoner; they were given their freedom only after Lewis had sworn on the Gospels that he would never again enter the territory of the Duchy under arms. He soon obtained papal dispensation from his enforced oath and in 872 actually managed to drive the Saracens

1 See p. 13n.

from Capua; but thereafter his strength began to fail and he retired to the north, where three years later he died near Brescia, leaving no male heir.

While the Byzantine fleet was occupied – or, more accurately, unoccupied – in the Adriatic, the bulk of the army was engaged in the East. Here the Empire had not one enemy but two: the Saracens and the Paulicians, whose numbers were once again on the increase and who were now spreading westward across Asia Minor. In two whirlwind campaigns Basil and his brother-in-law Christopher drove deep into their heartland, and in 872 destroyed the fortified city of Tephriké,[1] the principal base for their raiding operations, killing their leader Chrysocheirus. Then, having effectively eliminated the Paulician threat in the region, they turned their attention to the Saracens, for the next ten years keeping up a continual pressure which won them Zapetra and Samosata, together with several other strongholds in the Euphrates Valley. Admittedly there were failures too: Melitene, always a trouble spot, stubbornly resisted all attempts to take it by storm, and in 883 the imperial forces suffered a serious setback near Tarsus which briefly robbed them of their momentum. But not for long: those first victories by Bardas and Petronas almost thirty years before could now be seen for what they were: not just a few neglible flashes in the pan, but the beginning of a sustained and spectacular advance which would reach its climax only with the campaigns of the Emperors Nicephorus Phocas and John Tzimisces, a hundred years into the future.

In Western Europe, Byzantine successes were on much the same scale. True, Basil failed in his attempts to recover Crete and Sicily – whose last major stronghold, Syracuse, was to fall in 878; but he was able to expel the Saracens from the entire Dalmatian coast (which became an imperial Theme) and in 873 established his suzerainty over Adelchis of Benevento. The same year saw the recovery of Otranto, and three years later Bari too recognized him as its overlord. With this vital bridgehead under his control he was able to launch a major offensive in the following decade as a result of which, thanks to the brilliant general Nicephorus Phocas,[2] virtually the whole of south Italy was restored to Byzantine authority before the end of the century. To the Papacy and the Western Empire alike, there could be no clearer indication that Byzantium had surrendered

---

1 The modern Divriği – where, three and a half centuries later, the Seljuk Turks were to build one of the most remarkable mosques in all Anatolia.

2 Not, of course, to be confused with his grandson the Emperor.

none of its claims to Italian dominion. Nor were these victories confined to operations on land. The imperial navy, after a long period of neglect, had been taken in hand by Theoctistus and Bardas, who had made it once again a force to be reckoned with; Basil now energetically continued the work that they had begun, and it was thanks above all to him – and to his son and grandson after him – that it was to become the envy of all their rivals, the most efficient and highly trained that the world had ever seen, patrolling the coasts, policing the high seas and attacking the Saracen raiding parties whenever and wherever they might be found.

Missionary work too went on apace. One by one the Slav tribes of the Balkans embraced the Christian faith; and although Roman influence was to prevail in Croatia and the northern part of the Dalmatian coast – and also in Moravia, where Cyril and Methodius had had to admit defeat – in Serbia, Macedonia and Greece the Orthodox rule and the supremacy of Constantinople were alike enthusiastically adopted.

Much of this success can be dated to the second Patriarchate of Ignatius. Paradoxically, however, it was precisely these ecclesiastical triumphs which led to the return of Photius from exile. His recall is unlikely to have caused him much surprise. He knew that his followers were just as numerous as those of his rival, and a good deal more intelligent; and during his seven-year banishment it became patently obvious that the sudden and dramatic expansion of the Orthodox faith was creating huge problems, both theological and administrative, with which the ill-educated old Patriarch was totally unfitted to deal. Ignatius had watched, helpless but perhaps secretly relieved, as more and more self-confessed Photians were promoted to key positions in the hierarchy; he seems to have raised no objection when, in 874 or 875, their leader himself was recalled to the capital, given charge of the University of The Magnaura and, in a surely conclusive demonstration of confidence, entrusted with the education of the Emperor's sons; and when, on 23 October 877, he finally expired at the age of eighty, it was Photius who for the second time assumed the patriarchal throne[1] and who three

---

1 The Continuator tells an extraordinary story of how Photius engineered his own recall by fabricating a document that purported to trace Basil's descent from the Parthians of ancient Persia. This he arranged to be placed in the imperial library and produced, as if by chance, during a visit by the Emperor – who, when he sought an interpretation, was to be told that only Photius was sufficiently learned to provide one. This story could just possibly be true: Basil was for ever trying to glorify his ancestry, and Photius was certainly more than capable of such a deception.

years later received – not that he particularly wanted it – official recognition from Pope John VIII.

During this Indian summer of his extraordinary career, Photius composed what must be considered a form of testament, setting out for posterity his view of the office of Patriarch and its relationship with the imperial throne. To place this in its proper context, however, we must look for a moment at another of Basil's achievements, and a particularly remarkable one for the illiterate 'Macedonian' that he was: his revision of Roman law. Such a revision, on such a scale, had not been attempted since the days of Justinian, over three centuries before; and although Leo III had produced a short work known as the *Ecloga*, designed as a practical companion for working judges, this itself was now inadequate and obsolete. Basil's intention was to produce a mighty compendium which he described as an *anacatharsis* – or purification – of the old laws, which would once again be collected, collated and where necessary reconciled; but it was never completed in his lifetime, nor ever as originally conceived. What did appear was a shorter work known as the *Procheiron*, or Handbook, which contained a résumé of the most important and regularly applicable legislation, grouped for convenience under forty principal headings. This was followed, towards the end of Basil's reign – indeed it bears the names of his sons Leo and Alexander as well as his own – by the *Epanagogē*, or Summary. Much of this second work is little more than a rearrangement of the first, but it is supplemented by a body of new material dealing with the rights and responsibilities of the Emperor, the Patriarch and various other high dignitaries of Church and State; and in it the hand of Photius is unmistakable. According to the theory there propounded, the Byzantine Empire is a single polity headed jointly by Emperor and Patriarch, working together in parallel for the material and spiritual well-being of their subjects. Such, it is true, had by no means been the pattern during most of the past century; but though the hypothesis might represent an ideal dispensation rather than the real one it was no less valid on that account. The pity was that it was not to enjoy universal endorsement – as the Patriarch was soon to discover to his cost.

There seems little doubt that – at least during the final decade of his reign – Basil began to see himself as another Justinian and to act accordingly. He was reconquering Italy; he was collecting and revising the laws; and he had also embarked on a vast building programme, with all the enthusiasm of his illustrious exemplar and on a similarly ambitious scale. There had been few new constructions under the ninth-century iconoclasts until the days of Theophilus, who had deliberately restricted his own programme to domestic architecture. Not only had no new churches been built; many of the older ones had been culpably neglected and were now in urgent need of repair – including St Sophia itself, where the great western arch had been damaged in the severe earthquake of 9 January 869 and was now in imminent danger of collapse. Basil saved it in the nick of time, and adorned it with a mosaic of the Virgin and Child, flanked by SS. Peter and Paul.[1] The old Church of the Holy Apostles was in a still sorrier state. Originally founded by Constantine, it had been completely rebuilt by Justinian; but the foundations had always been inadequate and it was now crumbling again. Basil repaired it from top to bottom, revetting the lower walls with slabs of polychrome marble and covering the upper parts with mosaics depicting the entire life of Christ from the Annunciation to the Passion. Many other, humbler shrines were similarly restored and in several cases re-roofed, the old wooden roofs – always a dangerous fire risk – being replaced by new ones of stone, frequently domed.

But the Emperor's greatest architectural triumph was his new church which – although formally dedicated to St Michael, the Prophet Elijah,[2] the Mother of God and St Nicholas – was always called just that: the Nea. It stood within the precincts of the Great Palace, immediately to the east of the Emperor's private apartments, and no expense was spared on either its construction or its decoration. If Basil was the Justinian of his day, this was his St Sophia. Its cluster of gilded domes could be seen from all over the city and from far out at sea; within the central rotunda was a dazzling mosaic of Christ Pantocrator – the Ruler of All – while the others carried representations of angels and archangels, martyrs and apostles, patriarchs and prophets. Most sumptuous of all – according to Photius, who has left us a detailed description of the whole church – was the iconostasis, which was of gold and silver, studded with precious stones. Behind it, the high altar was 'of a material more precious than gold' – presumably it too was set with jewels and enamels – and surmounted by a ciborium on columns of silver-gilt. Of the three apses

---

1 This was to be destroyed, alas, in the even greater earthquake of 26 October 989. See C. Mango, *The Mosaics of St Sophia at Istanbul*, pp. 76–80.

2 Who was said to have appeared to Basil's mother in a dream, encouraging her to allow her son to travel to Constantinople, where a glorious future awaited him.

that closed the east end, the central one contained a mosaic of the Virgin 'extending her pure hands towards us and granting to the Emperor long life and victory over his enemies'.

For the Great Palace itself, Basil provided a new treasury, resplendent new baths and another triclinium; he also largely rebuilt the Chalkē, endowing it with new marbles and mosaics appropriate to what was, after all, the principal gateway into the imperial residence. It was the same with the other palaces – the Mangana, the Magnaura, the Eleuthera, the Hieria, St Mamas: none escaped his attention. Few Emperors if any did more to ensure that Constantinople remained what it had always been – the most opulent city in the world, a vast treasure-house that was itself a treasure. It is a sad irony indeed that, in the whole of that city, there now survives of his work not one stone resting on another.

By the high summer of the year 879, Basil the Macedonian could look back on twelve years of quite remarkable success. His armed forces were stronger than they had ever been. To both east and west, the Saracens were in retreat. The Paulicians had been crushed. The Bulgars and the Serbs had been converted, and had entered the Orthodox fold. The Photian schism was over, having effectively proved to the Pope in Rome that Byzantium was not to be trifled with. The revision of the laws was well under way, with the *Procheiron* already published and work on the *Epanagogē* proceeding apace. The principal buildings of the capital had been restored and embellished, while at the point where the grounds of the Palace swept down to the Marmara his own great church, the Nea, rose tall and triumphant, a continuing reminder to the world of the majesty and magnificence of its founder. In little over a decade the coarse and illiterate Armenian peasant, who had reached the throne by way of two of the vilest murders that even Byzantine history could recall, had proved himself the greatest Emperor since Justinian.

And Justinian had had no son to succeed him; Basil, truthfully or not, could claim four. For the three younger ones he cared little – his second, Leo, he loathed – but his eldest son, Constantine, the only child of his first wife Maria, was the apple of his eye: the only human being, perhaps, whom he ever really loved. Outstandingly handsome and possessed of all Basil's superb physique, Constantine had been little more than a boy when he had first accompanied his father into battle, mounted on a snow-white horse and wearing, we are told, golden armour. In 869 he had been crowned co-Emperor and, if the preliminary

97

negotiations had not turned sour, might well have married the daughter of Lewis II, thus uniting both Eastern and Western Empires under his sway. He nevertheless showed high promise of proving himself, in the fullness of time, as great a ruler as his father – perhaps even greater.

And then, suddenly, at the beginning of September 879, he was dead. The circumstances of his death are unknown, but Basil never recovered from the blow. This, as he saw it, was divine retribution – God's punishment for the murder of His anointed. Despite all that he had achieved, despite even the building of the most resplendent church in Christendom, he had not been forgiven. From that moment he began to withdraw further and further into himself, lapsing into deep depressions which occasionally led to bouts of insanity. At such times, one man only could hope to control him: Photius. He would humour the distracted Emperor by arranging ever more elaborate Masses for the soul of Constantine, whom he ultimately went so far as to canonize; when that was no longer enough, he and his close friend Theodore Santabarenus, Archbishop of Euchaites, even engineered a séance in which Basil was confronted with what he believed to be the shade of his son on a white charger, carrying a lance and clad from head to foot in gold – only to see the apparition fade away as he approached to embrace it.[1]

In all these activities, if the Continuator is to be believed, the Patriarch had one overriding object in view: to prevent the succession of Basil's second son and now his heir apparent, Leo. We do not know why this should be: the boy was quick-tempered and generally judged to be somewhat overfond of women – his relationship with the beautiful Zoe Zautsina was already causing much clicking of tongues – but there was no reason to think that he might not make a fine *basileus*, nor is it easy to accept the theory that Photius was working for the restoration of the Amorian dynasty, to which he was related only distantly and by marriage. However that may be, he did all he could to work on Basil's known dislike of his son – and to considerable effect.

When Leo was just sixteen he had been married off, much against his will, to a relative of Eudocia's, an ill-favoured girl of asphyxiating piety named Theophano; he had, however, steadfastly refused to give up Zoe. Theophano had complained to Basil, who had flown into a fury and flogged his son with his own hands till the blood came, Zoe for her part being banished from the capital and married off in turn to a certain

1 However this trick was performed, there can be little doubt that the story itself is true, since Basil is known to have built a church on the spot where he saw the vision.

Theodore Gutzuniates, of whom little is known – or needs to be. Meanwhile the Patriarch continued his whispering campaign, dropping ever darker hints of conspiracies and treachery. Given his mental and emotional state, the old Emperor proved all too easily persuaded. Only a year or so later, the young prince was arrested and imprisoned without trial, narrowly escaping with his eyes. He remained a captive for the next three months,[1] after which his father reluctantly freed him.

What prompted his release is unclear. Leo himself attributed it to the merciful intervention of the Prophet Elijah; hardly more probable is the claim of certain chroniclers that the Emperor's decision was largely due to a parrot, persistently squawking 'Alas, poor Leo!' from its cage in the imperial dining hall: such a lamentation, one suspects, would have been far more likely to result in Basil's wringing the bird's neck with his own hands. More probably he simply gave in to public pressure, for Leo was highly popular everywhere outside his immediate family and had never been charged with any crime. The Emperor, however, remained unconvinced: not long afterwards when his son, restored to his honours and dignities and marching in a state procession, was suddenly greeted by the crowd with a round of applause, the old man could not resist shouting back to them that their cheers were unjustified, since the boy would surely cause them much sorrow and distress in the future.

In these last tormented years, Basil found some slight relief from his sufferings in the chase; and it was while hunting near his country palace of Apamea in the summer of 886 that he met his end. How he did so remains a mystery. Most of the chroniclers record that he died as a result of a hunting accident, and leave it at that; two, Simeon the Logothete and the anonymous author of the *Vita S. Euthymii*, give us a detailed account of what they claim to have occurred, but the story they tell is so improbable that our suspicions are immediately aroused. According to their version Basil was riding alone – 'for his companions were tired' – when he surprised an enormous stag drinking at a stream. He spurred his horse towards it, but the animal suddenly turned and charged, somehow contriving to hook its antlers under his belt and pull him from

---

1 The fourteenth-century chronicler Nicephorus Gregoras, whose history does not cover this period, mentions in passing that Leo's imprisonment lasted three *years* – a statement that has been almost universally accepted by modern historians. Our tenth-century sources, on the other hand, either give its duration as three months or take refuge in vague phrases which nevertheless suggest a relatively short period. See Vogt, 'La Jeunesse de Léon VI le Sage' in *Revue Historique*, Vol. clxxiv, p. 424.

his saddle. It then galloped off into the forest, dragging the helpless Emperor with it.

The rest of the party were unaware of what had happened until they saw their master's riderless horse approaching; a small group of Farghanese[1] then started off in pursuit and finally caught up with the stag, surrounding it and slowly closing in until one of them was able to cut Basil free with his sword. The Emperor fell senseless to the ground, and while the others crowded round him the stag escaped. (It was never caught.) When he recovered consciousness, his first act was to order the immediate execution of the guard who had freed him, on the grounds that he had raised his sword against his sovereign; he next commanded that the distance should be measured from the place where the accident had occurred. (This was later calculated to be sixteen miles.) Only then would he allow himself to be carried back to the Palace, where he was found to have suffered a severe haemorrhage of the stomach. After lingering nine days in agony, he died on 29 August. He was seventy-four years old.

What are we to make of this absurd farrago? Why, first of all, in the name of elementary prudence – let alone imperial protocol – was a mentally disturbed Emperor in his middle seventies left completely unattended? How, experienced hunter that he was, did he allow such an accident to occur? Why did he not himself slash through his belt, with the knife that he always carried? Why, come to that, did the stag not free itself from its burden before making its escape? And, having failed to do so, could it really have dragged a man famous for his colossal physique sixteen miles across rough forest country? All this sounds suspicious enough; but it becomes still more so when we discover that the rescue party was led by the Armenian Stylian Zautses, father of the mistress of young Leo and soon to be the most powerful man in the Empire after the Emperor himself.

And so we come to the last and most important question of all: did Basil the Macedonian meet his death, as the chroniclers claim, through an unfortunate (and extremely improbable) hunting accident, or was he murdered by Stylian – presumably with the knowledge and approval of his son Leo? Motives, certainly, would not have been lacking. The old man was growing increasingly unbalanced. Once already he had thrown Leo into prison; and he was perfectly capable, from one moment to the next, of ordering his execution. Stylian was in similar danger; he was

1 The Emperor's Turkish bodyguard, composed of slaves imported from the lands beyond the Oxus. So many of them came from Farghana that the name was indiscriminately applied to them all.

known to be one of the closest associates of the young prince who, if he were to replace his father on the throne, would almost certainly manage to rid himself of the insufferable Theophano and make Stylian's daughter Zoe his Empress – as indeed he subsequently did.

But for none of this do we have any hard evidence, let alone a shred of proof; and the verdict must remain open. We can only say that, if there is ever any possible justification for patricide – always assuming that Basil was in fact his father – Leo might have claimed it; and that none of the benefits that the old man had conferred upon his Empire – his military victories, his settlement of religious conflicts, his legal revisions, his financial and administrative reforms, the political stability that he created, the arts and sciences that he encouraged, the superb buildings with which he adorned his capital and, by no means least, the vastly increased prestige that he won for Byzantium in both the East and the West – could mitigate the brutality and bloodshed by which he had come to power. If, as seems likely, he himself died by an assassin's hand, his fate was not undeserved.

8
Leo the Wise

[886–912]

Most animals, when their mate is dead, retire into perpetual widowhood. Human beings, on the contrary, unconscious of the shameful nature of their weakness, are not satisfied with one marriage, but proceed immodestly to contract a second and, not content with that, go from the second to a third.

The Emperor Leo VI

In view of the relations existing between Basil and his successor, who now ascended the throne under the title of Leo VI, it is hardly surprising that the old Emperor's obsequies should have been kept to a minimum. Returned to Constantinople and clothed in full imperial regalia, his body was exposed according to tradition in the Triclinium of the Nineteen Beds.[1] Here the requiem was chanted, at the close of which the Master of Ceremonies repeated thrice the time-honoured formula: *'Come forth, Basileus, the King of Kings and Lord of Lords summons thee. Take thy crown from off thy head.'* The *praepositus* then removed the diadem and replaced it with a simple purple cap. And that, so far as the records go, is all. The coffin was presumably transferred to the Church of the Holy Apostles for burial, but even this is far from certain; what we do know for a fact is that one of Leo's first actions as *basileus* was to bring back the remains of Michael III from his burial-place at Chrysopolis, and to reinter them in that same church, in a sarcophagus that had formerly held those of Justin I or II. Now to do such honour to the murdered Emperor while deliberately flouting the dispensations ordered by his murderer seems – even if we make allowance for Leo's never-concealed hatred of Basil – an unnecessarily blatant insult to the latter's memory; if, on the other hand, Leo knew himself to be the son not of Basil but of Michael, such a gesture was no more than might have been expected.

---

1 So called because of the nineteen couches on which guests reclined in the antique manner during certain ceremonial banquets, particularly between Christmas and Epiphany.

At the time of his consecration, the new Emperor was just twenty years old. His life up to that time had not been a happy one. He had been only thirteen when the death of his brother Constantine had changed his father's feelings towards him from mild dislike to bitter loathing; less than three years later, there had been the enforced marriage, the banishment of his beloved mistress and his own incarceration – made a good deal more irksome by the presence of his wife Theophano, who had insisted on sharing it together with their infant daughter. So much adversity during his formative years might well have had a catastrophic effect on Leo's character. It is greatly to his credit that it did nothing of the kind. There is, admittedly, the possibility that he may have been privy to the plot – if such existed – to murder Basil; but this can never be proved. For the rest, he seems to have been kind, generous, highly intelligent and possessed of considerable charm. He was also – unlike Basil – a scholar.

The one point upon which all the chroniclers agree is Leo's intellectual calibre. The first Emperor to have been able to benefit from the cultural renaissance inaugurated by Theoctistus and Bardas and exemplified by Photius, Constantine-Cyril and Leo the Philosopher, he had shown himself from his earliest years to possess a first-rate academic mind, with the strong inclinations typical of his time towards philosophy and theology. He was never, it need hardly be said, the astrologer-soothsayer of his later reputation, nor could he conceivably have been the author of the immensely popular but utterly spurious collection of prophecies about the Empire and its destiny with which he was to be universally credited in later centuries. He was, on the other hand, a man of very considerable learning – more, almost certainly, than could have been claimed by any of his predecessors on the Byzantine throne: one who had read widely on many subjects and who spent his leisure hours composing not only liturgical poems and hymns but also a vast collection of sermons and homilies which he was wont to deliver personally, on the great feasts of the Church, from the pulpit of St Sophia. These effusions occasionally reveal a somewhat disconcerting lack of self-consciousness: diatribes against those who 'instead of bathing in the pure waters of matrimony prefer to wallow in the mud of fornication' come strangely from the lips of a man who kept a regular and recognized mistress from the age of fifteen; while the words at the head of this chapter must surely have caused him considerable embarrassment towards the end of his life. The general tenor of his writings, however, leaves us in no doubt of the breadth of his scholarship, which was enough to earn him, while still in his twenties, the sobriquet of *sophōtatos*, 'the most wise'; and although outside the Greek world we tend to drop the superlative form of the adjective, it is as Leo the Wise that – rightly or wrongly – he is still known today.

In the circumstances it was only to be expected that when Leo succeeded to the throne – in theory he shared it with his brother Alexander, but Alexander was a pleasure-loving nonentity who took no interest in government and asked nothing better than to be relieved of all responsibilities – he should have made radical changes in the administration; nor does it come as a surprise to learn that the chief beneficiary of these changes was Stylian Zautses – he who had played so questionable a part in the mystery surrounding Basil's death – who now became Master of the Offices and Logothete of the Course, effectively the director of imperial policy at home and abroad. The chief casualty, equally predictably, was Photius. After all that he had suffered, directly and indirectly, at the Patriarch's hands, Leo would have had sufficient cause to dismiss him for personal reasons alone; but there was more to it than that. The long years of the quarrel with Ignatius had revealed all too clearly the danger of allowing the Church too much independence or freedom of action; and Photius's views on the relationship between the political and spiritual thrones as set out in the *Epanagogē* seemed to the new Emperor to savour more than a little of treason. For the second time the Patriarch found himself obliged to sign an act of abdication; on this occasion, however, he did not escape so easily. Early in 887 he and Theodore Santabarenus were brought before a specially-convened tribunal and accused of having been involved, four years previously, in a conspiracy against the State. Santabarenus, found guilty, was blinded and exiled; Photius, devious to the last, was permitted to retire to a remote monastery in the Armeniakon Theme, where he was able to continue his theological and literary work undisturbed, and where he died in obscurity a few years later.

The choice of his successor showed clearly enough the way Leo's mind was working: on Christmas Day 886 he audaciously raised to the patriarchal throne his own youngest brother Stephen, not yet sixteen years old. Never in the history of the Eastern Church had the supreme ecclesiastical authority been entrusted to one so young; surprisingly, however, Stephen's appointment seems to have aroused little opposition.[1] It may be that the bishops and abbots had simply had enough of the endless squabbling of the past forty years and genuinely welcomed the prospect of a period of peace and understanding between Church and State, even at some cost to their effective independence. There was after all no other obvious candidate for the post, and Stephen – who was a weak and sickly youth, unlikely to last very long – may well have struck them as a harmless stopgap who would ensure his brother a few years' respite while he settled on to his throne. If so, they were right: the new Patriarch was to prove every bit as cooperative as expected. Alas, only six and a half years later he was dead; his successors, as we shall see, were to prove distinctly less amenable.

With Stylian Zautses as his political adviser and Stephen as his willing instrument in Church affairs, Leo was now admirably equipped to govern his Empire. On the domestic front there were no major upheavals for the rest of the century, which was to end on a particularly happy note when an important synod – it may even have been a General Council – was summoned in 899 and did much to restore relations between the Eastern and Western Churches. (At the time it seemed also to have settled the still-smouldering dispute that divided the Photian and Ignatian factions; but this, as we shall shortly see, was soon to be rekindled by the affair of the Emperor's fourth marriage.) Leo was consequently able to give his full attention to the tremendous work initiated by his father – the revision and recodification of the Roman law.

His reputation as a lawgiver – and indeed as the most important in Byzantine history since Justinian himself – was, it must be said, partly due to Basil and his commission of distinguished legists, under the chairmanship of the *protospatharius*[2] Symbatius, to whom he had entrusted the task of 'purification' mentioned in the preceding chapter. Not a little of the credit must also go to Stylian, who inspired him and drove him forward, and after whose death the whole project seems to have lost a certain impetus. But Leo too applied himself to the work, at least in those early years, with energy and enthusiasm; and there can be no doubt that it gained much from both his erudition and his literary skills.

---

1 Forty-seven years later, Romanus I was to elevate his own youngest son Theophylact, who was only a month or two older.

2 One of the eighteen honorary ranks of the Byzantine imperial service. The three highest – *Caesar, nobilissimus* and *curopalates* – were normally reserved for members of the Emperor's family; they were followed by *magister, antihypatus, patricius, protospatharius* and eleven others.

The results were published in series over the years: known as the *Basilica* and consisting of six mighty volumes, each containing ten books, they were largely based on Justinian's *Codex* and *Digest*; they did, however, incorporate a good deal of later work – including parts of the *Procheiron* – and in addition possessed two inestimable advantages. First, the laws were systematically arranged: a given subject was treated *in extenso* in a given book, and nowhere else. Second, they were written in Greek rather than Latin, which for well over two centuries had been a dead language in Constantinople, comprehensible only to scholars. Thus, from the reign of Leo VI onwards, the work of Justinian was effectively superseded; it is henceforth the *Basilica*, rather than the *Codex*, *Digest* or *Institutes*, on which the medieval legal structure of Byzantium is founded.

For all their importance, however, the *Basilica* deal mainly with first principles of right and wrong; they tell us disappointingly little about their time. A good deal more illuminating in this respect are Leo's so-called *Novels*, the 113 separate decrees by which he revises or revokes older laws according to developments in political or religious ideas. Once again we must be chary of ascribing too much responsibility for them to the Emperor personally: the seventeen which deal with exclusively ecclesiastical matters may well be from his own hand; the remainder, however, though ostensibly addressed to Stylian, are more probably the work of the Logothete himself. Of the latter, the most significant are those revoking the ancient rights of the Curia and the Senate. For a hundred years and more these two institutions – whose functions had formerly been to provide checks on imperial power – had been declining in importance; at last, in *Novels* 46, 47 and 78, they received their quietus. This is not to say that they were dissolved. The Senate in particular remained active and was not afraid to express its opinions; and it is worth noting that when Leo was at the point of death he specifically committed his son to its care. But it no longer existed as a political force in the State, nor did it enjoy any constitutional power.

Only in ecclesiastical matters was the Emperor still something less than omnipotent. God's Vice-Gerent on Earth he may have been; yet he remained after all a layman, while the Church had its own leader in the Patriarch of Constantinople. Admittedly it was he who appointed the Patriarch; but the appointment, like that to all high ecclesiastical offices, required the consent of the clergy. He was also bound by the decisions of the Councils, his duty where matters of dogma were concerned being merely to safeguard the Orthodox creed as defined by those authorized to do so. In all other fields, however, his power was absolute: chosen by God, Equal of the Apostles, he was master of the government of the Empire, commander-in-chief of its forces, sole lawgiver and supreme judge, whose decisions were subject to no appeal and irrevocable by all but himself.

That blessed period of domestic quiet which accounts in large measure for the remarkable speed with which the new legislation was published in the last decade of the ninth century was not, unfortunately for Leo, reflected by a similar degree of tranquillity abroad. In the Eastern Mediterranean and the Aegean, the Arabs kept up the pressure: some years were worse than others, but there had been few indeed since the fall of Sicily and Crete to Saracen arms when an imperial city had not been raided or imperial shipping attacked. A more immediate threat, however – and a very much more unexpected one – came in 894 from Bulgaria. After the conversion of King Boris twenty-nine years before, the Byzantines had hoped that the two Christian peoples might henceforth live together in peace; but Boris had abdicated in 889 and had retired to the monastery of St Panteleimon near Preslav, leaving the throne to his elder son, Vladimir; and Vladimir had proved a disaster. In a violent reaction against his father and all that he had stood for, he had identified himself with the once-powerful boyar aristocracy which Boris had done his utmost to crush. The boyars were old-fashioned reactionaries who detested Christianity and asked nothing better than to return to the bad old days of privilege and paganism; Vladimir agreed with them entirely, and with their support was rapidly undoing all his father's work and encouraging a return to the ancient tribal gods.

Had he waited another few years, he might even have succeeded. The Bulgarian Church had got off to a fairly shaky start and had had little time to take root; many of its members may well have felt a similar nostalgia. But he had reckoned without Boris, whose espousal of the contemplative life had not prevented him from closely following developments in the outside world. In an explosion of rage which can almost be heard down the centuries the old king burst out of his monastery, took over the government without a struggle, deposed and blinded Vladimir and, summoning a great conference from every corner of his kingdom, bade the assembled delegates acclaim his younger son, Symeon, as their ruler. Unhesitatingly, they did so; whereupon he returned to his cloister, never to leave it again.

Symeon was now twenty-nine. As a boy he had been sent to be educated in Constantinople, where he may have studied, along with Leo, at the feet of Photius himself. Returning to his homeland, he too had become a monk; but monastic disciplines had done nothing to curb a warlike and ambitious spirit, and when the call came to assume the throne of his father he was not slow to respond. In Byzantium, the news of his accession was received with considerable relief, and for a year all went well. Then in 894 Stylian Zautses, for reasons at which we can only guess, awarded the monopoly of trade with Bulgaria to two of his own protégés. Immediately they imposed a dramatic increase on the customs dues payable by Bulgar merchants on all goods imported into the Empire, simultaneously transferring the entrepôt from Constantinople to Thessalonica, where sharp practices were a good deal less likely to be detected. The Bulgars were appalled. At a single stroke, the substantial freight trade from the Black Sea down the Bosphorus to the Golden Horn had been destroyed; to make matters worse, the Thessalonica road was rough and frequently impassable in winter, and meant far greater distances to cover. Symeon at once sent an embassy to Constantinople in protest, but Leo as always supported his Logothete and nothing was done.

He had underestimated Symeon; but he did not do so for long. Within weeks, a Bulgar army had invaded Thrace. The imperial forces were already fully occupied in south Italy and on the eastern frontier. The Empire's one outstanding general, Nicephorus Phocas, was urgently recalled; and although the troops that he was given to command were raw and only semi-trained, he and the *drungarius*[1] Eustathius — who blockaded the mouth of the Danube — were able to hold the situation while the Emperor, by now seriously alarmed, turned for assistance to the Magyars. These savage warrior people, after several centuries of slow westward migration from Siberia, were now occupying the Moldavian and Transylvanian lands beyond the Danube and were consequently the northern neighbours of the Bulgars, for whom they had no very great liking. They needed little enough encouragement to swarm across the river — the Byzantines providing the boats — into

[1] The *drungarius* was the commander-in-chief of the imperial navy – though not of the local levies raised from the cities along the coast, which were under the authority of the *strategoi* of their respective Themes. At this period the *drungarius*, despite his importance, ranked below these *strategoi*; within another half-century, however, he would occupy a place in the military hierarchy second only to that of the commander-in-chief of the land forces, the Domestic of the Schools.

Bulgar territory, leaving the usual trail of devastation and destruction in their wake. But if Leo could summon a barbarian tribe to his aid, so too could Symeon. Beyond the lands of the Magyars, in the plains of southern Russia, dwelt another nomadic tribe, the Pechenegs. Bribed with Bulgar gold, they fell on the Magyar rear, with results even more catastrophic than their victims had inflicted on Symeon's kingdom. The Magyars, as soon as they heard the news, returned with all speed to save their wives and children from this new terror, only to find their way blocked by a huge Pecheneg host. Unable to remain in Bulgaria, where Symeon was now advancing against them, they had no choice but to continue their old westward migration through the Carpathian passes into the great Pannonian plain – the land which we now call Hungary, and which is still their home.

With the Magyars finally off his back, Symeon was able once again to devote his full attention to the Byzantines, on whom in 896 he inflicted a crushing defeat at Bulgarophygon, near the modern Babaeski, in European Turkey. Unfortunately for the Empire, Nicephorus Phocas had been recalled by Stylian to Constantinople; his successor Catacalon possessed little of his energy and strategic imagination. Somehow this lacklustre commander managed to escape with his life; few of those who fought with him were equally fortunate.[1] Leo had no choice but to sue for peace; but it was only after five years of long and patient diplomacy, and a reluctant agreement to pay a large annual tribute, that he obtained it. The staple at Thessalonica was closed, and Constantinople once again became the centre for Bulgarian trade. The war, which had been caused by what should have remained a minor commercial dispute, had proved an unmitigated disaster for the Empire. It had also permanently and decisively changed the map of Central Europe. Bulgar susceptibilities could no longer be ignored: Symeon had shown that he was a force to be reckoned with.

He had also succeeded in dangerously reducing Byzantine military power at a time when the Empire needed to mobilize all its available resources against the Arabs. With the departure of Nicephorus Phocas, the Saracen advance in south Italy could no longer be held in check: 1 August 902 saw the fall of Taormina, the last imperial stronghold in

---

1 One of the other survivors was so revolted by the carnage that he retired to Mount Joannitsa near Corinth, where he spent the rest of his life on top of a pillar – earning later canonization as St Luke the Stylite.

Sicily; while in the East, Armenia was left practically defenceless and the Muslim forces began a new advance into Cilicia. The situation in the Aegean was no better; that same year also saw the destruction of the wealthy and well-defended port of Demetrias – now Volos – in Thessaly. The worst catastrophe of all, however, occurred two years later when a Greek renegade, Leo of Tripoli, led a Saracen fleet up the Hellespont and into the Marmara. Eustathius sailed out against him, but lost his nerve at the last moment and retired without risking an engagement. The command was hastily transferred to a certain Himerius, who succeeded in forcing the Saracens to retire; instead of returning to their home waters, however, they made straight for Thessalonica. The city resisted for three days, but its walls were in disrepair and its two commanders at loggerheads; the sudden death of one of them after a fall from his horse might in other circumstances have proved a blessing in disguise, but it came too late. On 29 July 904 the defences crumbled and the Saracens poured through the breach. The bloodshed and butchery continued for a full week; only then did the raiders re-embark with their priceless plunder and – we are told – more than 30,000 prisoners, leaving the second city and port of the Empire a smoking ruin behind them.

It was more than a disaster; it was a disgrace. Leo determined on revenge. The shattered fortifications of Thessalonica were rebuilt and strengthened; an intensive programme of ship-building considerably enlarged the fleet; and a plan was prepared for the autumn of 905 according to which Himerius, who had by now succeeded Stylian as Logothete of the Course, would sail round the coast to Attaleia – the modern Antalya – embark a land army under the command of the local military governor, Andronicus Ducas, and then continue to Tarsus, a port which was roughly commensurate with Thessalonica in size and importance and which would now, it was intended, suffer a similar fate. Himerius duly arrived at Attaleia with his fleet – only to find that Ducas had no intention of joining him and had effectively come out in open revolt against the Empire. At this point a lesser man, suddenly denied the forces he had been promised, might well have given up the whole operation; but Himerius, ill-equipped and inexperienced as he was, had no intention of doing any such thing. He pressed on regardless; and a few days later, having utterly destroyed the Saracen fleet that had sailed out to intercept him, he reduced Tarsus in its turn to ashes. Byzantine honour had been saved.

Andronicus Ducas had meanwhile retired, with as many of his army as he had been able to persuade to follow him, some 150 miles north-east to a fortress near Iconium (the modern Konya). There he remained throughout the winter until March 906 when, learning of the approach of an imperial army, he withdrew with his son Constantine across the Saracen frontier and, after a brief pause in what was left of Tarsus, sought refuge in Baghdad. His story is neither edifying nor, in itself, particularly important; but it serves admirably to illustrate a grave new danger that was beginning to threaten the Empire: the rise of an increasingly powerful social class which had grown up in the course of the ninth century and was to cause serious problems during the tenth and eleventh. It consisted of a number of immensely rich families – in view of their size and ramifications, perhaps 'clans' would be a better word – possessed of extensive estates all over Asia Minor and sharing a long militaristic tradition, intermarrying among each other and showing little loyalty to the crown – if only because many of them had designs on it for themselves. Of these clans, that of the Ducas was probably the largest and certainly the most formidable; and Andronicus stood at its head. In the past he had given good service to the Empire, notably in 904 when he had led an expedition into Syria with extremely satisfactory results; but his sudden betrayal – prompted so far as we know by nothing more than resentment at finding himself subordinated to a commander whom he considered his inferior – demonstrates clearly enough the tenuousness of the ties that attached him, and many others like him, to the throne.

As things turned out it was the Emperor himself who was to be responsible, all unwittingly, for the ultimate downfall of Andronicus Ducas. He had arranged for an embassy to be dispatched to Baghdad, there to negotiate with the eleven-year-old Sultan al-Muqtadir an exchange of prisoners; and to it he now entrusted a secret letter to his former *strategos*, offering him pardon and reinstatement if he would only return to his old allegiance. Unfortunately, the letter was discovered; and its discovery proved Andronicus's undoing. Until then, the Sultan had believed him worthy of his trust; now, he was not so sure. Summoning the renegade into his presence, he gave him the choice between death and immediate conversion to Islam. Not altogether surprisingly, Andronicus chose the latter, but even this did not secure his freedom. He was placed, if not in confinement, at least under close surveillance; and shortly afterwards he died.

*

Leo's struggle against the Saracens was not quite over: it was to continue, indeed, for the rest of his life. The time has now come, however, to return to Constantinople, there to trace the vicissitudes of his emotional life during the second half of his reign.

His troubles had begun with his wife Theophano. During his father's lifetime the pair had been obliged to keep up appearances as best they could; after his own accession, however, relations between them had deteriorated fast. He had never liked her at the best of times, but now – perhaps to compensate for the love he could never give her – she had turned all her thoughts to religion, growing more and more devout until she became, even by Byzantine standards, mildly ridiculous. 'With morbid zeal,' writes her own biographer,

the Augusta applied herself to the salvation of her soul, treating all the pleasures of worldly life as dirt beneath her feet. Day and night her soul ascended to God in the chanting of psalms and in constant prayer; and unceasingly she drew near to Him through her works of charity. In public she wore the flowers of the purple and was clad in all the splendour of majesty. In private, secretly, she dressed in rags. Preferring the ascetic life to all others, she despised sumptuous food, and when delicate dishes were set before her she took bread and vegetables instead. All the money that she received, all the things so highly esteemed by people of this world, she distributed to the poor; her magnificent robes she gave to the needy; she ministered to the needs of widows and orphans; she enriched the monasteries, and loved the monks as if they were her own brothers.

At night, he continues, the Empress forsook her husband's bed, preferring a rough mat in a corner, from which every hour she rose to pray. A more unsatisfactory consort for a lusty young prince could hardly be imagined; moreover, Leo desperately wanted a son – and, as the anonymous biographer admits, 'he could not hope to have another child by her since her body, weakened and consumed by spiritual contemplation, was no longer capable of giving itself up to the delights of the flesh'.

In the winter of 892 their only child, Eudocia, died; Theophano withdrew into deeper and deeper seclusion and a year or two later, to her husband's unconcealed relief, retired to the convent attached to the Church of St Mary Theotokos at Blachernae where on 10 November 897, not yet thirty years old, she followed her daughter to the grave. Leo gave her a magnificent funeral – considering the way he had treated her in her lifetime, it was the least he could do – and immediately summoned his beloved Zoe to Constantinople. There remained the problem of her husband; but fortunately – some people thought a little too fortunately, but in the circumstances no inquiries were made and nothing was ever proved – Theodore Gutzuniates chose this peculiarly opportune moment to die in his turn. With unseemly dispatch his widow was installed in the Palace, and early in 898 the two lovers were married at last.

For a short time all was well. Zoe soon found herself pregnant, and the Emperor eagerly awaited the son that the astrologers had promised him. Alas, the child proved to be another girl, who was given the name of Anna; but this was only the first – and least – of the misfortunes that he was called upon to suffer as the century drew to its close. The second was the death, in the spring of 899, of Stylian Zautses. As Leo's chief minister he had served the Emperor faithfully – if not always selflessly – for thirteen years, and being also his father-in-law had been granted the unprecedented title of *basileopator*. Leo had given him his total trust, and implicitly relied on his judgement and experience; his loss came as a bitter blow. But worse yet was in store: at the end of that same year Zoe herself succumbed to some mysterious disease. Their long-awaited idyll had lasted just two years.

Leo's grief was, there is every reason to believe, deep and genuine; but there was no doubt in his mind that he must take a third wife. He had never been strong, and his health was causing him increasing concern; meanwhile his brother Alexander, with whom he theoretically shared the throne, was rapidly destroying himself with drink and debauchery and showed every sign of predeceasing him. In such an event, and in the absence of any son to succeed, the Empire would once again be imperilled, the prize of any adventurer who might attempt to seize it. And there was another consideration too: that only if an ordered and regular succession were guaranteed could there be any hope of a consistent long-term policy. The century that was just closing had proved both these points beyond any reasonable doubt: again and again the throne had been acquired by guile, or violence, or both. On the iconoclast question alone, the pendulum had swung so wildly to and fro that the majority of the Emperor's subjects could have been forgiven for feeling heartily sick of the whole business. What was required was a single, numerous, imperial family: a family whose members would all share similar opinions on the major issues of the day and in which the diadem would pass smoothly, ineluctably, from father to son or uncle to nephew, each pursuing the policies of his predecessor and giving the

Empire the consistency and continuity that it had so notably lacked in the recent past. But such a desirable a state of affairs could never be achieved in the absence of a generally accepted heir. Inevitably, this led to a disputed succession, which was in turn the fundamental evil from which all the others sprang: the plots and intrigues, the palace revolutions and the *coups d'état*, the pointless and bewildering changes of policy. The conclusion was obvious: the Emperor must marry a third time, and have a son.

But was such a thing permitted? The early Fathers of the Church – including SS. Jerome, Ambrose and Augustine – had adopted a fairly lenient view. Premature deaths from disease or childbirth were frequent in those days, and for a man to take a second wife after the loss of his first, or even a third after that of his second, seemed to them pardonable enough – particularly since it was, in the majority of cases, bound to happen anyway. In the East, on the other hand, the accepted code of conduct was more stringent. St Basil – always the most authoritative voice – had reluctantly permitted second marriages, so long as those concerned did suitable penance; third marriages, however, he firmly disallowed. They were at best what he called 'moderated fornication', and carried the penalty for both parties of four years' denial of the Sacrament. As for anyone ill-advised enough to attempt matrimony for the fourth time, they were guilty of something far worse than fornication, moderated or not. Their crime was polygamy, 'a practice bestial and wholly alien to humankind', for which a canonical penalty of no less than eight years was enjoined.

But Emperors were not necessarily bound by the same laws as their subjects, least of all when state interests were involved. Leo's brother, the Patriarch Stephen, had unfortunately died in 893; but his successor, the moderate and easy-going Antony Cauleas, was quite ready to grant the necessary dispensation and during the summer of 900, in the last of those curious beauty competitions or 'bride shows' ever held at the court of Constantinople, Leo selected a ravishing girl from Phrygia named Eudocia Baiana as his new consort. She tried hard, and on Easter Sunday, 12 April 901 presented her husband with a son. Alas, she died while doing so, and the baby prince survived her by only a few days.[1]

Leo, however, refused to give up. He was still only thirty-five, and

---

[1] An indication of the disapproval felt by many of the more strait-laced clerics of Constantinople was afforded by the abbot of the monastery of St Lazarus, who refused point-blank to allow her to be buried within the monastic precincts.

his determination to propagate his dynasty was as firm as ever. A fourth marriage, on the other hand, would be a good deal harder to arrange than the third had been, and even if he succeeded would unquestionably be his last chance. Before embarking on it, he had to be sure of his ground. His first step was, therefore, to take as his mistress the strikingly beautiful niece of the admiral Himerius, Zoe Carbonopsina – 'with eyes as black as coal'. (One feels throughout this story that however pressing may have been the reasons of state that impelled Leo to continue on his quest for a son, the process was not altogether uncongenial to him.) Illicit as it was, he made no secret of this union, which the Church – while not in any way condoning it – infinitely preferred to the idea of yet another marriage; nor was there any great wave of indignation or censure when, a year or two later, Zoe gave birth to a girl. Finally, however, in September 905, she produced a son. Small and sickly though he was, the Emperor's immediate ambition was achieved. The Patriarch, on the other hand, found himself in a quandary. He could not contemplate the possibility of the Emperor's marrying again; neither, however, could there be any question of Leo and his mistress living indefinitely in open sin. Finally agreement was reached: the Emperor would remove Zoe from the Palace, after which the Patriarch would consent to baptize his son in St Sophia. And so it came about: on the Epiphany following, 6 January 906, the baptism took place, the baby prince being given the name of Constantine.

That hurdle having been successfully crossed, however, Leo had no intention of maintaining a celibate life. Only three days later he brought Zoe back to the Palace, where he was already contemplating his next step. His son had been received into the Church, but he was still a bastard and, as such, debarred from the throne. Somehow he must be legitimized, and that could be achieved in one way only – by presenting the Patriarch with a *fait accompli*. And so Leo did the only sensible thing. He asked no permissions, gave no warnings. Quietly, almost secretly, in the private chapel of the Palace and before a simple parish priest, he and Zoe went through a form of marriage. Only when the ceremony was over did he make public what he had done and proclaim his new wife Empress.

For eight years the storm had been gathering; now it broke. The Church exploded in fury. St Basil was quoted *ad nauseam*; the Patriarch publicly reminded the Emperor that he had consented to perform the baptism of his son only on the understanding that his unseemly liaison was to be broken off forthwith. There could be no question of the fourth marriage being recognized: Leo himself had been joint signatory, with his father and his brother Constantine, of the article in the civil code which read:

Let it now be absolutely clear to all, that if any shall dare to proceed to a fourth marriage, which is no marriage, not merely shall such a pretended marriage be of no validity and the offspring of it be illegitimate, but it shall be subject to the punishment prescribed for those who are soiled with the filth of fornication, it being understood that the persons who have indulged in it shall be separated from each other.

In fact, where the civil code was concerned, Leo could have claimed immunity. He could even have issued a new decree annulling the former one and declaring fourth marriages lawful. Against canon law, on the other hand, he was powerless. Somehow, therefore, he must obtain a special dispensation; but how was this to be done? Had his brother still been alive and in occupation of the patriarchal chair, things might have been arranged without too much difficulty – though Stephen might have had a hard time carrying his colleagues with him. But he and his successor Antony Cauleas were both dead, the latter having been succeeded in 901 by a certain Nicholas, a nephew of Photius who had formerly served as the Emperor's private secretary. Left to himself, Nicholas too would probably have agreed to the dispensation; it was his misfortune to find himself confronted with Arethas, Bishop of Caesarea, the foremost scholar of the day and now to prove his most implacable enemy.

Although Leo liked to congratulate himself that he had brought peace to the Church through the Synod of 899, and although the two protagonists of the recent schism had long been in their graves, the Photian and Ignatian factions were still very much alive and continuing to threaten the unity of Orthodoxy. Both by training and inclination, Arethas had been for the first half-century of his life a dedicated Photian. Intellectually he was probably the only man in the Empire who could hold a candle to his master; he had published scholarly editions of several classical writers and was himself the author of one of the earliest Greek commentaries on the Apocalypse. Unfortunately, however, his writings had given mortal offence to the Ignatians, who at Easter 900 had had him arraigned on a charge of atheism. The proceedings had in fact ended in his acquittal, but he was a bitter and vindictive man who never forgot an injury; and when Nicholas, his friend and fellow-Photian, had been appointed Patriarch in the following year the bishop had pressed him to take immediate action against those who had done him wrong. Nicholas however had refused, pointing out that he had promised the Emperor as a condition of his appointment that he would do everything in his power to heal the breach between the two sides; the incident was closed, and to resurrect it would serve only to stir up the old animosities again to no purpose. Arethas, furious, had sworn revenge.

The issue of the Emperor's fourth marriage gave him just the opportunity he wanted. Inevitably, it had developed on factional lines, with the intellectual, worldly-wise Photians inclined to allow Leo his dispensation for the greater good of the State while the Ignatians, bigoted and doctrinaire to the last, ranged themselves inflexibly against it. Everything that Arethas stood for should have placed him squarely in the Photian camp; his vindictiveness alone drove him to adopt the line taken by the Ignatians, who welcomed him with open arms. Ill-educated as they were, they could never have hoped to hold their own in argument with the sophisticated followers of Photius. Now, suddenly, they had found a voice: a man of deep theological erudition, thoroughly trained in the arts of disputation and dialectic,[1] more than a match for any of his former friends who might champion the Emperor's cause.

All through the year the debate continued, while the Ignatians – thanks entirely to Arethas – steadily gained ground and the position of Patriarch Nicholas grew ever more impossible. The Emperor, meanwhile, was losing patience; and some time during the autumn a new and daring idea seems to have formulated itself in his mind. The Photians alone, obviously, would never be strong enough to gain him his dispensation. Very well, he would seek it from the Ignatians. True, they had set their faces firmly against it; but what might they not do in return for the Patriarchate? Discreet inquiries were made – not of Arethas, who had spoken out too strongly against the fourth marriage for any compact to be possible, but of Euthymius, abbot of the monastery of Psamathia, the leader and most widely respected member of the Ignatian party before the Archbishop's adherence.

Euthymius occupies a somewhat questionable place in the history of

---

1 Less so, however, in those of diplomacy – or he would hardly have written in a letter to the Emperor, 'Why can you not now dismiss with thanks the woman who has given you the child you desired, as we dismiss a ship when her cargo is discharged or throw away the husk which has brought the fruit to maturity?'

the Orthodox Church. Whether or not he deserved the canonization that he later received, he was certainly a profoundly religious man and a genuine ascetic. Early in his youth Leo had chosen him as his spiritual father and had built and endowed Psamathia specifically for him; but Euthymius had made no secret of his disapproval of the Emperor's treatment of Theophano or of his two subsequent marriages, and – though Leo had never lost his respect for his former mentor – relations between the two had understandably cooled. In view of both his record and his reputation – he was well known for his strict interpretations of canon law and all Church observances – one would have expected so stern a moralist to reject out of hand the proposal that was now made to him; but Leo clearly knew his man. After a decent moment of hesitation Euthymius accepted the offer of the Patriarchate and pronounced himself ready to issue the required dispensation, provided only that some respectable pretext could be found.

The Emperor was ready for this. Knowing full well that the Ignatians had always been staunch upholders of papal authority, and had indeed received invaluable support from Rome during the stormy days of the Photian dispute forty years before, he now revealed that he had recently submitted the whole question of the *tetragamy* (as it had come to be called) to Pope Sergius III, from whom he confidently expected a favourable reply. If the Supreme Pontiff were now to give his blessing, what better authority could Euthymius require? He could issue the dispensation forthwith – and, Leo might have added, save his face as well.

How, we may ask, could Leo be so sure that the Pope would react as he hoped? First, there was the fact that the early Catholic Fathers had never been unduly exercised over the question of plural marriages; what caused far more concern in Rome was the ever-widening rift between the Eastern and the Western Churches, and no Pope worthy of his throne would let slip so golden an opportunity of seeming to impose his authority on Constantinople. Second, Sergius was in desperate need of military assistance in south Italy where the Saracens were showing every sign of strengthening their hold, and the Emperor had no doubt that the Pope would consider his approval for the fourth marriage a more than acceptable *quid pro quo*.

Meanwhile, he was prepared to bide his time. Not a word was said publicly about his negotiations with Euthymius or his appeal to the Pope. He refused any suggestion that Zoe should be separated from him while the question remained unresolved, insisting that she should be treated with all the honour and respect due to an Empress; when, on the other hand, at Christmas 906 and on the Feast of Epiphany following, Patriarch Nicholas denied him entry into St Sophia, he turned back without protest to the Palace. Then, in February 907, the night before the papal legates were due to reach the capital, he struck. Nicholas was accused – with what justification we shall never know – of having been in secret communication with the rebel Andronicus Ducas, put under close arrest and forced to sign an act of abdication from the Patriarchate.

Now such an abdication, even if the Patriarch had been guilty of treasonable activities, would not have been valid without the approval of his fellow-Patriarchs and, at least in theory, of the Pope in Rome. Once again, however, Leo had made his preparations in good time. That same embassy that had been sent to Baghdad to negotiate the exchange of prisoners – and that had, incidentally, proved so disastrous for Andronicus Ducas – had also been entrusted with a further task: to bring back to the capital accredited representatives of the three Eastern Patriarchates – Alexandria, Antioch and Jerusalem. Pope Sergius, too, had been secretly apprised of Leo's intentions. It was gratifying enough to him to have been asked to pronounce on the fourth marriage; an additional appeal by an Emperor against his own Patriarch was an even more valuable testimonial to the respect in which the Papacy was held in the East, and was certainly not to be refused.

The letter from Sergius, which the legates delivered on their arrival the next day, justified the Emperor's highest hopes: in the circumstances, His Holiness could see no objection to his remarriage. Before the end of the month Euthymius, newly enthroned as Patriarch, duly granted the long-awaited dispensation. He did not, it should be emphasized, even now *sanction* the marriage: for as long as he continued to associate with Zoe Leo would be admitted to the Great Church only as a penitent, being debarred from the sanctuary and forbidden to sit at any time during the service. For the Emperor, however, this was a minor humiliation – little enough price to pay for a happy married life. Sinful as it might be, his marriage was at least reluctantly recognized. He and Zoe were man and wife, and the baby Constantine, now eighteen months old, was held to be *porphyrogenitus*, 'born in the purple' – a title by which he is still known to this day. Insofar as it ever could be in those uncertain times, the succession was assured.

*

The autumn of the year 905 was, for the Emperor Leo the Wise, a blessed season. September had seen the birth of his son, October the destruction of a Saracen fleet and the destruction of Tarsus. At last, it seemed, the wind was beginning to blow in his favour; and though the following year had brought a further deterioration in his relations with Nicholas, his triumph over the Patriarch during the first weeks of 907 must have provided further confirmation of his changing fortunes. The baby was crowned co-Emperor on 15 May 908, and two years later Himerius sailed against the Syrian port of Laodicea (now Lattakia), sacked the city, plundered and ravaged the hinterland and returned safely to Constantinople without the loss of a single ship.

It would have been better for Leo if he had died there and then. Instead, in the autumn of 911 he sent off his admiral on a final attempt to recapture Crete. For five years he had been working to improve the imperial navy, and the force at Himerius's disposal was stronger and infinitely better equipped than any that had been previously thrown against the island. Alas, the occupying Saracens had been working simultaneously on their defences, and the expedition proved no more successful than its predecessors. For six months – all through the winter and into the spring – Himerius kept up the siege; but the defenders held firm, and the Byzantines could make no appreciable impact on the massive fortifications. Then, in April 912, there arrived an urgent message from the capital: the Emperor's health, which had been giving cause for anxiety since the beginning of the year, had taken a sudden turn for the worse. He was now gravely ill, and unlikely to live. Reluctantly, the admiral gave orders for the raising of the siege and set sail for the Bosphorus. His ships were just rounding the island of Chios when they found themselves surrounded by a huge Saracen fleet under the command of Leo of Tripoli – he who had practically annihilated Thessalonica eight years before. Now he subjected the Byzantine vessels to much the same fate. Nearly all were sent to the bottom, Himerius himself narrowly escaping to Mitylene whence, slowly and with a heavy heart, he made his way back to Constantinople.

By the time news of the disaster reached the Imperial Palace, Leo's life was ebbing fast. He lived just long enough to hear it, then turned his face to the wall. On the night of 11 May he died. In a reign of just over a quarter of a century he had proved himself, if not perhaps a great Emperor, at any rate an outstandingly good one. He had, it is true, split the Church more deeply than ever; but this was the inevitable result of his fourth marriage, without which there would have been no obvious heir to the throne after the death of the childless Alexander. By his determination to marry Zoe Carbonopsina and to legitimize their son, he ensured both a universally recognized succession and the continuation of the Macedonian house, which was to survive for another 150 years – the greatest dynasty in the history of Byzantium. Compared with those two inestimable benefits, the damage done to the Church was of little long-term account.

For the rest, although he lacked that combination of relentless ambition, superhuman energy and boundless self-confidence that had distinguished his father – and is probably as good a definition of greatness as any other – he had ruled wisely and conscientiously over his subjects; and although his armed forces suffered more than their fair share of defeats at the hands of their Arab and Bulgar enemies, there can be no question but that he left the Empire, at least internally, in far better shape than when he inherited it. As befitted an intellectual and a scholar, he was not an exhibitionist: no great churches or sumptuous additions to the imperial palaces stand to his memory, and his mosaic portrait over the Imperial Door of St Sophia – which shows him, incidentally, in an attitude of prostration before Christ – dates almost certainly from several years after his death.[1] His most enduring achievements – the codification of the law, the reorganization of the provincial administration, the restructuring of the armed forces – were by definition unspectacular; but they were no less valuable for that. In his lifetime Leo was genuinely loved and respected by his people; and after his death posterity had good cause to be grateful to him.

1 This mosaic, in the lunette above the central doorway of the nine leading from the narthex into the main body of the church, carries – most exceptionally – no identifying inscription, and has consequently been the subject of much learned argument. By far the most convincing interpretation is that given by N. Oikonomides, who believes it to represent Leo's repentance after his fourth marriage and his salvation after the intercession of the Virgin – pictured in a medallion above him, with the Recording Angel opposite her. According to this theory the mosaic would be connected with the Council of 920, intended to illustrate the subjection of the earthly ruler to the King of Heaven and placed over the very door before which Leo was twice denied entrance to the church. See 'Leo VI and the Narthex Mosaic at St Sophia' in the *Dumbarton Oaks Papers*, Vol. 30 (1976).

9
The Rise of Romanus
[912–20]

Thirteen months – and an evil time.
Leo the Wise, on his deathbed[1]

The only good thing that can be said of the reign of the Emperor Alexander is that it was mercifully short. Already at the age of forty-one worn out by dissipation and debauchery, he was to occupy the throne of Byzantium for a little under thirteen months. Even in that short time, however, he managed to do a remarkable amount of damage. His normal behaviour could be compared only to that of Michael the Drunkard at his worst: the people of Constantinople were forced to witness the same senseless cruelties, the same drunken roisterings in public places, the same acts of wanton sacrilege. Sometimes it looked as though he intended to follow the example of Vladimir in Bulgaria and attempt the reintroduction of the ancient gods throughout the Empire; on one occasion at least, his pagan superstition brought him close to insanity – when he somehow persuaded himself that the bronze boar in the Hippodrome was his other self,[2] and had it provided with new teeth and genitals in an attempt to remedy the extraordinary wear and tear that he had inflicted on his own.

He had long hated his brother, and in 903 had almost certainly been involved in an unsuccessful plot to assassinate him during a service in

---

1 Scholars are undecided about these last words of Leo. His use of the preposition *meta* suggests that he meant that the evil time would come *in* thirteen months; on the other hand, if we could interpret his utterance to mean '*for* thirteen months' it would be a remarkable prophecy about the reign of Alexander. The above admittedly free translation keeps the ambiguity of the original, if nothing else.

2 In fairness to Alexander it should be pointed out that this curious belief that every human being possessed an inanimate *stoicheion*, a second repository of his physical and spiritual essence, was widely held in tenth-century Byzantium. It may well have been shared by Romanus Lecapenus himself: see p. 146n.

the Church of St Mocius. (It was probably as a result of this that in the following year he was deprived of his rank as co-Emperor – although his strong position as sole heir to the throne ensured that the demotion was only temporary.) Once he had achieved the power that he had so long awaited, he lost no time in giving that hatred open expression, reversing all Leo's policies, countermanding all his orders – striving, in short, to undo all that his brother had ever done, regardless of the consequences. The Empress Zoe was unceremoniously turned out of the Palace, together with all her friends and advisers; her uncle Himerius, who had given such sterling service to the Empire, was disgraced and thrown into prison, where he died six months later.

Meanwhile a Bulgarian embassy had arrived in Constantinople, sent by Symeon to congratulate him on his accession and to suggest a renewal of the peace treaty of 901. To Alexander, who had been with difficulty torn away from one of his orgiastic carousals to receive them, the treaty had been the work of his brother, and for that reason alone must be abrogated. In a sudden access of drunken braggadocio he shouted at the ambassador that he wanted no more treaties and, more-over, that Byzantium would be paying no further tribute. Then he dismissed them. They in their turn, probably more distressed by what they had seen than by what they had heard, returned with much sad shaking of heads to their master. To Symeon, we may be sure, their report was not entirely unwelcome. Confident in the strength of his army and concluding that he had nothing to fear from any Empire ruled by so pathetic a figure, he began preparations for war.

By this time, too, Alexander had taken another step which was to prove, in its own way, almost as disastrous as his reception of the Bulgars. Once again for no other apparent reason than to go against his brother, he had declared the abdication of Patriarch Nicholas invalid, recalled him from banishment and restored him to his former throne. (Nicholas himself was to claim that his restitution had been ordered by Leo, in a moving scene of deathbed repentance.) Adversity had not improved the Patriarch's character. He had spent his five-year exile brooding over the injustice he had suffered and, in particular, over his betrayal by Euthymius and the Ignatians – who, having originally stood firm with him against Leo's fourth marriage, had then joined with the Emperor to plot his overthrow, seized power for themselves and finally, in giving the required dispensa-tion, had done the one thing that they had always forbidden to him. He now returned with but a single thought in his mind: revenge.

Admittedly, he had a case. His mistake was to allow his resentment to blind him to all other considerations. Had he been content with his victory, directing his still considerable energies towards reconciliation with the Ignatians and permitting Euthymius to return quietly to the monastery that he should never have left, he might with time and patience have healed the controversy and reunited the Church. Instead he brought it, in a way that no Patriarch had ever brought it before, to the point of open mutiny. Euthymius was arraigned before a tribunal in the Palace of The Magnaura, whose proceedings are reported in detail by his contemporary biographer, who was quite possibly an eye-witness. Nicholas opened the cross-examination:

'Tell me, thou most witless of men, interpreter of the libidinous dreams of the deceased sovereign Leo, why, while yet I was among the living, didst thou take to wife the Church that was wedded to me, defiling her while driving me out?'

Replied Euthymius: 'Thou it was who broughtest her into defilement, and drovest thyself out, not once but thrice tendering thy resignation. And if thou askest me, I will tell thee the nature of thy defilement, and the cause of thine expulsion. For I am able, if God gives me the strength, to convict thee and set thine injustices before thy face.'

Struck dumb by these words and boiling with anger at the liberty with which the other spoke, the Patriarch ordered him to be publicly and shamefully stripped of his robes, and declared him fallen from his holy office.

Then was there a sight to be seen more pitiful than any before. Dragging off his bishop's scarf, they trampled upon it, not sparing even the figure of the Cross; similarly, they tore off all his sacred vestments and trampled upon them too, even his monk's cowl. And when the servants saw their master rejoicing and delighting in these things, they laid hands on his beard and pulled it, and pushed him with such violence that he fell on his back to the ground, and there they kicked him where he lay, spitting upon him, beating him with their fists and striking him in the face. Then the Patriarch ordered him to be set on his feet again, that the interrogation might be continued. But one of his henchmen, a giant of huge physical strength, stood looking on until, at a nod from his master, he struck him two blows, knocking out two of his teeth, and continued to pummel him at the back of the neck until he had no breath left, nor speech, and was on the point of falling down the staircase. Had not a nobleman named Petronas caught hold of him with three others, he would quickly have died a martyr's death.[1]

---

[1] The above is an edited and slightly shortened version of the translation by P. Karlin-Hayter, *Byzantion*, Vols. xxv–xxvii (1955–7). According to the Continuator of Theophanes, the man who pulled Euthymius's beard returned home to find his house burnt down and his daughter struck dumb and paralysed, in which state she lived on until the reign of Nicephorus.

Having banished Euthymius to the monastery of Agathon, and having persuaded the Emperor to remove his name and that of the Pope from the diptychs[1] (thereby breaking off all communion with Rome) the Patriarch now initiated a major purge of the entire hierarchy, aimed at nothing less than the elimination of all bishops and clergy with Ignatian – or, more properly, Euthymian – sympathies. How he expected the Church to function after such drastic surgery – where the episcopal bench alone was concerned, the Euthymians represented some two-thirds of the total – was never explained, but the problem was ultimately solved in another way: those dismissed flatly refused to go. The opposition, predictably, was led by Nicholas's arch-enemy Arethas of Caesarea, who made a public statement to the effect that he would leave his see only when the Emperor sent armed troops to remove him by force. Till then, he proposed to remain where he was and to carry out his duties as usual. Many others followed his example; meanwhile several Photian bishops who had tried to get rid of their Euthymian clergy found themselves besieged in their palaces by their mutinous flocks, and in one or two cities the disturbances led to serious rioting. Too late, the Patriarch realized that he had stirred up a hornets' nest. Back-pedalling desperately, he countermanded all his former orders; his voluminous correspondence from this time forth advocates a degree of tolerance and understanding far removed indeed from the spirit of his earlier fulminations. When the dust eventually settled, although several bishops had been transferred to other, equivalent, sees, only four had been dismissed absolutely. Arethas, we may not be surprised to learn, was not among them.

By this time, however, the Emperor Alexander was dead. The Continuator claims that he died as a result of a stroke, brought on by an ill-advised game of polo played in the heat of the day after a heavy lunch. More reliable sources, however, claim that his collapse followed immediately after various pagan sacrifices that he was making to the statues in the Hippodrome – including, presumably, the boar – in the hope of curing his impotence. It hardly matters: the important thing was his death, which occurred two days later, on Sunday, 6 June 913. His mosaic portrait in the north gallery of St Sophia must unquestionably

---

1 The tablets on which were inscribed the names of those, living and dead, who were to be specifically remembered during the service of the Eucharist.

date from his reign. After his death, his subjects wished only to forget him.

The moment that she heard that the Emperor was dying, his sister-in-law Zoe had forced her way back into the Palace, desperately worried for the future of her son. Some months before, she knew, Alexander had proposed to castrate him, thus rendering him permanently ineligible for the throne; he had been persuaded to reconsider only by the argument that such a step would provoke a potentially dangerous outcry, and that the boy was so weak and sickly that he could not be expected to live very long in any case. Now that it appeared that the Patriarch was to be the most powerful figure in the State, her anxieties were multiplied. Nicholas had never accepted the dispensation given by his enemy Euthymius that had recognized her marriage and her son's legitimacy; she had no doubt that he would do everything in his power to keep young Constantine from the throne, and she was determined to frustrate his efforts.

Her suspicions were well founded: the Patriarch did indeed have an alternative candidate. It was Constantine Ducas, Domestic of the Schools,[1] son of that Andronicus with whom Nicholas had been accused of maintaining treasonable contacts six years before: a man who felt no greater loyalty to the Macedonian house than his father had before him. He could probably rely on the support of much of the army, and had connections of one kind or another with most of the leading aristocratic families of the Empire; if he were to attempt a *coup* his chances of success would be high, and once on the throne his natural gratitude to Nicholas would ensure the final victory of the Patriarchate over its enemies. For some time already he and the Patriarch had been in secret correspondence; when the moment came, their plans would be already laid.

Zoe was still battling to regain her old position when the dying Emperor recovered sufficient consciousness to nominate his successor – which, to her relief, was indeed her son Constantine. She must, however, have been a good deal less pleased when he went on to appoint the necessary Council of Regency. Its president was to be Patriarch Nicholas; she herself was not included. She protested vigorously: never in the history of Byzantium had the mother of an Emperor and a crowned

---

1 I.e. Commander-in-chief of the land forces of the Empire.

Augusta[1] been denied a place on such a council. But Nicholas knew that he could take no chances. Zoe was the virtual embodiment of the Euthymian party – more so even than the old abbot himself – beholden to it for both her own crown and that of her son, and thus the Patriarch's most implacable enemy. One of his first actions as Regent was to have her arrested, shorn of her hair and dispatched to the distant convent of St Euphemia in Petrium. Even her name was no longer her own: henceforth she would be known as Sister Anna, and nothing more.

For the moment at least, her seven-year-old son was sole Emperor; but, with a Regent who denied him any legal right to the throne, how long could he be expected to survive? The first threat to his position – and probably to his life – came within days of his accession, with the attempted *coup* of Constantine Ducas. Marching eastward from his Thracian camp, Ducas entered the city by night with only a handful of men – few enough to suggest that he expected the Palace gates to be opened to him from within. If so, it was he who was taken by surprise. The *magister* John Eladas, one of the Regency Council, had been forewarned and was waiting for him with a hastily assembled company of militia. Several of Ducas's men, including his son Gregory, were killed in the fighting; and just as he was trying to escape his own horse slipped on the wet pavement. He fell heavily to the ground, where one of the defenders severed his head from his body with a single stroke.

The Patriarch, it need hardly be said, disclaimed any association with the plot and, as if to emphasize his innocence, instituted a reign of terror against all those whose complicity was known or even suspected. Whole companies were massacred, their bodies impaled along the Asiatic shore of the Bosphorus; others were flogged or blinded. Those who had sought sanctuary in St Sophia were dragged out, tonsured and driven into monasteries. Ducas's widow was exiled to the family's distant estates in Paphlagonia; his younger son, who had played no part in the affair, was castrated. Only when the Regency Council itself began to protest at the relentless bloodshed did Nicholas reluctantly call a halt.

He did so just in time; for less than two months after the Ducas fiasco, Symeon of Bulgaria appeared before Constantinople at the head

---

1 It should be remembered that an Augusta was not simply an Emperor's wife; she was the holder of a recognized rank, which carried considerable power and for which a special coronation was necessary. Once crowned, she had a court of her own and absolute control over her own immense revenues; and she played an indispensable part in many of the chief ceremonies of the Empire. See Diehl, *Figures Byzantines*, I, i.

of an army so immense that its camp occupied the entire four-mile stretch of the land walls between the Marmara and the upper reaches of the Golden Horn. Once there, however, he discovered what so many would-be conquerors of the Empire – including his own great-great-grandfather Krum – had discovered before him: that the fortifications of the city were impregnable. But he made no move to retire. By the threat of a land blockade, combined with the systematic devastation of the surrounding countryside, he could still make a considerable nuisance of himself and, with any luck, obtain favourable terms without the loss of any of his men. From the Palace of the Hebdomon he sent messengers to the Regency Council, announcing that he was ready to negotiate a settlement.

Nicholas was only too pleased to agree. To preserve peace with Symeon he was prepared to make almost any sacrifice, for war would be virtually certain to lead to the breaking away of the Bulgarian Church – which was at present still part of his Patriarchate – and, even worse, might even drive it back into the arms of Rome. He invited Symeon's two sons into the city and entertained them at a lavish banquet, in the presence of the boy Emperor, at Blachernae; and a day or two later himself secretly visited Symeon at the Hebdomon, where he was much gratified by the respect with which he was received. In the surprisingly friendly discussions that followed, the Bulgar King predictably insisted on being paid the arrears of tribute, and seems also to have demanded that Constantine should take one of his daughters to wife. Then, loaded with gifts, he returned to his homeland.

At first reading, we may be astonished at Symeon's moderation. Why, having brought this vast army to the very gates of the city, did he not drive a harder bargain? Simply because his policy had changed. His ambitions where Byzantium was concerned were greater than ever, being by now focused on nothing less than the crown itself[1] – which, once he had made himself the Emperor's father-in-law, would be within his grasp.[2] But his examination of the walls had convinced him that this was a prize that could be won only by diplomacy, while his discussions with Nicholas had revealed to him a hitherto unsuspected ally. Not only

1 There is reason to believe that Symeon received some sort of coronation at the hands of the Patriarch during the latter's visit; but this could only have been as ruler of Bulgaria. Romilly Jenkins's suggestion (*Byzantium: The Imperial Centuries*, p. 232) – that Nicholas actually crowned him Emperor of Byzantium, with a makeshift diadem 'improvised from his own patriarchal veil' – is surely absurd.

2 Just how right he was in this assumption was to be proved only six years later by Romanus Lecapenus, though not in quite the way that Symeon would have wished.

did the Patriarch obviously feel little or no loyalty to the Macedonian house; his obvious terror at the thought of losing control of the Bulgarian Church gave Symeon immense bargaining strength – particularly since he himself cared not a straw for the independence of his Church, one way or another: since he himself intended to be Emperor, what difference could it make? For both these reasons, to have adopted an aggressive or threatening attitude at this juncture would have been folly. His interests (and his daughter's) would best be served by showing himself in as favourable a light as possible: as a man whose decisions were governed by reason and good sense – he had after all been educated in Constantinople – and whose family was in every respect worthy of an imperial alliance. Only one indication did he give that an iron hand still lurked within the velvet glove – a hint so slight as to be almost imperceptible, and negative at that: he avoided any further mention of a treaty of peace. With the Empire in its present enfeebled state, there was no point in needlessly limiting his freedom of action.

But if Symeon had played his hand beautifully, Patriarch Nicholas had badly overplayed his. His fellow-members of the Council were increasingly irritated by his arrogance and like everyone else had been revolted by his cruelty, first to Euthymius and then to the whole Ducas clan. They were also appalled by his treatment of Zoe, whose claims to a share in the Regency were undeniable, and they could not but be moved at the sight of the pale, delicate little Emperor, wandering miserably around the Palace crying for his mother. The news that the Patriarch, who was by now strongly suspected of collusion in at least the early stages of the Ducas affair, had been in secret negotiations with the Bulgar King – for as usual he had not bothered to inform them in advance – was the last straw. From that moment on, the Council began to fall apart. In February 914 Sister Anna was recalled from her nunnery and, once again an Empress, took over the Regency, reappointing all her old friends and advisers.

The new government was to be contemptuously described by Symeon as a 'council of eunuchs' – which in a very large measure it was. But eunuchs in the Byzantine Empire were neither the mincing male sopranos of later Western Europe nor the overweight and epicene harem-keepers of the Oriental tradition. For at least the four centuries since the age of Justinian – one of whose generals, Narses, must despite his castration be numbered among the greatest soldiers in imperial history – they had been highly respected members of society and holders of many of the most distinguished offices of Church and State, among which they were denied only those of Prefect of the City, Quaestor, Domestic of the four imperial regiments and the throne itself. By the tenth century to be a eunuch was, for a promising youth about to enter the imperial service, a virtual guarantee of advancement; many an ambitious parent would have a younger son castrated as a matter of course. The practice may seem strange, even barbarous; but the reasons are in fact not far to seek. Eunuchs, with no wives or family to support, tended to be far more industrious and dedicated than their more completely-endowed colleagues. Since they left no sons, there was no tendency for certain offices to become hereditary, as happened so often in the West: posts could be awarded on merit alone. By the same token they constituted an invaluable bulwark against that feudalism which was to cause the Empire more and more trouble, particularly in Asia Minor, as the century progressed. Finally and most important of all, they were safe. A eunuch might – and frequently did – engage in a little mild intrigue on behalf of a brother or a nephew; but never, however powerful he might be, could he make a bid for the throne.

Small wonder, then, that the Empress and her eunuchs soon showed themselves far more capable administrators of the Empire than Nicholas and his Regency Council had ever been. The old Patriarch himself, on the other hand, presented them with something of a problem. Zoe's first intention had been to replace him for the second time with Euthymius, but Euthymius had demurred; not surprisingly, he had had enough. With some reluctance, therefore, she allowed Nicholas to continue in office – though with dire warnings as to what he could expect if he meddled any further in affairs which did not concern him. Back he went to his pastoral duties – setting foot in St Sophia, according to one (admittedly hostile) source, for the first time since his assumption of the Regency some eight months before – and accepting his fate with as much grace as he could muster; though it doubtless galled him not a little when Zoe almost immediately raised her already considerable popularity still higher with a trio of military and political triumphs of very considerable importance to the security of her Empire.

The first of these was the enthronement of Ashot, King of Armenia.[1]

---

1 The title of 'King', or more properly 'King of Kings', was periodically bestowed upon whichever leader of the principal Armenian clans was for the time being the most powerful. Though it might on occasion pass from father to son it was never in any real sense hereditary, and frequently fell into abeyance altogether.

That bleak, inhospitable region around Mount Ararat, long the most sensitive point of confrontation between the Byzantines and the Saracens, occupied a delicate and ambiguous political position. To the Emperor at Constantinople, the Armenian princes – the land was never truly united – were his vassals; unfortunately the Caliph in Baghdad took a similar view, and for well over a century had regularly appointed an Arab *ostigan*, or Governor. As for the Armenians, they prided themselves on their intelligence and their ancient culture, and claimed to have been the first people to have adopted Christianity as their national faith. They were however – like most of their Christian neighbours in the East – convinced monophysites, and felt little loyalty or affection for Byzantium: many of them indeed, following that well-known tendency of the dogmatist to prefer infidels to heretics, frankly welcomed the Muslim influence.

Given the natural disputatiousness of the Armenians and the basic instability of their situation, it was little wonder that they seemed to pass from one political crisis to the next. In 909, however, they found themselves faced with a threat which was, even by their standards, unusually grave when the Caliph's *ostigan*, the Persian Emir Yusuf, determined to eliminate Byzantine influence altogether and to reduce them to a state of total subjection to Baghdad. First sparking off a civil war – never difficult in Armenia – Yusuf swept across the strife-torn country, massacring all who resisted him and committing unspeakable atrocities in the towns and villages through which he passed. For four years the terror continued, until in 913 the Armenian King Smbat, in the vain hope of saving his subjects' lives, finally surrendered to Yusuf and was rewarded by a particularly hideous martyrdom.

To Byzantium, Armenia constituted a vital bulwark; and one of Zoe's first actions on her return to power in 914 had been to invite Smbat's son and heir, the young Prince Ashot, to Constantinople to decide on a plan of campaign. Thus it came about that in the spring of the following year Ashot returned to his native land at the head of a large Greek army. Yusuf put up a stiff resistance, but was hopelessly outnumbered; and by the first snowfall – winter comes early in those regions – all western and much of eastern Armenia was back in Ashot's firmly pro-Byzantine hands. It was to be another four years before the land was properly at peace – the inevitable internal squabbling saw to that – but its integrity had been saved, and both Zoe and Ashot had good reason to congratulate themselves.

The Empress's second success was the decisive defeat of a large Muslim army that had launched a major raid on imperial territory from its base at Tarsus. There was much jubilation when the news reached Constantinople; but this triumph was as nothing compared with the third, achieved just as Ashot was re-establishing himself in Armenia, in the very opposite corner of the Empire – the south Italian Theme of Langobardia. Here, just outside the city of Capua, the imperial *strategos* totally destroyed the Saracen army, thereby restoring Byzantine prestige in the peninsula to its highest level since the departure of Nicephorus Phocas in 886. By the end of 915, in the minds of the large majority of her subjects, the Empress Zoe could do no wrong.

Even Symeon of Bulgaria suffered a reverse, if only a temporary one. To him Patriarch Nicholas's fall from power and the return of Zoe had been a devastating blow: the Empress, he knew, would never for a moment countenance that all-important marriage on which he had set his heart. His careful diplomacy had gone for nothing; it would have to be war after all. In September he appeared with his army before Adrianople (Edirne), which was immediately surrendered by the local governor without even a show of resistance. He seems to have been genuinely astonished when the Empress sent a massive force to recover the city, and in his turn hastily withdrew.

For the next two years he contented himself with harassing the cities and towns of Thessaly and Epirus; but in 917 his armies were back again in Thrace, and Zoe decided on a pre-emptive strike. Her *strategos* at Cherson in the Crimea, a certain John Bogas, had succeeded in bribing Symeon's erstwhile allies, the notoriously venal Pechenegs, to invade Bulgaria from the north; and the Byzantine fleet had been enlisted to carry them across the Danube, just as it had carried the Magyars a quarter of a century before. Meanwhile the army was to march up from Constantinople to the southern frontier. Trapped between the two arms of a gigantic pincer movement, Symeon would have no alternative but to accept the terms he was offered; it would be a long time before he were once more in a position to make trouble for the Empire.

As a plan it seemed almost foolproof; and so it might have proved, but for a sudden, unexpected twist of fate: a twist so surprising, indeed, that we may be forgiven for suspecting that Symeon had again exercised his remarkable talent for bribery. John Bogas arrived with his Pechenegs on the banks of the Danube to keep his rendezvous with the fleet, which was commanded by its *drungarius* – an Armenian named Romanus Lecapenus; the moment they met, however, the two men became involved in a furious argument, each denying the authority of the other. The upshot was that Romanus categorically refused to transport the invaders across the river; and the Pechenegs, soon tired of waiting, drifted away to their homes.

The army meanwhile, under the command of the Domesticus Leo Phocas – son of the great general Nicephorus – had advanced from the capital along the Black Sea coast and had entered Bulgar territory at the southern end of the Gulf of Burgas, where dawn on 20 August found it encamped outside the little port of Anchialus. It was then that Symeon, who had been carefully monitoring its progress, saw his chance. Sweeping down on it from the hills to the west, he took it entirely by surprise and showed it no mercy. What exactly happened is uncertain: George Cedrenus claims that Leo's horse suddenly took fright while its master was bathing and galloped riderless through the ranks, causing a panic among the soldiers who immediately concluded that their general must be dead. This story may or may not be true; what is beyond doubt is that virtually the entire Byzantine army was massacred. The navy, which should have been standing by to pick up survivors, had already returned to the Bosphorus; those who managed to flee from the butchery found themselves with no means of escape and were cut down by their pursuers. Leo the Deacon, writing the better part of a century later, reports that even in his day the battlefield was still covered with the bones of the fallen, lying bleached in the sun. One of the few to get away with his life was Leo Phocas himself, who somehow managed to make his way northward along the coast to Mesembria whence, some time later, he took ship for Constantinople.

The anger of the Empress on hearing the news of the disaster can easily be imagined. She at once ordered an official inquiry into the conduct of Romanus Lecapenus, who was sentenced to be blinded; it was fortunate for him – and, as it turned out, for the Empire – that some of his influential friends were able to intercede on his behalf and win him a last-minute reprieve. Strangely enough, her confidence in Leo Phocas remained apparently unshaken; that same winter she entrusted him with another army, with which to drive back the Bulgars who had once again overrun eastern Thrace up to the very walls of the capital. But Leo had inherited none of his father's military genius. He had got no further than Casasyrtae in the western suburbs before his second army was destroyed almost as completely as his first had been.

For Symeon it was another victory – of a kind; but there soon came additional confirmation of what he already knew all too well: that whatever damage he might do to the imperial soldiery, he could still make not the slightest impression on the defences of Constantinople. He had no choice but to return, frustrated and furious, to Bulgaria for what was left of the winter. In the capital, however, the year 918 opened to reveal a situation of growing chaos. After two annihilating defeats, Zoe's reputation was in ruins and her regime in serious danger. There was, she knew, no chance of any accommodation with Symeon; he continued to insist on the marriage between young Constantine and his daughter as a *sine qua non* of any settlement, and the Empress still could not bring herself to contemplate the idea of a barbarian daughter-in-law. If she were to find the support she needed to shore up her tottering throne, she would have to look for it within the Empire.

But where was it to be found? Not, certainly, with the Patriarch, who was by now sniffing the possibility of his own return to power and could be trusted to do her down at every opportunity. There were in fact but two alternatives. The first was Leo Phocas, discredited as he was, who after the disgrace of Casasyrtae had crossed over to Asia in an attempt to rally the army of Anatolia. Since the downfall of Constantine Ducas, the family of Phocas was the recognized leader of the rich landed aristocracy; Leo was moreover a widower, with whom the Empress may have been contemplating marriage – a step which would have immeasurably strengthened her own position, to say nothing of that of her son.

The other alternative was Romanus Lecapenus. He differed from Leo in two important respects. First, he was a man of neither birth nor breeding, an Armenian peasant's son who had risen to his present rank entirely on his own merit. Second, although he too had signally failed to distinguish himself during the recent hostilities, he had not been defeated. His great flagship was even now riding proudly at anchor in the Golden Horn, surrounded by the rest of the imperial fleet: a proclamation of naval might that was not lost on the Byzantines, particularly when they remembered the condition of their army – for which, as they well knew, Leo Phocas was principally to blame.

Of the two, the Empress not surprisingly preferred the handsome, aristocratic general to the jumped-up foreign parvenu. She therefore summoned Leo to the Palace where, within a few weeks, he became one of her closest associates and most trusted advisers. She had, however, seriously underestimated the strength of public opinion. The people of Constantinople – a political element which, especially in times of crisis, sovereigns ignored at their peril – had always mistrusted these feudal lords from Anatolia; their traditional loyalties were to the established imperial dynasty, and their opinions were shared by most of the old urban aristocracy and many members of the court itself. Little Constantine was now thirteen years old; although his health remained poor, he was clearly a child of quite unusual intelligence who appeared to have the makings of a first-class Emperor. But what chance would he stand against the ambitions of a Phocas, when not even his own mother seemed aware of the danger?

It was at this moment that a member of the imperial household took matters into his own hands. Theodore, Constantine's personal tutor, now wrote a letter in his pupil's name to Romanus Lecapenus appealing for his protection. Why Romanus was considered any more trustworthy than Leo is not altogether clear: perhaps his modest beginnings told in his favour. But he was certainly no less ambitious, and unhesitatingly proclaimed his readiness to serve the young Emperor as his protector and champion. In doing so, he can have had no delusions as to the effect that such a pronouncement would have on the Empress. Doubtless encouraged by Phocas, she instructed her old friend and counsellor, the *parakoimomenos* Constantine, to order Romanus in her name to pay off his sailors and disband the fleet forthwith. The admiral replied with the utmost courtesy, inviting Constantine to come on board the flagship to see for himself how conscientiously the imperial commands were being obeyed. All unsuspecting, the Chamberlain did so – only to be immediately seized and put under arrest.

To lay hands on her chief representative was a deliberate affront to the Empress herself; but when Zoe sent envoys to the admiral to demand an explanation they were greeted by a hail of stones. Now seriously alarmed, she called a meeting of her ministers at the Bucoleon[1] – only to find that they too had turned against her. She was obliged to listen in silence while the young Constantine Porphyrogenitus read from a prepared script, informing his mother that her Regency was at an end:

---

1 The area between the southern end of the Hippodrome and the Marmara, which included the private harbour and maritime entrance to the Great Palace.

henceforth the government would be entrusted jointly to Patriarch Nicholas and another member of the former Council, the *magister* Stephen. The next morning a body of soldiers arrived to escort her back to the convent of St Euphemia; only in response to long and tearful entreaties on the part of her son was she at length permitted to remain, powerless but at least uncloistered, in the *gynaeceum* of the Palace.

Nicholas had triumphed; but he soon discovered that the condition of the Empire was very different from what it had been five years before. Zoe had been dealt with satisfactorily enough; but Leo Phocas and Romanus Lecapenus were now locked in an open struggle for supremacy. Floundering hopelessly between them, the unhappy Patriarch did his utmost to play one off against the other, but succeeded only in making his own position more and more untenable. Finally, on 25 March 919, Romanus appeared with his fleet at the Bucoleon, entered the Palace by the Marine Gate and announced that he had taken over the government of the Empire; and only a month later, in St Sophia, he gave away his exquisite young daughter Helena to Constantine in marriage, taking for himself that same title of *basileopator* that Leo the Wise had invented for his own father-in-law, Stylian Zautses.

For the second time in just over half a century, an Armenian upstart stood but one short step from the throne of Byzantium.

Of the obstacles remaining in the path of Romanus Lecapenus, the greatest was Leo Phocas, who had returned to his army across the Bosphorus and there, from his camp at Chrysopolis, had raised the standard of revolt. To ensure the loyalty of his troops, he gave it out that he was acting to free the Emperor from the clutches of the usurping *basileopator*; Romanus countered this by using two undercover agents, one a priest and the other a prostitute, to disseminate copies of a letter ostensibly signed by the boy Emperor himself, making it clear that his father-in-law enjoyed his complete confidence and trust, while Leo Phocas was nothing more than a contemptible rebel with the temerity to rise up against his legitimate sovereign. The priest was soon arrested, but the prostitute did her work admirably and hundreds of Leo's men laid down their arms. Leo himself saw that he had failed, and that his only chance of survival lay in flight; but he was caught in a Bithynian village, where his eyes were put out before he was brought back in chains to Constantinople.

When he heard of the blinding of his rival, Romanus is said to have flown into a fury – though his anger did not prevent him, on the discovery of another conspiracy a few weeks later, from parading the wretched Leo round the Forum on a mule to the jeers and taunts of the populace. But Leo Phocas was now a spent force; a far more important consideration in the mind of Romanus was to smooth his own path to the throne – an objective which, since he clearly had no right to it, could be achieved only by undermining the claims of Constantine. Thus, with the enthusiastic cooperation of the Patriarch, a formal synod was summoned to Constantinople in the summer of 920, with the express purpose of putting an end to the turmoil in the Church; and on 9 July this synod published the famous *Tomus Unionis* in which was set out, finally and authoritatively, the revised canon law on the subject of remarriage. According to its meticulously drafted provisions, for a man to marry a second time was perfectly legitimate, while even a third wife might be permitted to a childless widower under the age of forty, provided that their nuptials were followed by an appropriate act of penance; but fourth marriages were out of the question in any circumstances at all, and would be punished by excommunication until such time as the fourth partner were permanently repudiated. Fortunately, the decree was not retrospective. Leo VI's last two marriages were however condemned in the strongest possible terms, and the legitimacy of his son accepted only reluctantly and on sufferance.

The feelings of the fourteen-year-old Constantine, obliged to put his signature to such a document, may well be imagined; but the *Tomus*, hateful to him as it must have been, did not mark the end of his tribulations. Barely a month later, his mother Zoe was accused by Romanus of attempting to poison him. Whether there was any truth in the charge we shall never know, although in the circumstances there seems nothing inherently improbable about it. But it was enough to settle the Empress's fate once and for all. Again her hair was shorn; again she was obliged to don the coarse nun's habit that she detested; and again the great doors of St Euphemia slammed shut behind the reluctant Sister Anna.

There remained one last adversary. Constantine's tutor Theodore had played a crucial part in Romanus's rise to power. He had first invited him to act as the young Emperor's protector; and there is reason to believe that it was he, when the admiral had appeared off the Bucoleon the previous March, who had actually unlocked the gate and admitted him into the Palace. In all this, however, Theodore had been acting in what he innocently believed to be the best interests of his pupil; he now saw that his intrigues had placed Constantine in precisely the position that he had most wished to avoid. Imperial champion or not, Romanus had shown himself every bit as self-seeking as Leo Phocas. The moment that he realized this, Theodore's attitude to him abruptly changed, and it did not take Romanus long to understand that the man who had started as his accomplice had become his enemy. It was probably some time in early September that Theodore and his brother Symeon were invited to a banquet given by the Patrician Theophylact, Count of the Stable. Half-way through the meal they were both arrested on a charge of conspiracy, and exiled to their country estate in north-west Anatolia.

With the departure of Theodore, Constantine lost his last true friend. He was now nothing but a pawn in the hands of his father-in-law, whom on 24 September 920 – just a few days after his fifteenth birthday – he dutifully appointed Caesar. Less than three months later, on 17 December, he marked the culmination of the astonishing career of Romanus Lecapenus by laying on his head the imperial diadem[1]. Theoretically, of course, he – Constantine – still remained the senior Emperor; but within a year it was Romanus whose portrait – slightly larger and in more resplendent robes – began to appear in the place of honour on the coinage, and to the vast majority of his subjects it must have seemed only a matter of time before that of the young Porphyrogenitus disappeared altogether.

---

1 Earlier historians, including Sir Steven Runciman (*The Emperor Romanus Lecapenus*, p. 62) place these last two events in the previous year, 919. But – as has been pointed out by both Grumel and Ostrogorsky (p. 264) – Romanus appeared at the Synod of 920 as *basileopator*, a title which he would not conceivably have used if he were already Caesar, let alone Emperor.

IO

The Gentle Usurper

[920–48]

You are a mortal; you await death, resurrection and judgement. Today you live and tomorrow you are dust; one fever will quench all your pride. What will you say, when you come before God, of your unrighteous slaughter? How will you face the terrible, just Judge? If it is for love of riches that you do this, I will grant all your desires and more: only hold out your hand. Welcome peace, love concord, that you yourself may live a peaceful, bloodless and untroubled life, and that Christians may see an end to their woes and may cease destroying their fellow-Christians.

Romanus Lecapenus to Symeon
of Bulgaria, 9 September 924

Of the early history of Romanus Lecapenus – or, as we must now call him, the Emperor Romanus I – all too little has come down to us. His father, known universally to contemporaries as Theophylact the Unbearable, was an Armenian peasant whose good fortune it was to have rescued Basil I from the Saracens at the battle of Tephrikē in 872. This earned him a place in the imperial guard, but probably little more: there is no indication that he was in any way ambitious either for himself or his son, and he certainly took no trouble over Romanus's education, as Constantine VII was scornfully to point out when circumstances allowed him to do so. It was left for the boy to make his own way in the world. Born around 870 – even the exact date is unknown – he had entered the imperial service in the navy, and whether or not we choose to accept the suggestion by Liudprand of Cremona that his early promotion was the direct result of a heroic encounter with a lion, he was probably still in his thirties when he was appointed *strategos* of the Samian Theme, which included most of the western coast of Asia Minor and the neighbouring islands – a position of considerable authority since it gave him, although a serving officer, full responsibility for the civil as well as the military administration. He seems to have performed his duties with distinction, and after the disgrace of Himerius in 912 was the obvious choice for *drungarius*, or High Admiral.

At the time of Romanus's seizure of power his wife Theodora – whom he was to proclaim Augusta at Epiphany, 921 – had borne him at least six children, and before her death in 923 was to present him with two more. Of their four sons, no less than three were to be crowned co-Emperor by the end of 924; the youngest, Theophylact, was a eunuch intended for the Patriarchate. It is clear that, like his fellow-Armenian Basil I, the new Emperor intended to found a dynasty. Where he differed from his predecessor was in the comparative gentleness of his character. Basil's road to power had been marked by at least two proved assassinations; Romanus Lecapenus had employed trickery and deceit in plenty, but he was not by nature either violent or brutal. When his arch-rival Leo Phocas was blinded by his captors – a common enough fate in tenth-century Byzantium – he had been quick to express his horror and disgust; for the vast majority of his enemies, he would always consider exile to be punishment enough. The persistency with which his young son-in-law clung to life must have infuriated him – while the Porphyrogenitus lived, there could be little long-term future for the house of Lecapenus – and given the boy's permanently fragile state of health it would have been an easy matter to poison him without arousing suspicions: Basil, in similar circumstances, would not have hesitated for an instant. But Romanus was cast in a different mould. He might – indeed he did – do everything in his power to displace the young Emperor, promoting both himself and his son to superior positions; but never did he lay a finger upon his son-in-law – who, as it turned out, was comfortably to outlive the two of them.

For Constantine it must, nevertheless, have been a miserably unhappy childhood, shot through with uncertainty and fear: a father dead, a mother branded as a concubine and twice exiled, he himself facing constant accusations of bastardy and forced to accept in silence the gradual removal of everyone in whom he could put his trust. All this would have been bad enough for a sickly, sensitive boy, without finding himself alone, unwanted and unloved amid a huge and fundamentally hostile family; and a marriage of convenience at the age of thirteen to a member of that family (a girl whom he hardly knew) can hardly have improved matters. Later, it is only fair to point out, that marriage was to prove a surprisingly happy one, with two of the couple's children eventually succeeding their father on the throne; be that as it may, there can be little doubt that the young Emperor passed his adolescence in desperate loneliness and very largely ignored. Fortunately for him, his physical weakness was offset by an unusually lively mind, and a wide range of artistic and intellectual interests: he seems to have been a talented painter, he was fascinated by everything he could discover about the great world that lay beyond the immediate confines of the capital and even the Empire, and he would spend hours and days at a time studying the intricacies of Byzantine court ceremonial, the one subject which his position, intolerable as it was, gave him limitless opportunity to observe and on which his exhaustive survey, *De Ceremoniis Aulae Byzantinae*, remains our most valuable authority.

He was fortunate too in possessing, at least in those early years, neither political ambition nor – so far as can be seen – very much in the way of moral courage. Wisely, he made no attempt to assert himself. When his father-in-law elbowed him aside as senior Emperor; when in May 921 Romanus elevated his eldest son Christopher to be yet another occupant of the throne; when, on the death of the Augusta Theodora in February 923, he crowned Christopher's wife Sophia in her place; when, two years later still, he elevated two more sons, thus producing a somewhat ridiculous total of five simultaneous Emperors; even when in 927 he proclaimed Christopher second only to himself, relegating the Porphyrogenitus to third position in the State – on none of these occasions did Constantine utter a word of protest. Silence, however, did not mean indifference: as his later writings show, each successive insult wounded him to the quick – though none, one suspects, more than the *Tomus Unionis*, whose insinuations were made still harder to bear by the stipulation that it was to be read every year, on the second Sunday in July, from the ambo of every church in the Empire, and was to be annually commemorated in the capital by a procession between the churches of St Irene and St Sophia in which all the co-Emperors, together with the Patriarch, were obliged to participate. Yet on these occasions too, obediently and uncomplainingly, Constantine did what was required of him. He knew that he had one duty that took precedence over all the others: to survive.

'We have glad tidings for you, O my son, which will delight your heart as much as it delights our own to impart them: the Church of God is once again united.' So wrote Patriarch Nicholas to Symeon of Bulgaria, informing him of the *Tomus Unionis* and the end of the quarrel between his own party and that of the Euthymians. Symeon was not delighted in the least. The Byzantine Church was of no interest to him: he cared only for the throne – that throne which seven years before had been almost within his grasp but which, since its appropriation by Romanus Lecapenus, now seemed as far away as ever. The Emperor, from the moment of his accession, had done everything in his power to restore good relations with his turbulent neighbour, whom he was perfectly prepared to buy off with an annual tribute or even, if necessary, with a cession of imperial territory; but Symeon would accept no terms that did not begin with Romanus's abdication, and so hostilities continued. The Byzantines reverted once again to their old trick of stirring up trouble elsewhere around the enemy's border – this time in Serbia, where the local princes, struggling to shake off the Bulgar yoke, were only too happy to accept imperial subsidies; but the pressure was never relaxed for long. In 919 Symeon pushed south as far as the Hellespont; in 921 he was back at Casasyrtae, within sight of the land walls; in 922 he advanced to the European shore of the Bosphorus, inflicted a humiliating defeat on a Byzantine army, sacked the whole area around Stenum (the modern Istinye) and burnt one of Romanus's favourite palaces at Pegae;[1] while 923 saw his recapture of Adrianople – whose Governor, Moroleon, he punished for his heroic resistance by torturing him to death.

But none of these small triumphs brought him any nearer to his ultimate goal; however much damage he might do in Thrace, however many towns and cities he might capture or destroy, Constantinople remained impregnable from the landward side. In 924 he therefore resolved on a final onslaught, this time from the sea. He himself had no fleet; but it seemed possible that the Fatimid Caliph in North Africa[2]

---

1 Pegae poses something of a problem. The Greek τιηγή means a stream, or source. According to R. Janin, our leading authority on the topography of Constantinople (*Constantinople Byzantine*, Paris 1950), there was a Palace 'of the Stream' (τῆς Πηγῆς) just outside the gate of the same name – now Silivri Kapi – in the land walls, and another 'of the Streams' (τῶν Πηγῶν) on the further side of the Golden Horn, in the quarter known today as Kasimpaşa. Neither of these locations, however, can be reconciled with the account of the Continuator of Theophanes, who twice associates it with the district of Stenum on the Bosphorus. Surely there could not have been a *third* palace of the same, or similar, name? Or is M. Janin mistaken?

2 The Fatimids began as a Shi'ite Arab clan which claimed descent from the Prophet's daughter Fatima and her husband Ali. In 909 one of their members, Abu Abdullah, had driven out the Arab prince of Kairouan and installed the Fatimid Obaidullah, who took the title of Mahdi and openly challenged the authority of the Abbasid Caliph in Baghdad. After their conquest of Egypt in 969 the Fatimids were to rule in Egypt till 1171, when Saladin put an end to them.

might be prepared to put his own magnificent navy at his disposal for a joint expedition, and he accordingly dispatched an embassy to the court at Mahdiya to discuss the idea. These initial overtures were distinctly encouraging, and it was agreed that the discussions should be continued with Symeon in person; but when the ambassadors sailed for home accompanied by an Arab delegation, they were intercepted on the high seas by a Byzantine squadron of Calabrian Greeks and escorted under heavy guard to Constantinople. There the Bulgars were interned; but Romanus, subtle diplomat that he was, loaded the Arabs with presents and sent them back to their Caliph with a promise of peace and an annual tribute far more certain than anything that could have been hoped for from Symeon.

We do not know when, or how, the news of this misfortune reached the Bulgar court. It may well be that when in the high summer of 924 Symeon led his army – for at least the tenth time – into Thrace he expected to find the Fatimid navy already mobilized in the Marmara. If so, he was disappointed. At any rate, he changed his tactics. According to well-established precedent, he could now have been expected to launch another campaign of devastation in the surrounding country; but he did not do so. Instead, he sent to the city with a request for a meeting with his old friend the Patriarch.

Once again the aged Nicholas – he was now seventy-two and beginning to fail – made his laborious way through the city to the walls, where one of the gates was cautiously unbarred to allow him to slip out to the Bulgar camp. This time, however, he did not do so by stealth, but in the company of a number of distinguished court officials; nor did he find the Bulgar King in as amenable a mood as he had eleven years before. Symeon had by now decided that he would no longer negotiate with inferiors. If the Patriarch was prepared to come hurrying out at his bidding, why should not the Emperor do likewise? Curtly, he informed Nicholas that since summoning him he had changed his mind. If the Empire wanted peace, he would discuss it only with Romanus himself.

The Emperor had no objection. He always preferred talking to fighting, and he was determined to put a stop to these constant Bulgar incursions. There remained, however, the question of security. He did not trust Symeon any more than Symeon trusted him, and neither had forgotten what had happened at the meeting between Khan Krum and Leo V a century before. And so a great pier was constructed at

Cosmidium at the northern end of the Golden Horn,[1] projecting into the water with a fence extending transversely across the middle. It was agreed that Symeon would approach from the landward side, while Romanus sailed up the Horn on his imperial barge; the barrier would remain between them throughout their conversation.

The meeting took place on Thursday, 9 September.[2] Symeon rode up with much swagger and in considerable state, with a numerous escort which he ostentatiously ordered to make a thorough examination of the security arrangements before he approached the fence. Romanus, who was accompanied by the Patriarch, appeared by contrast thoughtful and subdued; with him he carried the city's holiest relic, the mantle of the Blessed Virgin, which he had borrowed from her church at Blachernae as a token of the importance he attached to the occasion. And so, after another brief delay during which hostages were exchanged, the two monarchs finally found themselves face to face.

Our sources for the discussion that followed are all Greek, and inevitably biased; there seems little doubt, however, that it was dominated by Romanus who, in typical Byzantine fashion, treated his adversary to a sermon: instead of begging for peace as Symeon had expected, he appealed to his better nature as a Christian and pressed him earnestly to mend his ways while there was still time. True, he also suggested increasing his own annual tribute; but the proposal was so deftly incorporated into the homily that many of his hearers may well have missed it altogether. Even to those who noticed, it must have sounded less like a concession than a price that was being willingly offered by a benevolent patron for the salvation of a sinner's soul.

It was, by all accounts, a masterly performance; and it succeeded better than either Emperor or Patriarch could have hoped. Romanus spoke, as everyone knew, from a position of weakness: it was he, not the Bulgar, who was suing for peace. As the son, moreover, of an Armenian peasant, his origins were considerably humbler than those of Symeon, who could boast a proud ancestry of Khans going back at least four generations to the great Krum, and possibly a good deal further. But, when he spoke, he did so with the majesty and authority of the

---

1 The modern Eyüp. The Byzantine village took its name from the great monastery of SS. Cosmas and Damian – of which, alas, not a brick now remains.

2 There has been a good deal of argument about the date, and even the year. I follow Sir Steven Runciman (*The Emperor Romanus Lecapenus*, pp. 246–8), who devotes a complete appendix to the question and makes what seems to me an unanswerable case.

thousand-year-old Roman Empire, compared with which Bulgaria was still nothing more than a parvenu principality of semi-civilized barbarians. And Symeon knew it.

At that moment two eagles were seen in the sky above, first wheeling together and then suddenly separating, one to continue its sweeping circles over the towers of Constantinople while the other headed off westward towards Thrace. None of those who saw it could doubt that it was a sign; and its meaning was unmistakable. Strive as he might, Symeon would never be lord of Byzantium: there were to be two rulers in the Balkan peninsula, not one.

After that, there was little more to be said. Details of the subsidy that Romanus himself had proposed were soon settled. It was to include an annual gift of 100 *scaramangia* – those richly embroidered silken robes that counted among the greatest luxuries that even Constantinople had to offer – in return for which Symeon agreed to withdraw from imperial territory and from the fortresses that he had captured on the Black Sea coast. Then he turned in silence from the fence, remounted his horse and rode back to his homeland. He never invaded the Empire again.

This is not to say that he became a reformed character. He was now over sixty, and had occupied the throne for more than thirty years: the old leopard could not be expected altogether to change his spots. No longer, however, did he dream of reigning in Constantinople; and his almost pathetic assumption in 925 of the title of *basileus* – adding the words 'of the Romans and the Bulgars' for good measure – was, in its way, an admission of defeat: the action not of a statesman but of a spoilt, petulant child. As Romanus very sensibly remarked, Symeon could call himself the Caliph of Baghdad if he wanted to. In the following year, showing the same spirit of impotent defiance, Symeon at last declared the independence of the Bulgarian Church, elevating its archbishop to the rank of Patriarch. Nicholas would have been horrified to see his old nightmare come true at last; but Nicholas had died in May 925, and nobody else seemed to care very much. From Constantinople there came not a single word of protest – a fact which, we may imagine, caused Symeon no little irritation in itself.

But he was trying not to think about Constantinople. Instead, he had turned his attention towards his enemies in the West: to the Serbs and, beyond them, to the maritime, militarist Kingdom of Croatia. The former he easily crushed; but the latter fought back and in 926 destroyed the Bulgar army almost to a man. Symeon never recovered. Obliged to accept a humiliating peace, he stumbled on into the spring of the following year; but the spirit had gone out of him and on 27 May 927, disillusioned and disappointed, he died at sixty-nine.[1]

Symeon left behind him clear orders as to the succession: the Bulgarian crown should go to the eldest of the three sons of his second marriage, a boy named Peter,[2] during whose minority his maternal uncle, one George Sursubul, was to act as Regent. Regencies, however, are dangerous things – particularly when they follow a ruler as strong as Symeon – and George soon realized that if he were to survive he must consolidate the recent understanding with Byzantium by means of a more formal treaty of peace, cemented if possible by a marriage alliance. He sent ambassadors to Romanus, who responded with alacrity; and at a conference held soon afterwards in the frontier city of Mesembria agreement was quickly reached. The Emperor and his suite then returned to Constantinople, whither the Bulgarian delegation followed them and where George was presented to – and enchanted by – the young Maria Lecapena, daughter of Romanus's eldest son Christopher. When his tentative inquiries met with encouraging replies he immediately sent for his nephew to join him.

The imperial wedding – the first time in over five hundred years that a Byzantine princess had married outside the Empire – was held in the Palace at Pegae on 8 October, only four and a half months after Symeon's death. The pair were duly blessed by Patriarch Stephen II – who had succeeded Nicholas in 925, the Emperor's son Theophylact being considered, at the age of eight, still a little too young for office – and the bride, now rechristened Irene in honour of the peace, returned briefly to Constantinople (for reasons probably gynaecological) while Peter waited at Pegae. Only three days later did she rejoin him for the sumptuous wedding feast. Then, tearfully – because she, like her husband, was still little more than a child, had never before left home and can have had no idea of the life that awaited her in the barbarian

---

1 The Byzantines always believed that it was they rather than the Croats who were responsible for his death. According to the Continuator, Romanus was informed by an astrologer that one of the statues in the Forum was Symeon's *stoicheion*. (See p. 122n.) He at once had it decapitated, and Symeon expired on the instant.

2 Symeon's son by his first marriage, Michael, was packed off to a monastery for reasons unexplained. Of Peter's two full brothers the younger, Benjamin, was to become one of the earliest – and certainly the most aristocratic – of that long and notorious line of Balkan werewolves, 'so adept in the art of magic that he could suddenly transform himself before men's eyes into a wolf or any other beast you pleased'. (Liudprand of Cremona, *Anapodosis*, iii, 29.)

land to which she was going – she kissed her family goodbye and set off with a vast baggage train on the long road to the north-west.

So dazzled are the chroniclers by the splendour of the wedding celebrations that they tell us next to nothing about the peace treaty that was signed at the same time. There seem to have been one or two minor territorial adjustments, together with provisions for the payment to Peter of an annual tribute – which may have been merely a confirmation of what had already been agreed upon by Symeon and Romanus on the Golden Horn but which now apparently carried an additional proviso that it should be payable only during Maria-Irene's lifetime, in which case it may have been nothing more than a subsidy to ensure that she would be able to maintain a degree of state appropriate to a Byzantine princess.[1] Finally – and here the contemporary sources leave no room for doubt – Romanus agreed formally to recognize the independence of the Bulgarian Patriarchate and Peter's imperial title of Tsar – or, in Greek, *basileus*. The first of these obligations did not worry him unduly: the independence of the Patriarchate was after all a *fait accompli* and, though mildly galling to Constantinople, effectively deprived the Bulgars of one of their favourite blackmailing threats, that of secession to Rome. The second must have been a little harder to stomach; in practice, however, it was simply ignored. Not until Constantine Porphyrogenitus assumed effective power in 945 was Peter to be addressed as anything more elevated than *archon* – 'ruler' – in missives from the Bosphorus.

For Romanus was above all a realist. The peace treaty to which he had set his seal left no question in anyone's mind that, although there had been no outright victor of the Bulgarian War, the Bulgars had had the better of it. Arguably, with patient and persistent diplomacy, he might have achieved more favourable terms, but the game was scarcely worth the candle: in the interests of a quick and uncontentious agreement, with a marriage alliance as a further guarantee of lasting Bulgar friendship, he was quite prepared to accept a few minor humiliations. In the first four years of his reign, with two open revolts to contend with (one in Apulia, the other in the Chaldian Theme in the far north-east) and new conspiracies being uncovered every few months, he could never have afforded such a luxury; but now he had consolidated his position. All those government and court officials who had opposed him had been sent

1 Such at least is the hypothesis of Sir Steven Runciman (*The Emperor Romanus Lecapenus*, p. 99), who suggests – perhaps a trifle unkindly – that the money would really have been used 'to pay for the titled ambassadress or spy that the Emperor kept at the Bulgarian court'.

off into exile or confined in monasteries; every key post was now in the hands of one of his own supporters. The navy was behind him to a man, together with the immense majority of the army. The Church, under a new and subservient Patriarch, gave no further trouble. Romanus himself was not only the crowned and anointed Emperor but head of a numerous imperial family, whose only possible rival was completely under his control and, incidentally, his son-in-law. At last he was secure.

Moreover, within a year or two of Symeon's death it became clear that Bulgaria was a spent force. She could never have become truly great until she had conquered Byzantium, and Byzantium had once again proved unconquerable. Symeon had had no choice but to turn back, time and time again, from those tremendous walls, and to exhaust himself instead against the tribes of the Balkans and the steppes; and this was a war that could never be won. Young Peter, in any case – quite apart from being the son-in-law of the Byzantine Emperor – possessed none of his father's natural aggression. Though infinitely superior in his moral life – many of his subjects looked upon him as a saint – he was to prove a weak and feckless ruler, who in a reign of forty-two years never learned to control his boyars, still less to hold his kingdom together. Thus, for half a century, Bulgaria was to give the Empire no further cause for concern; and when at last a new ruler, representing a new dynasty, was once again to challenge the authority of Constantinople, he was to find himself faced with an adversary worthy of his steel.

The Bulgarian peace finally allowed Romanus Lecapenus to concentrate his energies in the East – a region infinitely more vital to the health and security of Byzantium than the Balkans could ever be. Here were the richest and most fertile fields and farms, here the seemingly bottomless human reservoir that had for centuries provided the Empire with the steadiest and the sturdiest of its fighting men. Here – most important of all – was the front line of Christendom, on whose integrity and inviolability all Europe depended.

Some time around 900, Leo VI had managed to annex the lands of a minor Armenian princeling, Manuel of Teces, which – with the addition of one or two neighbouring cities – he had incorporated into a new Theme which he called Mesopotamia.[1] With this not very

---

1 Not quite the area, however, to which the name – 'between the rivers' – is normally applied today. The two rivers here referred to are not the Euphrates and the Tigris but the two main branches of the Euphrates.

important exception, the Empire's eastern frontier had remained, at the time of his death, substantially as it had been for the past two centuries. Raiding, on the part of both sides, had long been an institution; seldom did a summer pass without the launching of at least one naval or military expedition from one side against the territory of the other. But these expeditions, though often involving forces of considerable size, were prompted more by the desire for plunder and pillage than for territorial expansion, and for the most part had little long-term effect.

Then, in 923, there was appointed as commander-in-chief of the army one of the most brilliant generals that Byzantium was ever to produce. John Curcuas – sometimes known by his baptismal name of Gourgen – was, like the Emperor himself, an Armenian from the extreme north: the region we now know as Georgia. The two were, so far as we can gather, old friends; it was Curcuas who had been primarily responsible for the rounding-up of all potentially subversive elements in the capital at the time of Romanus's assumption of power, and for the next quarter-century no man in the Empire was to give his master more loyal or devoted service. In the first year of his command, the one outstanding victory was in fact naval rather than military: the final defeat of the renegade pirate Leo of Tripoli, the destroyer of Thessalonica nineteen years previously; and in 924, the better to deal with Symeon, Romanus concluded a two-year peace with the Caliph. But from 926, with the Bulgar threat behind him, he was ready to take on the Arabs; and over the next eighteen years the whole complexion of the age-long and hitherto indecisive struggle in the East was to be changed. Since the earliest days of Saracen conquest, the initiative had remained firmly with the forces of Islam. After their first onslaught they had made no further major advance; but though the Byzantines had scored several notable victories under Michael III in the previous century there had never been a question of a large-scale invasion of traditionally Saracen territory. The first six years of Curcuas's campaigns were aimed at the further consolidation of imperial authority in Armenia, and ended in 932 with the capture of Manzikert: a city later to acquire terrible significance in Byzantine history, but which at this time – together with Percri, Khelat (the modern Ahlat) and other towns on or around the northern shore of Lake Van – simply enabled him to control the roads into central Armenia and the more southerly district of Vaspurakan. Only two years later, on 19 May 934, there came an even greater triumph: the capture of

Melitene, the first important Arab Emirate to be incorporated into the Empire.

The years immediately following were less eventful, largely owing to a counter-offensive on the part of the powerful Hamdanid Emir of Mosul, Saïf ed-Daula, 'Sword of the Empire'. By 940 Saïf was causing Curcuas serious anxiety; and matters might have taken a dramatically different turn had not a new crisis in Baghdad – where the Abbasid Caliphate was by now fast disintegrating – recalled him in haste to the capital. For the Byzantines, their good fortune proved even greater than they knew: had the Emir kept up the pressure, they would have been hard put to it indeed to meet the utterly unexpected thunderbolt that descended on them, out of an apparently clear blue sky, during the following summer.

In the year 941 there may have been old men and women still alive in Constantinople who remembered their parents' stories of the terrible – though fortunately short-lived – Russian raid on the city eighty-one years before.[1] In those days the Russians had been a primitive and fairly heterogeneous collection of mainly Slav tribes, held together by a feudal, probably Scandinavian, aristocracy; in the intervening period, however, they had come – both literally and figuratively – a long way. In 882 or thereabouts the Viking Oleg had headed south from Novgorod and sailed down the Dnieper to Kiev, which he had captured and made the capital of a new Russian state; since then trade had steadily expanded and, where Byzantium was concerned, had been regulated by a commercial treaty signed with Leo VI in 911, according to which preferential treatment was to be accorded – though with certain safeguards – to all Russian merchants in Constantinople. The Slavonic chronicler known – wrongly, as it happens – by the name of Nestor maintains that this treaty had been intended to settle matters after Oleg had launched an immense land and sea expedition, with 2,000 ships and an unspecified number of men, against the city four years previously, in 907; it even relates how, at one stage during the fighting, he had carried his ships on rollers over the hill of Pera and down into the Golden Horn, just as Mehmet II was to do in 1453. This raid is not mentioned by any other source and is almost certainly apocryphal; Oleg had anyway died in the following year and had been succeeded by Igor, son of Rurik, as Grand Prince of Kiev.

1 See pp. 66–8.

But the armada that Igor dispatched at the beginning of June 941 was all too real.

This time the Greek chroniclers put the number of vessels in the Russian fleet at ten or, in one case, fifteen thousand; Liudprand of Cremona, on the other hand (whose stepfather, then the Italian ambassador at Constantinople, was able to give him a first-hand account of what had occurred) speaks, rather more moderately, of *mille et eo amplius* – 'a thousand and more' – and is almost certainly a good deal nearer the mark. Nevertheless, when Romanus first heard from his Bulgar friends of the Russian approach, his heart sank within him: his army was away on the eastern frontier, his navy divided between the Mediterranean and the Black Sea. Urgent messages were sent to both, with orders to return at once; meanwhile, the shipwrights worked round the clock trying to put into some kind of shape the only craft that could be mobilized in the capital: a pathetic collection of fifteen ancient hulks, long destined for the scrapyard but fortunately not yet dismantled. These were loaded to the gunwales with Greek fire and dispatched, under the *protovestiarius* Theophanes, to block the Bosphorus at its northern end. Theophanes arrived only just in time: on the morning of 11 June the Russian fleet appeared on the horizon. He attacked at once.

It is impossible to exaggerate the importance of Greek fire in Byzantine history. Time and time again, in naval engagements without number, it had wrenched victory from almost certain defeat. To Saracen fleets it was all too familiar – though they had never found an effective weapon against it. To the Russians, on the other hand, it came as a total surprise. As the first of their ships were engulfed in flames, the remainder turned abruptly away from the mouth of the Bosphorus and headed east along the Black Sea coast of Bithynia; there they landed in strength, venting on the maritime towns and villages all their pent-up anger and frustration at being blocked from the capital and perpetrating unspeakable horrors on the local populations – especially, we are told, on the clergy, some of whom were used for target practice while others, still less fortunate, had iron skewers driven through their skulls.

For many weeks the terror continued; but the military governor of the Armeniakon Theme, Bardas Phocas, hurried to the scene with his local levies and kept the marauders occupied as best he could pending the arrival of the main army under Curcuas. The fleet too was on its way, and as each new squadron arrived it went, just as Theophanes had done, straight into the attack. Before many days had passed it was the Russians who were on the defensive: they had failed in their primary purpose, autumn was approaching and they were increasingly anxious to sail for home. But it was too late. The Byzantine fleet was drawn up in strength between them and the open sea, and slowly closing in. Early in September they made a desperate attempt to slip through the blockade to the north-west, towards Thrace; again, Theophanes was too quick for them. Suddenly the whole sea was aflame with what Nestor's chronicle describes as 'winged fire'; the Russian ships went up like matchwood. The crews leaped overboard in their hundreds, but there was little hope for them: the lucky ones were dragged to the bottom by the weight of their armour, while the rest met their deaths in the oil-covered water, which blazed as fiercely as the vessels from which they had flung themselves. Few – very few – escaped the inferno and returned to break the news of the catastrophe to their master. In Constantinople, however, there was wild rejoicing: Theophanes was given a hero's welcome and promoted on the spot to the rank of *parakoimomenos*. Where the Russian prisoners were concerned, Romanus seems for once to have shown no mercy – not surprisingly, perhaps, in view of the outrages for which they had been responsible. If Liudprand is to be believed, they were all executed in the presence of his stepfather – though why a peaceable ambassador should have been called upon to witness so unpleasant a proceeding is nowhere explained.[1]

This was not quite the end of Romanus's difficulties with the Russians. Only three years later Igor tried again – this time with an amphibious operation, for which he had mobilized members of virtually every tribe in his dominions, to say nothing of a large force of Pecheneg mercenaries. As before, the Emperor was given advance warning: the Bulgars reported the approach of the land army, while the people of Cherson in the Crimea sent him a blood-curdling description of a fleet so huge that the vessels covered the whole surface of the sea. Romanus, however, had no intention of fighting if he could avoid it. His recent victory, complete as it was, had been won only after much bloodshed and devastation; besides, his army was once again away in Mesopotamia, even further from the capital than on the last occasion. He was by no means certain that it could be recalled in time, and was in any case reluctant to withdraw it from a campaign that was proving outstandingly successful. Instead, he decided to send ambassadors to Igor, who was leading the

---

1 Although Liudprand is probably right about the size of the Russian armament, he is not, it must be said, invariably to be relied upon.

land force, to negotiate a settlement. They met the Grand Prince on the Danube and, quite simply, bought him off; while a further *douceur* satisfied the Pechenegs, who were only too pleased to lay waste Bulgaria instead.

The following spring, a delegation arrived from Kiev to conclude a new political and commercial treaty. Drawn up in the names of Igor on the one side and those of Romanus and all his co-Emperors on the other – and transcribed verbatim in Nestor's chronicle – it laid down a detailed set of conditions regulating trade between the two states, the duties and responsibilities to be accepted and the privileges to be enjoyed by the merchants of each in the territories of the other. Article II, for example, stated that Russians wishing to enter Constantinople might do so only in unarmed groups of up to fifty at a time, accompanied by an imperial representative; any merchandise purchased for more than 50 *zolotniki* would be delivered in bond and excise duty levied.[1] Other articles related to the treatment of escaped slaves, extradition arrangements, punishments for crimes committed by Russians in the Empire or Byzantines in Russia and, in the event of threats from any third power, the duty of each of the signatories to send immediate and unlimited assistance to the other. After the Emperor had affixed his seal the Russians returned to Kiev, together with imperial representatives empowered to sign the ratification documents once the Grand Prince had similarly given his approval. Both sides were well pleased with what they had achieved, and so they might be: relations between Russia and Byzantium were to remain unruffled for a quarter of a century.

Immediately after the destruction of the Russian fleet in 941, John Curcuas had led his army back to the East. To his relief, he had found all his old positions intact: his chief enemy Saïf ed-Daula was still detained with the crumbling Caliphate in Baghdad, and everything seemed set fair for a continuation of the interrupted offensive. Early in 942 therefore, he swept down into the province of Aleppo where, although he failed to capture the city, he took prisoners in a quantity estimated by the Arabs' own sources at ten or fifteen thousand. By the high summer he was back in imperial territory, resting his troops, rearming and revictualling; and then, as autumn drew on – for the

---

1 The approximate value of a *zolotnik* may be judged from Article V, which prescribed the ransoms payable for Russian prisoners. An able-bodied young man or a pretty girl could be redeemed for 10 *zolotniki*; a person of middle age for 8; old people and children for 5.

Syrian climate, unlike the Armenian, allows campaigning throughout the year – he was off again, in a huge clockwise loop that led him past Lake Van and then westward to the great fortress city of Amida on the banks of the Tigris.[1] From here he swung south-east again to Nisibin, and thence west to Edessa.

Edessa, though it had fallen to Islam as early as 641 in the first wave of Muslim conquest, could boast a long and venerable history as a Christian city. In the fifth century it had been a refuge for the Nestorians expelled from the Empire after the Council of Ephesus,[2] and it was later to perform a similar service for persecuted monophysites. To the average Eastern Christian of the tenth century, however, Edessa was above all famous for its two priceless possessions: the letter which the ailing King Abgar I had received from Jesus Christ in reply to an invitation to come to Edessa and cure him, and the Saviour's own portrait, miraculously imprinted on a cloth.[3] Both these objects were known to be spurious – the portrait is nowhere heard of before the fifth century, while the letter had actually been declared a fake by Pope Gelasius in 494 – but their legends had refused to die; and by the tenth century there seem to have been no less than three rival portraits in the city, held respectively by the Jacobites, the Nestorians and the Melkites, each of them claiming their own to be authentic.[4]

So far as John Curcuas was concerned, however, there was only one; and he was determined to have it. He therefore sent word to the inhabitants offering peace and the return of all his prisoners in return for the famous image. This put the Edessans in a quandary. The vast majority of them were devout Muslims; but in the eyes of Islam Jesus was one of those 'close to God', and his portrait in consequence a sacred trust. So important a decision, they replied, must be referred to the Caliph in person; would the general therefore be so good as to stay his hand until they received instructions? Curcuas agreed; there was, after

---

1 Now known as Diyarbakir, the city has retained nearly all its tremendous medieval walls, more than four miles in circumference. The immense Islamic reliefs above the Harput Gate on the northern side almost certainly date from 910 – and had thus, by the time of which we are speaking, already been in place nearly forty years.

2 See *Byzantium: The Early Centuries*, p. 148n.

3 This tradition appears to have been the origin of the Veronica legend, which does not properly surface again until the fourteenth century – and then in France, whither it was probably brought back by the Crusaders. Compare also the Turin Shroud.

4 The fullest account of the letter and the portrait – together with much else about one of the most fascinating of ancient cities – is given by J. B. Segal (*Edessa, 'The Blessed City'*, Oxford 1970).

all, plenty of other work for him to do. He spent the better part of the next year laying waste large areas of Mesopotamia and capturing several cities, including Dara and Ras al-Ain (where he took another thousand prisoners); then he returned to Edessa to wait.

In the spring of 944 the Edessans received their answer. Since there was clearly no other way of saving the city – and, doubtless, many of their own lives – they had their Caliph's authority to surrender the image. With much ceremony it was carried from the town and reverently placed in the hands of Curcuas, who immediately forwarded it, under heavy escort, to Constantinople. Early in August it arrived on the Asiatic shore of the Bosphorus, where it was met by the *parakoimomenos* Theophanes and taken personally by him to the Emperor at Blachernae; only a few days later, on the Feast of the Dormition of the Virgin,[1] did it make its solemn entry into the capital by the Golden Gate. Here it was formally received by the three young co-Emperors still surviving – Christopher having died in 931 and Romanus being too ill to attend – together with the Patriarch; after which it was borne in triumph through the streets to St Sophia. Two embarrassing moments are, however, reported. The first was when Romanus's two sons failed absolutely to distinguish the lineaments of the Saviour on the cloth, though these were perfectly clear to the Porphyrogenitus; the second when a so-called madman amid the cheering crowd suddenly shouted: 'Constantinople, accept the glory and the blessing; and you, Constantine, accept your throne!'

There was, in point of fact, nothing remotely mad about this exhortation, of which the large majority of those who heard it must warmly have approved; for it was by now clear that the days of the house of Lecapenus were numbered. Romanus was no longer the man he had once been. By now well into his seventies, he was going the way that so many of his predecessors had gone before him, spending more of his time with monks than with ministers, gradually losing his grip on affairs of state as he sank deeper and deeper into morbid religiosity. Death, he felt, was approaching, and his conscience was troubled. True, he had been a hard-working Emperor and on the whole a successful one; but the fact remained that he had had no right to the throne, which he had acquired by perjury and deceit, depriving the legitimate Emperor of all but nominal power for a quarter of a century and promoting his own worthless sons to imperial rank.

---

1 The Dormition, or Falling Asleep, of the Virgin is the equivalent in the Eastern Church of the Assumption, and is celebrated on the same day, 15 August.

For worthless they were – or at least two of them. The eldest, Christopher, had showed some degree of promise and might have proved worthy of his father had he lived to succeed him; but the two younger brothers, Stephen and Constantine,[1] were notorious for their immorality and corruption – characteristics which they combined with a disastrous appetite for intrigue. Already in 943 they had moved against John Curcuas – of whose power and popularity they had become quite unreasonably jealous – successfully dissuading their father from marrying his eldest surviving grandson Romanus (the son of Constantine Porphyrogenitus and Helena) to Curcuas's daughter Euphrosyne, as he had very much hoped to do. Towards the end of the following year they carried their campaign a step further still, obliging Romanus to recall the most successful general of the century in the middle of a triumphant expedition and to replace him with one of their own relatives, Pantherius – who contrived, within a few months, to get his whole army smashed to pieces.

The readiness with which the old Emperor submitted to his sons' demands is a clear enough indication of his own decline. Superstitious as sailors are and uneducated to boot, he had succeeded by virtue of an immense capacity for hard work, unwavering self-confidence and any amount of good sound common sense. Now, it seemed, all three had deserted him. Terrified of death, he had but a single preoccupation: the salvation of his soul. Encouraged by a host of spiritual counsellors, he resorted to ever more desperate measures to achieve this end. On one occasion he remitted all government rents in Constantinople and cancelled all debts, at appalling cost to the imperial exchequer; on another he decreed the expulsion of every Jew and Armenian who would not immediately embrace the Orthodox faith. Almost his only sensible action of these last sad years was to make a new will, in which he expressly confirmed the seniority of Constantine Porphyrogenitus over his own sons, thus in effect eliminating them from power after his death.

Sensible, that is, insofar as the actual provisions of the will were concerned. In his decision to publicize those provisions, Romanus made one of the great mistakes of his life: for he left his sons in no doubt that, unless they acted quickly and decisively, they were lost. In

---

1 Gibbon calls him Constantine VIII, but most subsequent historians have deemed him unworthy to rank as an Emperor in his own right and have kept this title for the brother and co-Emperor of Basil II – who was, as we shall see, very little better.

view of their past record, if Constantine became senior Emperor, what was there for them to hope for? Banishment? Castration? Enforced seclusion in a monastery? Even worse fates were not impossible. There was but one alternative: a *coup d'état*. And so, five days before Christmas in the year 944, during the midday period when the government offices were closed, the two young Lecapeni and their supporters slipped into the Great Palace and made their way quickly to the chamber where the old Emperor lay on his sick-bed. He offered no resistance when they carried him down to the little harbour of Bucoleon, where a small boat was waiting; and a few minutes later, without any alarm having been raised, Romanus was on his way to Proti – now Kınalı – the nearest of the Princes' Islands. There he was tonsured and obliged to take monastic vows – which, one suspects, he was only too happy to do.

By the time his sons returned to the mainland, all Constantinople was agog. Nobody minded much about Romanus; he had not been treated unkindly, and though he was not unpopular the means by which he had seized the throne had never been forgotten. The name now on everyone's lips was that of Constantine Porphyrogenitus. Where was he? Before long, angry and suspicious crowds had gathered at the gates of the Palace. Only after Constantine had showed himself at a window, safe and sound if somewhat dishevelled,[1] did they agree to disperse.

Here was something that the conspirators had never suspected, any more, probably, than he had himself: Constantine was loved by his people. He had never set out to win their affection; on the contrary, he had deliberately kept as far in the background as possible, appearing in public only when absolutely obliged by state protocol to do so. But that was not the point. He possessed another virtue, infinitely more important than any other: legitimacy. Son of Leo the Wise, grandson of the great Basil himself, born in the purple, he and he alone was the rightful Emperor of Byzantium. As for the Lecapeni, they were nothing but upstart usurpers. Their so-called subjects had had enough of them.

The brothers now saw that they had fatally miscalculated. They had intended to deal with Constantine in due course, in just the same way as they had dealt with their father; but in the face of public opinion so forcibly expressed, this was no longer a possibility. They therefore took the only course open to them: reluctantly, and with ill grace, they

---

1 *Crines solutus*, writes Liudprand, 'with his hair unloosed'. Why, one wonders: had there been some sort of a struggle?

formally recognized Constantine as senior Emperor. It was, as may be imagined, an uneasy partnership, with the Porphyrogenitus on the one side and the Lecapeni on the other appointing their own men to as many as possible of the key positions. Left to himself, the gentle, retiring Constantine would probably have allowed the situation to drag on – although, had he done so, it is unlikely that he would have lasted very long. But Helena his wife was made of sterner stuff. For twenty-five years she had loyally defended her husband's interests against her own family, and now she urged him with all her strength to take action while there was still time. For a little while longer he wavered, but soon he received a warning that could not be ignored: his brothers-in-law were planning to kill him. He hesitated no more. Spurred on as always by Helena, he gave his orders. On 27 January 945 his two co-Emperors were arrested, tonsured in their turn and sent off to Proti to join their father. According to the Greek chroniclers, the old man greeted his sons with a well-chosen quotation from Isaiah: *'I have nourished and brought up children, and they have rebelled against me.'*[1] Liudprand, however – whose stepfather Bishop Sigefred was still in Constantinople as the ambassador from King Hugh of Italy and had, in company with other diplomatic representatives from Rome, Gaeta and Amalfi, strongly supported the cause of Constantine five weeks before – provides us with a rather more spirited version:

When their father Romanus heard of their arrival, he rendered thanks to God and with a glad face came to meet them outside the monastery door. 'O happy hour,' he cried, 'that has compelled Your Majesties to visit my humble estate. That filial affection which drove me from the palace, I suppose, has not allowed you yourselves to remain there any longer. How fortunate that you should have sent me here some time in advance: my brother-monks and fellow soldiers in Christ devote their days to things of the spirit, and would not have known how Emperors should be received had they not had me with them, an expert in imperial protocol. Here is boiled water for you, colder than the Gothic snows; here are soft beans, all manner of greenstuffs, and leeks freshly plucked. You will find none of those delicacies from the fishmongers that cause illness; such maladies as we have here are brought about by our frequent fasts. Our modest abode has no space for a large and extravagant company; but it is just large enough for Your Majesties, who have refused to desert your father in his old age.'[2]

---

1 Isaiah 1:2.
2 *Anapodosis*, v, 23.

If the old man persisted in this vein, his wretched sons must have been relieved indeed to learn that Proti was to be only a temporary place of exile, while their brother-in-law pondered their long-term future. Wisely, he resolved that they should be separated. Stephen was first sent to Proconnesus in the Marmara, then to Rhodes and finally to Lesbos; his brother, after a brief period on Tenedos, was transferred to Samothrace. Of the remaining Lecapeni, only the Empress Helena and the Patriarch Theophylact – and, away in Bulgaria, the Tsaritsa Maria-Irene – still occupied positions of power.[1]

As for the old Emperor, he lived on in his monastery, passing his days in prayer and penitence. His conscience still allowed him no rest: his fitful sleep was troubled by dreadful nightmares. In one of them he saw himself, accompanied by his son Constantine and the Bishop of Heraclea, being driven down into hell. At the last moment there appeared the Blessed Virgin, who extended her hand and drew him back; for the other two, however, there was no salvation, and a few days later he learned that they had both died on that very night – Constantine in the course of an attempt to escape from his captivity, during which he had first killed his gaoler and had then been himself cut down by the prison guards. So shattered was Romanus by this vision and its sinister fulfilment that he resolved on a public confession and penance. On Holy Thursday 946 there were assembled no less than 300 monks from all over the Empire – and even, we are told, from Rome itself – who chanted the *Kyrie Eleison* while the old man listed all his sins one by one, asking absolution for each. Finally, in front of the high altar, he was scourged and humiliated by a young novice before returning alone to his cell. The book of his sins was sent to Dermocaetes, a monk of renowned holiness who lived in the monastery on Mount Olympus in Bithynia, together with a gift of money and a request that the entire community there should fast for a fortnight and pray for his soul. They did so, after which Dermocaetes reported having heard a voice from heaven confirming that their prayer had been granted, and sent the book – its pages now miraculously blank – back to Romanus, who ordered that it should be buried with him.

Almost incredibly in the circumstances, a plot was even then being hatched, by his friend the *parakoimomenos* Theophanes and his son the

---

1 Although some years later Christopher's son Michael was to become *magister* and Rector, and Constantine Lecapenus's son Romanus rose – after castration – to the rank of Patrician.

Patriarch Theophylact,[1] to restore him to the throne. Stranger still, Romanus is said to have given it his support. But this was almost certainly due to weakness rather than strength, and in any case the conspiracy was revealed before any harm was done. The Patriarch was saved by virtue of his office; Theophanes, however, was sent into exile – a sad end to a career during which he served his Emperor loyally, but just a little too long. Romanus lived to see his old friend's disgrace; by this time, however, he was failing fast. He died on 15 June 948. His body was carried back to Constantinople and was buried in the monastery of the Myrelaeum, beside that of his wife.

He had been a good Emperor – perhaps even a great one. Having seized power by duplicity and deceit, he had thereafter wielded it with wisdom and moderation and, in the space of a quarter of a century, had given the Empire new direction. His immediate predecessors had had to cope with two principal problems: the Church, which had poisoned the last years of the unfortunate Leo VI; and Bulgaria, whose repeated victories had brought about the downfall of Zoe. Romanus – it seemed almost effortlessly – had solved them both, and both by the same technique: he had allowed his enemies their head, exhausted them and then made sure that they were not replaced. It had worked with Patriarch Nicholas, whom he had flattered and indulged until the insufferable old man died, after which he had replaced him with two short-lived nonentities and finally with his own son; and it had worked with the Bulgars, to whom he had been prepared to make a temporary sacrifice of Thrace in the sure knowledge that Constantinople was and would remain inviolate. Once Symeon was out of the way, he had showed himself ready to agree to any number of concessions – including that of his daughter – and so eliminated the problem altogether.

It was in the East that Romanus's quiet diplomacy proved useless. There armed force was the only argument understood, and there – since he had lost not a single fighting man to the Bulgars – he was able to throw the whole weight of his army and navy against his Saracen foes. Luck,

---

1 Theophylact, having been intended for the Patriarchate since his earliest years, had eventually achieved it in 931, at the age of fourteen. A harmless but essentially frivolous youth, he had given his father no trouble, devoting a good deal more time to his 2,000 horses than to his religious duties, which he would always unhesitatingly interrupt for the *accouchement* of one of his mares. As Sir Steven Runciman reminds us, 'he made one brave attempt to reconcile pleasure with piety by brightening up divine service on the lines of a pantomime; but it met with disapproval, though some of the turns lasted to shock the righteous more than a century later'. He was to enjoy the Patriarchate thoroughly for twenty-five years, dying in 956 as the result of a riding accident.

admittedly, was on his side – first in John Curcuas, in whom he found a general of quite exceptional merit, and secondly in the state of the Abbasid Caliphate, which was no longer capable of exercising any real authority; but it remains a fact that, for the first time since the rise of Islam, it was the Christian forces that were on the offensive.

At home, during a remarkably uneventful reign, Romanus displayed much the same qualities that he had shown in his dealings with the Bulgars. There can be no doubt of his unfeigned abhorrence of bloodshed, a rare virtue in those violent days: again and again, even in cases of conspiracy against his own person, we find him preferring sentences of exile to those of execution. He seems, too, to have been genuinely kind-hearted: in the dreadful winter of 928, the longest and coldest in Constantinople's history, it was he who personally directed the emergency food supply. And he was a devoted family man – rather too devoted, perhaps, where his sons were concerned.

Why, then, was he not better loved? Why, when his own sons rose against him, did none of his subjects utter a word of protest or lift a finger on his behalf? Was it simply that they disliked usurpers? Or was there also something in his character that failed to endear him? Here, perhaps, we can find at least a partial answer to the mystery; for Romanus's virtues and qualities were not such as ever to seize the popular imagination. He was not a great soldier, nor a great legislator: his ambitious attempts at land reform had little long-term effect, and were anyway of minimal interest to the people of Constantinople. He seems to have appeared rarely in public and never made much of a show at the Hippodrome. In short, although he did his utmost to see his subjects properly provided with bread, he was distinctly short on circuses. They consequently tended to ignore him and, when they thought of him at all, to remember the only deeply memorable thing in the life of this able, quiet and surprisingly colourless man: his path to the throne.

And he, as we know, remembered it too: remembered it so vividly, and with such consuming remorse, that his last few years were passed in unremitting mental torment. This, surely, was punishment enough; for if at the start he had laid predatory hands on the Empire, later he had served it well. And it is pleasant to reflect that he died at last with his spirit at peace, and his sins forgiven.

I I

The Scholar Emperor

[945–63]

He was devoid of that energy of character which could emerge into a life of action and glory; and the studies which had amused and dignified his leisure were incompatible with the serious duties of a sovereign. The emperor neglected the practice, to instruct his son Romanus in the theory, of government: while he indulged the habits of intemperance and sloth, he dropped the reins of the administration into the hands of Helena his wife; and, in the shifting scene of her favour and caprice, each minister was regretted in the promotion of a more worthless successor. Yet the birth and misfortunes of Constantine had endeared him to the Greeks; they excused his failings; they respected his learning, his innocence and charity, his love of justice; and the ceremony of his funeral was mourned with the unfeigned tears of his subjects.

Edward Gibbon
The Decline and Fall of the
Roman Empire, Chapter XLVIII

By the time Constantine Porphyrogenitus assumed sole power in the Byzantine State after the effective elimination of his brothers-in-law at the beginning of 945, he had long outgrown the sickliness of his youth. Tall and broad-shouldered, standing 'erect as a cypress tree',[1] his ruddy complexion half-hidden by a thick black beard above which shone eyes of a brilliant pale blue, he now looked as if he had never known a day's illness in his life. True, he was – by modern standards – distinctly overweight, the result of a largely sedentary life and an almost insatiable appetite; but a generous degree of *embonpoint* was considered no bad thing in the tenth century, when a man of thirty-nine was considered to be already well advanced in middle age.

For well over thirty-six of those thirty-nine years, Constantine had been a titular Emperor; and during practically the whole of that period,

1 Theophanes Continuatus, *Chronographia*, Book VI.

for reasons which the last two chapters should have made clear, he had played no part in the imperial government, confining his public appearances to the minimum required of him by his office. He had not, however, wasted his time. From his father Leo the Wise he had inherited a passion for books and scholarship which, unlike Leo, he had had plenty of time to indulge. He failed, it is true, to fulfil his great ambition, declared in the opening chapter of his life of Basil I,[1] of writing a complete history of Byzantium until his own day, nor even his more modest aspiration to give an account of the Macedonian house; none the less, the body of work which he left behind him is impressive by any standards. Few other writers – and certainly no other Emperors – have contributed so much to our knowledge of their time.

Apart from the biography of his grandfather, Constantine is known above all for two major works. The first, *De Ceremoniis Aulae Byzantinae*, is an encyclopedia of Byzantine ritual in which the Emperor sets out in detail the protocol to be followed on every feast of the Church and state occasions: coronations and birthdays, baptisms and funerals of Emperors and Augustae, promotions to the high offices of government and court, even games in the Hippodrome. Clothes and vestments to be worn, responses to be sung, acclamations required of the army and the people, the Blues and the Greens – nothing is omitted or ignored, nothing left to chance. To read even a few pages at random is to be almost suffocated by the sheer weight of the ceremonial described: how, one wonders, could any Emperor – whether he were active and energetic like Basil I or Romanus, or idle and pleasure-loving like Michael III or Alexander – have endured it for a moment? And yet, for all the oppression, here is a rare and precious glimpse of the court life of Byzantium: the mosaics and the marbles, the damasks and the brocades, the *basileus* in dalmatic and diadem, pavilioned in all the majesty of the New Rome.

But the Emperor was more than a great golden symbol: he was also the head of a vast administrative machine, the ruler of a state which still extended from the toe of Italy to the foothills of the Caucasus, an immense area which Constantine was well aware that his son Romanus would one day be called upon to govern. In 952, therefore – the year in which the young prince celebrated his fourteenth birthday – he set about the composition of what is, in essence, a practical textbook

1 Theophanes Continuatus, *Chronographia*, Book V, is believed to be entirely his work.

on the art of government which he quite simply entitled *Constantine to his son Romanus* but which we now know as *De Administrando Imperio*. The nucleus of this work seems to have been another, earlier, essay by the Emperor on the various barbarian races which occupied the lands surrounding the imperial frontiers; to this he now added a detailed assessment of the world situation as he saw it, together with a quantity of excellent advice for the boy's future guidance. It is significant that the Bulgars, to whom thirty years before he would almost certainly have devoted more attention than to any other people, are scarcely mentioned. Pride of place is now given to the Pechenegs, whose apparently limitless numbers and bestial cruelty made them by far the most feared of all the Empire's potential foes. Like his father-in-law, Constantine was instinctively opposed to war if it were not absolutely necessary; there is no suggestion in *De Administrando Imperio* that any military action should be taken against the tribe. On the contrary:

In my judgement it is always greatly to our advantage to keep the peace with the Pecheneg nation; to conclude conventions and treaties of friendship with them; to send to them every year an envoy with gifts of appropriate value and kind; and to welcome from their side sureties – that is, hostages – and a diplomatic representative who will confer, in this our God-protected city, with a competent minister and will enjoy all imperial attentions and honours which it is suitable for the Emperor to bestow.[1]

It is, he continues, an expensive business:

These Pechenegs are insatiable, fiercely covetous of those commodities that are rare among them, and shameless in their demands for generous presents . . . When the imperial envoy enters their country, their first reaction is to ask for the Emperor's gifts; and when the men have finally been satisfied they demand the same for their wives and their parents.[2]

They should, however, be given whatever they ask for, unhesitatingly and with a good grace; it will always be cheaper in the end.

With less powerful peoples, on the other hand, Constantine favours a distinctly tougher line. Foreign ambassadors should, as a general rule, be granted as little as possible. On no account should they be allowed to carry away state robes or vestments – items which seem to have been much coveted abroad, and for which the Byzantine government received innumerable requests – nor of course could there ever be any question

1 *De Administrando Imperio*, Chapter I.
2 Ibid., Chapter VII.

of revealing the secret of Greek fire. Romanus should also refuse all suggestions for marriage alliances, on the grounds that Constantine the Great himself had decreed that the imperial family should never marry outside the Empire except on occasion to the Franks.[1] At this point all his pent-up resentment of his father-in-law suddenly comes boiling up to the surface:

If they point out that the Lord Emperor Romanus himself made such an alliance when he gave the hand of his own granddaughter to the Bulgarian Tsar Peter, you should reply that the Lord Romanus was a vulgar illiterate who had been neither educated in the Palace nor initiated in the Roman traditions. His family was not imperial or even noble, and tended accordingly to be arrogant and headstrong. In this instance he heeded neither the prohibition of the Church nor the commandment of the great Constantine, but went his own arrogant and headstrong way . . . It was for this reason that he was in his lifetime much abused, and was hated and vilified by the Senate, the people and the Church itself, as was shown by the end to which he came; and that hatred and vilification continued after his death, even to the present day.[2]

All this – together with a historical and geographical description of the imperial provinces usually known as *De Thematibus* – was written, at least for the most part, by the Emperor's own hand, in the elegant and polished style of the scholar that he was. With the help of a regiment of scribes and copyists, however, he also compiled digests of all the available manuals and treatises on any number of other subjects: military strategy, history, diplomacy, jurisprudence, hagiography, medicine, agriculture, natural science, even veterinary surgery. The result was a veritable encyclopedia – a reference work which must have been of immense value to the imperial civil service and to all those private individuals fortunate enough to have access to it for many years to come, and which testifies both to the size and range of the Emperor's personal library and to the catholicity of his interests. He was, we are told, a passionate collector – not only of books and manuscripts but of works of art of every kind; more remarkable still for a man of his class

---

1 It is doubtful whether the Emperor would have inserted this proviso had he not been on fairly shaky ground himself. His half-sister Anna – Leo VI's daughter by his second wife Zoe – had married Lewis III (the Blind) of Provence, while his own son Romanus (to whom he was addressing these words) had at the age of five been married off to Bertha, the illegitimate daughter of Hugh of Arles, King of Italy, and was at the time the book was written betrothed to Hedwig of Bavaria, niece of Otto the Great.

2 *De Administrando Imperio*, Chapter XIII. The translation has been slightly abridged in the interests of concision, but accurately reflects the spirit of the original.

and background, he seems to have been a painter in his own right – and, if we are to believe Liudprand of Cremona, a very good one too. Finally, he was the most generous of patrons: to mosaicists and enamellers, to writers and scholars, to goldsmiths, silversmiths and jewellers.

Thus it is less as an Emperor than as a writer, scholar, compiler, collector, bibliophile, painter and patron that Constantine Porphyrogenitus deserves his place as the central figure of the tenth-century literary and artistic revival known as the 'Macedonian Renaissance'. But – the question can no longer be postponed – how effective was he as an Emperor? If we are to believe Gibbon, we shall have to rank him as a near-disaster; but Gibbon is obviously basing himself on two not entirely trustworthy sources, Cedrenus and Zonaras – both of whom derive from the same earlier authority, John Scylitzes – and seems to ignore the anonymous author of the second part of Theophanes Continuatus, Book VI, who paints a very different picture. Here Constantine emerges as a competent, conscientious and hard-working administrator and an excellent picker of men, who made appointments to military, naval, ecclesiastical, civil and academic posts that were both imaginative and successful. He also did much to develop the imperial system of higher education and took a special interest in the administration of justice, immediately investigating all reports of social abuses – particularly against the poor – and himself reviewing the sentences of long-term prisoners. That he ate and drank more than was good for him all our authorities seem to agree – though he was certainly not a drunkard in any sense of the word; and there is unanimity, too, on his constant good humour: he was unfailingly courteous to all classes of society and was never known to lose his temper.

Feeling as he did about his father-in-law, it is perhaps understandable that Constantine should have looked with instinctive favour on the family of Phocas. The Phocas had been arch-enemies of the Lecapeni ever since Romanus's original *coup*, and found his treatment of their relative Leo – whom, it will be remembered, he had held up to public ridicule, parading him round the Forum on a mule – impossible to forgive. From that time on they had made no secret of their sympathy for Constantine, and the Emperor was happy to repay their loyalty. As successor to John Curcuas in supreme command of the armies of the East he now named Leo's brother Bardas Phocas, giving his sons Nicephorus and Leo the military governorships of the Anatolikon and

Cappadocian Themes respectively. Of the Lecapeni, on the other hand, only one (apart from the Empress Helena herself) enjoyed his complete trust – though not, even then, until after he had been castrated. This was Romanus's natural son Basil, whom he appointed his *parakoimomenos* and who was later to lead a highly successful expedition against the dreaded Saïf ed-Daula.

Meanwhile both foreign and domestic policy continued unchanged. Where the Saracens were concerned, Constantine was determined to keep up the pressure. Bardas, it soon became clear, was no Curcuas; but after being seriously wounded in 953 he was succeeded by his son Nicephorus, who four years later gained one of the two greatest victories of the reign by capturing the city of Adata in Pamphylia and with it the control of one of the principal passes through the Taurus Mountains. The second triumph came in 958 when Samosata (now Samsat) on the Euphrates fell to the arms of another brilliant young general, John Tzimisces. It would have been pleasant to record a similar success against the Saracens of Crete; but an attempt in 949 to reconquer the island, in a campaign in which the Emperor hoped to involve both the German King, Otto the Saxon, and, rather more surprisingly, the Omayyad Caliph of Cordova, proved little short of a fiasco.

Some at least of the responsibility for this disaster must be taken by the expedition's leader, the eunuch Constantine Gongyles; but, as several previous attempts had shown, Crete was a notoriously tough nut to crack. Little of the blame attaches directly to the Porphyrogenitus and still less to King Otto, who had more important things on his mind. He was still building up the Kingdom he had inherited in 936, pushing out its frontiers ever further against the Slav tribes to the East and simultaneously extending his influence into neighbouring states, notably Bohemia and Burgundy. Constantine seems immediately to have sensed the ability – and thus the importance – of this dynamic young prince, since he opened up relations with him as soon as he assumed power; though he could not know that, less than three years after his own death, Otto would be crowned Western Emperor in Rome and would quickly raise his Empire to a level of strength and splendour that it had not enjoyed since the days of Charlemagne.

By then, of course, he would be master of Italy; but in the early years of Constantine's reign the Italian peninsula was still in the state of semi-chaos that had characterized it since the break-up of the Carolingian Empire in 888. Its crown was a prize open to anyone with the strength, ambition and lack of scruple to go after it; and since it had by now become the most obvious stepping-stone to that of the Western Empire itself, the struggle for it was not confined to the Italian feudal nobility but was frequently also joined by the kings and princes of neighbouring lands. To make matters worse, Lombardy and indeed much of north Italy was in the hands of the Magyars, while the coasts were subject to continual raids by the Saracens from Sicily, Africa and not least from their pirate stronghold at Le Frassinet in Provence.[1]

Worst of all was Rome, where the local aristocracy had established complete control over the Church and had made the Papacy their plaything: Nicholas I, who enters these pages at the time of the Photian schism, was virtually the last Pontiff of any ability or integrity to occupy the chair of St Peter for a century and a half.[2] His second successor, John VIII, had been hammered to death by jealous relations, while in 896 the dead body of Pope Formosus had been exhumed, brought to trial before a synod of bishops, stripped, mutilated and thrown into the Tiber.[3] As recently as 928, the infamous Marozia, Senatrix of Rome – mistress, mother and grandmother of Popes – had had her mother's lover, Pope John X, strangled in the Castel Sant'Angelo in order to instal – after three years during which a couple of nonentities kept the throne warm for him while he grew to manhood – her son by her own former paramour, Pope Sergius III. In 932 she had taken as her second husband Hugh of Arles (whom the unfortunate Pope John had crowned King of Italy and who had murdered his wife, defamed his mother and blinded his brother in order to marry her) and the two would unquestionably have become Emperor and Empress of the West had not her son by her first marriage – his name was Alberic – engineered a popular revolt against them. Hugh escaped; Marozia was thrown in her turn into a dungeon of the Castel Sant'Angelo, where she was to spend the rest of her life.

*

---

1 Now the little village of La Garde Freinet on the crest of the Chaîne de Maures in the Var. The Saracen enclave lasted for over a century, creating havoc for hundreds of miles around.

2 Unless we include the sadly apocryphal Pope Joan, the Englishwoman who is said to have concealed her sex throughout a three-year Pontificate until, by some unhappy miscalculation, she gave birth to a baby, half-way through a papal procession, on the steps of the Lateran. (A delightful engraving in which this event is depicted will be found in Spanheim, *Histoire de la Papesse Jeanne*, 2 vols., The Hague, 1720.)

3 It is only fair to add, however, that it was later miraculously recovered, rehabilitated and reinterred in its former tomb.

It was from this somewhat lurid background that there sprang one of the most valuable – and certainly the most colourful – of our sources of tenth-century history in both the Eastern and the Western Empires. Liudprand, Bishop of Cremona – whose name has already appeared several times in these pages – had been born in 920 into a well-to-do Lombard family. Both his father and his stepfather had travelled to Constantinople before him, as ambassadors from King Hugh; Liudprand himself had served as a singing pageboy at the royal court at Pavia, for he had a beautiful voice and the King was passionately fond of music. Hugh's other pastimes were, unfortunately, rather less innocent: Liudprand's characteristic combination of prudishness and prurience may well stem from an adolescence spent among the courtesans who came flocking to Pavia from all over Italy and beyond. However that may be, he decided to enter the Church and soon afterwards found himself private secretary and chancellor to Hugh's effective successor, Berengar of Ivrea; and it was on Berengar's behalf, on 1 August 949, that he himself set off down the Po on the first stage of a diplomatic mission to the Bosphorus.

Most irritatingly, Liudprand nowhere explains the reasons for this mission; but it seems more than likely, since an ambassador from Otto – a certain Liutefred of Mainz – was travelling to Constantinople at the same time, that Berengar was anxious to make his presence felt and to ensure that as ruler of Italy he would be party to any understanding reached between his rival and Constantine Porphyrogenitus. At all events the two envoys – who had travelled together on the same ship from Venice – arrived on 17 September and were soon afterwards received by the Emperor in audience.

Next to the imperial residence at Constantinople there is a palace of remarkable size and beauty which the Greeks call *Magnaura*, the name signifying 'fresh breeze' . . . Before the throne of the Emperor there rose a tree of gilded bronze, its branches full of birds fashioned of the same material, all singing different songs according to their kind. The throne itself was so contrived that at one moment it stood low on the ground and the next moment it would suddenly be raised high in the air. It was of immense size, made of either wood or bronze (for I cannot be sure), and guarded by gilded lions who beat the ground with their tails and emitted dreadful roars, their mouths open and their tongues quivering. Leaning on the shoulders of two eunuchs, I was led into the Emperor's presence. Immediately the lions began to roar and the birds to sing, but I myself displayed no terror or surprise at these marvels, having received prior warning from others who were already well acquainted with them. After I had three times made my obeisance I raised my head and lo! he whom I had seen only a moment before on a throne scarcely elevated from the ground was now clad in different robes and sitting on a level with the roof. How this was achieved I cannot tell, unless it was by a device similar to those we employ for lifting the timbers of a wine press. He did not address me on this occasion – in view of the distance between us any conversation would have been most unseemly – but inquired through his Logothete as to the life and health of Berengar. I made an appropriate reply, and then at a signal from the interpreter left the chamber and returned to my lodging.[1]

After this description, Liudprand goes on to tell of his embarrassment on discovering that whereas Otto's ambassador and those from Cordova had brought the Emperor magnificent presents, his own master had sent nothing but a letter – 'and that was full of lies'. Fortunately he had with him a number of gifts that he had intended to offer to Constantine on his own account; and these, most reluctantly, he now pretended had come from Berengar. They consisted of

nine excellent cuirasses, seven excellent shields with gilded bosses, two silver-gilt cups, some swords, spears and spits, and – more appreciated by the Emperor than anything else – four *carzimasia*, that being the Greek name for young eunuchs who have been deprived not only of their testicles but of their penises as well – an operation performed by merchants at Verdun, who export them to Spain at huge profit to themselves.

This last item raises more questions than can be discussed here, not least why these luckless youths should have been so sought after – particularly by Constantine, whose sexual tastes were, so far as we know, entirely normal and who already enjoyed a virtually limitless supply of slaves of every kind. Alas, Liudprand is once again silent – though he goes on to make it clear that the Emperor was not always as unapproachable as he had been at that first audience. Three days after the delivery of his presents he received an invitation to a banquet.

There is a palace near the Hippodrome looking northwards, of wondrous height and beauty, known as the *Decanneacubita*, since . . . on the day of the Nativity of our Lord Jesus Christ nineteen places are laid at the table. On this day the Emperor and his guests do not sit at dinner in the usual manner but

1 If the golden tree was the same as that installed by the Emperor Theophilus a century earlier (see p. 44), it says much for Byzantine standards of maintenance. The lifting gear, at all events, seems to have been a tenth-century innovation.

recline on couches; and all the dishes are served in vessels not of silver but of gold. After the meal fruit is brought on in three golden bowls, too heavy for men to lift ... Through openings in the ceiling there hang three ropes, covered with gilded leather, with golden rings at their ends. To these rings are attached the handles projecting from the bowls and, with the help of four or five men standing below, the huge vessels are swung on to the table and removed again in the same manner.

Whether Liudprand's own invitation was for this Christmas feast is not altogether clear, but the occasion was certainly memorable in other ways.

A man entered, balancing on his head, and without touching it with his hands, a wooden pole more than twenty-four feet long, with a three-foot cross-piece a foot and a half from the top. There then appeared two boys, naked except for loincloths, who climbed up the pole, performed various tricks on it and then descended head first, the pole remaining all the time as steady as if it had been rooted in the earth ... While they were both performing, the evenness of their weights gave the pole some equilibrium; but when one returned to the ground and the other, remaining on high, kept his balance so perfectly that he could both do his tricks and come down at last without mishap, I was so bewildered that the Emperor himself noticed my amazement. He therefore summoned an interpreter and asked me which seemed to me the more wonderful, the boy who had moved so carefully that the pole remained stable, or the man who had balanced it on his head so adroitly that neither the weight of the boys nor their performance had disturbed it in the least. I said that I did not know; he then gave a loud laugh and said that he was in the same difficulty: he did not know either.

Liudprand and Liutefred, the ambassadors from the Caliph of Cordova and their respective staffs were not the only foreign envoys to be received by Constantine Porphyrogenitus. In 946, a year after his coming to power, there had been a Saracen embassy from Saïf ed-Daula to discuss an exchange of prisoners; in 949, the same year as the other three, the Magyars sent a high-powered delegation which not only concluded a treaty of non-aggression but actually submitted itself to Christian baptism. Most important of all, however, in its long-term effect was the visit in 957 of Princess Olga of Russia, Igor's widow and now Regent of the young Kievan state, on a mission of peace and good will. After a series of magnificent receptions, the climax came with her own christening by the Patriarch in St Sophia – in the course of which she adopted the name of the Empress Helena, who stood proxy.[1] If the Byzantines had hoped that this ceremony would be immediately followed by the mass conversion of her people, they were disappointed. But the seed had been sown; and thirty years later, under Olga's grandson Vladimir, it would become clear that it had fallen on fertile ground.

On the domestic front, too, Constantine gladly continued the policies that Romanus Lecapenus had initiated. Much of Romanus's legislation had been concerned with the protection of the small-holding peasant militia against the rich feudal aristocracy, who had for years been buying up more and more of their land. It had made him deeply – at times even dangerously – unpopular with the latter, whose influence had grown to the point where they were now universally known as οἱ δυνατοί – 'the powerful'; but he had refused to be deflected from his object, knowing that ever since the days of Heraclius the small-holders, with their regular payments of state taxes and their obligations of armed service, had formed the foundation of the whole economic and military strength of the Empire.

It was inevitable that Constantine Porphyrogenitus should have felt a good deal more sympathetic to the aristocracy, to which he himself belonged, than did his Armenian *parvenu* father-in-law: as we have seen, he made no secret of his particular friendship for the family of Phocas, who represented everything that Romanus had most mistrusted. Yet from the moment that power was in his hands he had steadfastly continued the agrarian policy of his predecessor – in 947 going so far as to order the immediate restitution, without compensation, of all peasant lands that had been acquired by 'the powerful' since his effective accession. On earlier sales the purchase price was theoretically repayable, but even then only by those small-holders with a capital of more than fifty gold pieces. Other laws decreed that properties to which soldiers owed their livelihood and their means of equipping themselves for military service should be inalienable, and that no sale of a small-holding could be deemed incontrovertible and absolute until forty years after its first conclusion. Romanus's old law providing for the confiscation, again without compensation, of lands illicitly surrendered to 'the power-ful' was confirmed, and certain loopholes closed up. Thus, by the end of

1 There has been some controversy over Olga's baptism, certain historians believing that it had already taken place in Russia some two or three years before. I follow my old tutor, Professor D. Obolensky. (*Cambridge Medieval History*, Vol. IV, p. 511n.)

the reign, the condition of the landed peasantry was better than it had been for a century and more. It says much for the aristocracy that it accepted the new dispensations with so little protest.

The darkest shadow over Constantine's fourteen years of undivided reign came in fact not from the ranks of the nobility but from the eunuch monk Polyeuctus, whom he was rash enough to appoint as Patriarch in 956, after the death of his disreputable brother-in-law Theophylact.[1] There are two schools of thought about Polyeuctus. Professor Toynbee considers him 'irreproachable'; for Professor Jenkins, on the other hand – whose view seems to come a good deal closer to the truth – he was a tiresome fanatic who from the moment of his appointment did nothing but make trouble: first by publicly accusing Basil the *parakoimomenos* of extortion and then, even more contentiously, by resurrecting the whole vexed question of Leo the Wise's fourth marriage and demanding the restitution of the name of Patriarch Euthymius – who, it may be remembered, had given Leo his longed-for dispensation – to the holy diptychs.[2]

Forty years before, the Emperor might have welcomed such an initiative; by now, the last thing he wanted was to have the whole affair raked up again. On this occasion Polyeuctus was obliged to yield; but he continued his disruptive behaviour until at last Constantine could bear it no longer and in September 959 crossed over to Asia to consult his old friend the Bishop of Cyzicus on possible ways of getting rid of him. From Cyzicus he travelled to Bursa, in the hopes that its celebrated hot springs would cure him of a persistent fever from which he had been suffering, and when this treatment proved ineffective he passed on to the monastery high on the Mysian Mount Olympus (now Ulu Dağ), some twenty miles outside the town. By this time, however, it was plain that he was mortally ill: the monks, seeing that there was no hope, warned him that the end was near and bade him prepare for death. He returned hurriedly to the capital where, on 9 November 959, he died in his bed, aged fifty-four, surrounded by his sorrowing family: his wife Helena, his five daughters and his twenty-year-old son Romanus, now Emperor of Byzantium.

No reign ever opened more auspiciously than that of Romanus II. His

---

1 The immense stables that Theophylact had built next to St Sophia for his 2,000 horses were converted into a home for the aged.

2 See p. 125n.

great-grandfather Basil I, his two grandfathers Leo the Wise and Romanus Lecapenus and his father Constantine had built up the Empire to a point where its economic and military strength were greater than they had been for centuries; intellectually and artistically the Macedonian Renaissance was at its height. The indubitably legitimate son of a much-loved Emperor, born like his father in the purple, he had inherited both Constantine's magnificent build and his charm of manner, together with much of his mother's beauty. His detractors complained that he was frivolous, and that he spent too much time hunting, carousing and playing polo; but such faults are surely forgivable in the young, and there is no reason to believe that he would not have outgrown them had he only been given the chance to do so.

More seriously, but even more excusably, he fell in love. As a child he had been married off to Bertha, one of the countless natural progeny of the Italian King, Hugh of Arles; but she had died soon afterwards and in 958 he had firmly rejected his father's next choice for him, King Otto's niece Hedwig of Bavaria, in favour of a Peloponnesian innkeeper's daughter who had taken the name of Theophano. History offers no more striking example of the *femme fatale*. Her beauty, for a start, was breathtaking: we have no reason to doubt Leo the Deacon when he assures us that she was the loveliest woman of her day. She was also intensely ambitious and, so far as we can judge, utterly devoid of moral scruple: a compulsive intriguer, she would stick at nothing – not even, as we shall see, at murder itself – to gain her ends. And although only just eighteen when her husband succeeded to the throne, she dominated him completely. No rivals were tolerated: almost her first action as Empress was to deal with her mother-in-law and her husband's five sisters. Helena was relegated to a distant corner of the Palace, where she was to die, alone and unheeded, in September 961; all five princesses – one of whom, Agatha, had for years never left her father's side, serving as his confidential secretary and, more recently, his nurse – were obliged to take the veil. They did not do so willingly: for days the Palace echoed with their lamentations. In vain did their mother and their brother plead for them; the young Empress was inexorable. She stood by grimly as Patriarch Polyeuctus himself sheared off their hair and, as a final blow, dispatched them to five different convents.

Thanks in large measure to Theophano, many of the senior officials of government and court also lost their posts; two of the most important, however, remained in power – although with different functions. Basil, the former *parakoimomenos*, was given the new title of *proedrus*, which carried with it the presidency of the Senate and effectively made him the Emperor's right-hand man, while his previous post was inherited by the eunuch Joseph Bringas, who had combined the duties of chief minister and High Admiral (*drungarius*) during the last years of Constantine's reign. Bringas emerges from the chronicles as an able yet somewhat sinister figure. Highly intelligent and perceptive, with immense energy and a seemingly limitless capacity for hard work, he was also greedy, rapacious, self-seeking and cruel. Gradually he had made himself indispensable to Constantine, whose dying wish had been that he should continue in charge of the government; with the accession of Romanus his power in the Empire became virtually absolute. It was he who initiated the campaign which was to lead to the most signal achievement of the young Emperor's brief reign: the recapture, after nearly a century and a half, of the island of Crete.

A late Arab chronicler claims that, after the collapse of the disastrous expedition of 949, Constantine Porphyrogenitus tried to make terms with the Cretan Emir, according to which the latter would call a halt to his subjects' constant raiding in return for an annual subsidy amounting to twice the sum normally brought in by piracy. It may well be so, though no surviving Byzantine source confirms the fact. There can be little doubt, on the other hand, that the 949 fiasco rankled; and before the young Romanus had been more than a few weeks on the throne preparations were under way for a new expedition, conceived on a scale infinitely more ambitious than any that had gone before. We are not, unfortunately, given precise figures for the forces involved; but they included elements from all over the Empire, which were further sup-plemented by important contingents from Armenia – to say nothing of large numbers of Russian mercenaries and Varangian axe-men from Scandinavia. The total must have been well in excess of 50,000. On the size of the fleet we are rather more precisely informed: 1,000 heavy transports, 308 supply ships and no less than 2,000 carriers of Greek fire. Command of this tremendous armament was entrusted to the ugly, austere and deeply religious man of forty-seven who had by now proved himself to be the Empire's outstanding general – one of the greatest, indeed, in all its history.

His name was Nicephorus Phocas. His grandfather and namesake had been responsible for the reconquest of south Italy during Basil I's reign; his uncle, Leo Phocas, had led the resistance to Romanus Lecapenus in

919 and had been blinded for his pains; his father, Bardas Phocas, had been appointed Domestic of the Schools under Constantine Porphyrogenitus and had commanded the imperial armies against the Saracens of the East until in 953 a hideous wound in the face had put an end to his military career. Nicephorus himself, hitherto military governor of the Anatolikon Theme, had immediately taken over the command and four years later had given spectacular proof of his abilities with the all-important capture of Adata. He was – friends and enemies alike agree – a superb soldier, through and through: cool and fearless in battle, of enormous physical strength, quick as lightning to seize an opportunity and unfailingly considerate of his soldiers, who adored him and would follow him anywhere. Outside the army he had no interests save his religion, leading a life of almost monastic austerity and spending his leisure hours in conversation or correspondence with holy men. (Of these his particular favourite was the future St Athanasius, who had deserted his monastery rather than become its abbot and was at this time living as a hermit on Mount Athos.) He had absolutely no social graces. He was, in short, a cold fish.

The preparations continued all through the first six months of 960; then, in the last days of June, the great fleet sailed out of the Golden Horn into the Marmara. Some two weeks later, on 13 July, it appeared off the north coast of Crete. Exactly where the landing took place is uncertain, but it was watched in horror by a dense crowd of Saracens, on foot and on horseback, who were gathered on the heights above the bank. The enemy had obviously been taken by surprise, and at first there was no organized resistance: those who approached too close were met by hails of arrows and sling-bolts. As the disembarkation continued, however, squadrons of cavalry began to appear in increasing strength, and as soon as enough were assembled, flung themselves on the invaders. They fought, according to Leo the Deacon,[1] with almost superhuman courage; but they were hopelessly outnumbered and made little impression on the Byzantine forces. Hundreds were killed, while those who fell wounded were trampled to death by the cataphracts – armoured cavalry whose heavy coats of mail rendered them well-nigh invulnerable to anything other than the fierce Mediterranean sun.

Then, a few days later, the imperial army suffered its first reverse. Nicephorus had dispatched a large reconnaissance and foraging party

1 Whose account I follow here. Theophanes Continuatus tells a rather different story, laying a good deal less emphasis on Saracen resistance.

into the hinterland, under the command of one Pastilas, *strategos* of Thrace. Unfortunately it included a detachment of Russians, whom the extraordinary beauty, richness and fertility of the land seems to have sent into a kind of ecstasy, causing them to lose all sense of discipline. What actually happened is uncertain – presumably they got roaring drunk and went to sleep; in any case the Saracens, who had been watching their every move, suddenly saw their opportunity. Down they swept, catching their victims entirely unawares. Pastilas and the rest hastened to the rescue, but too late: nearly all were cut down in the ensuing mêlée, the *strategos* himself among them. Only a handful survived to bring news of the catastrophe back to the main body of the army.

Nicephorus was predictably furious, but saw no reason to change his plan, which was to advance directly on the city of Candia – which the Byzantines called Chandax and we today know as Heraklion. It was by far the largest town on the whole island and – insofar as such a thing existed in an essentially pirate community – its capital. If it were taken there was a good chance that there would be no other serious resistance anywhere on the island. A day or two later he drew up the army before its walls, and the siege began. It continued for eight months. Had the Byzantines managed to maintain an effective blockade by sea as well as by land, the whole thing might have been over in half that time; but there were no natural harbours and Nicephorus could not keep his ships indefinitely at sea through what was to prove an abnormally long and harsh winter. The beleaguered citizens could thus bring in all the provisions and supplies they needed; more important still, they could – and did – send urgent appeals for aid to their co-religionists in Sicily, Egypt and Spain.

But their appeals went unanswered and, as the weeks went by, their morale began to flag. Their only consolation was the sight of their half-frozen enemies huddling together round their fires and the knowledge that – as so often in medieval siege warfare – life, especially in winter, was often a good deal more uncomfortable for the besiegers than for the besieged. As the long, cold months dragged by, the imperial army was indeed beginning to suffer the pangs of serious hunger; under many another commander, open mutiny would have been a distinct possibility. But Nicephorus understood his men: somehow, on his daily rounds, he managed to imbue them with strength, hope and the courage to continue. In this task he seems to have been himself inspired by his friend and mentor Athanasius who by now, with several undoubted miracles to his credit, had reluctantly left his hermitage on Mount Athos at the general's urgent summons and joined him in the camp. It was – Nicephorus was convinced – entirely through his intercession that just in time, around the middle of February, the long-awaited relief fleet arrived with supplies from Constantinople; and before the end of the month the Byzantines, their morale considerably restored, had made two determined attempts to smash their way into the town. Both these first assaults failed; but a third succeeded, and on 7 March 961, for the first time in 136 years, the imperial standard flew again over Crete.

On the same day the massacre began. Women, old and young, were raped, murdered and thrown aside; children, even babies at the breast, were strangled or impaled on lances. Not even the immense prestige of Nicephorus was able to halt the carnage; only after three days did he succeed in making his voice heard, and even then there was little hope for the people of Candia. The survivors, both male and female, were sold into slavery; and the victorious fleet headed back to the Bosphorus, laden to the gunwales with the results of more than a century's plunder of the richest cities of the Eastern Mediterranean.

The fall of Candia, and the consequent collapse of Saracen power in Crete, was a victory for the Byzantines unparalleled since the days of Heraclius. When the news reached Constantinople there was celebration throughout the city: an all-night service of thanksgiving was held in St Sophia in the presence of the Emperor and Empress, the nobility and clergy, and as many of the populace as could squeeze themselves into the Great Church. Among the whole vast congregation there was perhaps one man only in whom the overriding emotion was not jubilation but anxiety. The eunuch Joseph Bringas had always hated the house of Phocas, of whom he was bitterly jealous. Heretofore, Nicephorus's popularity had been confined to the army; he had had no appeal for the people of Constantinople, to most of whom he was in any case little more than a name. Now all that would be changed: overnight he had become the Empire's hero. Victorious generals were dangerous at the best of times, and Nicephorus was known to be consumed by ambition. If that ambition was to be contained, both government and court must proceed with the most meticulous care; there would be difficult weeks ahead.

And so it came about that when Nicephorus Phocas sailed proudly back into the Golden Horn, to be greeted by Romanus and Theophano and publicly congratulated on his historic achievement, he was not on this occasion offered the full imperial triumph that he had so abundantly deserved. All that was permitted to him was an ovation in the Hippodrome, at which the people were given the chance to gaze upon their finest general and to salute him with their cheers; he, on the other hand, stood before them not in a four-horse chariot but on foot. There was no great military parade, no flaunting of prisoners and plunder. It was made clear to him, too, that he was not to remain in the capital any longer than was absolutely necessary. Saracen morale had suffered a bitter blow, and the Empire must quickly follow up the advantage it had gained. In short, he was needed in the East.

When Nicephorus had relinquished his eastern command two years before to prepare for the Cretan expedition, he had been succeeded by his younger brother Leo. Within weeks of his assumption of that command, however, Leo had found himself faced with a major challenge from the Empire's old enemy, Saïf ed-Daula. Saïf had come a long way since his first appearance in these pages in the 930s, as the most redoubtable opponent of John Curcuas. In 944 he had captured Aleppo, which he had made his permanent headquarters and from which he had rapidly extended his domains to embrace the greater part of Syria and northern Mesopotamia, including Damascus, Emesa and Antioch. All these conquests had further enhanced the reputation for valour that he had first acquired in his early youth; thus, well before the age of thirty-five – he had been born in 916 – he had become the *beau idéal* of the Arab Emir of the early Middle Ages: cruel and pitiless in war but chivalrous and merciful in peace, poet and scholar, patron of literature and the arts, possessor of the largest stable, the most extensive library and the most sumptuously stocked harem in the Muslim world.

Every year without fail, Saïf had led at least one major raid into Byzantine territory. None, however, had been so ambitious as that of the early summer of 960. The moment was perfectly chosen. The army of the East, seriously depleted by the demands of the Cretan expedition, was weaker than it had been for years. Leo Phocas was still mopping up after a successful campaign in south Syria and was thus several days' march away in the opposite direction. Saïf was not the man to miss that kind of opportunity; and at almost exactly the time that Nicephorus sailed for Crete – it may well have been on the very same day – he crossed the imperial border from the south-east at the head of a Saracen army estimated at 30,000 men, passing unhindered through the defiles of the eastern Taurus and advancing to the fortress of Charsian[1] near Melitene, where he massacred the garrison and took a large number of prisoners.

Leo Phocas pursued him, but without undue haste. He was heavily outnumbered, he knew, and such men as he had available were still exhausted after a long and arduous campaign; to meet such an enemy on open ground would be to invite disaster. He advanced only as far as the mountains, where he carefully disposed his men to command the principal passes. Then he settled down to wait.

It was early November before Saïf ed-Daula returned with his army. His expedition had been a huge success. Long trains of captives shuffled behind him, his carts groaned with the weight of his plunder; he himself, according to Leo the Deacon, rode proudly at the head of his men on a magnificent Arab mare, 'playing all the time skilfully with his lance, which he would throw high in the air and catch again as it descended, without once letting it fall or delaying the speed of the march'. Cheerfully and confidently the long procession made its way back through the mountains; then, just as it entered a pass that the Greeks called the *Kulindros*, or cylinder, there rang out the blast of a hidden trumpet. Within seconds, immense boulders came spinning down the mountainside on top of the defenceless column. As if from nowhere, Leo Phocas and his army appeared both before and behind, and Saïf suddenly found himself surrounded. At first he stood his ground, defending himself heroically, hacking to left and right with his scimitar. His horse was killed under him; seizing that of a servant, he returned to the fray. Only later, when he saw that the day was lost, did he wheel round and set off at a gallop. By scattering behind him handful after handful of gold coins he effectively slowed down his pursuers and so made good his escape, together with some 300 of his cavalry. Of the rest, nearly half lay dead; the survivors were all taken prisoner, being secured with the same ropes and fetters that had formerly held the Christian captives.

This famous victory shows clearly enough that Leo Phocas, even with diminished forces, was perfectly capable of defending the eastern frontier – and causes us yet again to question the real motives for the almost indecent speed with which Nicephorus was posted back to relieve him. As was only to be expected, however, the renewed presence of both

1 The Arab chroniclers call it Karchanah. I have been unable to identify it.

brothers, at the head of an army restored to its former size and with its morale higher than ever before, had a dramatic effect on the future of the fighting. In the space of just three weeks during February and March 962, the Byzantines regained no less than fifty-five walled towns in Cilicia; then, after a brief pause while they celebrated Easter, they advanced through the Syrian Gates near Alexandretta (Iskenderun). From here they moved slowly and methodically southward, burning and plundering as they went. A few months later they were beneath the walls of Aleppo itself, preparing to lay siege to the city.

Aleppo was at this moment enjoying the most brilliant chapter of its long history. Its capture by Saïf ed-Daula eighteen years before had made it, for the first time, the capital of an independent state and the chief residence of its ruler; and Saïf's magnificent palace, known as al-Hallaba, was one of the most beautiful and renowned buildings of the tenth-century Muslim world. The Emir himself had never ceased to enrich it with all the spoils taken in his countless campaigns, but it had one major drawback: a cruelly exposed position outside the city walls, which he had made little effort to protect. On the very night of their arrival, Nicephorus's men fell on it like locusts, first emptying it of all its treasures and then burning it to the ground. As well as 390,000 silver dinars, they took possession of 2,000 camels, 1,400 mules and so many Arab thoroughbreds that 'they could not be counted'. The building itself was stripped, inside and out: the Arab chroniclers speak sadly of the gold and silver plate, the bales of velvet and silken damask, the swords and breastplates and jewelled belts, even the gilded tiles from the walls and roofs. Only when there was nothing of the palace left to plunder did the imperial army turn its attention to Aleppo itself. Saïf, caught outside the walls, was once again obliged to flee for his life; the majority of the local garrison, deprived of his ever-inspiriting presence, lacked stomach for the fight; and two days before Christmas the triumphant Byzantines swarmed into the city. As at Candia, no mercy was shown: the carnage, writes an Arab historian, ceased only when the conquerors were too exhausted to go on.

But Aleppo, though occupied, had not quite fallen. A handful of soldiers in the citadel had dug themselves in and obstinately refused to surrender. Nicephorus simply ignored them. They could not hold out for long, and their provisions could not last for ever. The important thing was that Saïf was gone, and Aleppo was no longer a force to be reckoned with. There was no point in wasting any more time. He gave the order to retire, and the victorious army began the long journey home.

It had advanced no further than Cappadocia when a message arrived from Constantinople. The Emperor Romanus II was dead.

12

The White Death of the Saracens

[963–9]

He is a monstrosity of a man, a dwarf, with a broad, flat head and tiny eyes like a mole; disfigured by a short, thick, grizzled beard; disgraced by a neck scarcely an inch long; piglike by reason of the big close bristles on his head; in colour an Ethiopian. As the poet[1] says, 'you would not like to meet him in the dark'. A big belly, a small posterior, very long in the hip considering his short stature, small legs, fair-sized heels and feet; dressed in a robe made of fine linen but old, foul-smelling and discoloured by age; shod with Sicyonian slippers; bold of tongue, a fox by nature, in perjury and falsehood a Ulysses.

Liudprand of Cremona, describing
Nicephorus Phocas

Romanus had died on 15 March, 963; and already by the next morning the rumour was circulating that the Empress Theophano had poisoned her husband. Such a reaction was, perhaps, inevitable. In the intrigue-ridden atmosphere of Constantinople the death of any young nobleman, let alone the *basileus* himself, for no immediately apparent reason always set evil tongues a-wagging; and the beautiful young Empress, in the forty months since Romanus's accession, had acquired a formidable reputation. Few doubted that she was capable of such a crime; but capability is a very different thing from guilt, and it is hard indeed to see how her position might have been improved by widowhood, whether or not self-inflicted. Insofar as she was able to love anyone, there is every reason to believe that she loved her husband, to whom she had already given four children – the youngest, a daughter, born only two days before his death. While he lived she was all-powerful, with her own future and that of her children alike assured. Now that he was gone, they were all in danger. She herself still lay in childbed; her two sons, the co-Emperors Basil and Constantine, were six and three years old

---

1 Juvenal, V, 54.

respectively. The example of her own father-in-law was enough to illustrate the perils of a long minority, especially when there were ambitious generals in the offing; and while her predecessor Zoe had had only two of these to cope with, there were now three – the two brothers Phocas and John Tzimisces – all of whom would be sure to see the present situation as a possible path to the throne. To these potential contenders there could easily have been added a fourth, the *parakoimomenos* Joseph Bringas, but for the fact that as a eunuch he was disqualified for the supreme power; he too, however, was a compulsive intriguer, and though Theophano knew that he would never support the Phocas faction there was no telling what other candidates he had in mind.

Meanwhile she needed a protector, and a strong one. Secretly – for Bringas, had he known, would surely have prevented her – she sent an urgent appeal to Nicephorus Phocas in the East, begging him to return at once. When the messenger found him in his camp near Caesarea in Cappadocia, Nicephorus did not hesitate. Speed, he knew, was all-important: there was no time to gather together his troops, many of whom had already dispersed to their homes. Pausing only long enough to assemble all the most precious spoils from his Syrian campaigns, he set off with a small escort, and some time in early April entered the capital. By this time the Empress's summons was common knowledge. Bringas, furious, had protested violently and at a meeting of the Council of Regency had gone so far as to argue that the general had become a public danger who should be arrested immediately on his arrival. But he had found no support, and the crowds that had gathered in front of the Palace were loudly demanding that Nicephorus be given not only a hero's welcome but also that full-scale triumph of which he had been so unjustly deprived after the Cretan conquest.

And so the triumph was held: the most splendid, perhaps, since that of Heraclius over three centuries before, and given additional sanctity by the tattered tunic of John the Baptist, recently snatched from its long-time resting-place in Aleppo and now carried proudly before Nicephorus – 'the White Death of the Saracens' – as he rode through the streets to the Hippodrome. In the face of his immense popularity, Bringas was powerless; and the anger and resentment that he had long harboured against his old enemy were now joined by a third emotion: fear. The general was in daily consultation with the Empress; if he were now with her support to make a bid for the throne, what fate would be in store for himself? Blinding? Banishment? Or both? Nicephorus, it was true, gave no outward sign of having any such ambition; on the contrary, he lost no opportunity of proclaiming his indifference to worldly pomp and power and his eagerness to retire as soon as possible to the monastery that his friend Athanasius was already building at his request on Mount Athos.[1] But Bringas was not deceived. Quietly and secretly he made his plans, and when all was in readiness summoned his enemy to the Palace.

Nicephorus too was on his guard. His spies had been busy. He had no delusions about what the *parakoimomenos* was planning, and he was determined to regain the initiative. Instead of obeying the summons he went straight to St Sophia, where he publicly accused Bringas of plotting to murder him and appealed for asylum. It was a brilliant ploy, and a successful one. An indignant crowd soon collected, calling angrily for punishment of any who dared lay a finger on its hero, and was soon joined by Patriarch Polyeuctus himself. Now the Patriarch was, as we have seen, a narrow-minded bigot who had blighted the last years of Constantine Porphyrogenitus; this austere and deeply devout general was on the other hand a man after his own heart, and he had no hesitation in lending his own voice to that of the crowd. Joseph Bringas was a powerful man, but the united stand of both Empress and Patriarch, with the people obviously behind them to a man, was too much for him: he could only watch, fuming, while the Senate confirmed Nicephorus in his command and undertook to make no major decisions of policy without his consent. The general in his turn thanked them for their confidence and trust and, as soon as the Easter celebrations were over, returned to rejoin his army in Anatolia.

But not, as everyone knew, for long. Those secret discussions with the Empress had ended in an agreement which was – in the short term at any rate – to prove highly advantageous to both parties. Nicephorus would protect the rights, and the persons, of the two child-Emperors; in return, he would himself be proclaimed Emperor and join them on the throne. He might talk as much as he liked of the preparations he was making for a coming campaign in Cilicia, but by now few people if any believed him. Bringas had been right: he was indeed preparing the army

---

1 On their return from the Cretan expedition, Nicephorus had entrusted his own share of the spoils to Athanasius for the building of this foundation, 'where you and I can be alone with our brothers and together taste the joys of the Eucharist'. Now known as the Grand Lavra, the monastery remains, the oldest and most venerable on the Holy Mountain, with its great bronze doors – the personal gift of the Emperor – still in place.

to march. The object of that march, however, would be not Cilicia but Constantinople.

And so Bringas, by now desperate, played his last card. He sent letters to two of Nicephorus's senior commanders, Romanus Curcuas and John Tzimisces – respectively the son and great-nephew of the great John Curcuas who had won such splendid victories for Romanus Lecapenus – offering them the supreme commands of East and West respectively in return for the betrayal of their chief. How they were to do it was for them to decide: they might have him forcibly tonsured and immured in a monastery, or they could send him in chains to Constantinople. 'I depend on you,' he wrote to Tzimisces. 'First accept the command in Anatolia, then be patient a little and before long you will be *basileus* of the Romans.' Unfortunately his dependence was misplaced: Tzimisces went at once to Nicephorus, who was sleeping in his tent, woke him excitedly and showed him the letter. The general seemed momentarily stunned; one of our chroniclers, George Cedrenus, claims that it was only after his two commanders had threatened to kill him if he hesitated any longer that he was at last stirred into action. But this was probably little more than a token show of reluctance. At dawn on 3 July 963, before the entire army drawn up on a great plain just outside the walls of the Cappadocian Caesarea, Nicephorus Phocas was raised by his generals on a great shield in the ancient manner and proclaimed Emperor of the Romans. Then, after a short service of blessing in the cathedral, he set off for his capital.

In Constantinople, meanwhile, Joseph Bringas refused to admit defeat. He had summoned large numbers of European troops from Macedonia and elsewhere who traditionally mistrusted the Anatolians and on whose loyalty he believed he could rely; most of these he distributed not only along the land and sea walls but also at key points throughout the city, to deal with the first signs of popular uprising. The rest were dispatched to the Asiatic shore of the Bosphorus, there to commandeer all the vessels they could find and sail them over to Europe. Thus it was that when Nicephorus Phocas and his army arrived at Chrysopolis (better known to us as Scutari) on 9 August they found themselves unable to cross the strait. The new Emperor did not however seem unduly disturbed; now that his friends and supporters in the city could see his watch-fires, he knew that some at least of them would succeed in joining him under cover of darkness. He installed himself comfortably in the nearby imperial summer Palace of Hieria and settled down to wait. He was soon proved right in his expectations: one of the first to arrive was his own brother Leo, hero of the battle of the Kulindros Pass. But Leo brought disturbing news: their father, the old general Bardas Phocas – now well into his eighties – was being held by Bringas as a hostage. If Nicephorus were to advance any further, his chances of survival would be slim.

In fact, events were moving a good deal faster than Leo realized. Taking advantage of the growing confusion in the city, Bardas – quite possibly with the connivance of his guards – managed to escape and himself sought asylum in St Sophia. Bringas, the moment he heard what had happened, sent a detachment of militia after him, with orders to drag him from his refuge. It was a fatal mistake. The day was 9 August, a Sunday, and the Great Church was thronged with people. Bardas was a popular figure, both as a distinguished veteran of the Saracen wars and as the father of Nicephorus; and the soldiers immediately found themselves surrounded by a hostile crowd, who snatched their prisoner from them and drove them forcibly out of the building before returning the old man to his place of sanctuary.

Whatever his other faults, Bringas was no coward. Seeing his men returning empty-handed and visibly shaken, he leaped on to his horse and rode straight to the Patriarchate, which adjoined St Sophia; then, when Polyeuctus refused to intervene, he himself passed through into the church, pushed his way through the jostling crowd, mounted the ambo and, silencing the priests with an imperious hand, personally addressed the congregation. But once again he misjudged the strength of his opposition. A few words of conciliation might yet have saved the day; instead he blustered, roundly berating those who defied his orders, threatening to cut off all the city's supplies of food and thus, if necessary, to starve them into submission. Then he strode out of the church, pausing only to order the bread-sellers who occupied a permanent pitch outside the west doors to close down their stalls immediately.

It was, of course, an empty threat; Bringas knew it, and so did his listeners. He returned to the Palace as angry as ever, conscious only of the fact that he, the imperial *parakoimomenos* and chief minister of the Byzantine Empire, had lost the first round and had been made to look a fool. But he was not yet beaten. He waited, fuming, until the crowd began to stream from St Sophia. It was noon; the service was over, and it was time for the midday meal. Sending for the two child-Emperors, he took them firmly by the hand and returned with them to the Great Church, by now almost deserted except for the old general, sitting quietly among the shadows of the sanctuary. Their subsequent conversation is unrecorded – though the presence of the two little boys suggests a possible threat that any further attempt at resistance would be paid for with their lives. All we know is that Bardas allowed himself to be led away.

For the third time the eunuch had underestimated the strength of popular feeling. When the hour of Vespers drew near and St Sophia began once again to fill with people, their first thought was for Bardas; and when they failed to find him their mood became uglier than ever, the force of their anger this time being principally directed against the Patriarch and clergy, who at best had failed to protect their fugitive and at worst had deliberately betrayed him. Polyeuctus, now seriously alarmed, hurried to the Palace, found Bardas sitting sadly in an anteroom, seized him by the arm and returned with him to the church, where his appearance produced an immediate hush; but when Bringas arrived a few minutes later with a platoon of Macedonians and made yet another attempt to lay hands upon him, the people decided that they had had enough. While some took charge of the bewildered old man, carried him back to his house and mounted guard over him, the remainder seized bricks, stones and anything else – even church furniture – that might serve them as a weapon and flung themselves on Bringas's soldiers.

The riot, once started, spread like wildfire through the city. At the outset, in the manner of all riots, it was largely uncontrolled; but as it gathered momentum it also began to reveal a guiding force behind it: that of Basil, the natural son of Romanus Lecapenus. Presumably to protect the interests of his elder, legitimate, sons Romanus had had him castrated in infancy; but from his youth Basil had always shown outstanding intelligence and ability and had long played an important part in affairs of state. As early as 944 Constantine Porphyrogenitus had created him Patrician and appointed him Exarch of the Grand Hetaireia;[1] a few months later he was *parakoimomenos*. In 958 we find him commanding the army of the East, winning a splendid victory over Saïf ed-Daula and being granted a triumph on his return to the capital. With the death of Constantine the following year, it was he who had personally laid the

---

1 The imperial guard, recruited exclusively from the barbarian tribes (including Russians and the redoubtable Varangians, or Northmen), which provided the garrison of the Great Palace and attended the Emperor on campaign.

Emperor's body beside that of his father Leo, in the same sarcophagus. Then, on his promotion to *proedrus*, he found himself replaced by Joseph Bringas, whom he disliked and mistrusted.

As soon as he heard the first sounds of the insurrection, Basil knew that his opportunity had come. Quickly he gathered together all his servants and retainers – 4,000 of them if the chroniclers are to be believed, a figure which gives some idea of the state maintained by noble Byzantines at this period – and led them down to the Forum, where the crowd was thickest and where he quickly assumed control. His first action was to send men to every corner of the city to proclaim the imminent arrival of the new Emperor; next – one suspects with still more satisfaction – he led the mob to Bringas's private palace, which was first plundered of everything that it possessed of value and was then burnt to the ground. After this the burning and looting became general: what had begun as a legitimate protest rapidly deteriorated into a howling, hysterical rampage. It was three days – by which time half Constantinople lay in ruins – before Basil was able to reassert his authority and impose some semblance of order. Then and only then could he lead his men down to the Golden Horn, take possession of all the vessels that lay at anchor within the harbour and sail the vast flotilla across the Bosphorus to the Hieria, where Nicephorus was still patiently waiting for him.

At last, on Sunday 16 August 963, the Emperor Nicephorus Phocas was ready to enter his capital. With Basil, now reappointed *parakoimomenos*, at his side he boarded the imperial *dromond*, seating himself upon a great silver throne beneath a golden canopy supported by gilded caryatids; he was then rowed slowly across the strait and westward along the European shore to the Palace of the Hebdomon, just outside the land walls at their southern end. Here he changed into ceremonial attire, strapped on his golden breastplate and mounted the huge white charger, caparisoned in purple and gold, that was to bear him through the city; and so the great procession began, stopping first at the Abramite monastery of the Acheiropoietus[1] to revere the miraculous ('not made with hands') icon of the Virgin, then passing through the Golden Gate and along the Mesē to St Sophia where, in the

---

1 This had been founded in the sixth century by the monk Abraham, who went on to establish the Byzantine monastery on the Mount of Olives and who later still became Bishop of Ephesus. Inevitably, perhaps, in view of its exposed position, it was to be destroyed shortly before the Turkish siege of 1453 – together, presumably, with the miraculous icon.

presence of the two child-Emperors, Patriarch Polyeuctus laid the diadem on his head.

Bishop Liudprand of Cremona never made any effort to conceal his dislike of Nicephorus Phocas, and his description at the head of this chapter can hardly be called unprejudiced; Leo the Deacon, on the other hand, who knew the Emperor well and has no axe to grind, paints a not dissimilar picture: he confirms that Nicephorus was short and squat – an impression strengthened by his broad shoulders and barrel chest – that his complexion was distinctly swarthy, and rendered darker still by his long years of service under the Syrian sun; and that his eyes were indeed small and dark, under heavy brows. (He adds that they seemed thoughtful and somehow sad.) The only point of radical disagreement is on the Emperor's hair: Liudprand's reference to bristles suggests that Nicephorus wore it *en brosse*, whereas according to Leo it was black with tight curls, and unusually long.[1]

We have already touched in the previous chapter on the character and way of life of the new Emperor. Neither, it may be repeated, was particularly endearing. His interests were confined to the army and his religion. He was, it is true, a man of normally high moral integrity, intelligent if narrow-minded, serious and sober, utterly incorruptible, impervious to flattery and hard as nails; but he could also be pitiless and cruel, and his meanness and avarice were notorious. Duplicity, too, came easily to him. As for his habits, they may have been in the highest degree praiseworthy but it is difficult to feel much affection for a man who for years had eaten no meat, who abhorred women, who invariably slept in the hair-shirt of his uncle – a monk famed for his holiness named Michael Maleinus – and who spent several hours a day in prayer. But Nicephorus never courted popularity. Though he had now entered his sixth decade his energies were unabated, and he flung himself into the task of government with every appearance of enthusiasm.

His first concern was Bringas. He too, when the mob was baying for his blood, had taken refuge in St Sophia, but after the dust had settled he seems to have left it of his own accord. When the time came for him to prostrate himself before his old enemy, knowing already that he was dismissed from his high office and that his home had been destroyed with all his possessions, he must have trembled for his future. The

---

1 Since this style is quite clearly illustrated in the contemporary coinage, we can safely prefer the evidence of the deacon to that of the bishop.

Emperor, however, was not vindictive: he contented himself by banishing Bringas to his wild Paphlagonian homeland, forbidding him ever to return to Constantinople. Meanwhile there were rewards to be distributed as well as punishment. On old Bardas his father, the Emperor conferred the title of Caesar, in recognition of the courage he had shown during his recent tribulations; his brother Leo became *magister* and *curopalates*, or marshal of the imperial court; while John Tzimisces was confirmed as Domestic of the Schools, commander-in-chief of the army in Anatolia.

There remained Theophano: she who had first appealed to Nicephorus to assume the protection of herself and her children, she without whom he would have probably spent the rest of his active life in Syria, at war against the Saracen. The Emperor's first action where she was concerned was, perhaps, somewhat surprising: he expelled her from the Palace to the old fortress of the Petrion, in what is now the Phanar quarter along the upper reaches of the Golden Horn. For a month and four days she was obliged to languish in what was effectively little better than a prison, while Nicephorus, austere and frugal as ever, occupied the imperial apartments; then, on 20 September in the palatine church of the Nea,[1] he married her.

It would seem to be beyond reasonable doubt that Theophano's temporary banishment was in fact a measure agreed by both of them in advance, in order to preserve the proprieties and to prevent undesirable gossip – though why she should have been consigned to so uncomfortable a retreat, rather than to any one of the dozen or more palaces in the neighbourhood of the capital, is not immediately clear. A more intriguing question, however, concerns the background to the marriage. It was suggested at the time – though not, it must be said, by any of our more reliable sources – that Nicephorus, dazzled by the Empress's extraordinary beauty, had fallen passionately in love with her; and this theory has been eagerly espoused by a number of later historians. It is not hard to see why: the picture of the rough, unbending old general suddenly losing his head and heart to the loveliest – and most vicious – woman of her day is difficult to resist. But is it likely? Nicephorus was, after all, a natural and deeply religious ascetic, who after the death of his first wife had taken an oath of chastity and who throughout his life had seldom

---

1 Strictly speaking of course, 'the church of the Nea' is a misnomer – as if one referred to New College, Oxford, as 'the College of "the New"'. But since every more accurate translation is in one way or another even more unsatisfactory, 'the Nea' it will have to be.

missed an opportunity for further mortification of the flesh. Would he –
other historians have asked – really have proved so susceptible? Was this
not, quite simply, a contract agreed between the two of them in those
long private conversations after the general's first recall, by the terms of
which he would take the Empress and her little co-Emperors under his
protection in return for his own third share of the imperial crown?

For her, certainly, it could have been nothing else. We cannot
seriously imagine this exquisite and pleasure-loving young Empress,
immediately after a happy if short-lived marriage with the outstandingly
attractive Romanus, feeling anything but repugnance for a sanctimonious
puritan more than twice her age who – however much allowance we may
make for the obvious malice of Liudprand's description – still seems to
have been unattractive to a point bordering on the grotesque. But as for
Nicephorus – well, we cannot be so sure. If we had nothing but the
evidence of his character and background to guide us, we should
probably agree that his motives were purely political and were based on
ambition rather than love. On the other hand, Nicephorus would not
have been the first confirmed bachelor to have been swept off his feet
when he least expected it, and his subsequent conduct when the legality
of the union was called in question strongly suggests that this was for
him anything but a *mariage de convenance* and that he loved his young wife
to distraction.

For there were others a good deal less ready to overcome their
scruples than Nicephorus had been, and among them was Polyeuctus the
Patriarch. He had, so far as is known, voiced no prior objections to the
imperial marriage, or uttered any word of caution; indeed, it was he who
had personally led the Emperor by the hand up the nave of the Nea to
the iconostasis, in front of which the ceremony was to be performed.
But when, towards the end of the service, Nicephorus advanced alone
towards the middle door of the screen to implant the traditional kiss
upon the high altar which stood behind it, the Patriarch suddenly
stepped forward, hand upraised. Was the Emperor unaware, he asked, of
the penance imposed by the Church on all who contracted a second
marriage? After one full year had passed, he might once again be permitted within the sanctuary; until then it would remain closed to him.

Nicephorus had no choice but to accept the judgement; but he never
forgave Polyeuctus for what he considered a public insult. Neither was
this the end of his tribulations; for before many days had passed the
palace chaplain, one Stylianus, was foolish enough to mention an

extremely awkward fact, which all those aware of it had been doing their utmost to forget: that a few years before, on one of his brief visits to Constantinople, the Emperor had stood godfather to one of Theophano's children. By another law of the Orthodox Church, this had created a 'spiritual affinity' between them which put them within the proscribed degrees and would, if upheld, render the entire marriage null and void. When the Patriarch was informed, he did not hesitate. As he had already demonstrated on any number of previous occasions, he had no idea of tact or of diplomacy: for him the law was the law, and he was determined to obey every letter of it. He went straight to the Palace, strode into the Emperor's private apartment and offered him a simple choice: he must either immediately repudiate Theophano or suffer the ban of the Church in perpetuity.

At this point, had he cared nothing for his wife, Nicephorus might well have given in. The very thought of spending the rest of his life debarred from the Eucharist would have been inconceivable to a man of his temperament and beliefs. To have submitted with a good grace to the law of the Church, simultaneously consigning Theophano to a nunnery, would not only have reinstated him in divine favour; it would also have provided him with a perfect excuse to rid himself of a tiresome responsibility. But he did not submit. Accepting neither option, he immediately called a meeting of all the bishops who chanced to be in Constantinople – several of whom had come specifically to seek favours from him and might therefore be not unamenable to persuasion – together with a number of other prominent figures from Church and State, and made it clear that he looked to them to find a solution. It was not long before this distinguished gathering pronounced its decision: the canonical decree which at first sight appeared to cast doubt on the validity of the Emperor's marriage had been promulgated during the reign – and consequently in the name – of Constantine Copronymus, 'a heretic who held in contempt the Blessed Virgin and the Saints, infamous persecutor of their cult, worshipper of devils, vile executioner of monks, impious destroyer of the holy images'. The decree was consequently itself without validity. The marriage stood.

Not, however, in the eyes of the Patriarch. Inflexible as ever, he held with some justification that an *ad hoc* commission of this kind had no authority to pronounce on such matters, and simply repeated his ultimatum. Meanwhile the Emperor was excommunicate, the breach between Church and State complete. Once again, Nicephorus refused to submit. Even though his very soul were in jeopardy, he refused to leave Theophano. Once again, he began to look desperately for a way out. Finally, he himself hit upon a solution: not, perhaps, a particularly elegant or even honourable one, but the only one that offered any prospect of success. A few days later Stylianus – the cause of all the trouble – testified before a joint assembly of Church and Senate that he had never made the statement attributed to him or, if he had, that his memory had played him false. At this point old Bardas was brought in, and quaveringly confirmed that neither he nor his son had stood sponsor to any of Theophano's children. Polyeuctus, confronted with what he and everyone else knew were two bare-faced lies one after the other, knew that he was beaten. He might have been able to handle Stylianus alone; but the aged Caesar, who enjoyed not only the reverence due to the father of the Emperor but also that special kind of popularity which is exclusively reserved for those with one foot in the grave, was beyond his reach. He gave in.

Only one other opponent of the marriage remained to be dealt with: Athanasius, whose monastery on Mount Athos was now well on the way to completion. The church was finished but for the domes, and around it the monastic buildings were rising fast – concealing, somewhere in their depths, the small cell which had already been reserved for the Emperor. According to the *Vita Athanasii*, he had written Nicephorus a letter accusing him of having broken his promises and of having preferred the transitory pleasures of this world to the imperishable joys of the next, had immediately suspended all building operations and had withdrawn in high dudgeon to his old hermitage. The *Typicon* of the Grand Lavra, on the other hand, assures us that the saint went straight to Constantinople in person and told the Emperor what he thought of him, adding that after such a betrayal of trust he himself had lost all interest in his monastery and would not be returning. Nicephorus fell on his knees, pleading tearfully that he had had no option but to act as he did. He still cherished his monastic dream: one day, when the situation permitted, he would put away Theophano and join his old friend on the Holy Mountain as he had always promised to do. Meanwhile, he assured him, for all his wife's undoubted attractions he had never had and never would have carnal intercourse with her.[1] Pressing into his hand a *chrysobul* according formal recognition to the new monastery and rendering

---

1 True or false? If not simply an out-and-out lie to appease Athanasius, was this decision the result of Nicephorus's oath or of Theophano's repugnance? We shall never know.

it free from all but direct imperial control, he implored him to return and finish the task he had begun.

Loaded down with all the treasures, precious relics, endowments and privileges with which Nicephorus strove to appease his agonized conscience – including the great jewelled Bible and the golden reliquary containing a section of the True Cross which are still among the chief glories of the Holy Mountain – Athanasius did as he was bidden. Within a few months his monastery was complete – though it was never, alas, destined to shelter the two old men, one an Emperor and the other a saint, in the evening of their lives. The dreadful fate of Nicephorus is shortly to be told, but Athanasius was spared this further shock: soon after his resumption of building operations, the half-completed dome of his church collapsed on his head and killed him.

The Emperor Nicephorus II was – it hardly seems necessary to repeat – a soldier through and through, and one moreover for whom the war against the Saracens was nothing less than a crusade. It was, he devoutly believed, the will of God that the infidels should be driven back to the desert wastes from which they had come – and that he, Nicephorus, had been ordained to perform the task. Thus even his love for Theophano, great as it may have been, could not keep him from his duty; and in 964 he returned to the attack, which rapidly regained all its old momentum. The summer of 965 saw the first major conquest of this new campaign: the city of Tarsus, the Arabs' chief springboard for their annual incursions into Cilicia and for over 200 years one of the sharpest and most painful thorns in Byzantine flesh.

From Tarsus, too, it was but a short sail across to Cyprus. As early as 668 the island had been the subject of a treaty between Constantine IV and the Caliph Abdul-Malik, by the terms of which it had been demilitarized and ruled as a sort of neutral condominium by Emperor and Caliph together. To the bigoted mind of Nicephorus, however, this eminently civilized arrangement was anathema. That same summer of 965 his troops occupied the island in strength, such Muslims as were there at the time making not even a gesture of resistance or even protest; and Cyprus became a Byzantine Theme.

This lack of Saracen reaction to what was little better than an act of highway robbery was by now almost to be expected; for as the Abbasid Caliphate crumbled, so did its subjects grow ever more demoralized. As for Saïf ed-Daula of Aleppo, he had never really recovered from the destruction of his palace and the effective conquest of his capital in 962; five years later, a broken man and partially paralysed after what seems to have been a stroke, he died aged only fifty-one.[1] With his chief adversary gone, Nicephorus encountered no more serious obstacles to his progress. The position of Aleppo itself, whose garrison had never formally capitulated, was now regularized: the city became an imperial vassal and protectorate. And in 969, after 332 years, the ancient patriarchal city of Antioch returned once more to Christian hands.

Thus, so far as the war in the East is concerned, an account of the reign of Nicephorus II is one of virtually uninterrupted success; nor need this surprise us, since all that was required there was the military skill that the Emperor, his brother Leo and his companion-in-arms John Tzimisces – to say nothing of the young hero of Antioch, Michael Bourtzes – possessed in plenty. In the West, on the other hand, there is a less happy story to tell; for in dealing with Europe diplomacy was required; and in all the history of Byzantium there were few worse diplomats than Nicephorus Phocas. He seems to have allowed supreme power to go to his head: at the best of times singularly devoid of charm, we see him becoming ever more arrogant and overbearing as his reign goes on. He provided an excellent example of this blundering boorishness as early as 965, when an embassy arrived from Bulgaria to collect the annual subsidy agreed by Romanus Lecapenus and Tsar Peter at the time of the latter's marriage in 927. The Bulgars were, it is true, pressing their luck: the Tsaritsa Maria-Irene had died a month or two before, and Nicephorus might legitimately have objected that the arrangement had lapsed with her death.[2] On the other hand Bulgaria was an invaluable buffer state, protecting the Empire from both the Magyars and the Russians, and the modest subsidy – which had been annually handed over without question for thirty-eight years – might have been considered a small enough price to pay for friendly relations. Be that as it may, the Emperor had no possible justification for acting as he did. He turned on the ambassadors with a stream of invective, abusing them and their countrymen as a race of hideous and filthy beggars, triple slaves and sons of dogs, ruled by a prince dressed only in the skins of

1 The immediate cause of his death, according to *The Encyclopaedia of Islam*, was 'retention of the urine'. His body, it continues, 'was brought to Mayyafariqin and buried in the *türbe* of his mother outside the town. He had given orders for a brick made of soil that he had won in his campaigns to be placed under his head in his coffin.'

2 Still according to the theory of Sir Steven Runciman. See p. 147n.

animals. Then he had them scourged before sending them back empty-handed to Preslav.

Whatever the provocation, such conduct was obviously inexcusable – paralleled only by that of the Emperor Alexander in similar circumstances over half a century before. But while Alexander had been a drunken boor, Nicephorus was in deadly earnest. He advanced at once to the Bulgar frontier and captured several border strongholds to show that he meant what he had said, and in other circumstances he would doubtless have penetrated further; but the bulk of his army was fully – and profitably – engaged in the East and he had no wish to weaken it at such a time. He therefore concluded an agreement with Prince Svyatoslav of Kiev – the son of Igor and the recently baptized Olga – whereby Svyatoslav, in return for a handsome fee, undertook to subdue the Bulgars on his behalf. Svyatoslav was more than happy to accept Byzantine gold, but he was also greedy for conquest. Only a few years before, he had utterly destroyed the Kingdom of the Khazars; here was a heaven-sent opportunity to do the same to his Bulgar neighbours, pushing forward his already extensive frontiers as far as the banks of the Danube. The Bulgar Kingdom, now hopelessly divided, could put up no effective resistance: too late, the Emperor saw that he had succeeded only in replacing a weak and peace-loving neighbour with an ambitious and aggressive enemy.

In his dealings with Western Europe, Nicephorus's diplomacy – if it can so be described – was equally calamitous, and his chief adversary still more formidable. Otto the Saxon had come a long way since the time of his first appearance in this story, some fifteen years before. Although titular King of Italy since 952, he had at first been largely occupied in Germany, while the peninsula had been effectively ruled by the Marquis Berengar of Ivrea. In 961, however, in response to an appeal by the unspeakable John XII,[1] he had swept down into Italy, reasserted his control, taken Berengar prisoner and ridden on to Rome, where in February 962 the Pope had crowned him Emperor.

Attentive readers may remember that Otto in earlier years had welcomed the offers of an alliance made to him by Constantine

---

1 Most infamous of the tenth-century papal 'pornocracy', John had been made Pope in 955 at the age of sixteen. As Gibbon puts it, 'we read, with some surprise, that the worthy grandson of Marozia lived in public adultery with the matrons of Rome; that the Lateran Palace was turned into a school for prostitution; and that his rapes of virgins and widows had deterred the female pilgrims from visiting the shrine of St Peter, lest, in the devout act, they should be violated by his successor'.

Porphyrogenitus: an alliance which Constantine had hoped to seal by the marriage of his son Romanus (after the early death of the latter's first wife) to Otto's niece Hedwig. Romanus's rejection of this lady in favour of the lovely Theophano had greatly displeased the Saxon King, and when in 959 this arrogant and – in Otto's eyes – extremely ill-mannered young man succeeded his father on the throne relations between them became chillier still; but Otto continued to dream of a dynastic union, and in the last weeks of 967 – with Romanus in his turn now safely out of the way – he sent an embassy to Nicephorus to discuss the possibility. Thanks to misunderstandings on both sides, this proved unsuccessful – so unsuccessful indeed that, in an effort to bring the *basileus* to his senses, Otto launched a totally unprovoked attack on Byzantine-held Apulia, occupying much of the province; but when his army failed absolutely to capture Bari he resorted once again to diplomacy, and in the early summer of 968 dispatched a second embassy, more high-powered than the first and under a considerably more experienced ambassador: our old friend Liudprand of Cremona.

Liudprand's report to Otto of his second journey to the Bosphorus, the so-called *Relatio de legatione constantinopolitana*, is incontestably the most enjoyable – as well as the most malicious – account ever written of a diplomatic mission to the court of Byzantium; and if he has little good to say of it, this is hardly surprising when we consider the difficulties with which he had to contend. First of all there was the abrasive personality of the Emperor himself. On Liudprand's earlier mission he had got on well enough with Constantine Porphyrogenitus, for whose sophisticated and scholarly mind any Western intellectual probably had considerable appeal. To the rough and uncultivated Nicephorus, on the other hand, he was everything that was most abhorrent: a smooth-tongued trickster made still more dangerous by his fluent Greek, a man in whom no trust could possibly be reposed and a heretic to boot. On top of this he represented a German adventurer who called himself Emperor, whereas every right-thinking person knew that the Roman Empire was one and indivisible, with its seat at Constantinople: a pretender to his throne and a usurper of his title who had, moreover, recently broken faith with an entirely unjustified attack on imperial Byzantine territory.

Liudprand's lukewarm reception on his return to Constantinople was thus only to be expected; he was, none the less, deeply wounded in his

Charlemagne: reliquary bust, *c.*1350

(*Above*) The fight against iconoclasm: Patriarch Nicholas
triumphant over John the Grammarian. Optimistic marginalia
from the Chludov Psalter, ninth century

(*Opposite*) Emperors hunting: silk textile, Constantinople,
?ninth century

(*Above*) Christ, the Virgin, Archangels and Apostles:
cupola mosaic, late ninth century, in the Church of the Holy
Wisdom, Thessalonica

(*Opposite*) St Michael and warrior saints: gold, jewelled
and enamelled icon, eleventh or twelfth century, in the
Treasury of St Mark, Venice

(*Above*) The Emperor Constantine VII Porphyrogenitus
crowned by Christ: ivory relief, *c.*944

(*Opposite*) The Virgin and Child: ivory statuette, eleventh or
twelfth century. One of the very rare examples of
post-iconoclast sculpture in the round

The Western Emperor Otto II and his wife Theophano, holding
the future Otto III: detail of an ivory panel, c.980

The Western Emperor Otto III enthroned: from a Gospel Book
painted at Reichenau or at the imperial court, c.998

The Emperor Basil II: from a psalter, c.1017

The Empress Irene (797–802)   The Emperor Leo VI (886–912)

(*Left*) The Emperor Romanus I Lecapenus (920–44) crowned by Christ;
on the reverse (*right*) The Emperor Constantine VII Porphyrogenitus
(913–59) and his co-Emperor Christopher (921–31)

The Emperor Isaac I Comnenus (1057–9)

The Emperors Nicephorus II Phocas
(963–9) and Basil II (963–1025)

The Emperor Michael VII (1071–8)
and his wife, the Empress Maria Ducas

The Rock Churches, Monasteries and Hermitages of Cappadocia

(*Above*) General view of the Göreme Valley

(*Left*) Ninnazan Church

(*Opposite, top*) Frescoes in chapel (Kiliçlar Kusluk): eleventh or twelfth century

(*Opposite, bottom*) The Archangel Gabriel, fresco in the Church of Tokali: eleventh century

(*Above*) The capture of a city: ivory casket-lid, eleventh century

(*Opposite*) St Eudoxia: marble inlaid icon, tenth century

The Ascension, with a building thought to be a representation
of the Church of the Holy Apostles, Constantinople: from
The Sermons of James of Kokkinobaphos, twelfth century

amour propre. Nineteen years before, as emissary of a mere Italian marquis, he had been welcomed with at least a modicum of politeness; now, a plenipotentiary of the Emperor of the West, he described to his master the barely disguised hostility with which he had been received:

The palace in which we were confined, though large and open, neither kept out the cold nor afforded protection from the heat; furthermore we were placed under armed guards, who prevented my people from going out and anyone else from coming in. It was thus accessible only to us who were shut up inside it, and was so far from the residence of the Emperor that when we walked there – for we were not permitted to ride – we arrived exhausted. To make matters worse, the Greek wine was quite undrinkable, having been mixed with pitch, resin and plaster[1] . . .

On the fourth of June . . . we arrived at Constantinople and waited in heavy rain with our horses outside the Carian Gate until the eleventh hour [5 p.m.]. Only then did Nicephorus order us to be admitted on foot, for he did not deem us worthy to ride the horse with which Your Grace had provided us, and we were escorted to the aforesaid loathsome, waterless and draughty stone house. On the sixth of June, the Saturday before Pentecost, I was brought before the Emperor's brother Leo, marshal of the court and Logothete; and we wore ourselves out in a fierce argument over your title. He called you not 'Emperor', which is *basileus* in his tongue, but – most insultingly – *rex*, which is 'King' in ours. When I told him that the two words, different as they were, signified the same he accused me of having come not to make peace but to foment strife. Finally he rose from his seat in a fury and, greatly offended, received your letter not with his own hands but through an intermediary. Though he may appear humble he is in fact a man of considerable stature: if anyone were to lean upon him for support, he would pierce his hand.

On the following day Liudprand had his first audience of the Emperor – who came, he tells us, straight to the point. He regretted not having been able to give his guest a more courteous reception, but in view of Otto's conduct – invading Rome, and depriving Berengar and Adalbert of their lawful Kingdom, to say nothing of his attempted seizure of Apulia – he had had no choice. Liudprand – if his account is to be believed – gave as good as he got. His master, he pointed out, had not invaded Rome, but had liberated the city from a tyranny of libertines and harlots; if Nicephorus and his predecessors were truly the Roman Emperors they claimed to be, why had they allowed this state of affairs? Berengar and Adalbert had been Otto's vassals. They had rebelled

1 This must, I believe, be the first recorded reaction of a Western European to the taste of *retsina*.

against him; he had removed them. It was as simple as that. As to the Apulian problem, that could easily be solved: if Nicephorus would give the hand in marriage of one of Romanus's daughters to his master's son, the younger Otto – who since the previous Christmas had been reigning with his father as co-Emperor – among the several important concessions that he might expect in return was the total evacuation of all occupying forces in the region. To this proposal he received no immediate answer; the Emperor signified that the audience was at an end, and Liudprand withdrew. Six days later, however, he was summoned by Basil the *parakoimomenos* and informed that a princess born in the purple might indeed be available – but only if the Western Empire were prepared to cede in return Ravenna, Rome and all eastern Italy, together with Istria and the northern part of the Dalmatian coast.

Neither Nicephorus nor Basil can have imagined for a moment that Otto would consider such terms, which were virtually tantamount to the surrender of all Italy and a good deal more besides; nor would Liudprand have had the authority to accept them even if he had wished to do so. There was consequently no good reason for him to remain in Constantinople, and his alarm was all the greater when, instead of being sent on his way, he found himself confined even more closely to his detested lodgings, from which he was allowed to emerge only when the Emperor from time to time invited him to dinner. Even these occasions were less agreeable than they might have been, owing first to the perfectly disgusting food, 'washed down with oil after the manner of drunkards and moistened also with an exceedingly bad fish liquor', and second to the fact that Nicephorus saw them only as opportunities to bully him. How, he would be asked again and again, did his master have the temerity to occupy lands in south Italy which had been recognized for centuries as the property of Byzantium? How, come to that, did he dare to call himself an Emperor at all?

At the end of July, to the ambassador's intense relief, his host left for Syria to resume his campaign; now at last there seemed some chance that he might be permitted to return home. But obstacles continued to be put in his way, and on 15 August a further disaster struck: an embassy arrived from Pope John XIII with a letter which was intended to help the negotiations along but which unfortunately referred to Otto as 'the august Emperor of the Romans' while Nicephorus was simply addressed as 'Emperor of the Greeks'. Liudprand describes the reaction of the Byzantine court with morbid relish: had the new envoys been of higher rank, he quotes them as saying – had there been, for example, a bishop or a marquis among them – they would have been scourged and had their hair and beards plucked out before being sewn into sacks and hurled into the sea. Being a bishop himself, he confesses to having felt some concern for his own safety: he was of course the emissary of the Western Emperor and not that of the Pope, but it was common knowledge that John was Otto's nominee, and he was far from sure that in their present anti-Western mood the Byzantines would bother with such nice distinctions.

Subsequent events were to prove him right; for on 17 September he was once again summoned, this time by the Patrician Christopher, a eunuch, who began the conversation with one or two personal remarks:

The pallor of your face, the emaciation of your whole body, the unusual length of your hair and beard, all reveal the immense pain that is in your heart because the date of your return to your master has been delayed . . . The reason is this. The Pope of Rome – if indeed he may be called Pope when he has held communion and ministry with Alberic's son, the apostate, the adulterer, the sacrilegious – has sent a letter to our most sacred Emperor, worthy of himself and unworthy of Nicephorus, calling him 'Emperor of the Greeks' and not 'of the Romans'. Certainly this has been done at your master's instigation . . . That fatuous blockhead of a Pope does not know that the sacred Constantine transferred to this city the imperial sceptre, the senate and all the Roman knighthood, leaving in Rome nothing but vile slaves, fishermen, confectioners, poulterers, bastards, plebeians and underlings. Never would he have written this letter if your king had not suggested it.

Clearly this was no time for heroics. Liudprand tried to argue that since the days of Constantine the Byzantines had changed their language, customs and dress, and that the Pope had probably thought that by now the very name of Romans, like their sartorial style, might be distasteful to them; but he did not press the point. Finally he promised that all future letters would be addressed to 'Nicephorus, Constantine and Basil, the great and august Emperors of the Romans'.

Now at last he was allowed to leave – but there was still one further insult in store for him. During his stay in Constantinople he had managed to buy five lengths of sumptuous purple cloth for the adornment of his cathedral in Cremona. These he was now peremptorily ordered to surrender. In vain he argued that Nicephorus himself had given him authority to take with him as much as he liked, calling as his witnesses the interpreter and the Emperor's brother Leo, both of whom had been present during the conversation; Nicephorus, he was told, had never intended his permission to cover luxuries such as these. In vain he pleaded that when, as a mere deacon representing the Marquis Berengar, he had visited the city nearly twenty years before, he had returned with a far greater number of vestments even more sumptuous than those at present in question, and had suffered none of the prevarications and insults that now, as a bishop representing an Emperor, he was called upon to endure. Times, it was firmly pointed out to him, had changed. Constantine had been a mild man, who achieved his ends by peaceful methods, working from his Palace; Nicephorus was a man of more warlike temper, who preferred crushing his enemies to bribing them. And so at last on 2 October, after four months of misery, sickness and almost constant vilification,

. . . I boarded my vessel and left the city that was once so rich and prosperous and is now such a starveling, a city full of lies, tricks, perjury and greed, a city rapacious, avaricious and vainglorious. My guide was with me, and after forty-nine days of ass-riding, walking, horse-riding, fasting, thirsting, sighing, weeping and groaning, I arrived at Naupactus . . .

Even that was not the end of Liudprand's tribulations. He was delayed by contrary winds at Naupactus, deserted by his ship's crew at Patras, unkindly received by a eunuch bishop and half-starved on Leucas and subjected to three consecutive earthquakes on Corfu, where he subsequently fell among thieves. He was conscious, too, that it had all been in vain. The imperial marriage seemed no nearer, and relations between East and West were if anything even more strained than they had been before he set out: indeed, before he was back in Cremona war had erupted once again between the two Empires in south Italy. Poor Liudprand – he could not have known that his account of his journey would still be read a thousand years after his death, and found to be as fresh, funny and revealing as on the day it was written. A pity: it would have cheered him up.

It was only to be expected, in view of the character, manners and appearance of Nicephorus Phocas, that he should have been incapable of maintaining the affections of his subjects. At the beginning of his reign he had enjoyed the popularity due to a hero who had fought long and valiantly for the Empire, and whose exertions had been rewarded by the reconquest of Crete and the virtual annihilation of the Saracen threat in the East. It was on the wave of this popularity that he had risen to the throne – not, certainly, as his birthright but at least by invitation of the reigning Empress, who had almost immediately become his wife; and his worst enemies would have had to agree that, in the political vacuum prevailing after the death of Romanus, he – and she – were fully justified in acting as they did. But Nicephorus was, as we have seen, supremely ungifted in the arts of peace; and in the six years of his reign he rapidly antagonized almost all those with whom he came into contact, together with that all-important element in the Byzantine State, the people of Constantinople.

Political power – which he had never before enjoyed – went to his head, and as his arrogance increased so did his irritability and shortness of temper. His unforgivable treatment of the Bishop of Cremona – who was, after all, an imperial ambassador – and his reception of the Bulgarian envoys were, alas, all too characteristic of his diplomatic methods, and he seems to have dealt with the officials of his own court and government in a similarly high-handed manner. Their dislike – and, as time went on, their growing distrust – of their master was based, however, on more than personal grounds. There was also his lack of judgement in foreign affairs, illustrated by his invitation to Prince Svyatoslav of Kiev to destroy Bulgaria and his gratuitous insults to Otto the Great at a time when his army, already fully stretched on both the eastern and western frontiers, could not possibly undertake a third simultaneous campaign in south Italy. And there was the shameless favouritism which he showed to the only two sections of society that represented his own background: the army first, and then the Anatolian military aristocracy. The imperial garrison in the capital could, in his eyes, do no wrong, and took full advantage of the fact: at night the streets were loud with the carousings of drunken soldiery, to the point where honest citizens feared to leave their homes. Protests and petitions in plenty were addressed to the Emperor, only to be brushed roughly aside.

The fortunes of 'the powerful' underwent an even more dramatic change. Romanus Lecapenus and Constantine Porphyrogenitus had both done their utmost to limit their growing influence; Nicephorus Phocas deliberately legislated in their favour. Formerly, if a holding came up for sale, first refusal was given to the owners of the immediately adjoining land; henceforth it was to be available to the highest bidder – almost inevitably a landed nobleman bent on increasing his estates. Formerly again, the minimum value of property to be owned by a small-holder for him to qualify as an armed cavalryman was four pounds of gold; this figure Nicephorus now increased to twelve pounds, effectively disqualifying thousands of those landed peasant families who for centuries had constituted the backbone of the local militia and giving further power to the proprietorial class. Thus the rich threatened to become richer and the poor poorer; and the people of Constantinople, who took no interest in agrarian questions and very little in military ones – which they tended to leave so far as possible to their Asian compatriots – but who knew injustice when they saw it, did not attempt to conceal their displeasure.

Another, rather more surprising, source of opposition was the Church. The Emperor's extreme piety had initially predisposed the ecclesiastical authorities strongly in his favour; but they were soon made to understand that Nicephorus's views on their proper role in society differed radically from their own. His ascetic and puritanical sensibilities were profoundly shocked by the enormous wealth that the Church – and in particular the monasteries – had accumulated over the centuries. This problem was not new, but it had not been seriously tackled since the days of Constantine Copronymus 200 years before; and with vast tracts of superb agricultural land lying fallow under monastic mismanagement the time had clearly come for remedial action. Nicephorus's approach was characteristically uncompromising: all further such transfers were forbidden, whatever the circumstances. Would-be benefactors might if they wished restore churches or monasteries that were ruined or derelict, but that was all. Predictably, the edict called forth a storm of protest from monks and clergy alike, but worse was to follow: there now came a decree that no new bishop might be appointed without the Emperor's personal approval. This, in the opinion of the outraged priesthood, could mean but one thing: that he was determined on complete control of the Church, its hierarchy and its administration.

Finally, affecting rich and poor, cleric and layman, soldier and civilian alike, was the crippling taxation that Nicephorus had increased to unprecedented levels to finance his endless warfare, now raging simultaneously on three fronts: against the Saracens in the East, the Russians in Bulgaria and Otto in south Italy. Of these three wars, the first was already virtually won while the other two were unnecessary and should never have been allowed to begin; and the average taxpayer saw no reason why he should finance a grossly inflated army, which he in any case cordially detested and which – while its demands for further financial support grew ever more insistent – made no attempt to share its considerable spoils. To make matters worse, a series of disastrous harvests had sent the price of bread rocketing. On similar occasions in the past, previous Emperors had ordered a government subsidy; but Nicephorus showed no such concern, and was widely suspected of using the misfortunes of his subjects for the additional benefit of his beloved soldiers.

And so dissatisfaction grew; and, as it grew, so it was more and more openly expressed. The first signs of serious trouble came on Easter Sunday 967, when a quarrel between the Emperor's Armenian guard and some Thracian sailors developed into a full-scale riot; there were scores of casualties, several of them fatal. That afternoon, as the usual Easter games were about to start in the Hippodrome, a rumour spread to the effect that the Emperor intended to mark his displeasure by ordering random killings among the assembled crowd. Now Nicephorus, we can be perfectly sure, had no such intention; in an interval between the races, however, he gave the signal for certain companies of armed guards to descend into the arena. His reasons are uncertain. Leo the Deacon suggests that he may have decided on this show of military strength as a salutary warning, an indication that no repetition of the morning's disturbances would be tolerated; but mock battles were common enough in games of this kind, and he may have ordered one on this occasion simply as an amusement for the spectators. The immediate reaction, in any event, was panic: the thousands that thronged the stands had but a single thought in mind – escape. Only after many had been crushed to death in the sudden dash for the exits, and many more trampled underfoot, was it noticed that the soldiers in the arena had made no move against anyone and that the Emperor was still sitting, calm and utterly impassive, in his box. Gradually peace was restored; but the people persisted in blaming Nicephorus for the whole affair and he became more unpopular than ever.

Two months later, on Ascension Day, as the *basileus* was proceeding in state through the city after attending Matins in the Church of the Virgin at Pegae, abusive shouts were heard from the crowd – coming, it was said, from the families and friends of those who had perished during the Easter disturbances; and within moments he was surrounded by a hostile mob. As always when physical danger threatened, Nicephorus betrayed no trace of emotion, continuing his measured pace and looking neither to right nor left; but had it not been for his personal guard, who formed a dense phalanx around him and shielded him from blows and even missiles, he would have been lucky to return to the Palace alive.

The next morning two women, a mother and her daughter, who had been arrested for hurling bricks at the Emperor from a nearby rooftop, were burnt alive in the Amaratas district; and Nicephorus gave orders for the fortification of the Great Palace, sealing it off completely from the surrounding streets. Within this huge enclave, down towards the little harbour of the Bucoleon, he built what seems to have been a private citadel, for the use of himself, his family and his closest associates. By now it was clear to all of them that – perhaps for the first time in his life – the Emperor was afraid. On the battlefield he had not known the meaning of the word; but Constantinople, where the very air was loud with rumours of plots and portents, had become sinister and threatening. His aspect grew still more sombre, his religious observances ever more morbid and morose. He no longer slept in a bed, but on a panther-skin laid on the floor in the corner of the imperial bedchamber. The death of his father, old Bardas Phocas, who had finally expired at the age of ninety, had utterly prostrated him; and he seemed never to have fully recovered from the shock that he had suffered one day in the late summer when he had been accosted in the middle of a religious procession by an unknown monk of repellent aspect, who had thrust a note into his hand before disappearing into the crowd. It read: 'O *basileus*, although I am but a worm upon the earth, it has been revealed to me that in the third month after this coming September you shall die.'

What ultimately brought matters to a head was the fate of Bulgaria. By the summer of 968 King Peter was desperate. Partially incapacitated by a stroke, he sent first an ambassador[1] to Constantinople to appeal for military aid against Svyatoslav, and shortly afterwards two little Bulgar princesses, intended as brides for the young Emperors Constantine and Basil. But it was already too late. On 30 January 969 he died after forty-two years on the throne, leaving as his successor his elder son Boris, a callow youth unremarkable except for an enormous red beard. Six months or so later Peter was followed to the grave by Princess Olga of Kiev, the only restraining influence on her headstrong son Svyatoslav, who in the early autumn swept down, at the head of a huge and heterogeneous army of Russians, Magyars and Pechenegs, into the

---

1 This curious figure, 'unwashed, with his hair cropped short in the Hungarian fashion and girt about with brass chains', had been the unwitting cause of furious indignation on the part of Liudprand of Cremona when given precedence over him at the Emperor's table.

Bulgarian heartland. Preslav fell after scarcely a struggle, and young Boris with his entire family was taken off into captivity. Philippopolis by contrast put up a heroic resistance; but it too had to capitulate in the end, and paid dearly for its heroism when Svyatoslav impaled 20,000 of its citizens. By the onset of winter the Russians were ranged along the whole Thracian border, and few doubted that at the first signs of spring they would launch their attack upon the Empire.[1]

At this point there returns to the forefront of the stage the lovely but ever-fateful figure of the Empress Theophano. Unlikely as it is that she – or anyone else for that matter – could have felt any physical attraction for Nicephorus, there can be little doubt that at some moment during the previous six years she had fallen passionately in love with his erstwhile colleague, the outstandingly good-looking former Domestic of the Schools John Tzimisces. The degree to which the tiny but irresistible Armenian returned her love is perhaps somewhat less certain: there were plenty of other emotions – ambition, jealousy, resentment towards the Emperor, who had recently deprived him of his military command and exiled him to his Anatolian estates – that might have impelled him to act as he did. But Theophano at twenty-eight was still as beautiful as ever: whether or not his heart was engaged, her embraces cannot have been altogether distasteful.

Her first task was to convince her husband that he had been unjust towards his former friend – to whom, after all, he probably owed his crown – and to persuade him to rescind the sentence of banishment. This was not as difficult as might have been imagined: she could nearly always get what she wanted from him if she put her mind to it (another indication, perhaps, of the genuineness of his love for her) and he readily agreed to recall Tzimisces, on the condition that he remained in his family's house at Chalcedon on the Asiatic side of the Bosphorus, coming over to Constantinople only when given specific permission to do so. Obviously, from the lovers' point of view, the situation was still rather less than ideal; but dispositions were made, and before long the little general was slipping nightly across the strait under cover of darkness to a hidden corner of the Palace where the Empress was waiting – and where, among other less reprehensible occupations, the two of them cold-bloodedly planned her husband's murder.

*

1 Older historians tend to date the fall of Philippopolis to the early spring of 970; I prefer to follow Sir Steven Runciman's chronology (*First Bulgarian Empire*, pp. 205–6).

Accomplices were not hard to find. By now there were few in his immediate entourage who had a good word to say for Nicephorus Phocas, and those party to the plot included Basil the *parakoimomenos* and several other high court officials; also implicated was Michael Bourtzes, hero of Antioch, whose conquest of the city had been furiously resented by the jealous Nicephorus and who had shortly afterwards been relieved of his command.

The date of the assassination was fixed for 10 December. On the afternoon of that day the leading conspirators, disguised as women with their swords concealed beneath their robes, entered the *gynaeceum* of the Palace ostensibly on a visit to the Empress, who distributed them among various small rooms in which they could wait unobserved until the time came for action. As evening drew on, Nicephorus received another message of warning, this time from one of his chaplains, telling him that the danger was now imminent and that his intended murderers were already hidden in the Palace. He immediately dispatched Michael, his chief eunuch and major-domo, to investigate; but Michael too had been suborned by the Empress and returned to report that he had found nothing untoward.

Darkness came early during those December days, and as night fell there arose a dreadful blizzard. The conspirators remained in hiding in the darkened Palace. They dared not act without John Tzimisces – but would he be able, in such weather, to make his secret journey across the Bosphorus? Meanwhile it was for Theophano to allay her husband's suspicions and to make sure that there would be no problems of access when the moment came. She had decided, she told him, to pay a quick visit to the two little Bulgar princesses, to see if they were comfortable in their new accommodation. She would not be gone for very long, so he must be careful not to shut her out: they could lock up properly after her return. Nicephorus raised no objection. For some time he continued to read one of the devotional works of which his library was full; then, as usual, he settled down to his prayers. At last, with his wife still absent, he wrapped himself up in his uncle's hair-shirt and stretched himself out on the floor to sleep.

Outside, the storm continued. It was bitterly cold, and snowing hard; the wind had whipped up the waves on the Bosphorus and John Tzimisces, making his way from Chalcedon with three trusted friends in an unlit boat, had had a long and perilous crossing. It was not until eleven o'clock that his accomplices heard the low whistle by which he had promised to announce his arrival. Silently a rope was let down from a window of the Empress's apartments, and one by one the conspirators were drawn up into the building. Tzimisces was the last to enter. Once inside, they lost no time. A eunuch was waiting to lead them straight to the Emperor's bedchamber. There was a moment of alarm when the bed was found to be empty, but the eunuch quietly pointed to the far corner of the room where their victim lay on his panther-skin, fast asleep.

The last minutes of Nicephorus's life, dwelt upon with relish by the chroniclers, do not make pleasant reading. Awoken by the noise, he tried to rise; at the same time the *taxiarch* Leo Balantes struck him a violent blow with his sword. It was aimed at the neck, but the Emperor's sudden movement deflected it; he received its full force diagonally across the face. Streaming with blood, he called loudly upon the Holy Virgin Theotokos for aid while he was dragged to the foot of the great bed, on which John Tzimisces was sitting as if in judgement. There they tried to make him kneel, but he fell to the ground and lay motionless as his former companion-in-arms cursed him for his injustice and ingratitude, kicking him savagely and tearing out handfuls of his hair and beard. After Tzimisces had finished it was the turn of the others. Each had his own private score to settle. One smashed his jaw; another knocked out his front teeth with the end of his scabbard. At last – we do not know by whom – he was run through with a long, curved sword. It was the *coup de grâce*. Nicephorus Phocas was dead.

The news spread fast. Minutes after the deed was done Tzimisces's men were out in the snow-covered streets of the city, shouting 'John, Augustus and Emperor of the Romans!' at every corner; they were soon joined by others, led by the Chamberlain Basil himself, on whose instructions they shouted also for the two child-Emperors Basil and Constantine but were otherwise no less vocal in their support of the new regime. Meanwhile in the Palace complex itself – which never slept – the duty guard of Varangian Vikings, axes in hand, hurried down to the Bucoleon. There by the light of flaming torches they saw the head of Nicephorus, struck from his body and held triumphantly aloft at a window by one of the assassins. At once they were still. Had he been alive, they would have defended their Emperor to the last breath; dead, there was no point in avenging him. They had a new master, and that was that.

As to the identity of that new master, there too they were faced with a *fait accompli*. As soon as the deed was done, John Tzimisces had made his way to the *Chrysotriclinium*, the great golden throne room of the Palace, pulled on the purple buskins and decked himself in as much of the imperial regalia as he could find; already he was seated on the throne, Theophano and her two sons at his side, while his fellow-conspirators and a growing crowd of court officials hailed him as Emperor of the Romans.

Throughout the next day the city lay silent and apparently deserted. Basil – who was henceforth to be ever at John's right hand, his most experienced and trusted lieutenant – had proclaimed a curfew. The citizens were so far as was possible to stay at home; those obliged to venture abroad were forbidden to congregate or to make the slightest disturbance, on pain of instant execution. By now the wind had dropped. The storm had been succeeded by an eerie stillness, the fog hung thick over the Marmara – and the body of Nicephorus lay below the window from which it had been flung, an obscene bundle on the bloodstained snow. After such a death there could be no question of a state funeral. Instead, when night had fallen, it was picked up, thrown on to a makeshift wooden stretcher, covered with a rough blanket and carried quietly through the empty streets to the Church of the Holy Apostles, where it was laid in one of the marble sarcophagi ordered by Constantine the Great six centuries before. It was an honourable resting-place; but Nicephorus Phocas, the White Death of the Saracens, hero of Syria and Crete, saintly and hideous, magnificent and insufferable, had deserved a better end.

13
John Tzimisces
[969–76]

If you reject my proposals you will have no choice, you and your subjects, but to leave Europe for ever, where you have scarcely any territory left to call your own and where you have no right to dwell. Retire then to Asia, and leave Constantinople to us. Only then can you hope to achieve a genuine peace between the Russian nation and yourselves.

> Prince Svyatoslav of Kiev, to
> the Emperor John Tzimisces, 970

For the second time in ten years the throne of Byzantium had been snatched by a member of the Anatolian aristocracy. On both occasions the usurping Emperor had been a dramatically successful general; on both occasions he had succeeded through the machinations of the Empress Theophano, of whose two young sons he had proclaimed himself protector. Between Nicephorus Phocas and John Tzimisces there were, however, two crucial differences: one related to their respective positions, the other to the two men themselves.

Though neither had any legitimate claim to the imperial diadem, Nicephorus could at least argue that he had accepted it by invitation of the Empress, and had further regularized the situation by his subsequent marriage. John, on the other hand, had acquired it by violence and bloodshed; and it was his further misfortune that the Patriarchate was still in the hands of Polyeuctus, now old and beginning to fail in strength but as stern and inexorable as ever. Even he could not reject the new claimant out of hand, but he could – and did – impose conditions which John was compelled, however reluctantly, to accept; and the first of these concerned Theophano. The lovers had clearly hoped that by the murder of Nicephorus they were removing an obstacle not only to the throne but also to their own union; this, the Patriarch firmly declared, could on no account be contemplated. On the contrary, there could be no question of John Tzimisces being crowned Emperor until the Empress were put away, never again to show her face in Constantinople.

Perhaps, as has already been suggested, John had never really loved Theophano, and had seen her merely as the most direct instrument of his own ambitions; in any event he did not hesitate in making his choice. The Empress, humiliated and heartbroken, was unceremoniously packed off to that favourite repository of imperial waste, the island of Proti in the Marmara.[1] But Polyeuctus was not yet satisfied. He next demanded that John should do public penance and denounce all those who had been his accomplices in the crime. Finally he must undertake to abrogate all his predecessor's decrees against the Church. These conditions were accepted without hesitation; and on Christmas Day 969, just two weeks after the murder, the new Emperor proceeded to his coronation. It remained only for him to deal with his victim's family, notably Leo Phocas – the former *curopalates* – who, having failed to stage a counter-*coup* of his own, had lost his nerve and fled with his eldest son – called, like his uncle, Nicephorus – to St Sophia. Both were deprived of their dignities, offices and possessions and sent into exile on Lesbos. Leo's second son Bardas was consigned to the infinitely less congenial Amaseia in Pontus, a rainswept region near the shores of the Black Sea; only his youngest, a Patrician and yet another brilliant general, was left at liberty – perhaps because of his magnificent military record against the Saracens, but more probably because he was a eunuch and consequently less of a long-term danger.

Up to this point the story of John Tzimisces can hardly be described as edifying. When we come, however, to compare his character with that of Nicephorus, we find him emerging from the writings of his contemporaries with very much more credit than might have been imagined: indeed, it seems almost impossible to reconcile the brutal and cynical murderer of the last few pages with the *chevalier sans peur et sans reproche* depicted by the chroniclers. They dwell at length not only on his

---

1 She was, even then, to make one last appearance in the capital. Some months later she escaped from her confinement and sought asylum in St Sophia – whence, however, she was forcibly removed by order of the *parakoimomenos* Basil, who condemned her to a more distant exile in far-off Armenia. The only concession that he was prepared to grant her was that she should be permitted to see the Emperor for the last time. John, perhaps surprisingly, agreed to the interview, at which he was subjected to a torrent of invective. Theophano then turned her attention to Basil, who had insisted on being present – a decision he must have regretted when she attacked him physically, landing several telling blows before being finally pulled off by his attendants.

valour in the field but on his kindness and generosity, his integrity and intelligence, his dash and his magnificent panache. They speak of his devastating good looks – darkish-blond hair, red beard, a clear and direct gaze from a pair of brilliant blue eyes – and, despite his small size, of his extraordinary agility and strength. None of his men, it was said, could match his seat on a horse, his accuracy with an arrow, his range with a spear or javelin. He possessed, too, an easy-going charm that won all hearts. Like Nicephorus before him, he was a widower; unlike Nicephorus, however, he had taken no vow of chastity, and his way with women was irresistible. Even his vices were attractive: Leo the Deacon, who knew him well, mentions his love of wine, pleasure and all the good things of life. He presented, in short, an astonishing contrast to his ugly, uncouth and puritanical predecessor, against whose sombre asceticism his own qualities – and above all his sheer, uncomplicated *joie de vivre* – stood out in even greater relief. One chronicler, Constantine Manasses, goes so far as to liken him to 'a new paradise, from which flowed the four rivers of justice, wisdom, prudence and courage . . . Had he not stained his hands with the murder of Nicephorus, he would have shone in the firmament like some incomparable star.'

Of all his undoubted virtues, that which most endeared him to his subjects was his quick and instinctive generosity. The Patriarch had, it is true, insisted that he should make a distribution of his own personal wealth before taking possession of the imperial treasury; but what we know of John Tzimisces suggests that he might easily have done so anyway. The larger part of his fortune he distributed among those sections of the population who had suffered the most from the recent succession of disastrous harvests – above all the farming communities of Thrace, where the resulting famine had been particularly severe. (Here again the contrast with the attitude of Nicephorus could hardly have passed unnoticed.) Another major beneficiary was his favourite charitable institution, the *Nosocomium* or leper hospital across the Bosphorus at Chrysopolis. Throughout his life, writes Leo the Deacon, he was to visit it regularly, giving sympathy and encouragement to the patients and occasionally even bathing their sores with his own hands. No wonder that, within a matter of months, the perpetrator of one of the foulest murders that even the Byzantine Empire had ever seen became one of its best-loved rulers.

It was fortunate that he did, for Prince Svyatoslav of Kiev was already on the march. Bulgaria was his, but he had no intention of stopping at Bulgaria; for him, the only really worthwhile prize was Byzantium. True, the two previous Russian attacks on the city had failed; but the first, in 861, had been no more than a raid, while the second – launched by his own father, Igor, less than thirty years before – had also been an exclusively naval operation: Constantinople, Svyatoslav was quite ready to believe, was impregnable from the sea. From the landward side, however, it would be a different story. His army was immense; morale, after the Bulgarian victories and the subsequent pillage, had never been higher. What was to prevent him from advancing across the flat, featureless plain that extended almost as far as the Bosphorus, appropriating for himself the fabled wealth of the Emperors and finally seizing their throne – casting out the murderous usurper (who had no more right to it than he did himself) to the distant Anatolian wastes from which he had come?

John did his best to negotiate, promising to send Svyatoslav the unpaid balance of the sum offered him by Nicephorus to attack Bulgaria if he would then agree to leave imperial territory; but the Prince's reply made it clear that nothing was to be achieved by diplomacy. War, it now seemed, was inevitable. In Constantinople frantic steps were taken to repair the walls where necessary; and tension, inevitably, began to rise. The citizens had of course faced similar dangers in the past; but most of the recent threats had been from the Bulgars, whom they understood and whose numbers, though large, were at least finite. They were now confronted by a vast nation whose frontiers extended from the Balkans to the Baltic, a nation that comprised whole races of whose names they had scarcely heard – all capable, it was said, of hideous savagery.

The Byzantine army, however, was ready for them. Thanks in large measure to Nicephorus Phocas, it had been developed into a first-class war machine, boasting at least half a dozen generals of a quality unparalleled, perhaps, since the days of Belisarius, the Emperor himself among them. On this occasion – and, we can be sure, to his genuine regret – John knew that he must stay in the capital: his position there was not yet sufficiently secure to allow him the luxury of a military campaign. But he had every confidence in his commanders; and events were to show that that confidence was not misplaced. Of the two whom he selected to lead the advance guard, the first was the *magister* Bardas Sclerus, brother of John's wife Maria – 'loveliest and purest of them all', writes Leo the Deacon – who had died, childless, some years before. He had fought at the Emperor's side in Syria and was probably his brother-in-law's closest friend. The second was the eunuch Peter Phocas, Patrician and *stratopedarch*, a hero like Sclerus of the Saracen wars and also of a recent skirmish with the Magyars in Thrace, in the course of which he had confronted a tribal leader – a giant wearing a thick coat of mail – in single combat, and had run him through with such force that the point of his lance had appeared between the Hungarian's shoulder-blades. Nephew of the murdered Nicephorus, he was as we have seen the only one of his uncle's immediate family to have escaped sentence of exile; if he bore Tzimisces any resentment, he took pains not to show it.

Both generals had strict orders from their master not to engage in battle if it could be avoided. The Emperor seems to have thought that the sight of the imperial army *en masse* in the field might itself be enough to persuade Svyatoslav to retreat; his purpose in sending it out at this time – it was still early spring – was simply to impress the undisciplined Russians with its organization and strength, and to protect the Thracian countryside from their unwelcome attentions. But he had underestimated the Prince of Kiev: Svyatoslav intended to fight. To help him he had allied himself with both the Magyars and the Pechenegs, and had even won considerable support among the boyars of Bulgaria, whom he had wooed with promises of a restoration of all their former privileges and even a return to the old paganism – for which many of them still secretly yearned. Numbers are impossible to estimate with any accuracy. Early historians always try to exaggerate the strength of the enemy and the numerical weakness of their own side: thus Zonaras and John Scylitzes put the Russians at 300,000 and 308,000 respectively, while Nestor's chronicle suggests only about one-tenth of these obviously ludicrous figures. Perhaps 50,000 might not be too wide of the mark. Against this, we are told – probably truthfully – that the Byzantines numbered just 12,000; however, all were elite troops – superbly equipped, meticulously trained and hardened in many a battle under the Syrian sun.

Bardas Sclerus, who was in overall command, first advanced as far as Adrianople; then, as the enemy approached, he slowly retreated, deliberately suggesting that he was afraid to give battle, lulling them into a sense of security that soon led to overconfidence. Meanwhile, well behind his own line, he made his dispositions. On the appointed day he sent out as a decoy a detachment of cavalry under the Patrician John Alakas, with orders to employ a similar technique: first lightly engaging the enemy and then quickly retiring – daring, as it were, the Russians to pursue them. Once sure of this pursuit they should quicken their pace, occasionally turning to confront their pursuers before once more taking flight, always keeping a little way in front but never too far, until they had led their unwilling victims into the trap that had been prepared for them.

The trick worked perfectly. Svyatoslav's army marched in three main divisions: the first was made up of Russians and Bulgars, the second of Hungarians and other Magyar tribes, the third of Pechenegs. It was these last whom Alakas engaged and they pursued him eagerly, confident of being able quickly to catch up with him and his men, looking forward to killing them and robbing them of horses, armour, weapons and all that they possessed. Suddenly, as they entered a shallow valley, the Byzantine cavalry scattered; their pursuers did likewise; and Sclerus struck. Surrounded and hopelessly outnumbered, the Pechenegs perished almost to a man.

And this was only a preliminary; it was followed a few days later by a decisive engagement near the city of Arcadiopolis, about a third of the way from Adrianople to the capital. This was a pitched battle – the first ever fought on open ground between Byzantines and Russians – and an extremely bloody one. We can decide for ourselves whether or not to believe the incidents described by Leo the Deacon and Scylitzes: that of young Constantine Sclerus who, seeing his elder brother and chief locked in combat with a gigantic Russian, hurried to his aid and struck a tremendous blow at his assailant, only to have it deflected on to the latter's horse, which was instantly decapitated and deposited its rider on the ground for Constantine to strangle at leisure; or of Bardas himself, splitting a huge Viking chieftain down the middle with his sword in such a way that the two halves fell separately, one on each side of the horse. What we cannot doubt is that it was all a far cry from the warfare of former centuries – a dismal saga, all too often, of indiscipline, cowardice and betrayal. Here, once again, is a heroic – almost Homeric – age: of fearless captains in shining armour, always at the head of their men or where the fighting is thickest, never hesitating to engage an enemy champion in single combat, ever resolved to win victory for their Emperor or die in the attempt. For them, Arcadiopolis was a triumph; for the Russians, a massacre. It was a shamed and shattered army that Svyatoslav led back to Bulgaria – and a full year before he showed his face again.

*

While his brother-in-law had been fighting in Thrace, John Tzimisces had been consolidating his position in the capital, simultaneously bringing back the bulk of the army from the East, giving it new arms and equipment, swelling it with new recruits. The war, he knew, was not yet over. The Prince of Kiev had been taught a sharp lesson; but he remained very much alive and there was no reason to think that he had renounced his ambitions. Besides, he would want his revenge.

By the early spring of 971 John was ready for him. The army was in first-class condition, and this time he would lead it himself. If Svyatoslav made no move, he would invade Bulgaria and flush him out. Then, just before he was due to leave, there arrived news from the East. Bardas Phocas, nephew of Nicephorus, had escaped from his place of exile in Pontus and had returned to Caesarea (now Kayseri), his family's Cappadocian power base, where a large gathering of citizens and fellow-nobles had proclaimed him *basileus*. This was quite bad enough; but soon afterwards came another report, informing him that Leo Phocas and his son, away in exile on Lesbos, had somehow contrived through a local bishop to spread the news of the rebellion through Thrace, announcing their own imminent arrival and calling upon the people to rise up against the new usurper.

The Emperor acted with his usual speed. The bishop, arrested and interrogated, soon revealed all he knew; on the basis of his evidence Leo and his son were given a summary trial and condemned to death. Almost at once, however, John had second thoughts – in a way that the chroniclers suggest was typical of him and that makes his earlier brutality towards his predecessor still harder to understand. He commuted the death sentence to one of blinding, with perpetual exile; and then, stretching his compassion further still, sent secret instructions to Lesbos that the red-hot iron should at the last moment be withdrawn, leaving the two men their sight. It was, after all, not they but the pretender himself who presented the real danger. To him John sent envoys with the promise that his life and property would be spared if he would only renounce his claim; but Bardas Phocas replied much as Svyatoslav had done the year before and began slowly to advance, at the head of several thousand men, towards the capital.

By now the Emperor must have bitterly regretted his withdrawal of the army from Anatolia. As a result, he had no effective force capable of dealing with the situation on the spot – and of those soldiers who remained a considerable number had joined the rebels. There was only one course open to him: to send his best general, with his best men, from Thrace. A few days later Bardas Sclerus too was on the march. It was undeniably a risk, leaving as it did the way clear for Svyatoslav should he choose to invade before Sclerus could return; but the eastern threat was more immediate than the western and the chance had to be taken.

Even now John hoped to spare the Empire a civil war. He enjoined his brother-in-law to make every effort to avoid bloodshed, and to offer all those prepared to abandon Phocas not only a guarantee that they would go unpunished but even honours and financial rewards. Sclerus, for his part, was only too happy to obey. He was an old friend and companion-in-arms of Phocas – his younger brother Constantine, hero of Arcadiopolis, had married the pretender's sister – and the whole affair can have been little to his taste. Thus, when he reached what was then known as the Lake of the Forty Martyrs[1] and his scouts reported a sighting of Phocas's camp just ahead, he made no attempt to attack; instead, he sent a number of secret agents, disguised as wandering beggars, to suborn the rebels. Perhaps the speed and size of the imperial army had weakened their morale, perhaps the promises of generous rewards for desertion proved irresistible; in any event the agents were quite extraordinarily successful. Every night more and more of Phocas's adherents dropped away, slipping out of his camp and across to that of Sclerus, where they were welcomed with open arms. The pretender soon found his army reduced to a few hundred men – and not an arrow had yet been loosed in anger. Desperate and humiliated, and accompanied only by a small company of cavalry that had remained loyal, he himself fled under cover of darkness and took refuge with his family in the fortress of Tyropoion, just outside the modern town of Ilgin. But it was no use: Sclerus had followed him, and immediately put the little castle under siege. He held out as long as he could, then – after receiving confirmation that all their lives would be spared – marched out with his wife and children and surrendered.

John Tzimisces was as good as his word. He ordered Bardas Phocas to be tonsured, and then to be shipped off with his family to exile on Chios, one of the most delightful of all the Aegean islands. Few rulers anywhere would have dealt so leniently with a rebel pretender to their

1 Now Akşehir Gölü, some ten miles north of the present town of Akşehir.

throne; few such claimants could have congratulated themselves on so moderate a punishment.[1]

After the revolt of Bardas Phocas, John Tzimisces was to encounter no further threats to his throne; the fact remained, however, that he could claim no legitimate right to it unless he could make himself at least in some degree part of the imperial family. Marriage with his exquisite mistress Theophano would, leaving aside its obvious advantages to himself, have strengthened his position immeasurably; but that he now knew to be out of the question. Fortunately there were other possibilities, in the shape of the five sisters of Romanus II whom Theophano had packed off to convents; and it was to one of these, Theodora, that the Emperor announced his betrothal in the autumn of 971. Twelve years of monastic seclusion had done little to improve her appearance: 'she was,' writes Leo the Deacon – for whom all princesses (let alone Empresses) normally represent the summit of physical perfection – 'neither beautiful nor elegant.' But John was not marrying Theodora for her looks; he had, after all, the choice of the loveliest women in the Empire for his bed. He was marrying her because she was the great-granddaughter, granddaughter, daughter and sister of Emperors, and because by doing so he became, through her, a member of the most glorious dynasty of the Macedonians.

The wedding took place some time in November. Old Polyeuctus had died at last, only five weeks after the coronation – if John had delayed his *coup* another couple of months, his future life (and Theophano's) might have been very different – and the ceremony was performed by his successor, an unworldly ascetic of the Emperor's own choosing named Basil the Scamandrian.[2] The celebrations continued until well after Christmas – by which time, however, there was another imperial marriage in the air: a marriage of far greater long-term significance than the first, intended as it was to put an end to the five-year quarrel with Otto the Saxon and to forge an indissoluble link between the Eastern and the Western Empires. The idea of such a union had, as we know, been first considered in the reign of Constantine Porphyrogenitus; it had been resurrected by Otto in 967, and had been the chief reason for the

1 Hieronimo Giustiniani, in his *Storia di Scio* of 1586, records that in his time there were still descendants of the Phocas family living as peasants in the village of Volissos.

2 Doubtless after his birthplace, or the monastery that he had founded, on the river Scamander – now the Küçük Menderes – that flows through the plain of Troy.

ill-fated mission of Liudprand of Cremona in the following year. To the narrow and suspicious mind of Nicephorus Phocas it had been predictably repugnant; John Tzimisces on the other hand supported it for all he was worth, and it was at his invitation that an embassy under the Archbishop of Cologne arrived in Constantinople towards the end of December to collect the bride-to-be and to carry her back to her imperial bridegroom.[1]

This bridegroom was to be the seventeen-year-old Otto, son and heir of the Emperor of the West. As to the identity of the bride, historians are somewhat less clear. Her name was Theophano, and until quite recently it was generally supposed that she was the daughter of Romanus II and thus the sister of the two boy Emperors. Modern authorities, however, are now generally agreed that she was a blood relation of John Tzimisces – probably his niece – and thus not of the Macedonian dynasty at all. There seems to have been some consternation when the poor girl arrived in Rome and it was discovered that she was not the *porphyrogenita* that had been expected; Otto the Great at first considered sending her straight back to Constantinople. Fortunately, wiser counsels prevailed. It was pointed out that John was, since his marriage, a member of the imperial family and that so, therefore, was his niece;[2] she was finally accepted by the Ottonian court, and she and young Otto were married by Pope John XIII in St Peter's on 14 April 972.

Thus it came about that Theophano, whoever she may have been, was removed from her home and family by a party of elderly ecclesiastics to be carried off to an unknown land and a husband she had never seen, of whose character she knew nothing and of whose language she understood not a single word. In the long run, admittedly, she was lucky: the marriage proved a surprisingly happy one, she was treated with kindness and consideration and allowed to maintain all her Byzantine customs and ways of life – to the point where her son, the future Otto III, was to grow up far more of a Greek than a Saxon. And she could later congratulate herself on the transformation of relations between the two Empires, brought about not just by her marriage but also by her own intelligence and hard work. None the less, for a girl of just sixteen, those

1 There is some tenuous evidence to suggest that this embassy may have included old Liudprand, on his third diplomatic mission to the Byzantine court.

2 Could it be that John deliberately arranged his marriage with this particular issue in mind? It seems not unlikely. If, on the other hand, the old theory were correct and the princess was indeed Romanus's daughter, she would anyway have become John's niece by virtue of his marriage to her aunt. Of such riddles is history made.

first four months of 972 must have been little short of a nightmare; and it is only right that we should spare a thought for her misery, fear and loneliness before we return to her uncle, John Tzimisces – who was having the time of his life.

In the week before Holy Week, 972, John had left Constantinople for Thrace. He was in buoyant mood. He had, it is true, lost a whole year: the revolt of Bardas Phocas had taken up much of 971, and by the time it had been settled the season had been too far advanced for any major campaign to be practicable; but the remaining months had been spent profitably enough on diplomatic activity (which included an important treaty with Venice), the preparation of his Black Sea fleet and the constant training and exercising of his troops – an occupation of which he never tired. The danger that he had most feared had not material-ized: marauding bands of Russians might have taken advantage of the Byzantine withdrawal to roam the countryside, raiding and raping to their hearts' content, but the Prince of Kiev had not been able to launch his major attack and was still skulking in Bulgaria. The time had now come to deal with him once and for all.

John's last act before his departure from the Palace had been to pray in the little chapel by the great gate of the Chalkē. It had been begun by Romanus Lecapenus as a private oratory for the Emperor, but John had enlarged it and enriched it and chosen it for his eventual burial-place: an immense tomb, inlaid with gold and enamels, was already in the course of construction. Thence, at the head of a long and solemn procession and carrying in his right hand a tall cross in which was set a gold-framed fragment of the True Cross, he continued first to St Sophia, where the God of Battles was again besought to grant him victory, and then on to Blachernae where, after further prayers in the Church of the Virgin, he reviewed the fleet assembled in the Golden Horn before giving it the signal to sail to its appointed destination – the mouth of the Danube, where it would prevent any attempt by Svyatoslav to escape by sea. As soon as the first ships were under way he wheeled his horse and headed westward, his troops behind him.

At Adrianople he picked up the rump of the army that Bardas Sclerus had left in Thrace the year before. Under the temporary command of the *magister* John Curcuas – who, with his deep mistrust of any strenuous activity and his fondness for the bottle, made a deplorable contrast to his illustrious namesake – the men had become not a little demoralized; but the sight of the Emperor in his gilded armour cap-à-pie, and his generals almost as magnificent on their splendidly caparisoned horses, put new life into them as they headed northward into the Bulgarian heartland. To John's relief, the defiles that twisted through the Balkan range – scene of earlier catastrophes to Constantine Copronymus in 757 and Nicephorus I in 811, to mention but two – were found to be unguarded. The first part of his plan had worked perfectly: the Prince of Kiev, expecting him to celebrate Easter as usual in Constantinople and to set off on campaign in mid-April at the earliest, had as yet made no defensive arrangements. On the Wednesday of Holy Week John emerged from the mountains above the old Bulgarian capital of Preslav and found himself looking down on the Russian camp. Surprise was everything: he attacked at once.

The battle, fought by the banks of the river now known as the Goljama Kamciya, was long, furious and for a long time indecisive. It was only after John had loosed his own personal regiment, the 'Immortals' – which he had raised and trained himself and had hitherto kept in reserve – in a murderous charge against their left flank that the Russians suddenly lost their nerve and broke up in disorder, fleeing for their lives towards Preslav with the imperial cavalry in hot pursuit. Few of them reached the city alive. The massacre continued till nightfall, and dawn broke next day on a field strewn thick with the bodies of the dead. By then the Emperor was at the gates of Preslav, calling upon the garrison to surrender. They refused, and immediately the siege began, the Byzantine catapults and ballistas hurling heavy rocks or flaming bolts of Greek fire over the walls. Meanwhile the ladders were hauled into position for the final assault.

The first into the city was a young man, 'still beardless', named Theodosius Mesonyctes. He was quickly followed by a hundred others, and Preslav was soon overrun. At its centre, however, was a fortified *enceinte*, part palace, part citadel, part treasury; hither the surviving Russians retreated to make their last stand. After more heavy fighting, during which his army failed absolutely to penetrate these inner defences, John ordered the walls to be put to the torch. The houses within were all of timber and went up like matchwood. The Russians were burnt alive, or struck down as they fled. Among those who delivered themselves up to the conquerors was the deposed Tsar Boris – he of the red beard – who for the past two years had been held by Svyatoslav as his prisoner. The Emperor received him with the utmost courtesy; his

mission, he told Boris, was not to conquer Bulgaria but to set it free –
an assurance which, in view of his later actions, he had better not have
made.

Easter was celebrated amid the ruins of Preslav, while John considered
the problem of Svyatoslav himself. The Prince, he now learned, was
away at Dristra – to the Greeks Dorystolon, the modern Silistra –
Bulgaria's chief port on the Danube, struggling, presumably to keep
open his lines of communication in spite of the Byzantine fleet. An
embassy was dispatched at once, informing him of the fate of Preslav
and calling upon him in the Emperor's name to surrender. Then,
pausing only to rebuild the shattered defences of the city – which he
renamed, after himself, Ioannopolis – John set off once more for the
north. It was a long and arduous march, but at last on St George's Day
he drew up his army before Dristra. The pattern was very much the
same as at Preslav, with a desperate battle outside the walls followed by
an attack on the city itself. On this occasion, however, he met tougher
opposition. Dristra successfully resisted every attempt to take it by
storm and both sides settled down to a siege, with a squadron from the
Byzantine fleet completing the blockade from the river.

The siege continued for three months, until supplies within the city
were virtually exhausted. At last Svyatoslav resolved to risk everything
on a last throw, and on 24 July burst out of the main gate with the
remainder of his men. So great was their impetus, so desperate their
determination, that they almost succeeded – and would have, according
to Leo the Deacon, but for the miraculous intervention of the warrior St
Theodore Stratilates, whom the Emperor and many of the soldiers saw,
mounted on a snow-white horse, laying valiantly about him in the midst
of the mêlée. In fact, the day was eventually won by means of John's
favourite trick, a feigned retreat; and at nightfall the Prince of Kiev sued
for peace. He would, he promised, evacuate the whole country and
deliver over every prisoner he had taken since his arrival in Bulgaria,
adding a further undertaking never to attack or invade the Byzantine
city of Cherson in the Crimea. All he asked in return was safe conduct
across the Danube, and a little food for his few surviving men. John
Tzimisces was only too happy to agree.

Before they left for their respective homes the two rulers met, at
Svyatoslav's request, for the first time face to face. John rode down in
state to the meeting-place on the river bank, mounted on his charger;
the Prince of Kiev arrived by boat, rowing alongside his men and

distinguishable from them only by the relative cleanliness of his white robe, his jewelled earring and the two long strands of fair hair – badges of rank – that fell from his otherwise shaven head. (That hair, together with his blue eyes and drooping moustache, testified, despite his name, to his Viking forebears.) In the course of a short but friendly conversation he expressed the hope that the old commercial treaty – governing, *inter alia*, visits of Russians to Constantinople – might be renewed. Then, with a dignified bow to the Emperor, he climbed back into his boat and rowed away.

He was never to see Russia again. As he passed through the land of the Pechenegs on his return journey he was stopped and interrogated: where was the rich plunder that he had promised them in return for their alliance? Alas, he told them, there was none. The spoils had gone to the victor: he, the vanquished, had been lucky to escape with his life. For the Pechenegs it was not a satisfactory outcome. The following spring, as Svyatoslav was negotiating the cataracts of the Dnieper, they ambushed him and killed him – subsequently making his skull into a drinking cup, just as the Bulgar Krum had done with that of the first Nicephorus, 161 years before.

John Tzimisces enjoyed a happier homecoming. Before leaving Dristra he renamed it Theodoropolis in honour of the saint who, he believed, had fought shoulder to shoulder with him beneath the walls. Then he headed south towards Constantinople, Tsar Boris and family following in his train. He could congratulate himself on two major achievements. Not only had he driven a dangerous enemy out of the Balkan peninsula; he had also regained Bulgaria for the Empire – for, whatever he might have said to Boris at Preslav, he had no intention of reinstating him on his throne. Indeed, anyone witnessing his triumphal entry into his capital that August might have been forgiven for supposing that it was the Bulgars rather than the Russians who had been defeated. Place of honour in the procession – in the gilded chariot, drawn by four white horses, that had been intended for his own use – he had accorded to the most revered of all Bulgarian icons, a portrait of the Virgin which he believed to have been, with St Theodore, partly instrumental in his victory and which he had brought back with him as one of the spoils of war. He himself rode behind it in his shining armour. At the rear of the procession, on foot, walked Tsar Boris, his wife and children. The crowds lining the streets could draw their own conclusions.

If, after this, there were any that still doubted the Empire's intentions towards its ravaged and devastated neighbour, they were soon to be enlightened. When the procession reached St Sophia, John laid upon the high altar not only the holy icon but the crown and other regalia of the Bulgar state. Shortly afterwards, in a civil ceremony at the Palace, he obliged the young Tsar to perform a formal act of abdication. Henceforth Bulgaria would be an imperial province. The Bulgar Patriarchate was declared abolished, and all its dependent bishoprics subjected once again to Constantinople. Characteristically, John tried to soften the blow by giving to Boris the honorary Byzantine rank of *magister*; the Tsar's younger brother Romanus, less fortunate, was castrated – presumably to prevent his returning to his homeland as pretender to the throne. It was a sad and inglorious end to the house of Krum, which had more than once caused Byzantium itself to tremble.[1]

Nations, however, are not killed so easily. A glance at the map will show that the Bulgaria of the tenth century was considerably larger than the Bulgarian Republic of today, extending as it did to within a few miles of the Adriatic; and that only the eastern region had been directly affected by the recent war. The western section – perhaps two-thirds of the whole – saw no reason to surrender its sovereignty, and remained a living ember from which there was soon to spring, briefly but gloriously, the final flame of the first Bulgarian Empire. But the story of Samuel the Cometopulus, his meteoric rise and his tragic downfall, must await the next chapter.

After the success of his Bulgarian campaign, John Tzimisces paid little further heed to Europe – at least so far as secular affairs were concerned. There was more important work to be done in the East. The Abbasid Caliphate at Baghdad was no longer a threat, with the weak and sickly al-Muti shorn of all effective power, a virtual prisoner within his palace; but danger was looming in the south. Only three years before, in 969, the rival Caliphate of the Fatimids had embarked on a new policy of expansion: advancing eastward from their capital at Mahdiya – on the east coast of what is now Tunisia – Fatimid troops had swept through the Nile Valley and on across Sinai into Palestine and southern Syria. In 971 they had attacked Antioch. It was already clear that they must be halted before serious damage was done; and when in July 973 they

---

1 Of the rest of Boris's family we know little. There is no further record of his wife, nor of his two children – which suggests either that they were daughters or that they died young.

almost annihilated a Byzantine army before the walls of Amida, John was already preparing to move against them.

By the spring of 974 he was ready; but at that moment there came news of a further crisis. This time the scene was Armenia, where the princes and barons – normally at each other's throats – had suddenly coalesced around their 'King of Kings' Ashot III, with an army estimated at 80,000 men.[1] Why they did so we do not know – our principal source, the Armenian Matthew of Edessa, is lamentably vague on the subject. We can only assume that they had heard of John's preparations and had somehow concluded that his coming campaign was to be directed against themselves. The Emperor – who was, after all, an Armenian himself – was able to allay their fears; but he decided none the less, instead of marching into Syria by the normal route through the Taurus passes, to make a detour northward into Armenia, reassure Ashot personally of his peaceable intentions and, he hoped, persuade the King of Kings to put some or all of the Armenian army at his disposal. This decision added some three or four hundred miles to the length of the march, but was fully justified by results: Ashot readily allied himself with the Empire for the coming campaign and immediately made available 10,000 of his best fighting men, fully equipped and ready for battle.

The combined force then headed south to Amida and Martyropolis (Mayyafariqin) – which escaped pillage and sack only by the payment of a heavy ransom – and onward via Nisibin (whence the entire population had fled at its approach) to the plains of Mesopotamia, nowhere meeting any opposition worthy of the name. Why the Emperor did not press on to Baghdad itself is once again unexplained; in its present condition the city could hardly have resisted any major offensive. Instead, laden with plunder, he retraced his steps to Antioch, where he left the army in its winter quarters while he himself returned hurriedly to Constantinople.

What obliged him to take the long and tedious road westward to his capital – conscious as he was that he would have to retrace his steps a month or two later – was, almost certainly, a religious crisis: a crisis precipitated not in Constantinople but in Rome. Otto the Great had died in 973; his son Otto was away in Germany; and in the early summer of 974 the Cardinal Deacon Franco – a noble Roman who hated the Saxon Emperor for having, as he saw it, made a plaything of the Papacy – had

1 See p. 130n.

seized the opportunity to stage a *coup* against Otto's puppet Pope Benedict VI, to imprisoning him in the Castel Sant'Angelo, where he was shortly afterwards strangled. Franco had then mounted the throne himself, under the name of Boniface VII; but a counter-revolution in the Emperor's favour had obliged him almost immediately to flee for his life to Constantinople. Meanwhile the young Emperor had appointed in his stead the Bishop of Sutri, one of whose first actions as Pope Benedict VII was to excommunicate his predecessor.

The arrival of Boniface on the Bosphorus put the Byzantines in something of a quandary. His long opposition to the Western Empire had led him to forge strong links with Constantinople, and he had steadfastly supported Nicephorus Phocas in all the latter's differences with Otto I. How much he chose to tell them of his treatment of Benedict VI we do not know; the Palace, at all events, seems to have decided that he deserved their support and that relations with Rome must be at once broken off; they also probably sent an urgent appeal to the Emperor in Mesopotamia to return as soon as he could and settle the matter once and for all. Patriarch Basil, on the other hand, took the opposite view. He had, it was true, been personally selected by John for the Patriarchate; but he was not prepared to be dictated to. He had never questioned the essential unity of the Church or the supremacy of the legitimate Pontiff, whose edict of excommunication he was determined to uphold.

As may already have been noticed, it was nearly always the urbane and ambitious Patriarchs of Constantinople who tended to challenge the status of the Pope in Rome; the unworldly ascetics had no such doubts. Basil the Scamandrian fell squarely into the second category; in the eyes of his flock, indeed, he was almost too holy, living on a near-starvation diet of berries and water, wearing the same filthy robe until it fell to pieces, sleeping always on the bare earth. 'His only fault,' writes Leo the Deacon, 'was a tendency to scrutinize too closely the behaviour of others, and to involve himself more than was proper in their affairs.' In consequence he had made himself thoroughly unpopular; and when the decision was taken to get rid of him in favour of someone more amenable there was no shortage of bishops and clergy to give evidence against him. He had been guilty, they testified, of maladministration, of contravention of the canon law, even of intrigue regarding the succession. Basil himself made no defence against the charges, in- sisting however that he could be deposed only by an Ecumenical

Council – one, that is to say, on which the Pope was properly represented. An imperial tribunal, meeting soon after the Emperor had returned to the capital, was only too happy to prove him wrong.

So Basil was exiled, Benedict was refused recognition and Boniface remained in Constantinople until April 984 when, with Byzantine help, he managed to depose his rival's successor John XIV (who also came to an unpleasant end in Sant'Angelo) and regain the pontifical throne. This time he held it for fifteen months – until his death, almost certainly by poison, in the following year. His corpse, we are told, was dragged naked through the city and eventually left 'beneath the horse of Constantine' on the Capitol,[1] where it lay ignored until a passing group of priests recovered it and arranged for its burial.

In the early spring of 975, with the religious crisis behind him and a new Patriarch, Antony III of the Studium, safely installed at St Sophia, John Tzimisces returned to the East and set off on the last, and the most spectacularly successful, of all his campaigns. From Antioch he first marched against Emesa (Homs), which surrendered without a struggle, passing on to Baalbek, which fell after little more than a token resistance. Damascus followed, after which the way was clear into Palestine. Tiberias, Nazareth, Caesarea – it seemed as though the triumphal progress would continue for ever; but the African garrisons from all these cities were now entrenching themselves in a line of fortresses along the coast, and rather than continue to Jerusalem John turned back to deal with them before they became a serious danger to his rear. Sidon fell, then – despite a heroic resistance – Beirut, then Byblos. Of all the coastal cities, only Tripoli resisted capture. By the end of the summer most of Palestine, Syria and the Lebanon – regions where no Emperor had set foot since the days of Heraclius – were under Byzantine control.

It was an astonishing achievement; but when John returned to Constantinople towards the end of the year he was a dying man. The nature of his illness is uncertain. Our three most authoritative sources – Scylitzes, Zonaras and Leo the Deacon – all point an accusing finger at Basil the *parakoimomenos*. They tell us that the Emperor, inquiring on his return journey through Anatolia about the ownership of all the most prosperous estates through which he passed, was informed that every

---

1 *Liber Pontificalis*. The equestrian statue of Marcus Aurelius was believed throughout the Middle Ages to be a representation of Constantine – a fortunate misconception which alone preserved it from destruction as a pagan monument.

one of them belonged to Basil. The discovery – which could only mean peculation on a scale of which he had never dreamed – threw him into a fury, and he made no secret of his intention of confronting his Chamberlain immediately on his return and demanding an explanation. He would have done better to keep silent. One of the daily couriers that shuttled between the army and the Palace reported his words to Basil; and Basil, sensing danger, made his dispositions accordingly. A week or two later, when John was dining with one of his rich vassals in Bithynia, a slow-acting poison was slipped into his cup; he awoke the next morning scarcely able to move his limbs, his eyes streaming with blood and his neck and shoulders covered with suppurating sores. Henceforth he had one idea only: to get home before he died. Messengers sped to Constantinople with orders to prepare for his imminent arrival and to speed up work on his tomb.

By the time he reached the Bosphorus he was breathing only with great difficulty. Somehow he seems to have risen from his litter for long enough to attend the service at which the two principal prizes he had brought back from the East – a pair of sandals worn by Christ and the hair of John the Baptist – were rededicated and installed in St Sophia; then he took to his bed, never to leave it again. All his own personal wealth he left to the poor and the sick; then he made a long and tearful confession to Bishop Nicholas of Adrianople, calling repeatedly on the Holy Virgin Theotokos to intercede on his behalf. He was still invoking her aid when he died on 10 January 976, after a reign of just six years and a month. He was fifty-one.

What are we to make of this poisoning story? At least seven chroniclers repeat it in one form or another, though not all of them accuse Basil; but as previous chapters have already made clear, foul play was invariably suspected on such occasions. Besides, if Basil had really done the deed, would he have remained in power as he did, acting as effective Regent for the two young Emperors? And what was this mysterious poison, so slow-acting and yet so grimly effective? (The secret of it must have been lost – or, at any rate, they don't seem to make it any more.) In short, is it not far likelier that John died – as many thousands of humbler soldiers must have died during those eastern wars – of typhoid, or malaria, or dysentery, or any of those other deadly infections which, even now, can only with difficulty be held at bay?

Yes – but we can never be sure. John Tzimisces is a mystery in his death, just as he was in his life. In his short reign he proved himself one of the very greatest of Byzantine Emperors. He had conquered the Russians, the Bulgars and the Caliphs of both Baghdad and Cairo; he had regained the greater part of Syria and the Lebanon, of Mesopotamia and Palestine. He had been admired by allies and enemies alike for his courage, his chivalry, his compassion. In peace he had been a ruler both wise and just, a friend to the poor and, above all, to the sick, with whom he always seems to have felt a particular affinity – although he himself never knew a day's illness until the end. His radiant personality, like his golden armour, leaves us dazzled. Yet it can never quite blind us to another, darker vision: that of a pitiful, misshapen heap lying huddled on a palace floor, while another figure – spare, sinewy and immensely strong – gazes contemptuously down, and kicks.

14

The Young Basil

[976–89]

Cut down the governors who become overproud. Let no generals on campaign have too many resources. Exhaust them with unjust exactions, to keep them busy with their own affairs. Admit no women to the imperial councils. Be accessible to no one. Share with few your most intimate plans.

Bardas Sclerus, to Basil II,
Bithynia, 989

With the death of John Tzimisces, the way seemed clear at last for the assumption of power by the two young sons of Romanus II, the eighteen-year-old Basil and his brother Constantine, two years his junior. The two could scarcely have been more dissimilar. Whereas Constantine was never to display, either then or in later life, the slightest interest in politics or statecraft, nor to ask anything more than to be left to his own mildly unsavoury devices, Basil impressed everyone by his alertness, his quickness of mind and his apparently inexhaustible energy. Still less did he resemble his forebears. For all his intelligence, he was in no sense an intellectual as Leo the Wise and Constantine Porphyrogenitus had been; he showed no inclination towards scholarship or literature, while the crude simplicity of his Greek grated on the ears of the ever-fastidious Byzantines. Whereas Leo and Constantine had taken care always to emphasize their power and majesty by dazzling panoply and sumptuous costume, surrounding themselves with priceless treasures and *objets d'art*, Basil spent practically nothing on himself, cut state ceremonial to a minimum and went about the Palace and the city in drab, workaday clothes quite unbefitting an Emperor and, it was noted, none too clean. Physically, too, he bore little resemblance to his father and grandfather. They had been tall and dark; Basil was short and stocky, with a round, heavily-bearded face and light blue eyes that shone with unusual brilliance from beneath high, arched eyebrows. The chronicler Michael

Psellus (who makes the first of his many appearances at this point in the story) tells us that when not in the saddle his appearance was undistinguished; it was only when mounted – for he was a superb horseman – that he came fully into his own.[1]

In one other respect, too, did Basil differ from his father. Romanus had been, throughout the adult years of his short life, a pleasure-loving voluptuary. Basil had shown similar tendencies in his early youth, but with his accession to power he put self-indulgence behind him and thenceforth led a life of quite exceptional austerity, eating and drinking sparingly and avoiding women altogether. Almost alone among Byzantine Emperors – and indeed among contemporary princes of Europe – he never married: an omission that appears still more extra-ordinary in view of the importance of providing for a legitimate succession, particularly since his brother's wife, Helena Alypina, was to produce only daughters. Could it be, one cannot help wondering, that there was indeed a marriage, of which all records have somehow been lost? Several Empresses, after all – the wife of John Tzimisces is a case in point – are mentioned only once in the chronicles and then never again; and our sources for the reign of Basil II are lamentably thin. But such a hypothesis, attractive as it may be, cannot really be sustained. For the half-century that Basil and his brother were to reign in tandem, several descriptions of state functions have come down to us; and in every one of them Helena is mentioned as the only Empress, performing all the duties appropriate to her rank. There can thus be no serious doubt that Basil lived and died a bachelor. Why he did so, on the other hand, remains a mystery.

From the moment that he found himself senior Emperor, he seems to have been determined to rule as well as reign; and with a brother grateful to be relieved of the burdens of responsibility he should have experienced no difficulty in doing so. Two obstacles, however, stood in his path. The first was his great-uncle and namesake, Basil the *parakoimomenos*. It was now some thirty years since this natural son of Romanus Lecapenus had been raised – while still in his twenties – by

---

1 Psellus was admittedly only seven years old when Basil died, but he himself assures us that he had many friends and acquaintances who had known the Emperor well. Such was the contrast between Basil and his predecessors that at least one historian has suggested that he may not in fact have been the son of Romanus II at all, but the result of some momentary collision between his mother Theophano and a Norman member of her husband's Varangian guard. But there is too little evidence for the theory to be convincing.

Constantine Porphyrogenitus to the highest office in the Byzantine State after the Emperor himself. Since then he had held it under Romanus II, Nicephorus Phocas and John Tzimisces; and whether or not (as has often been maintained) he deliberately encouraged the two co-Emperors in their early dissipations in order to keep power in his own hands, he certainly had no intention of letting go of it without a struggle.

The second obstacle was a good deal more serious, since it concerned the nature of the throne itself. The first Roman Emperors, it must be remembered, had gained power not by inheritance but by the acclamation of their army; and although the hereditary principle had long been accepted in Constantinople, it had never been an integral or essential feature of the body politic. Now, after the seizure of power by three victorious generals in less than sixty years, it was – especially in the minds of the Anatolian military aristocracy – wearing distinctly thin: would it not be better, they reasoned, to return to the old tradition, whereby the imperial diadem was the preserve of mature men who had proved themselves in battle, rather than of callow, untried youths whose only recommendation was that they had been born in the purple?

Thus it came about that the first nine years of Basil's theoretically autocratic reign were largely overshadowed by his formidable Chamberlain, and the first thirteen occupied in defending his throne against the attacks of two rebel generals determined to wrest it from him. Both have already made their appearance in these pages. One was Bardas Sclerus, Domestic of the armies of the East, who had served his brother-in-law John Tzimisces with unwavering loyalty and saw himself as his legitimate successor; the other – more predictably perhaps – was Bardas Phocas, nephew of the Emperor Nicephorus, who having failed in his first rebellion against Tzimisces was resolved to launch a second against Basil as soon as the opportunity offered. Sclerus was the first to act. In the spring of 976, only a month or two after his brother-in-law's death, he had himself proclaimed *basileus* by his troops, took possession of his army's treasury and marched on Caesarea. By the autumn of 977 he had won two decisive battles – during the second of which the commander of the loyalist forces, his erstwhile companion-in-arms Peter Phocas, met his death – and gained the support of the southern fleet based on Attaleia; and a few months later, having captured Nicaea, he drew up his army on the Asiatic shore of the Bosphorus and settled down to an amphibious siege of the capital.

At sea the issue was quickly settled. The home fleet, traditionally loyal to the reigning Emperor, streamed out of the Golden Horn and made short work of the rebel ships. On land, however, the situation seemed grave; and so it might have continued had not the eunuch Basil (who was at this time still in effective control of the government) had the imagination – and, it must be said, the courage – to entrust the command of the army to Bardas Phocas. It was a surprising appointment, to say the least. The loyalty of Phocas to the throne was scarcely less questionable than that of Sclerus himself; indeed, when the decision was taken, he was still in exile on Chios. On the other hand the entire army was now controlled by the Anatolian barons, and no other general would have been any more reliable; besides, even if Phocas did dream of acquiring the supreme power for himself, he would still have to get rid of Sclerus first. The only danger was that the two generals might combine, making common cause against Constantinople; but on balance this seemed unlikely. In any case, it was a risk that had to be taken.

So Bardas Phocas, having been brought back with all speed from Chios, flung off his monastic habit, swore an oath of loyalty to the *porphyrogeniti* and secretly made his way back to his own power base at Caesarea, where it was an easy matter for him to raise an army. Sclerus, seeing a dangerous threat to his rear, had no choice but to retire. The civil war that followed lasted nearly three years. There were several fierce engagements; but Bardas Sclerus, despite repeated tactical victories, was never able to destroy the forces of his rival, who always managed to retreat in good order, collect reinforcements and return a month or two later with renewed vigour to the fray. Finally, on a date which is disputed but which must certainly have been some time in the spring of 979, the two armies fought for the last time and Bardas Phocas, seeing the tide of battle turning against him, challenged the rebel to decide the issue by single combat. Courageously – for Phocas was a giant among men[1] – Sclerus accepted the challenge; the soldiers on both sides gathered round to watch; and, in a scene that seems to come straight out of the *Iliad*, the contest began. The two combatants galloped towards each other, then struck simultaneously. Phocas managed to parry Sclerus's thrust, which fell instead on his horse, splitting its bridle and severing its right ear. His own blow, meanwhile, found its mark. Sclerus pitched forward on his saddle and slid to the ground, blood streaming

---

1 'Anyone who received a blow from his hand was a dead man straightway, and whole armies trembled even when he shouted from afar.' (Psellus, *Chronographia*. The translation, like all others from this source, is based on that of E. R. A. Sewter.)

from his head. A few of his men carried him, unconscious, to a nearby stream to bathe the wound; the remainder fled from the field. The war was over.

For the moment, at least. The Emperor Basil, following events from Constantinople, knew that his grasp on the throne remained uncertain. Apart from anything else, both his rivals were still very much alive and doubtless making new plans for the future. Bardas Sclerus, having somewhat dented the reputation of Bardas Phocas by surviving his blow on the head, had sought refuge with the Saracens and had been borne off in semi-captivity to Baghdad – whence, sooner or later, he was bound to return; while Bardas Phocas was stronger than ever and, despite his oath of loyalty, equally certain to make another bid for power. None the less, here was a much-needed respite; and it afforded Basil time and opportunity to prepare himself for the tremendous tasks that lay ahead. For the six years following the defeat of Sclerus we hear little of him, but we may be sure that he was hard at work, familiarizing himself with the innermost workings of the army, the navy, the Church, the monasteries and every department of state. If he were to be what he was determined to be – an Emperor in the fullest sense of the word, in complete charge of his own government, responsible for every aspect of its foreign policy and ready when the need arose to lead his own troops in the field – he could afford to leave nothing to chance.

In 985 he was ready; only his great-uncle stood in his way. Basil the *parakoimomenos*, however, was not easy to shift. A eunuch he might be, but there were few men in Constantinople who did not tremble before this tremendous figure, whose every word and movement seemed to proclaim his own imperial origins and to radiate authority. After a lifetime of loyalty to the Macedonian house – of which, after all, he was himself indirectly a member – he seems to have been at first genuinely attached to the young Emperor; his mistake was to underestimate him. By turns patronizing and domineering, he insisted on treating his great-nephew like the child he no longer was, dismissing his ideas, ignoring his suggestions, countermanding his orders without hesitation or apology. As Basil found himself blocked and frustrated at every step, his long-felt resentment gradually gave way to hatred: he knew that he could never breathe freely until he had rid himself of this insufferable incubus once and for all. Fortunately there were grounds in plenty for doing so. His Chamberlain's corruption was notorious, and had brought him enormous wealth which he flaunted shamelessly, maintaining a degree of state that put the Emperor himself in the shade. More serious still, he had recently been discovered – doubtless suspecting a coming attempt to unseat him – to be in secret and potentially treasonable correspondence with Bardas Phocas. Basil laid his plans carefully; then he struck. The capital awoke one morning to the news that the most feared man in the Empire had been arrested and exiled, and all his property confiscated.

That, one might think – particularly considering the amount of the property involved, the *parakoimomenos* having been by far the greatest landowner in all the imperial dominions – should have been enough; but there was in the Emperor's character a streak of brutal vindictiveness which he never managed to control. Not content with having broken and dispossessed his old enemy, he even turned against the immense monastery which the latter had built in the capital and had richly endowed in honour of his namesake St Basil. He was tempted, we are told, to demolish it completely; not wishing, however, to encourage accusations of impiety, he contented himself with stripping it of all its movable furniture and mosaic decoration and reducing the luckless monks to penury.[1] More extraordinary still, he then issued an edict by which all laws promulgated by his great-uncle should be considered null and void unless they bore a mark in his own hand signifying his approval; 'for,' he explained, 'at the beginning of our own reign, until the deposition of Basil the *parakoimomenos* . . . many things happened which were not according to our wish, for he decided and appointed everything according to his own will.' To the old man in his place of exile, it must have seemed as if his very existence were being denied. He sank quickly into senility and died soon afterwards.

At last Basil was master in his own house. But less than a year later his Empire was facing a new threat, and one that was to bring him greater humiliation than any that he had yet suffered. Samuel, self-proclaimed Tsar of the Bulgarian Empire, had invaded Thessaly and captured its chief city, Larissa.

Of the origins of Tsar Samuel we know little. His father, the *comes*

---

1 Psellus, who tells this story, records a distinctly bad-taste pun of which the Emperor is also said to have been guilty at this time. Like all puns it is untranslatable; but the following adaptation, gleefully repeated by several modern English and French historians, probably comes as close as we shall ever get to the original: 'I have turned their refectory into a reflectory, since all they can now do is to reflect on how to feed themselves.'

Nicholas, seems to have been governor of all or part of western Bulgaria around the time of Svyatoslav's invasion; and when he died his influence, if not his position, passed to his four sons. These young men thus became the natural leaders of an insurrection which broke out soon after the death of John Tzimisces and soon developed into a full-blown war of independence. When the news of it reached Constantinople, Tsar Boris escaped with his brother Romanus to join the insurgents; but the Tsar was accidentally killed at the frontier by his own subjects while Romanus, being a eunuch, was debarred from the throne. The leadership therefore remained with the sons of the *comes* – known collectively as the *Cometopuli* – and, in particular, with the youngest and ablest of the four, Samuel.

The revolt of Bardas Sclerus had played perfectly into Samuel's hands, providing him with just the opportunity he needed to extend his dominions without opposition. Gradually he had managed to impose control over all Bulgaria west of a line drawn south from the Danube and passing roughly midway between his first capital Serdica (the modern Sofia) and Philippopolis; he had then assumed the old title of Tsar and simultaneously revived the old Bulgarian Patriarchate abolished by Tzimisces. Thus, both politically and ecclesiastically, the new State came to be seen by the Bulgars not so much as the descendant of its predecessor as its continuation – the continuity being further emphasized by the close association of Prince Romanus, whom Samuel took care to load with honours and titles.

By 980 Samuel was secure enough to make his presence felt beyond his own borders, and thenceforth not a summer went by without one or more Bulgar incursions into Thessaly; but it was not for another five years that he put Larissa seriously under siege. The citizens held out as long as they could; but early in 986, when a woman was found eating the thigh of her dead husband, they understandably decided to surrender. With the exception of a single quisling family, the Nicoulitzes, all were sold into slavery; while the city's holiest relic, the body of its former bishop St Achilleus, was carried off to adorn the cathedral of Prespa, to which Samuel had recently transferred his capital.[1]

Here was an outrage that could not go unpunished. On hearing the news Basil gave orders for the immediate mobilization of the army, personally assumed the supreme command and marched on Sardica,

1 Runciman, *The First Bulgarian Empire*, pp. 221–2.

following the valley of the river Maritsa before turning north-west through the pass known as Trajan's Gate and out on to the plain on which the city lies. Just short of his objective, however, he stopped to await his rearguard: a disastrous mistake, since it allowed Samuel – who, accompanied by his brother Aaron and Prince Romanus, had meanwhile hurried up from Thessaly – to occupy the surrounding mountains. Not till the end of July did the Emperor pass on to the city and lay siege to it; and even then he met with little success. The weather was stiflingly hot, morale was low, and Samuel's constant harassment of the imperial foraging parties meant that the besiegers were often almost as short of food as the besieged. After only three weeks, Basil decided to give up the struggle and return home. But worse was to come. On Tuesday, 17 August, as the Byzantine troops passed for the second time through Trajan's Gate, they marched straight into Samuel's carefully-prepared ambush – the Bulgarian cavalry streaming down from the mountains to each side and taking them totally by surprise. The vast majority were cut down where they stood; all the baggage, including the treasury, was lost. It was but a poor shambling rump of his former army that followed the distraught Emperor into Philippopolis a day or two later.[1]

Basil's own feelings of humiliation can easily be imagined. Never one to lack confidence in his own abilities, he had schooled himself to be the most efficient ruler Byzantium had ever known. His years under the shadow of his great-uncle had been intolerable to him because he was convinced that he could govern his Empire better than anyone else: only he, once his hands were untied, could restore it to the strength and prosperity it had known under his great-great-grandfather Basil I, under Heraclius, even under the great Justinian himself. He had had to wait until his twenty-ninth year – by which time he had been titular Emperor for over a quarter of a century – for the opportunity to undertake an important foreign campaign on his own initiative; and it had been a catastrophe. He was bitterly ashamed; but he was also angry. Somehow, too, he had retained his fundamental belief in himself. When he arrived back in Constantinople, he vowed a solemn oath that he would have his revenge on the entire Bulgar nation, until it would rue the day that it had ever raised a finger against him.

He was, as we shall see, as good as his word.

*

1 Among the survivors was Leo the Deacon, who owed his survival, he tells us, only to the agility of his horse.

Basil's time would indeed come; but it would not come yet. News of Trajan's Gate persuaded Bardas Sclerus, now effectively a prisoner in Baghdad, that the Empire was at last his for the taking; and he had no difficulty in persuading the Caliph al-Tai to release him, in return for a promise to restore certain frontier fortresses as soon as he gained the throne. The Caliph supplied him with men, money and provisions, and it was thus with quite a sizeable and well-equipped force that Sclerus returned to Asia Minor and, at Melitene in the first weeks of 987, for the second time proclaimed himself *basileus*.

Initially at any rate, he must have been gratified to find the Anatolian barons already on the point of revolt. The imperial army, they firmly believed, was their own special preserve; and they were outraged that the Emperor should have appropriated it to invade Bulgaria without so much as informing them of his intentions. Without one of their own number in command, the defeat had, they agreed, been inevitable. Basil had brought it on himself, and had only himself to blame. Here, in short, was conclusive proof, if any were needed, that they should never have allowed the crown out of their own hands. The sooner it returned to them, the better.

But whose, precisely, should it be? Here Sclerus must have been rather less pleased, for he soon discovered that many of his fellow-nobles favoured Bardas Phocas rather than himself: so many in fact that Phocas, instead of leading a loyalist army against him as he had eight years before, once again turned his coat and on 15 August formally claimed the Empire on his own account. Of the two claimants, Phocas was now substantially the stronger, enjoying as he did the support of the majority of the senior officers as well as that of the landed aristocracy; but he did not dare march on the capital leaving Sclerus in his rear. Clearly some sort of compact was necessary between the two, and he therefore proposed what amounted to a partition of the Empire, whereby he would be satisfied with the European part – including, of course, Constantinople – leaving Sclerus all Anatolia from the Marmara to the eastern frontier. Sclerus, against the advice of all his associates, accepted, dropped his guard – and walked straight into the trap. Soon afterwards he was arrested, and spent the next two years immured in the fortress of Tyropoion – the same, ironically enough, from which he had starved out Bardas Phocas after the latter's first rebellion sixteen years before – while his rival made a final bid for power.

At that time Phocas can have been in little doubt of his eventual success. On his long march through Asia Minor he encountered no opposition of any kind, while more and more recruits flocked enthusiastically to his banner. Against him stood a young and inexperienced Emperor, whose only military exploit had ended in disaster and whose army – what was left of it – was broken and utterly demoralized. How, in such circumstances, could he possibly fail? When he reached the Marmara he divided his army, sending half of it west to Abydos on the Hellespont while the other half dug itself in at Chrysopolis opposite Constantinople, and began to prepare a two-pronged attack on the capital.

Basil's situation was indeed desperate; but he kept his head. If he could not hope to defend his Empire unaided, he must seek foreign help; and help on the necessary scale could come from one quarter only: Vladimir, Prince of Kiev. Even before Bardas Phocas had arrived on the Bosphorus shore the imperial ambassadors were on their way, though it was months later before they returned with the Prince's answer. Vladimir, they reported, considered himself bound by his father Svyatoslav's agreement with John Tzimisces to send the force required: a *druzhina* of 6,000 fully-equipped Varangians[1] would be dispatched as soon as possible. In return, he asked one thing only: the hand in marriage of the Emperor's sister, the *porphyrogenita* Anna.

The effect of this demand on the Byzantine court can hardly be imagined. In the whole history of the Empire, no princess born in the purple had ever been given in marriage to a foreigner; and Vladimir was not only a foreigner but – despite the conversion of his grandmother Olga – a heathen, a man who was known to have killed his own brother and who already boasted at least four wives and 800 concubines: a fact which however in no way discouraged him from cutting an almost legendary swath through the matrons and maidens of any town or village in which he happened to be. He possessed, in the minds of the Byzantines, only one redeeming feature: he had given it out that he was seeking, for himself and his people, a respectable religion. If we are to believe that curious document known as Nestor's chronicle, he had already ordered a survey of all the principal faiths of the known world and had personally made searching inquiries of Muslims, Jews and

---

1 The name (which comes from an Old Norse word meaning 'plighted faith') was given to those Russianized Vikings whose forefathers had sailed across the Baltic and up the rivers of northern Russia, easily dominating the Slav tribes of the interior.

Roman Catholics – by none of whom, however, had he been particularly impressed. Finally, in that very year of 987, he had sent emissaries to Constantinople where, in their honour, a special service had been held in St Sophia. So captivated had they been by its beauty that, as they subsequently reported to their master, they had not known whether they were on earth or in heaven: 'all we can tell is that in that place is God's dwelling among men.' It seemed likely therefore that Vladimir might soon be forswearing his pagan gods and, with any luck, some of his more reprehensible habits; and Basil accordingly gave his consent to the match, on the sole condition that the Prince of Kiev were to embrace the Orthodox faith. Then he settled down to wait.

He waited for the best part of a year: a year he survived thanks to the imperial navy which, by its constant patrolling of the Hellespont, the Marmara and the Bosphorus, successfully prevented Bardas Phocas and his army from crossing over into Europe. Only around the time of the winter solstice[1] did the Black Sea lookouts espy the first of a great fleet of Viking ships on the northern horizon; but a week or so later the whole of that fleet was safely anchored in the Golden Horn and 6,000 burly giants drawn up for the inspection of the Emperor. He made his plans quickly. One night in late February 989 the Norsemen, with Basil himself at their head, crossed the straits under cover of darkness and took up their positions a few hundred yards from the main rebel camp, spread out along the coast at Chrysopolis. Then, at first light, they attacked, while a squadron of imperial flame-throwers sprayed the shore with Greek fire. Phocas's men, roused from sleep to find this terrible horde bearing down upon them, could do little to defend themselves; but their assailants swung their swords and battle-axes without mercy until they stood ankle-deep in blood. Few of the victims escaped with their lives; three subordinate commanders, delivered into the hands of the Emperor, were respectively hanged, impaled and crucified.

Bardas Phocas seems – fortunately for him – to have remained with his reserves, if not actually at Nicaea, at any rate some little distance

---

1 The chronology at this point presents something of a problem, since our principal sources – to say nothing of modern historians – are in considerable disagreement. If however we accept Yahya's precise date of 13 April 989 as the date of the battle of Abydos, it is hard to see how the massacre at Chrysopolis could have preceded it by more than a few weeks, or that the latter could have occurred long after the Norsemen's arrival.

away from Chrysopolis. As soon as he heard of the massacre, he hastened to join the rest of his army outside Abydos; if he could but capture this port at the mouth of the Hellespont he would, he knew, find vessels enough in its harbour to transport his men across to the Gallipoli peninsula, whence they could launch their assault on Constantinople. On his arrival he immediately laid siege to the city; but the town put up a determined resistance, and with the imperial navy in firm control of the straits a proper blockade proved impossible. Meanwhile the Emperor, who had returned to the capital, set about preparing a relief expedition. By mid-March 989 it was ready, and he at once sent off an advance contingent under the command – rather surprisingly – of his brother and co-Emperor Constantine: the only time in his long life, so far as we know, that this unsatisfactory prince led an army in the field. Basil himself embarked a few days later, landed near Lampsacus a few miles to the north-east and immediately set off for the besieged city, his gigantic Varangians following behind.

The next morning saw the two opposing armies drawn up facing each other on the open plain to the landward side of Abydos, where they remained for several days manoeuvring for position. Only at dawn on Saturday 13 April did the Emperor give the order to attack. At first it seemed as if this initial onslaught might prove decisive. The rebel troops scattered: many were cut down, others simply turned and ran. Only with the greatest difficulty did Phocas manage to restore order and regroup the survivors. Then, we are told, as he gazed across the plain, he caught sight of Basil himself, riding up and down the lines of Norsemen, congratulating them and encouraging them to still greater feats of valour, with young Constantine, carrying a long lance, at his side; and his expression changed as he remembered how, during his last encounter with Bardas Sclerus, he had turned defeat into victory by proposing that the issue be decided by single combat. Ignoring all attempts to dissuade him he suddenly called for his horse, spurred it to a gallop and, as both armies watched, silent and incredulous, thundered towards the imperial lines, his sword pointing directly at the Emperor. Basil stood his ground, his own drawn sword clasped in his right hand, while in his left he clutched an icon of the Virgin, well known for its miraculous powers.[1]

---

1 Was this the icon that was to be stolen by the Venetians during the Fourth Crusade and, now known as the *Nicopoeia* or Bringer of Victory, still hangs in the north aisle of the Basilica of St Mark? It may well have been: see Canon Ag. Molin, *Dell' antica Immagine di Maria santissima che si conserva nella basilica di San Marco in Venezia*, Venice, 1821.

Nearer and nearer came his assailant – 'like a cloud driven by a hurricane' as Psellus describes him; then, suddenly, he seemed to falter. Swaying as if overcome by a fit of dizziness, he reined in his horse, slipped slowly from the saddle and lay motionless on the ground. When Basil, Constantine and their followers rode up a moment or two later they found that he was already dead. At first they assumed that he had been hit by an arrow, but his body bore no trace of a wound. He had in fact suffered a sudden stroke, presumably brought on by excitement and exertion, which had killed him instantly. His troops, seeing what had occurred, panicked and fled; but they were no match for the Norsemen, who pursued them and cheerfully hacked them to pieces.

Bardas Sclerus was left the only pretender to the throne of Byzantium. During his two years' captivity at Tyropoion, his gaoler had been none other than Phocas's wife; with her husband's death, however, seeing him no longer as her prisoner but as her one hope of revenge, she immediately set him free to raise a new army. Almost from the first, however, Sclerus realized that it was too late: he was getting old, and his sight was rapidly failing. In the comparative darkness of his prison he had scarcely noticed the cataracts that were by now clouding both his eyes; back once again under the brilliant Anatolian sky, he knew that there was no hope – blindness would soon be upon him. Basil – his usual vindictiveness for once put aside – had already offered him almost unbelievably generous terms: he asked only that Sclerus should formally renounce all imperial attributes and the title of *basileus*; in return he would be accorded that of *curopalates*. His officers, once they had taken a new oath of loyalty, would retain all their ranks and titles and suffer no further penalties, while the rank and file would be allowed to return peaceably to their homes.

And so Bardas Sclerus made his submission; and on one of the imperial estates in Bithynia, for the first time in thirteen years, the young Emperor and the old general met face to face. When Basil saw his former enemy, now almost blind, being led into the audience chamber by two of the court ushers, he could barely suppress a gasp. 'Can this old dotard,' he asked those around him, 'truly be he whom I have feared for so long? See, he can scarcely walk by himself!' Then his eye fell on Sclerus's feet, which unaccountably still wore the imperial purple buskins; and he turned away his head. Only when the old man had removed the offending boots was he allowed to approach his sovereign and prostrate himself at the foot of the throne. Basil continued to treat him with surprising courtesy and consideration, listening carefully to his explanation of his past conduct which – if Psellus is to be believed – he simply ascribed to the will of God; at the dinner that followed, as a further gesture of reconciliation – though also, perhaps, to allay any suspicions of poison – he seized the wine-cup and took a copious draught before handing it to his guest. Then the two settled down to talk.

The Emperor opened the conversation by seeking the old general's advice. How, he asked him, could he best guard against any further rebellions by the powerful Anatolian barons, similar to those which Bardas Phocas and he himself had so recently led? Sclerus's reply is quoted at the head of this chapter. He did not propose that the barons should be suppressed: not even Basil at his most ruthless could have succeeded in doing that. But he did recommend that they should be kept on the tightest of reins, that they should be taxed to the hilt, harassed, plagued, financially persecuted, even deliberately and unfairly victimized, in such a way that they would be far too preoccupied in keeping their own heads above water to pursue any schemes of personal ambition. To Basil, these words alone would have occasioned little astonishment, expressing as they did his own opinions to the letter. What was interesting was the source from which they came. Now at last, as his life was drawing to a close and after the collapse of all his own ambitions, Bardas Sclerus was putting the interests of the Empire above those of himself and his class. His words may have been cynical, but they were also wise. Not only would Basil remember them for the rest of his life; he would act upon them, making them the keystone of his domestic policy. And he would never regret having done so.

In view of all the momentous events of the past two years, it is perhaps understandable that Basil should have given little time to the question of his sister's promised marriage to the Prince of Kiev. But Vladimir soon made clear that he was not to be trifled with. By responding to the Emperor's appeal he had saved Byzantium, and he was impatient for his reward. It was thus by way of reminding Basil of his responsibilities that in the summer of 989 he suddenly seized the imperial colony of Cherson in the Crimea, the last Byzantine outpost on the northern Black Sea coast, simultaneously sending him an ominous message to the effect that if his forgetfulness continued, Constantinople itself would suffer a similar fate.[1]

For Basil, the fall of Cherson was quite enough to be getting on with. Not only was the colony financially and strategically valuable in its own right; its capture also suggested the withdrawal of Russian support at a time when Bardas Sclerus was still at large and, worse still, the real possibility of a *rapprochement* between Vladimir and Tsar Samuel of Bulgaria. The 6,000 Varangians were still in Constantinople: they needed only a word from their sovereign for their present friendship to change to open hostility, in which event the damage that they might do would be incalculable. There was, in short, nothing for it: the agreement must be honoured. When the twenty-five-year-old princess was told by her brothers of her fate, she wept long and bitterly, accusing them of selling her into slavery – which, in the light of what was known about Vladimir, was not far from the truth. Finally, however, she was persuaded to accept the inevitable, and reluctantly embarked on the ship that was to take her to Cherson, where her betrothed awaited her. There the two were duly married, the colony being immediately returned to Basil as the *veno* – the traditional gift from the bridegroom; there too, immediately before the ceremony, the Prince of Kiev was baptized by the local bishop in what was perhaps the most fateful religious ceremony in Russian history.[2]

For it was the conversion of Vladimir, far more than that of his grandmother thirty-two years before, that marked the entry of Russia itself into the Christian fold. After their marriage, he and his bride were escorted to Kiev by the local clergy of Cherson, who immediately set about proselytizing and converting whole towns and villages *en masse*. The new Russian Church was thus from the outset subordinated to the the Patriarchate of Constantinople, forming part of the Eastern Church and tied culturally to Byzantium. There is consequently some reason to hope that poor Anna may have found her new life a degree or two less intolerable than she had feared it might be. Kiev, admittedly, was no Constantinople; but her husband became, after his baptism, a changed man. Away went the four previous wives and the 800 concubines;

---

1 Prince Svyatoslav's undertaking never to attack or invade this city (p. 223) had presumably lapsed on his death.

2 It is in fact possible that this was Vladimir's second baptism – the first having already taken place two years previously, after the return of his representatives from Constantinople and the conclusion of his agreement with the Emperor.

henceforth he was to give her no cause for complaint, spending all his time instead on supervising conversions, standing godfather at innumerable baptisms and building churches and monasteries wherever he went. Saints, one feels, can never be the easiest of husbands, and St Vladimir of Kiev is unlikely to have been an exception to the rule; but for a girl who had expected to share her bed with an ogre it must, all the same, have been something of a relief.

15
The Bulgar-Slayer

[989–1025]

His cruelty inflicted a cool and exquisite vengeance on the fifteen thousand captives who had been guilty of the defence of their country. They were deprived of sight, but to one of each hundred a single eye was left, that he might conduct his blind century to the presence of their king. Their king is said to have expired of grief and horror; the nation was awed by this terrible example; the Bulgarians were swept away from their settlements, and circumscribed within a narrow province; the surviving chiefs bequeathed to their children the advice of patience and the duty of revenge.

Edward Gibbon, *The Decline and Fall of the*
Roman Empire, Chapter LV

In the sixty-five-year reign of Basil II, the year 989 marks the watershed. Though still only thirty-one, he had held the title of Emperor for twenty-nine years. Of those years, the first sixteen – covering the period of his minority – had been overshadowed by the two military adventurers who had successively seized the throne, Nicephorus Phocas and John Tzimisces. The next nine had seen him the puppet – albeit a most unwilling one – of his great-uncle. The last four had been chiefly notable for his defeat and humiliation by Tsar Samuel at Trajan's Gate; for a major rebellion which had been contained only with outside help and which might still have been threatening him but for the sudden death of its leader; and, most recently, for his own submission to a piece of shameless blackmail on the part of the Prince of Kiev. It was not a distinguished record.

But by the end of 989 his luck had changed. The year itself had provided more than its share of disasters. After one of the cruellest winters in living memory, during which the sea itself was frozen, there had been the struggle with Bardas Phocas, and another with Bardas Sclerus; within days of the Russian capture of Cherson had come news of the fall to the Bulgars of Berrhoea (the modern Verria), a strategic fortress town guarding the approaches to Thessalonica; while serious disturbances had broken out in Antioch. The significance of the aurora borealis on 7 April, and of the brilliant comet which illuminated the sky for three weeks during July and August, was variously interpreted; but there could be no two minds about the calamitous earthquake which on the night of 25 October destroyed or damaged over forty churches in the capital alone – including St Sophia itself, whose central dome was split right across and had to be completely redesigned,[1] while part of the eastern apse simply subsided into a pile of rubble. A more unmistakable manifestation of the divine wrath could scarcely be imagined: yet the year was to close with the Empire enjoying internal peace for the first time since the death of John Tzimisces in 976 and its Emperor, with his defeats and disappointments behind him, standing at last on the threshold of glory.

Now that he had no longer anything to fear from the Anatolian barons, he was free to concentrate on the great task that was to occupy him for the next three decades: the annihilation of the Bulgar Empire. It was, however, typical of his farsightedness that he should first turn his attention to a small piece of unfinished business concerning David, Prince of the region of Upper Tao in Georgia. In 978 David, as a loyal vassal of the Empire, had been awarded temporary possession of a large area of imperial territory to the north of Lake Van. Since then, however, he had rather spoilt his record by supporting the rebellious Bardas Phocas – an error of judgement which he must bitterly have regretted when, in the autumn of 989, an imperial army marched eastward with obviously punitive intent. Fortunately for him the commanding general, a certain John of Chaldia, had authority from the Emperor to offer terms: David might keep the ceded territory for his lifetime and would be additionally awarded the title of *curopalates*, provided that *all* his lands – including his own birthplace and patrimony – reverted on his death to the imperial crown. With the army sharpening its swords only a mile or two away, the prince had little choice but to agree; and Basil considerably extended his eastern frontiers without the loss of a single life.

Unfortunately, as he well knew, diplomacy of this kind would have

---

1 The new design, by an Armenian named Trdat, was to collapse in its turn in 1346. (See *Byzantium: The Early Centuries*, p. 203n.) Another casualty of the earthquake was the Aqueduct of Valens, the subsequent repair of which put it back into working order, enabling it to bring fresh water to the city for the first time in several hundred years.

little impact on Tsar Samuel; and in the early spring of 991 he set off with his army for Thessalonica, where he strengthened the defences, prostrated himself before the altar of the city's patron St Demetrius,[1] and tracked down to a remote monastery a living local saint named Photius, who had been present at his baptism – after the ceremony he had actually carried him in his arms back to the Palace – and who now promised to pray for him nightly during the coming campaign.[2] This was to continue for the next four years, during which Basil never once relaxed his pressure. Gone were the days when warfare was restricted to the summer months; the new imperial army, trained and toughened by the Emperor in person and now in superb physical condition, showed itself as impervious to the January snows as to the August sun. Many cities – including Berrhoea – were recaptured. Some were garrisoned; others, less lucky, were razed to the ground.

There were, however, no dramatic advances, no great victories. Trajan's Gate had taught Basil a lesson he would never forget. Success for him depended above all else on faultless organization. The army must act as a single, perfectly coordinated body. Psellus tells us how at first sight of the enemy he would draw up his troops 'like a solid tower', establishing unbreakable lines of communication between himself and the cavalry, the cavalry and the heavy infantry, the heavy infantry and the light. When battle began, he would absolutely forbid any soldier to break ranks or advance independently in front of the line. Heroics of any kind were not simply discouraged, but punished with instant dismissal – or, on occasion, worse. His men complained openly about their master's endless inspections, and the attention he paid to every minute detail of their weapons and equipment; but they gave him their confidence and their trust because they knew that he left nothing to chance, that he never undertook an operation until he was certain of victory and that he valued their lives as he did his own.

In such circumstances progress might be sure; but it was also undeniably slow, and it comes as little surprise to find that when the Emperor was summoned urgently to Syria early in 995 he had achieved relatively

1 St Demetrius was, with St Theodore Stratilates, St Theodore of Tyre and St George, one of that great quartet (or possibly trio, since the two Theodores may have been one and the same) of warrior saints who protected Byzantine armies in battle.

2 There is a theory that Photius may have left his monastery and accompanied Basil throughout his four-year campaign, much as St Athanasius had accompanied Nicephorus Phocas; but on this point – as on so many others – our sadly inadequate sources are dumb.

little. Despite the reconquered towns, the situation was still very much as it had been fifteen years before, with the Bulgar Tsar as strong and determined as ever and the threat to Byzantium not a jot diminished. Samuel too had moved with caution, adopting the traditional Bulgar tactic of keeping to the mountains and avoiding pitched battles. He possessed, he knew, one great advantage over his enemy: he was on home ground. Over a prolonged campaign Basil might well gain the upper hand; but sooner or later he would be called away, quite possibly with a fair proportion of his army, leaving the remainder under the command of lesser men; and Samuel's turn would come. He would keep his powder dry, and play a waiting game.

When he had the choice, Basil preferred to move slowly and with caution; but he was also capable of astonishing speed when the occasion demanded, as he showed during his whirlwind Syrian expedition of 995. The crisis had been precipitated by the designs of the Egyptian Fatimid Caliph Aziz on the city of Aleppo, a Byzantine protectorate since the days of Nicephorus Phocas. Already in 994 its Emir had appealed to the Emperor, who had sent reinforcements to Antioch with instructions to the local governor, Michael Bourtzes – he who had recaptured the city for the Empire in 969 – to intervene; but Bourtzes was, alas, no longer the dashing young general he had been a quarter of a century before and was certainly no match for the Fatimid commander Manjutekin, who on 15 September had virtually destroyed his army on the banks of the Orontes.

The Emir, now desperate, dispatched a second appeal, stressing that Antioch itself was now in grave danger; and this time Basil recognized the emergency for what it was – one in which he could trust no one but himself. Hurrying back to the capital with as many troops as he dared, he collected all available reserves until he could boast a new army of some 40,000 men.[1] There remained, however, the problem of getting them to Syria. For such a force, with full arms, armour and equipment, the 600 miles across Anatolia would represent a good three months' march. By the time it arrived, in all probability, both Antioch and Aleppo would be lost. Every day counted. What was to be done?

Basil's solution, simple as it was, seems to have been unprecedented in

---

1 Once again our sources are miserably thin and uninformative. The Byzantine chroniclers tell us next to nothing; we are left with the Jews and the Arabs, of whom Yahya (who gives this figure) seems to be usually the most reliable.

all Byzantine history. He mounted his entire army. Every soldier was provided with two mules, one to ride and one for his equipment, serving also as a reserve. Even then, some travelled faster than others; but the Emperor, himself riding at the head of the column, could not wait for stragglers. Towards the end of April 995, he drew up the first 17,000 of his troops beneath the walls of Aleppo. They had taken just sixteen days – but they arrived not a day too soon. The city was already under heavy siege; a week more and it would have fallen, with much of northern Syria, into Fatimid hands. Now it was saved. Caught unawares and hopelessly outnumbered, Manjutekin fled back to Damascus. A few days later the Emperor himself headed south, sacking Emesa and sowing a trail of devastation as far as Tripoli. Returning, he established a strong garrison in Tortosa (Tartus) and in place of Bourtzes – whom he put under house arrest – appointed a new and younger Governor of Antioch with instructions to emphasize his supremacy in the region by annual shows of strength. Then he started back to his capital.

Even on his breakneck outward journey, Basil had had time to observe the countryside through which he rode; he drew his own conclusions, and during his more leisurely return his first impressions were confirmed. This was, so far as we can tell, his first visit to Asia since he had accompanied his stepfather Nicephorus Phocas to Cilicia as a child; and he was amazed at the size and splendour of the estates built up by the Anatolian 'powerful' on what was legally either imperial property or, more probably, that of the local village communes. Several of them – including old Eustathius Maleinus, in whose territory Bardas Phocas had raised the standard of revolt in 986 – made the mistake of attempting to assure him of their loyalty by receiving him in a style that he himself could hardly have equalled: mindless displays of wealth which, given his own hatred of empty ostentation, invariably aroused his fury. It was a sombre, pensive Emperor who returned that autumn to Constantinople.

On 1 January 996 there was promulgated over the Emperor's seal an edict the very title of which must have struck horror into the hearts of those Anatolian noblemen who had so recently tried to impress him: 'New Constitution,' it read, 'of the pious Emperor Basil the Young, by which are Condemned those Rich Men who Amass their Wealth at the Expense of the Poor', going on to make specific reference to a similar – though far less stringent – decree of Romanus Lecapenus in 935. In that decree Romanus had stipulated a forty-year period of grace, during which claims could be made for the restitution of unjustly expropriated property; the trouble, as Basil well knew, was that any rich landowner could easily suppress such claims, by bribery, blackmail or a combination of the two; and he did not hesitate to name the guilty:

The Patrician Constantine Maleinus and his son the *magister* Eustathius have enjoyed for a hundred years, perhaps 120, the uncontested possession of property unlawfully acquired by them. The same is true of the Phocas who, from father to son over more than a century, have also succeeded in retaining estates to which they have no legal title . . .

Basil abolished the forty-year period altogether, requiring that any territorial claim, to be valid, must go back at least to the decree of his great-grandfather Romanus, sixty-one years before. All property acquired since that time was to be restored immediately to its previous owner or his family, without compensation or payment for any improvements made. Even imperial *chrysobuls* – including those signed with the name of Basil himself – were to be inadmissible as a defence, while any deed of grant issued between 976 and 985 in the name of Basil the eunuch was automatically null and void unless specially revalidated in the Emperor's own hand.

The results were dramatic – and, to the Anatolian aristocracy, calamitous. Maleinus was not only expropriated but imprisoned for life. The Phocas lost all but a minute fraction of their vast estates. Some noble families were reduced literally to beggary, others to the level of the peasants around them. But for those peasants, and for the local small-holders – the traditional backbone of imperial armies for hundreds of years – the way was open to return to the lands of their forefathers. Meanwhile vast tracts of formerly imperial land reverted again to the Empire, while the Emperor himself gained immeasurably in strength. For thirteen years he had been obliged to defend his lawful throne against 'the powerful'. Now their power was gone; and his revenge, we may be sure, was sweet.

Even after the publication of his fateful edict, the Emperor did not at once return to Bulgaria. There was, inevitably, serious disaffection in Anatolia, and it was important that he should be at hand in the capital, ready to deal with any trouble. Besides, he had now been absent for nearly five years from the imperial chancery, where a vast backlog of work had accumulated. The Patriarchate – to take but one example –

had been vacant since 991; on 12 April 996 Basil appointed a learned physician named Sisinnius to the post. In one respect it was an unfortunate choice – not so much because Sisinnius was a layman, but because he shared all his master's dislike and distrust of the Western Empire; and scarcely had he assumed his new office when there arrived in Constantinople an embassy from the court of young Otto III. Otto, it appeared, wanted a Byzantine wife, just as his father had done; and he was now making a formal request for the hand in marriage of one of Basil's three nieces Eudocia, Zoe or Theodora – he did not greatly mind which – the daughters of his brother Constantine.

On the face of it, Otto's embassy was a surprising one. Admittedly his father Otto II had married the Greek princess Theophano,[1] who had made him an excellent wife and had done much for the spread of Byzantine culture in the West; but he had unfortunately seen the marriage as grounds for claiming the 'restitution', as part of her dowry, of all Byzantine lands in Italy, and war had been the inevitable result. This had continued intermittently until 981, when Otto II had marched into Apulia, his wrath on this occasion directed principally against the occupying Saracens; and Basil – or more probably his great-uncle the *parakoimomenos* – had seen his chance. A temporary alliance had quickly been arranged with the Saracens, who soon afterwards cut Otto's army to pieces near Stilo in Calabria. Luckily for the Western Emperor, he was a strong swimmer: he swam to a passing ship, managed somehow to conceal his identity and later, as the vessel passed Rossano, jumped overboard again and struck out for the shore. But he never recovered from the humiliation and died in Rome the following year, aged twenty-eight.[2]

His son by Theophano, Otto III, was an extraordinary child. Succeeding to the imperial throne at the age of three, he grew up combining the traditional ambitions of his line with a romantic mysticism clearly inherited from his mother, forever dreaming of a great Byzantinesque theocracy that would embrace Germans and Greeks, Italians and Slavs alike, with God at its head and himself and the Pope – in that order – His twin Viceroys. Who could be more suited than he – born as he was of a Greek mother – to make this dream a reality? And what better foundation for that reality than another marriage alliance between the two Empires? Otto chose his ambassadors carefully. They were Bishop

1 See p. 220.
2 He is the only Holy Roman Emperor to be buried in St Peter's.

Bernward of Würzburg[1] and John Philagathus, Archbishop of Piacenza, a Greek from Calabria who, having begun life as a slave, had become the close friend, protégé and finally chaplain of Theophano, and had retained the favour of her son after her death.

Alas, we have no Bishop of Cremona to give us an account of this embassy; but it is safe to assume that it was received in Constantinople a good deal more cordially than Liudprand had been. Basil would have asked nothing better than a marriage which would, with any luck, preserve the peace in south Italy and give him a free hand to pursue his struggle with the Bulgars, and it is recorded that when Philagathus returned to Rome[2] he took with him Byzantine ambassadors to negotiate the details with Otto in person. If those ambassadors had found the Emperor in the city, there is little doubt that all would have been swiftly arranged: the marriage would have taken place and the future would have been very different – not only for those directly concerned. Unfortunately Otto had left some weeks before, with consequences that would be unhappy for him, deeply unpleasant for them and, for John Philagathus, nothing short of catastrophic.

Early that same year, 996, the fifteen-year-old Emperor had crossed the snow-covered Brenner Pass and entered Italy in full imperial state, with the Holy Lance that had pierced Christ's side[3] carried before him and a sizeable army marching behind. In Pavia he had heard of the death of Pope John XV; and in Ravenna, at the request of delegates from the Roman nobility who had come to greet him, he had personally designated as John's successor his own cousin Bruno of Carinthia, then aged twenty-four, who took the name of Gregory V. On Ascension Day – 21 May – Otto was crowned by Gregory in St Peter's. When he left for Germany a few weeks later, it seemed to everyone that the imperial power had once again been firmly established in the Eternal City, and that Western Christendom was in safer hands than for many years past.

Pope Gregory, however, now made a disastrous mistake. He revoked

---

1 Not Bishop – later St – Bernward of Hildesheim, as Schlumberger rather surprisingly assumes.

2 Minus, unfortunately, the Bishop of Würzburg, who expired *en route*. Such is the paucity of our information on this period that we do not even know whether his death occurred on the outward or the return journey; only that he was buried in the monastery of Politika, on the island of Euboea.

3 Another Holy Lance, with equal claims to authenticity, had been cherished in Constantinople since the seventh century and was to remain there till 1492, when Sultan Beyazit II presented it to Pope Innocent VIII. Yet another was to be discovered at Antioch during the First Crusade; this is almost certainly the one which is still preserved in the Armenian cathedral at Etchmiadzin. We may take our choice.

the sentence of banishment that had been passed on the Patrician Crescentius, head of the most influential family in Rome, who had been responsible for the election of John XV and had, until shortly before Otto's arrival, held the city in his grip; and Crescentius, heedless of the oath of fidelity that he had been obliged to swear, at once reverted to his old ways. One of his first actions on returning to power was to seize Basil's ambassadors (who were apparently still in Rome, recovering from their long sea voyage) and throw them into prison – more, it seems, to spite Otto by spoiling his marriage plans than for any other reason. Gregory, panic-stricken, sent urgently to his cousin, begging him to return and restore imperial–papal authority; but Otto refused – on the somewhat surprising grounds that he could not stand the climate – and the poor Pope had no alternative but to flee, early in 997, to Pavia, whereupon Crescentius appointed in his place none other than the Archbishop of Piacenza, John Philagathus.

Why one of the Emperor's most trusted servants should have lent himself to such villainy is hard to understand. Having successfully concluded the preliminary negotiations for the imperial marriage, Philagathus could confidently have expected high preferment in the near future; to have betrayed his master by throwing in his lot with an unscrupulous adventurer seems little short of lunacy. But he was eaten up by ambition, and the immediate prospect of the papal throne, even if he were to occupy it only as Anti-Pope, seems to have been more than he could resist. In May 997 he installed himself in the Lateran Palace under the name of John XVI.

He soon had cause to regret his decision. Already excommunicated by his rival, he spent a miserable summer under a hail of abuse from every bishop in Italy, scarcely able to show himself in the streets of the city, dealing with the remonstrations of both Gregory and Otto by the simple expedient of throwing their ambassadors too into prison. Then, towards the end of the year, came retribution. The Emperor of the West – trusting, presumably, that the Roman winter would prove less of a trial to his constitution than the Roman summer – marched into the peninsula for the second time, joined the Pope at Pavia (where they celebrated Christmas together) and then, with a mixed force of Germans and Italians, advanced on Rome. Two years before, he had come peaceably, as a friend. This time he was angry – and pitiless. As confusion spread through the city Crescentius shut himself up with a dozen faithful henchmen in the Castel Sant'Angelo. John Philagathus meanwhile fled the city and took refuge in a tower that was said to be impregnable; but a few days later he was tracked down by a party of Germans who quickly proved that it was nothing of the kind. On Pope Gregory's orders – but, we are assured, without the knowledge of the Emperor – he was taken prisoner and hideously mutilated. His captors cut off his ears, nose and hands, put out his eyes and tore out his tongue; then they dragged him back to Rome and flung him into a monastic cell to await trial.

Some time during Lent in 998, what was left of John Philagathus was brought before Pope and Emperor, sitting side by side. John's fellow-countryman St Nilus, abbot of Rossano in Calabria, pleaded earnestly that he had already suffered enough; but Pope Gregory thought otherwise. The unfortunate man was now seated backwards on a mule and paraded through the streets of Rome to jeers and catcalls; only then was he permitted to retire to a distant retreat – probably the German monastery of Fulda, near Frankfurt-am-Main – where he lived on, after a fashion, till 1013.

As for Crescentius, he held out in the Castel Sant'Angelo until 29 April, when he was finally obliged to surrender. His punishment was comparatively merciful: at the highest point of the castle, where he could be seen by all Rome, he was publicly beheaded. His body was flung into the surrounding ditch, whence it was later retrieved and, together with those of his twelve followers who had suffered a similar fate, hung by the heels from a gallows on Monte Mario.

For Basil II, who seems – though we cannot be sure – to have remained throughout this period in Constantinople, news of the fate of John Philagathus and the events leading up to it could hardly have been more unwelcome. Not that he would have been moved by any description of the archbishop's sufferings; he was not that sort of man. But it would have suited him to have a Greek on the throne of St Peter almost as much as to have a niece as Empress of the West;[1] now the first was out of the question, and even the second had run into difficulties. His ambassadors, who had left Constantinople nearly two years before, had finally been released from prison; but they had not yet made contact with Otto – whose pro-Greek sympathies might well have been, after the Philagathus affair, not quite what they were.

---

1 It has even been suggested – by St Peter Damian (most uncharitable of chroniclers) and by many others after him – that John's elevation might have been due less to Crescentius's powers of persuasion than to the sacks of Byzantine gold that he had brought with him from Constantinople.

But Basil had other more immediate preoccupations: and the most important of these was the fact that the past three years had seen an alarming increase in the power of Tsar Samuel. In 996, taking full advantage of the Emperor's absence in the East, Samuel had ambushed and killed the Governor of Thessalonica and had taken prisoner both his son and his successor, John of Chaldia. He had then invaded the defenceless Theme of Hellas, which he had sacked and plundered as far south as Corinth. The following year, admittedly, had seen a decisive defeat of the Bulgar army – on the banks of the river Spercheus, near Thermopylae – by the best of the new generation of imperial generals, Nicephorus Uranus; Samuel himself had been lucky to escape with his life. Soon afterwards, however, the Tsar had seized the important Adriatic harbour of Dyrrachium (Durazzo, now Dürres in Albania) and begun a long, triumphant advance through the Dalmatian hinterland and into Bosnia. If he were not stopped quickly it might soon be too late to stop him at all.

The Byzantine lands along the shores of the Adriatic had always presented something of an administrative problem. In terms of distance they were no further from Constantinople than was Syria; but the roads were steep and rocky and the populations, even in peaceful times, tended to be a good deal less friendly than those of Asia Minor. In present circumstances, Basil would have had to fight every inch of the way. There was, as he saw it, only one solution: the Republic of Venice, with which he was already on excellent terms. Already in 992 he had concluded a treaty with Pietro Orseolo II – one of the most brilliant Doges in Venetian history – by the terms of which Venice was granted generous commercial privileges in Constantinople in return for her agreement to transport imperial troops in time of war; why should the republic not now take over responsibility for the entire Dalmatian coast, ruling it as a protectorate under Byzantine suzerainty?

Pietro Orseolo asked nothing better. Here was an offer of a practically inexhaustible new source of corn for Venice's rapidly growing population, and of timber for ship-building. Furthermore, for some time Venetian merchantmen had been suffering severely at the hands of Croatian pirates; such an arrangement as was now proposed would allow him to move against them far more effectively than before. His son Giovanni hastened to Constantinople, and the matter was soon settled. On Ascension Day, AD 1000, Orseolo – newly dubbed *Dux Dalmatiae* – attended Mass in the cathedral of S. Pietro di Castello and received from the Bishop of Olivolo a consecrated standard.[1] He then boarded his flagship and set sail at the head of a huge fleet to receive the homage of his new subjects. Tsar Samuel might control the hinterland and the fastnesses of Bosnia; but the Greek-speaking cities of the coast were henceforth in safe hands.

The Emperor meanwhile turned his attention back to Bulgaria itself, employing precisely the same tactics as before: first, the establishment of an impregnable base camp – now Philippopolis (Plovdiv); then a slow, methodical spreading-out to north, west and south, consolidating every conquest and garrisoning every captured town before advancing to the next. In 999 another Fatimid victory in Syria caused a repetition of the crisis of five years before and called him back to the East – fortunately as it happened, since he chanced to be in Tarsus when, on Easter Sunday 1000, Prince David of Upper Tao was assassinated; he was thus able to move in immediately with the army to claim his new inheritance. The governorship of this vast region to the north of Lake Van he entrusted to the dead man's cousin Bagrat, King of Abasgia, to whom he also transferred David's title of *curopalates*; but it was already late autumn before he was back on the Bosphorus. A few months later he was able to conclude a ten-year truce with the Fatimid Caliphate. Now at last, with both his eastern and western frontiers properly protected, he was free to concentrate on Bulgaria; and in the summer of 1001 he succeeded both in recapturing Berrhoea and in expelling the Bulgar garrisons from Thessaly before returning to the capital – where important business awaited him.

The Emperor Otto, far from giving up his idea of a Byzantine marriage, had sent a second embassy to Constantinople with instructions not only to conclude any outstanding arrangements but to bring him back his bride. It was consequently a far larger and more impressive mission than its predecessor. At its head was Archbishop Arnulf of Milan, the richest and most magnificent ecclesiastic in the West, who appeared at the Palace on a superbly caparisoned steed whose very horseshoes were of gold, secured with silver nails. Although he made no attempt to match his guest either in sartorial splendour or in the social graces – for Arnulf was renowned for his cultivation, intelligence and charm – Basil received him with every honour, bade him sit by his side and, calling for an interpreter, engaged him in long and earnest conversa-

1 There is reason to believe that on it the Venetian emblem of the winged lion of St Mark, holding in its paw an open book, appeared for the first time.

tion while all the other high dignitaries of East and West remained standing. He made no difficulties: the sooner the marriage were to take place, the sooner he could be off to Bulgaria where he belonged. Of his three nieces the eldest, Eudocia, was badly disfigured by smallpox and destined to spend her life in the cloister while the youngest, Theodora, is said to have been almost as unpleasing in appearance; she too – as we shall see – never married. The middle sister, the Princess Zoe, was however a good-looking and eminently nubile girl of twenty-three, in every respect suitable for the match. The archbishop was delighted with her, and had no doubt that his imperial master would be equally enthusiastic; while Zoe herself seems to have displayed none of the reluctance that had characterized the departure of her aunt Anna to Kiev a dozen years before. In January 1002, accompanied by Arnulf and his suite and a retinue appropriate to a *porphyrogenita* and an Empress, she set sail for her new home.

Alas, it was not to be. When her ship reached Bari, she found tragic news awaiting her. Her betrothed, stricken by a sudden fever, had died on 24 January at the castle of Paterno near Rome, aged twenty-two. Poor Zoe: by his death she had lost far more than a husband – far more, even, than the imperial crown of the West. If she and Otto had had a son, he might in due course have inherited not only the Western Empire but – in the absence of any other male heir – the Eastern as well, uniting the two for the first time and ruling over a territory extending from the borders of France to those of Persia; and the whole subsequent history of the world might have been changed. Now those dreams had vanished. Sadly she bade farewell to the archbishop and re-embarked on the same vessel by which she had come.

We may indeed grieve for Zoe; we need not, on the other hand, grieve for her too much. The Western Empire might have slipped from her grasp; but the Eastern remained her inheritance and, as we shall see in the next chapter, for more than twenty years after the death of her father she was to enjoy all the power – and all the marriages – that she could have wished.

The spirits of the young princess can hardly have been much lifted when, in the spring of 1004, there was celebrated in Constantinople another dynastic marriage with all the pomp and panoply that she might have expected for her own. The bride on this occasion was a distant relative of the two Emperors, a certain Maria Argyra; the groom was

Giovanni, the son of the Doge of Venice Pietro Orseolo, whom his father had recently raised to share the ducal throne. The ceremony took place in the imperial chapel and was performed by the Patriarch himself, the two Emperors Basil and Constantine both being present to crown the bridal pair in the Eastern fashion. When the festivities were over, a magnificent palace was put at their disposal in which they stayed for several months. Autumn was already far advanced – as was Maria's pregnancy – by the time they returned to Venice.

But if Zoe envied the couple their happiness, she did not do so for long. In 1006, after a series of disastrous harvests, north Italy and Dalmatia were stricken by famine; and in the wake of famine, as so often in the Middle Ages, came plague – carrying off, among many thousands of humbler victims, Giovanni Orseolo, his wife and their baby son. The death of the young Dogaressa was recorded, with ill-concealed satisfaction, by St Peter Damian; vindictive as always, however, he ascribes it to a rather different cause:

Such was the luxury of her habits that she scorned even to wash herself in common water, obliging her servants instead to collect the dew that fell from the heavens for her to bathe in. Nor did she deign to touch her food with her fingers, but would command her eunuchs to cut it up in small pieces, which she would impale on a certain golden instrument with two prongs and thus carry to her mouth. Her rooms, too, were so heavy with incense and various perfumes that it is nauseating for me to speak of them, nor would my readers readily believe it. But this woman's vanity was hateful to Almighty God; and so, unmistakably, did He take His revenge. For He raised over her the sword of His divine justice, so that her whole body did putrefy and all her limbs began to wither, filling her bedchamber with an unbearable odour such that no one – not a handmaiden, nor even a slave – could withstand this dreadful attack on the nostrils; except for one serving-girl who, with the help of aromatic concoctions, conscientiously remained to do her bidding. And even she could only approach her mistress hurriedly, and then immediately withdraw. So, after a slow decline and agonizing torments, to the joyful relief of her friends she breathed her last.

Almost as soon as the Venetian wedding was over, Basil had returned to Bulgaria, where he was devoting all his energies to the eradication of Tsar Samuel and his Empire. By dint of almost continuous campaigning between 1000 and 1004, he had regained virtually all the eastern half of the Balkan peninsula, from Thessalonica to the Iron Gates of the Danube; Samuel, who had always trusted to what might today be called guerrilla tactics, now found himself struggling against an enemy who could move through rough country as quickly as he could himself, who never gave him an opportunity for ambush or surprise attack and who seemed alike impervious to heat and cold, wind and weather. Throughout the next decade the Emperor continued to advance, though our sources – such as they are – give us infuriatingly little detail. We know, for example, that in 1005 Samuel was betrayed by his father-in-law John Chryselius, his daughter Miroslava and her husband Ashot the Taronite, who handed over Dyrrachium to Basil in return for money and titles; and that in 1009 the Tsar suffered a crippling defeat at a village called Creta, near Thessalonica. But that is about all. It is only in 1014 that the mists clear away sufficiently to allow us a glimpse of a battle which, though it by no means marked the end of the war, certainly put its eventual outcome beyond reasonable doubt.

It was fought in the narrow defile of Cimbalongus, or Clidion, leading from Serrae (Seres) into the valley of the Upper Struma. Fifteen years before, Samuel would probably have prepared an ambush; but by this time any such plan, as he knew all too well, was doomed to failure. Instead, he decided to occupy it with his own troops, blocking Basil's way forward and obliging him to undertake a long and dangerous detour. Thus, when the Emperor arrived with his army, he found the entry to the defile closed by row after row of wooden palisades. He was still wondering how to proceed when one of his generals, the *strategos* of Philippopolis Nicephorus Xiphias, suggested leading a detachment secretly up the wooded hillside, along the ridge and down again to attack the Bulgars in the rear. At first Basil was sceptical – the plan smacked of risk and daring, two qualities he always mistrusted – but finally, seeing no other way out of the difficulty, he reluctantly agreed.

So Xiphias stole out of the imperial camp with a small body of carefully chosen men, made his way through the forest and eventually emerged at the further end of the defile, behind Samuel's army; and on 29 July he attacked, while the Emperor simultaneously launched a determined assault on the palisades. The Bulgars, taken entirely by surprise and unable to defend both extremities of the pass at once, panicked and fled. Many were cut down as they ran, many more were captured – some 14,000 to 15,000, if our sources are to be believed.[1] The Tsar himself would have been among them but for the heroism of his son, who somehow remounted him and brought him back to the

---

1 Cecaumenus, writing some sixty years after the event, gives a figure of 14,000; Cedrenus 15,000.

fortress of Prilapon (the modern Prilep). The two of them were especially lucky, for Basil was in vengeful mood: it was now that he meted out the punishment for which – more than for any of his conquests, or any of his legislation – he is chiefly remembered, and which is described by Gibbon at the head of this chapter.

It was the beginning of October before the dreadful procession shuffled into the Tsar's castle at Prespa. Samuel was already a sick man, broken by the misfortunes of his nation and the failure of his hopes; and at the sight of his once-splendid army in its pitiful state he collapsed in a fit of apoplexy. A draught of cold water revived him for a few moments; but he soon lapsed into a coma and died two days later. Most of those who mourned his death knew full well that they were also mourning that of his Empire; and yet, with all the courage of their despair, the Bulgars still fought on – first under his son Gabriel Radomir and then, after the latter's murder in 1016, under his murderer (who was also his cousin), John Vladislav. Only when John in his turn was killed while besieging Dyrrachium in February 1018 did they surrender. Soon afterwards Basil made his formal entry into their capital, Ochrid. He was met at the gates of the city by John's widow, Maria, and as many of their family as she had been able to gather: three sons[1] and six daughters, together with two daughters of Gabriel Radomir and five of his sons, one of whom had been blinded. There was even a bastard son of Samuel's. Basil received them with friendliness and courtesy and took all eighteen under his protection.

He had been twenty-eight years old when he first took up arms against the Bulgar Empire; he was now sixty. Its annihilation had taken him most of his active life, but now at last the task was triumphantly accomplished. For the first time since the arrival of the Slavs the entire Balkan peninsula was under Byzantine control. All that he had to do now was to show himself in as many cities as possible, to receive homage, to exact oaths of fealty and to establish himself in the minds of the populations as their overlord. From Ochrid he passed on with his royal protégés to Prespa, where one of the bravest of the Bulgar generals, Ivatsia, was blinded when he refused to submit; thence to Castoria, where two daughters of Tsar Samuel were brought before him and, suddenly catching sight of the Tsaritsa Maria, were with difficulty

---

1 Their eldest son Prusian and two more of his brothers had escaped to the mountains, where they were resolved to continue the struggle; but it was not long before they too gave themselves up.

prevented from tearing her limb from limb; thence to Thermopylae, where he gazed upon the bleached bones of the thousands of Bulgar soldiers slaughtered by Nicephorus Uranus twenty-three years before and – with still greater interest – upon the mighty fortifications built by another of his commanders, Roupen the Armenian, to protect the pass against further assault; thence finally to Athens itself, where he climbed up to the Acropolis to attend a service of thanksgiving in the Church of the Theotokos, the Mother of God – originally dedicated to a very different goddess, and known to us as the Parthenon.

In war Basil II – called *Bulgaroctonus*, the Bulgar-Slayer – had been merciless and brutal; with the coming of peace he proved moderate and understanding. The Bulgars were no longer his enemies; they were his subjects, and as such they deserved every consideration. Taxes were kept deliberately low, and payable not in gold as elsewhere in the Empire but in kind. The Patriarchate of Ochrid was downgraded to the status of an archbishopric, but not subordinated to the see of Constantinople: the Bulgarian Church thus continued to be autocephalous in every respect save one: the appointment of the archbishop was kept by the Emperor in his own hands. Most of the conquered territory was divided into two main Themes, Bulgaria and Paristrium, the latter being essentially the old Danubian province to the north. Certain areas in the west, however – notably Croatia, Dioclea, Rascia and Bosnia – continued to be ruled by their own native princes under imperial suzerainty. As for the Bulgars themselves, the vast majority welcomed the peace and caused no trouble (except on two later occasions when they very understandably protested against corrupt imperial governors); the aristocracy, for their part, were integrated into the Byzantine social and official hierarchy, several of them being given high office. Thus Prusian, the eldest son of John Vladislav, received the rank of *magister* and subsequently became *strategos* of the important Brucellarian Theme, covering roughly the area between Nicaea and Ancyra. His brother Aaron was later to be *catapan* (military governor) of Vaspurakan and, as we shall see, brother-in-law of the Emperor Isaac Comnenus.

And so the Bulgarian problem was settled; but the Emperor's work was not yet done. The eastern *curopalates*, King Bagrat of Abasgia, had died in 1014, whereupon his son George had immediately renounced the agreement of fourteen years before, invading and occupying Tao and Phasiane. Basil had sent a fleet to the far end of the Black Sea in an attempt to contain the damage, but now was his first chance of dealing effectively and conclusively with the rebel prince. In 1021 he set out on his third and last Asian expedition; in the following year George surrendered, leaving his three-year-old son in the Emperor's hands as a hostage for his good behaviour.[1] At this point Basil could easily have turned back; instead, he seized the opportunity to improve his position along his ever-troublesome eastern frontier. By astute diplomacy and without any threat or even suggestion of military aggression, he annexed the region of Vaspurakan; equally peacefully, he persuaded John Smbat, the Armenian King of Ani, to bequeath his kingdom to the Empire on his death. By the time he returned to the capital in 1023 he had established no less than eight new Themes – running in a huge arc from that of Antioch in the far south and then north-eastward with those of Teluch, 'the Euphrates Cities' (later to be known as the Theme of Edessa), Melitene, Taron, Vaspurakan, Iberia and Theodosiopolis. He himself now reigned supreme from the Adriatic to Azerbaijan.

He was just sixty-five: a good age by medieval standards. Almost half his life had been spent on campaign. Most other men of his years and achievements would have been only too ready to lay down their swords and live out the rest of their days in peace and tranquillity. But Basil was not like other men: his energies were undiminished, and the reports that he found awaiting him at Constantinople immediately suggested a new channel into which they might be directed. These reports came from the imperial *catapan* in south Italy, Basil Boioannes. The political situation in that region had been greatly complicated since 1017 by the arrival of large numbers of young Norman adventurers and freebooters, who had entered the peninsula in search of fame and fortune and had willingly allied themselves with the local Lombard separatists in the latter's efforts to free all Apulia and Calabria from Byzantine rule. For a year they had had considerable success; but in October 1019, at Cannae on the River Ofanto – where in 216 BC the Carthaginians under Hannibal had destroyed the army of Republican Rome – Boioannes had won a similar (if smaller) victory over a mixed force of Lombards and Normans. Three years later he had blocked a huge military expedition led by the Western Emperor

---

1 The little prince was returned three years later, and only just in time. A day or two after he had been safely delivered into the hands of his parents, Constantine VIII – who had just become sole ruler – made a determined effort to have him brought back to Constantinople. Fortunately the attempt failed; less than two years later, on George's death at the age of thirty, he succeeded to the throne under the name of Bagrat IV, and ruled over almost all Georgia for nearly half a century.

Henry II in person, and forced it back over the Alps. Now, surely, was the moment to strike again while the iron was still hot, consolidating past gains, re-establishing traditional frontiers and clearing Byzantine territory once and for all of foreign upstarts.

In south Italy, thanks to Boioannes, the job was already half done; there remained, however, the problem of Sicily which, reconquered for the Empire by Belisarius in 535, had been invaded by the Arabs three centuries later[1] and had long been effectively part of the Muslim world. Now at long last this unsatisfactory state of affairs could be rectified. A great new army was prepared, and Boioannes was ordered to draw up a comprehensive plan for the invasion of the island in 1026. It was to be another twelve years, however, before that invasion took place; and when it did, neither the Emperor or his splendid *catapan* were there to lead it. Ten days before Christmas 1025, at the ninth hour of the day, Basil II died in the Great Palace of Constantinople, aged sixty-seven.

He had been a phenomenon: the most astonishing, perhaps, in all Byzantine history. For reasons which should be clear from the previous chapter, he had come late to maturity; but once he had found his touch it never deserted him. Despising as he did the outward trappings of power – by which almost all Emperors before and after him set so much store – he none the less effortlessly dominated and directed, by the impact of his personality alone, every branch of the administration of Church and State. He made and unmade Patriarchs, framed laws which revolutionized the whole social structure of Anatolia, summoned foreign princes again and again to do his bidding and – by virtue of the way in which he uniquely combined the strategic vision of a commander-in-chief with the meticulous attention to detail of a drill-sergeant – showed himself one of the most brilliant generals that the Empire had ever seen.

This last quality is the more surprising in that, apart from what must inevitably surround the figure of an Emperor, he was utterly devoid of glamour. Throughout history, nearly every outstanding leader in the field has had something charismatic about him, some indefinable spark that fires the imagination of his men, persuading them to follow him into battle not only willingly but with energy and enthusiasm. Of this, so far as we can judge, Basil possessed scarcely a trace. His campaigns generated no thunder or lightning. Under him the imperial army was more like a flood of volcanic lava, advancing slowly but inexorably, as

1 See pp. 37–8.

impervious to direct frontal resistance as it was to attack from the sides or the rear. After his youthful humiliation at Trajan's Gate – which he never forgot, and for which the entire Bulgarian war was, in a sense, an act of revenge – he took few risks, and suffered few casualties. But although he was trusted by his troops, they never loved him.

No one – with the possible exception of his mother – ever did. Love as an emotion seems never to have touched him, either as lover or beloved. Indeed, there is no evidence that anyone even liked him much. The chroniclers mention no close associates. No lonelier man ever occupied the Byzantine throne – or any other, for that matter. And it is hardly surprising: Basil was ugly, dirty, coarse, boorish, totally philistine and almost pathologically mean. He was, in short, profoundly un-Byzantine. And all these things, one suspects, he would have readily admitted. He was not concerned with the social graces, not interested even in personal happiness, in laughter and the love of friends. He cared only for the greatness and prosperity of his Empire. No wonder that in his hands it reached its apogee.

In one respect only did he fail; but it was a failure so calamitous as to outweigh much of his success and to bring to naught much of his achievement. He left no children, and no one to continue his work after he was gone. He knew – better than anyone – the hopeless inadequacy of his brother Constantine, still as frivolous and pleasure-loving in his middle sixties as he had been half a century before. His own attitude to women – whether he hated them, or despised them, or (as is most likely) feared them – remains a mystery; and yet, one wonders, with all that steel discipline of his, could he not somehow have forced himself to take a wife, and engender a son or two, for the Empire's sake? Had he done so, it might have continued to prosper, might have spread still further across Europe and Asia, might have risen to yet greater heights of influence and power. Dying as he did without issue, he virtually ensured its decline.

He died on 15 December. By the 16th, that decline had already begun.

16
The Decline Begins

[1025–41]

Not one of the Emperors in my time – and I say this with experience of many in my life, for most of them lasted only a year – not one of them, to my knowledge, bore the burden of Empire entirely free from blame to the end.

Michael Psellus,
Chronographia, IV, 11

Constantine VIII, the sixty-five-year-old widower who now found himself sole Emperor of Byzantium, was as different from his brother as it is possible to be. Physically, he was magnificent: tall and well-proportioned where Basil had been short and stocky, and with a natural grace of movement and manner. A superb horseman, he had a passion for the chase and the circus, and habitually trained his own horses; in his youth he had also been an active competitor in athletic events – running, wrestling, javelin-throwing and the like – which had long been out of fashion but which he once again made popular. By the time of his succession, it need hardly be said, his athletic days were over; years of excess had ravaged his constitution and had led to chronic gout, so severe that in his last years he could hardly put a foot to the ground; but he remained to the end an impressive figure. Like his brother, he had received little formal schooling; a lively intellectual curiosity had however given him a modicum of culture – 'enough for a child', sniffs Psellus – which enabled him to hold his own with foreign ambassadors. Those whom he received in audience for the first time would frequently comment on his remarkable eloquence, the effect of which was further increased by a beautiful speaking voice. So easily, indeed, did words come to him that his secretaries were obliged to develop a shorthand of their own to keep pace with his dictation.

With all these advantages, he should – and could – have made a perfectly adequate Emperor. Why then was his reign of less than three years an unmitigated disaster? Above all, because he was devoid of any semblance of moral fibre. He was terrified of his own power, and since he knew himself incapable of handling it he reacted to every challenge with mindless cruelty. He believed every rumour and, lacking the courage for trials or confrontations, ordered the execution or mutilation of hundreds of innocent men. Blinding was his favourite punishment. 'He had a true predilection for this form of torture,' writes Zonaras, 'since it paralyses the sufferer and renders him powerless without depriving him of life . . . ' The sentence was known in Constantinople, with tragic irony, as 'the divine clemency of the Emperor'. His tendency to indulge later in an orgy of remorse, tearfully flinging his arms around his sightless victims and imploring their forgiveness, did little to increase his popularity.

A man so dedicated to the pursuit of pleasure – 'when he held the dice in his hand,' Psellus tells us, 'the affairs of the world, however important they might be, were suspended' – could have been expected to give careful consideration to the choice of his closest ministers and counsellors, to whom the tedious business of government might safely be entrusted. If Constantine did anything of the kind, it says little for him as a judge of men. The all-important posts of *parakoimomenos* and Domestic of the Schools – or commander-in-chief – in the East were given to his chief valet, the eunuch Nicholas; another eunuch, Symeon – heretofore a very minor Palace functionary – was appointed chief of police in Constantinople; yet a third, Eustathius, was raised from equally humble duties to that of Grand Heteriarch, responsible for all the foreign or barbarian mercenaries of the Imperial Guard; while a fourth, a well-known ruffian named Spondylus, became Duke of Antioch, castellan of the greatest and most strategic fortress in the Empire and chief protector of the newly conquered southern frontier against the Saracen hordes.

Only one class of Byzantines welcomed the weakness of the new regime: the Anatolian aristocracy. Their first reaction was to stage a *coup d'état*, sweep Constantine away and replace him with an Emperor of their own; but they foolishly tried to act independently rather than in unison, and since the greater part of Basil's army remained loyal to his brother their attempts came to nothing. In the event it hardly mattered: the Emperor was quite unable to resist their demands, and within months the detested land laws were buried. Once again 'the powerful' descended on their erstwhile estates, snapping up every available acre while the poor peasant small-holders were left to survive as best they might – their distress still further increased by a decade of droughts and visitations of locusts that reduced many to literal starvation. Once more, as in the sixth century, Asia Minor became a country of *latifundia* – vast estates owned more often than not by absentee landlords and worked by serfs.

Meanwhile Constantine VIII carried on as he always had: hunting, feasting, gaming, carousing with his cronies, cavorting with his concubines, watching obscene performances in his private theatre, experimenting with more and more elaborate sauces – for he was a passionate gourmet with the digestion of an ostrich – and avoiding whenever possible the affairs of state. But such a life could not endure for ever, and on 9 November 1028 he fell mortally ill. Then, and only then, did he give a thought to the question which must long have been troubling every other citizen of Constantinople: who was to succeed him? He had, as we saw in the last chapter, no sons. Of his three daughters, the eldest had long been vowed to the religious life. The second, Zoe, had experienced one near-encounter with matrimony when she had set off to marry Otto III, only to find on her arrival in Italy that he was already dead; but that was twenty-six years in the past, and ever since then she had dragged out a mournful existence in the imperial *gynaeceum*, in the company of her younger sister Theodora – a good deal more intelligent, but less attractive in appearance – whom she cordially detested.

Theodora, while still only in her middle forties, had become distinctly spinsterish; but Zoe, though now approaching fifty and well past the age of child-bearing, still dreamed voluptuously of the marriage that she had never had and longed passionately for liberation from her Palace prison.[1] She consoled herself with the knowledge that that liberation must come sooner or later; for she was her father's heir, and it was through her that the imperial diadem would be passed on to her husband. There was only one question: who was it to be? Feverish discussions by the bedside of the dying Emperor first raised the possibility of the Patrician Constantine Dalassenus, a member of one of the few families of 'the powerful' who had never wavered in their loyalty to the Macedonian house, and a

1 Her spirits may have risen when, early that same year, an embassy arrived from the Empire of the West with another proposal for an imperial marriage; but they almost certainly sank again when it was discovered that the intended bridegroom – Henry, son of the Emperor Conrad II – was only ten years old. The idea, it need hardly be said, came to nothing.

messenger was dispatched to summon him urgently to Constantinople; but when word of what had happened reached the civil bureaucracy of the capital there was an immediate storm of protest and the Emperor, timorous even on his deathbed, immediately gave in. Another messenger followed the first with instructions to intercept Dalassenus and tell him to come no further. Meanwhile the bureaucracy proposed its own candidate: a sexagenarian senator named Romanus Argyrus.

Romanus came from an old aristocratic family of Constantinople. A distant relative of the Emperor[1] (and a brother of the ill-starred Maria who had married young Giovanni Orseolo twenty-four years before), he was a Patrician, a Supreme Judge of one of the principal tribunals, Administrator (*economos*) of St Sophia and, finally, Imperial Prefect of the city – an office roughly equivalent to that of mayor. For all these reasons he seemed admirably suited for the throne. As it happened, he was already happily married; but Constantine had made up his mind, and anyway there was no time to be lost. The senator and his wife were both put under arrest; they were then brought to the Emperor and given a simple choice. Either there was an immediate divorce and Romanus married Zoe, in which case he would receive the rank of Caesar and, in due course, *basileus*; or his eyes would be put out.

Psellus suggests that all this was nothing more than a charade and that, if Romanus had had the courage to call the bluff, he and his wife could have lived out the rest of their lives together unharmed. It seems unlikely. In the past three years Constantine had shown himself perfectly capable of greater brutalities than this; meanwhile the question of Zoe's marriage – and, with it, the succession – was of desperate urgency and could be no longer postponed. In any case, the old couple can surely be forgiven for not taking the risk. He, loving his wife as dearly as he did, was agonized; but she did not hesitate. Tearfully she cut off all her hair and declared herself ready, for his sake, to enter a convent – which she immediately did. On the very next day – it was 10 November – Romanus, with some reluctance, married Zoe[2] in the imperial chapel of the Palace; on the 11th, he stood at his father-in-law's bedside as he

---

1 They were in fact third cousins, their great-grandfathers having both married daughters of Romanus Lecapenus.

2 Zonaras claims that Constantine had originally intended to marry Argyrus to his youngest daughter, Theodora, on the grounds that she was more intelligent and that, being a few years younger, she might just possibly still manage to produce a son; but, he continues, Theodora refused categorically on the grounds of their blood relationship. Zoe, on the other hand, seems to have been almost embarrassingly enthusiastic.

breathed his last; and on the 12th he found himself Romanus III, seated beside his beaming wife on the imperial throne.

Before we continue the story, it may be a good idea to pause for a moment to make a proper introduction to the greatest scholar of his day, author of the most valuable – and by far the most entertaining – Byzantine memoir since that of Procopius, 500 years before. The name of Michael Psellus has appeared already more than once in these pages, but only as a reporter of what he has heard, never of what he has seen: henceforth his *Chronographia* – still covering almost half a century – can be considered an eye-witness account. As he himself puts it at the beginning of his chapter on Romanus III:

From now on, this history will be more accurate than it was before, for the Emperor Basil died when I was a child, while Constantine ended his reign just after I had begun my elementary studies. Consequently I was never admitted to their presence, nor did I hear them speak. Whether I even saw them I cannot say, for I was too young to remember at the time. On the other hand, I saw Romanus with my own eyes and, on one occasion, actually talked with him.

Psellus was born in 1018, of a respectable middle-class family in Constantinople. His social advancement was probably due in large measure to John Mauropous, the future Archbishop of Euchaita, who was then working as a private tutor in the capital and under whose roof he was able to meet, as fellow-students, several rich and influential young men – including his close friend John Xiphilinus (who would one day become Patriarch) and Constantine Ducas, better known as the Emperor Constantine X. He soon entered the imperial service, where his quick intelligence and profound scholarship – always highly prized in Byzantium – won him rapid promotion. He thus writes of events which he not only experienced but frequently himself helped to shape and control. Though his last chapters are unashamedly tendentious – they were commissioned by his friend Ducas, then reigning in Constantinople – few medieval writers can boast his eye for detail; fewer still have the gift of bringing a character to life in a few lines; and none has produced a more brilliant and evocative picture of the world in which he lived. Of Romanus Argyrus he writes:

This man, nurtured on Greek literature, also had some acquaintance with the literary works of the Italians. He had a graceful turn of speech and a majestic utterance. A man of heroic stature, he looked every inch an Emperor. His idea of his own range of knowledge was vastly exaggerated, but wishing to model his reign on those of the great Antonines of the past . . . he paid particular attention to two things: the study of letters and the science of war. Of the latter he was completely ignorant, and as for literature, his knowledge was far from profound . . . This belief in his own knowledge, this straining beyond his own intellectual limits, led him to make mistakes on a grand scale.

In short, the besetting sin of Romanus – in striking contrast to his predecessor – was over-confidence. He was far from stupid, and had been an admirable magistrate; but imperial power went straight to his head and seems to have convinced him that, now that he was an Emperor himself, he could equal any of the great Emperors of the past in their own fields. If Marcus Aurelius was a philosopher, then so was he: whole days would pass while he discussed abstruse problems of theology and metaphysics, but since he had had no proper grounding in syllogisms or dialectical argument no purpose was served, no conclusion reached. If Augustus or Constantine could found a dynasty, then – despite his wife's advanced age – he must do likewise. To increase his chances, he made himself easy game for all the charlatans in Constantinople, swallowing their nostrums and aphrodisiacs, rubbing himself with their ointments and performing extraordinary exercises that would, he was promised, restore to him the vigour of his youth. Meanwhile Zoe did much the same, draping herself with chains and charms, stuffing herself with amulets and falling for the most transparently ridiculous mumbo-jumbo in her determination, somehow, to conceive – though no one, with the possible exceptions of herself and her husband, was surprised when she failed to do so.

When the Emperor chose to play the philosopher or the dynast, no great harm was done; it was a very different matter when he tried to prove himself a strategist, as was seen in 1030 when he decided to teach the obstreperous Emir of Aleppo a lesson. His generals warned him against it; on his arrival at Antioch, however, he found ambassadors from the Emir reminding him of the existing treaty of peace and offering reparations for any damage that might have been done. But Romanus – who had already ordered the crown that he intended to wear for his triumphal procession – refused to listen. Instead, he set out for Aleppo at the head of his army. He and his men were already in Syria, and were just about to enter a narrow pass, when they heard the Saracen war-cry; and there, suddenly, were the Emir's men galloping down on them from both sides, their scimitars flashing in the sun. Nicephorus Phocas or John Tzimisces, had they allowed themselves to be ambushed in such a manner, would have fought it out where they stood; Romanus Argyrus fled, his troops with him. Indeed, if one of his aides had not quickly helped him on to his horse, he would almost certainly have been taken prisoner. It was worse than a disaster; it was a disgrace. The enemy, Psellus tells us, watched the flight in utter astonishment – as well they might. When Basil died, the imperial army had been the finest fighting machine in the civilized world; now, after just five years of mismanagement and neglect, it was well on the way to becoming the laughing-stock of the East.

All, however, was not lost. A little way to the north of Antioch lay a small and relatively unimportant Theme known by the name of its chief city, Teluch, and governed by a young *strategos* of colossal size and exceptional ability called George Maniakes. Some days later a body of some 800 Saracen cavalry, loaded with plunder from the imperial camp, rode up insolently to Teluch with the town's first news of the débâcle – a somewhat exaggerated account as it happened, according to which the Emperor had been killed and the entire Byzantine army annihilated. As night was already falling, they gave the garrison until the following morning to surrender, adding threats of dire retribution if it failed to do so. Maniakes, showing every sign of fear, agreed at once, sending out copious quantities of food and wine to the infidel camp as an earnest of his good intentions and promising that he and his men would give themselves up at first light with all the gold and treasure the town possessed.

His plan worked perfectly. The Saracens, suspecting nothing and as delighted to receive the wine as they were unaccustomed to its effects, polished off the lot. Maniakes waited until they were in a logged sleep, fell on them and then, when every one of the 800 lay dead on the ground, gave orders that each corpse should have its nose and ears cut off. The next morning he set out in search of his defeated sovereign. Finding him in Cappadocia, he produced a blood-stained sack from which he proudly poured the grisly trophies at Romanus's feet, whereupon the delighted Emperor immediately appointed him *catapan* of Lower Media – effectively Governor of all the cities of the upper Euphrates Valley, with his residence at Samosata. From here he was to launch a whole series of victorious campaigns, culminating two years later in a heroic recovery of Edessa for the first time since the days of Heraclius, four centuries before.

On his return to Constantinople, the Emperor wisely forsook military matters and devoted himself instead to the cares of government. In the first months of his reign his acts of generosity – probably sincerely meant – had won him a good deal of support: that of the Church, when he increased by eighty pounds of gold the annual government subsidy to St Sophia; that of the monasteries and the greater landowners, when he repealed Basil's law known as the *allelengyon*, according to which they had been responsible for any shortfall in the tax payable by their local communities; that of government debtors, for whom he declared an amnesty – resulting in the release of several hundred from prison; and that of the victims of Constantine VIII's agrarian policy, to whom princely compensation was paid. It was a promising start; but the promise was not fulfilled. As time went on Romanus showed himself to be hardly more successful as a legislator than he had been in other fields. The appalling results of Constantine VIII's legislation should by now have been obvious to all; but the new Emperor continued the work of his predecessor, even going so far as to revive the farming of taxes – that most pernicious of all abuses, whereby some speculator would purchase from the treasury for an agreed sum the right to collect revenue on its behalf, then would himself demand double or treble that sum from the unfortunate taxpayers. 'The powerful' – by now more powerful than ever – were of course well able to resist this sort of skulduggery; once again the burden fell on the defenceless small-holder, who had no means of fighting back.

It was perhaps inevitable, sooner or later, that Romanus should have turned his attention to church-building. He had already spent a small fortune on gilding the capitals in St Sophia and the Church of the Theotokos in Blachernae, but this was not enough: like his great predecessor Justinian, he too must leave a lasting memorial behind him. The result of this decision was an enormous edifice dedicated to the Virgin *Peribleptos*, or All-Seeing,[1] on the Seventh Hill as it slopes down to the Marmara shore. It was unquestionably magnificent; but, as Psellus makes all too clear, it scarcely added to the Emperor's reputation:

What was intended as an act of piety turned out to be the cause of evil and the occasion for many injustices. The expenditure incurred over the church was constantly increased. Every day he collected more contributions than were necessary for the work, and woe betide the man who tried to limit the building.

---

1 Not, surely, 'the Virgin who must be seen by all and from all sides', as Schlumberger suggests.

On the other hand, anyone who invented fresh extravagances and new variations of style was sure of winning the Emperor's friendship at once . . .

Nothing in the whole world was thought good enough for this church. All the royal treasure was made available, every golden stream poured into it. Even when funds were exhausted the construction went on, for new parts were added one on top of another while other parts were pulled down again.

The church, however, was not enough by itself; it must have a dependent monastery. Soon this second building was as grandiose as the first, so huge indeed that it became almost impossible to find monks enough to fill it. Together, these two monuments to imperial megalomania are said to have brought the people of Constantinople to the verge of rebellion, such was their fury over the Emperor's continual demands for more and more money. But did they, one wonders, admire them none the less? It seems unlikely. The *Peribleptos*, if Psellus is to be believed, must have been an appalling hotchpotch. It can certainly have borne little trace of any overall architectural conception, of the kind that gives the Church of the Holy Wisdom its simplicity and strength. But we shall never know for sure: for on its site there now rises the wonderfully uninteresting mass of the Armenian church of Surp Kevork (St George), known locally as Sulu Monastir. Of the vast edifice that Romanus Argyrus intended to stand for ever to the glory of God and His Mother – and of course himself – not a trace remains.[1]

What, meanwhile, of the Empress Zoe, without whom her husband would never have attained the supreme power, or had the money to squander as he did? She was, as she had been for most of her life, frustrated and dissatisfied; and – like the people of Constantinople, though for a rather different reason – she was furious with her husband. Her anger was due principally to the fact that, from the moment he had given up hope of posterity, he had refused to share her bed and had taken a mistress; indeed, he had conceived so intense a dislike of her that he could hardly bear to be in the same room. It was further increased by

---

1 The *Peribleptos* was one of the few churches in Constantinople that continued as a Christian sanctuary after the Turkish conquest. According to the *Blue Guide to Istanbul*, 'the generally accepted tradition is that the church remained in the hands of the Greeks until 1643, when it was given to the Armenians by Sultan Ibrahim under the influence of a favourite Armenian concubine. (This lady's name was şeker Parça, or Piece of Sugar; she is said to have weighed more than 300 pounds.)' The *Guide* adds, however, that more recent evidence suggests that it was already in the Armenian Patriarchate in 1608.

his having refused her access to the imperial treasury, giving her instead a meagre annual pension which she was formally forbidden to exceed. Unfortunately for him, Zoe was intensely proud; she had also, for the first fifty years of her life, been thoroughly spoilt by a father who had denied her nothing. At first she had vented her feelings on her sister Theodora – now a morbidly religious old maid of fifty who had hardly ever left the *gynaeceum* – whom in 1031 she ordered into a convent 'to put an end to her constant intrigues and the scandals of her life'; soon, however, she took more direct action, and it is at this moment that there enters upon the scene the strange and sinister figure of John the Orphanotrophus.

This man – destined to play a leading role in our story over the coming decade – was a eunuch who had risen, through his own intelligence and industry, from obscure and humble origins in Paphlagonia to be a highly influential member of the civil bureaucracy. For many years already he had been a friend and confidant of the Emperor, who had recently appointed him director of the city's principal orphanage, whence he took his name. He possessed four younger brothers, of whom the two eldest were eunuchs like himself; the other two called themselves money-changers but were more probably strikers of false coin. The youngest, Michael, an outstandingly handsome youth still in his teens, was one day in 1033 brought by his brother to the Palace and presented to Romanus and Zoe in formal audience. Romanus scarcely noticed him; Zoe, on the other hand, fell – precisely as John had intended her to fall – instantly and besottedly in love.

From that moment she thought of nothing but the young Paphlagonian, whom she invited regularly to her private apartments and, after having overcome first his shyness and later his understandable reluctance, successfully seduced. Michael remained far from enthusiastic where sex was concerned, though he was naturally flattered to be the lover of the Empress; but he received careful instruction from his brother, and – particularly after Zoe began to flaunt her new *amour* in public and speak openly about her intention to make him Emperor – his own slowly awakening ambition did the rest. As for Romanus, for a long time he seems to have had no inkling of what was going on; far from treating Michael with suspicion, he actually appointed him his own personal servant, regularly sending for him to massage his legs and feet (for his health was becoming rapidly worse and he was beginning to have difficulty in walking) and – or so it appeared to those around him –

deliberately shutting his eyes to his wife's increasingly blatant infidelity. Finally his sister Pulcheria could bear the gossip no longer and told him in so many words what was going on, warning him in addition that there might be a plot against his life. Only then did he send for Michael and make him swear on some holy relics that there was no truth in what he had heard; when the lad unhesitatingly did so, he showed every sign of being completely reassured.

There were those at court who believed that he was only feigning ignorance: that he was perfectly well aware of his wife's insatiable sexual appetite and was only too pleased that her infatuation with Michael was keeping her out of worse trouble. Others suggested that as the young man was known to be an epileptic, Romanus had dismissed the rumours as impossible. As the months went by, however, the question became less and less important; for by now it was plain to all that the Emperor was himself very seriously ill. Though he still appeared in ceremonial processions, he looked (writes Psellus) like a walking corpse: his face was grotesquely swollen, his breathing short and rapid, and every few paces he had to stop to rest. His appetite left him and he could not sleep. His character, too, had changed. In the past he had been a friendly, accessible sort of man, easily moved to laughter; now he was irritable and peevish, hating to be disturbed and losing his temper on the slightest provocation.

All too often already in this history, we have seen how circumstances such as these at the court of Byzantium would immediately give rise to rumours of poison. Such rumours had been rife after the death Romanus II, and again after that of John Tzimisces; but on both those occasions they were almost certainly unfounded. With Romanus III, we cannot be so sure. We know for a fact that his wife hated him and had every reason to want him out of the way, enabling her to instal Michael in his place. We know too that she had plenty of opportunity, while it is clear from her subsequent behaviour that she would have been fully capable of the crime. As far as local opinion was concerned, we have it on the authority of Psellus that no one at the Palace doubted her guilt for an instant. Already the case against Zoe – and with her, almost certainly, John the Orphanotrophus and Michael himself – looks black; what makes it blacker still is the highly suspicious manner in which, on the Thursday before Good Friday 1034, her husband met his death. Once again we must quote Psellus, since his account is the fullest and, if we are to make up our minds, his carefully-worded testimony is vital:

He was making himself ready for the public services on the morrow. Before dawn he set out to bathe in one of the huge and beautifully decorated baths near the imperial apartments. There was no one to assist him, and he was certainly not then at the point of death . . . He washed his head and body; then, as he was breathing strongly, he proceeded to the swimming bath, which had been deepened in the middle. At first he amused himself by swimming and floating on the surface, blowing out and refreshing himself with every sign of pleasure. Soon, as he had ordered, some of his retinue arrived to help him rest and to dress him.

I cannot swear that it was these men who killed him, but I know that all those who tell the story maintain that, at the moment that the Emperor dived as was his custom, they held his head for a long time beneath the water, attempting at the same time to strangle him. Then they departed. Later the unhappy Emperor was found floating on the surface like a cork. He was still breathing feebly, and reached out his arm in an imploring gesture for help. Someone, seized with pity, picked him up in his arms, carried him from the bath and laid him on a couch.

By this time the shouts of those who had first discovered him brought many people running to the spot, among them the Empress herself, unattended and making an immense show of grief. She gazed long at her husband; then, satisfied that he was past help, went away. Romanus moaned, looking round this way and that. He could not speak, and tried to express himself with signs and gestures; then, seeing that these were not understood, he closed his eyes and his breathing became faster again. Suddenly his mouth gaped open and there flowed from it some dark-coloured, coagulated matter. He gasped two or three times more, then gave up the ghost.

It is a curious story, and not altogether conclusive. The murder – if murder it was – is unsubstantiated, with no eye-witnesses; Psellus's only evidence is based on hearsay, and the victim was unable to testify one way or the other before he died. For all we know, the Emperor might have suffered a sudden stroke or heart attack while bathing. On the other hand it is worth mentioning that Scylitzes states as a point of fact – though again without substantiation – that Romanus was strangled by Michael's men, in the main pool or *kolymbithra* in the Baths of the Great Palace, while Matthew of Edessa maintains that he died of poison administered by his wife. We are consequently left with two suspected murders of the same victim, and four separate theories. The first is that that there was no foul play at all: the Emperor was simply a very sick man, suffering in all probability from some cardiac or arterial complaint, which finally struck him down while bathing. The second also accepts that his sickness sprang from natural causes, but holds that the

Empress and her friends administered – or caused to be administered – the *coup de grâce*. According to the third, Romanus was dying of slow poison – Psellus suggests hellebore – which weakened him to the point where the swim was too much for him, so that he died, quite naturally, of his exertions.

And so we come to the fourth theory: that Zoe, John and Michael at first planned to kill Romanus by poison but then, when he took much longer to die than they had expected, lost patience and decided to force the issue. This seems on the face of it the most probable of all, but there – once again we shall never know, and perhaps it hardly matters. The essential point is that unless we accept the first hypothesis – which surely strains our credulity too far – we must conclude that in some way or another Zoe killed her husband.

Once he was dead, she made no pretence of grieving for him. At dawn on that Good Friday morning – it was 12 April 1034 – Alexis of the Studium, Patriarch of Constantinople, was summoned urgently from St Sophia to the Palace, where the first sight that met his eyes was the near-naked body of the dead Emperor. Scarcely had he recovered from the shock when a pair of enormous doors opened – and there, in the great Coronation Hall or *Chrysotriclinium*, sat the Empress enthroned in state. On her head was the imperial diadem, in her hand the sceptre, over her shoulders the gold brocade robe of the Emperors, heavy with jewels. And there at her side, to the unconcealed horror of the Patriarch, sat young Michael, similarly robed and crowned. She spoke firmly and steadily; Alexis could not fail to understand her commands, nor could he refuse them. There and then he joined the hand of the fifty-six-year-old Empress – widowed only a few hours before – with that of her fellow-murderer and paramour, an epileptic young Paphlagonian forger nearly forty years her junior;[1] consecrated him as *basileus*, Equal of the Apostles; and called the blessing of God down upon them both.

That same evening, after all the high functionaries of Church and State – bishops and abbots, senators and generals, ministers and bureaucrats – had filed past the sovereign pair, touching their foreheads to the ground and kissing Michael's hand (though not Zoe's) in homage, the body of Romanus Argyrus was carried in an open coffin through the streets of Constantinople to his own Church of the

---

1 Scylitzes claims that for some time the Patriarch was too shocked to speak, and found his voice only after the Empress had thrust into his hand fifty pounds of gold for himself and fifty more for his clergy.

Peribleptos, the new Emperor and his brother leading the procession. The eighteen-year-old Psellus, recently arrived in the capital, watched it pass. Had it not been for the imperial insignia, he tells us, he would never have recognized the old man. The face was not wasted away but curiously swollen, drained of colour 'like those who have been poisoned', while the sparseness of the hair and beard reminded him of 'an empty cornfield after the harvest'. No tears were shed: the people of the city had cordially disliked Romanus while he was alive, and they were not sorry to see him go.

If the Empress had hoped for a second husband who would in effect be little more than a crowned slave, ready to indulge her every whim and obey her every command, she was soon to be disappointed. For a few months she was indeed able to enjoy such a desirable state of affairs; but long before that fateful year of 1034 was at its end, Michael was beginning to show signs of impatience. He had never loved Zoe or even much respected her; and it soon became clear to him that he was capable of governing the Empire very much better than she. If, on the other hand, he were to take over the reins – which he was determined to do – might he not risk a similar fate to that which had befallen his predecessor? His brother the Orphanotrophus certainly believed so, and it was probably at his insistence that Zoe once again found herself confined to the *gynaeceum* under constant surveillance, forbidden even to receive visits from her friends without permission, her liberty – and her spending – even more curtailed than in the days of Romanus.

There were other reasons too – apart from fear and personal dislike – why Michael should wish to distance himself from his wife. One was his health, which was fast deteriorating. His epileptic fits were becoming ever more frequent, to the point where he had red curtains hung about his throne, which could be drawn immediately his eyes began to glaze or his head suddenly to shake from side to side; but there was clearly no way in which he could conceal his humiliation from his family and close associates, and since on these occasions he minded the presence of Zoe more than that of anyone else, he preferred to avoid her altogether. He was also, despite his youth, becoming dropsical – a disability which apparently made him incapable of normal sexual relations. Finally there was his conscience. He owed everything to the Empress: his position, his wealth, his power. That debt, he knew, had been ill repaid, and he could not bear to meet her eye.

But he also knew that this betrayal of his wife was as nothing compared to his faithlessness towards Romanus. The memory of it tortured him, and the rest of his short life was one desperate attempt to save his soul. He spent hours a day in church; he established monasteries and convents by the dozen; he set up a vast refuge for the pious poor together with another, even larger, for reformed prostitutes; he sought out holy men and ascetics from every corner of the Empire, washing their feet, personally tending their sores, even putting them to rest in his own bed, while he himself stretched out by its side on a humble pallet; and he transformed Justinian's old Church of St Cosmas and St Damian – the two doctor saints in whom he naturally took a special interest – into what, according to Psellus, must have been one of the loveliest buildings in the city:

So far as the building of sacred churches was concerned, Michael surpassed all his predecessors, both in workmanship and in magnificence. The depths and heights of this edifice were given a new symmetry, and the new chapels harmonized with the church to give it an infinite beauty. The most wondrous stones were used in the floors and walls, and the whole church was made resplendent with gold mosaics and the painter's art. Images that seemed almost to live, set in every corner of the building, filled it with glory. Besides all this, near the church and practically incorporated in it, were luxurious baths, countless fountains, beautiful lawns and whatever else could attract or delight the eye.[1]

At those times when he was not preoccupied with spiritual matters (and once his wife was out of the way) the Emperor devoted himself to the business of government – at which, it must be said, he proved a good deal more adept than might have been expected. Suddenly he seemed to grow up: the Empire was no longer a plaything, but a responsibility. Psellus notes with approval that he made no dramatic changes in the administration after the manner of so many new Emperors: there were no abolitions of established customs, no reversals of policy, no removals of old or experienced advisers. Such changes as were made came about only gradually, while those men to whom he was under some obligation and who had hoped for high office under the new regime were started off in junior positions to gain experience until he felt them to be ready for promotion. Questions of finance and taxation

---

1 In Michael's day the church was usually known as the *Anargyroi* – 'the unpaid ones' – owing to the tradition that the two saintly physicians never accepted fees for their services. Nothing, alas, remains of it today.

he left to his brother the Orphanotrophus; everything else he kept firmly in his own hands, paying particular attention to local administration, to foreign affairs and to the army, whose shattered morale he managed in large measure to restore.

Although he had had little formal education, Michael learned fast. Within months of his assumption of effective power he was ruling the Empire with a sure and steady hand. His advisers marvelled at his industry, his quickness of perception, his sure political instinct and, despite his epilepsy, his emotional balance: he never lost his temper or raised his voice – which was, we are told, unusually resonant – but spoke evenly and rapidly, with a ready wit and a natural ease of expression. In his presence, the baseness of his origins and his shameful path to the throne were alike forgotten. Men were conscious only of his intelligence, his gentleness of manner and his obviously genuine desire to serve his Empire to the best of his ability; and those who knew him well had nothing but admiration for the courage with which he struggled against his two cruellest handicaps – his health and his family.

Of his four elder brothers, three were little better than parasites, living off the court and interested only in what they could get. The eldest, John the Orphanotrophus, was a far more formidable figure. He also lacked Michael's new-found selflessness and high moral principle; where intelligence and industry were concerned, however, he was cast in a similar mould. While the Emperor, progressively weakened by disease, was on occasion almost prostrate with exhaustion, John's energy was boundless. So, too, was his vigilance. He would work indefatigably late into the night, and then spend hours wandering through the streets of Constantinople, watching and listening, unrecognized in the monastic habit which he always wore. There was, it appeared, nothing that he did not know. Like his brother he was without malice, and would never do anyone a gratuitous injury; but he deliberately cultivated a fierce, intimidating manner, and if this did not make him hated it did at least ensure that he was almost universally feared. He drank heavily, and occasionally abandoned himself to unspeakable debaucheries; yet his shrewdness and watchfulness never left him, and his drinking companions soon discovered that every careless word spoken in their cups was remembered when, early the following morning, they were summoned into his presence to explain themselves. Psellus – who knew him well – was not the only man to conclude that the Orphanotrophus was still more dangerous drunk than sober.

He differed from his brother the Emperor in one other important respect. While the latter strove for fairness and impartiality in all that he did, John thought only of the advancement of his family. To be sure, this failing had its advantages: without it, Michael would never have come to the throne in the first place, and once he had attained the supreme power he found in the Orphanotrophus a source of constant strength. It was not that the conduct of the other three brothers was a whit less embarrassing to John than to everyone else; it was simply that he felt bound to protect them. He would go to any length to keep the Emperor in ignorance of their misdeeds or, if this proved impossible, to minimize them or shift the blame elsewhere. This and this alone explains why Michael did not take firm action against them, as he would have been well capable of doing; but John had no similar excuse. Had he treated them as firmly as he treated everyone and everything else, all might have been well. By refusing to do so he did a serious disservice both to his brother's reputation and to his own.

More serious still, he extended this family feeling to a certain Stephen, husband of his sister Maria. In his early days, before suddenly waking up to find himself the Emperor's brother-in-law, Stephen had exercised the humble profession of ships' caulker in the harbour of Constantinople. A man of no intelligence, education or aptitude, it would have been better had he remained there. Psellus gives us an unforgettable description:

I saw him after the metamorphosis . . . His horse, his clothes, everything else that alters a man's appearance – all were out of place. It was as if a pygmy wanted to play Hercules . . . The more such a person tries, the more his appearance belies him – clothed in a lion's skin, but weighed down by the club.

Had the Orphanotrophus been content to weigh his brother-in-law down with honours and titles and leave it at that, no great harm would have been done. Unfortunately, he went further. In 1038 he arranged for Stephen to be given command of the transport fleet for the most ambitious – and what, but for him, might have been the most triumphant – military undertaking of Michael's reign: the long-delayed Sicilian expedition.

Originally planned by Basil II for 1026 but indefinitely postponed as a result of his death in the previous year, this expedition now seemed to Michael and his advisers more necessary than ever. The continual raids on Byzantine territory in south Italy by the Sicilian-based Saracens were no longer an annoyance; they were rapidly becoming a threat to imperial security. Nor was it only the coastal towns that were suffering from their depredations: the city merchants complained that the Middle Sea was alive with pirates, prices of imports were rising accordingly and the level of foreign trade was beginning to decline. To every Byzantine, Sicily remained part of the imperial birthright; it continued to boast a considerable Greek population. That it should still be occupied by the heathen after more than two centuries was an affront not only to national security but also to national pride.

But if the necessity of the expedition had increased in the twelve years since Basil's death, so too had its chances of success. Among the Arab Emirs of the island, civil war had broken out. The ruler of Palermo, al-Akhal, had suddenly found himself confronted with an insurgent army led by his brother Abu Hafs, stiffened by 6,000 warriors from Africa under the command of Abdullah, son of the Zirid Emir of Kairouan; in 1035, growing desperate, he had actually appealed to Constantinople for help. Michael had agreed: such an opportunity, he knew, was unlikely to be repeated. The Emir's assassination almost immediately afterwards unfortunately removed this useful pretext for an unopposed landing; but revolt was now spreading throughout Sicily and the Saracens, more and more hopelessly divided, seemed unlikely to be able to offer much resistance to a concerted Byzantine attack.

The expedition sailed in the early summer of 1038. It had been put under the overall command of George Maniakes, still glorious from his Syrian triumphs and by now the foremost general of the Empire. Psellus has left us a fearsome description:

I myself saw the man, and marvelled at him; for nature had combined in his person all the qualities necessary for a military commander. He stood to the height of ten feet, so that to look at him men would tilt back their heads as if towards the top of a hill or a high mountain. His countenance was neither gentle nor pleasing, but put one in mind of a tempest; his voice was like thunder and his hands seemed made for tearing down walls or for smashing doors of bronze. He could spring like a lion and his frown was terrible. And everything else about him was in proportion. Those who saw him for the first time discovered that every description that they had heard of him was an understatement.

The army which this magnificent ogre was to command was as usual heterogeneous. Its strongest element was an impressive Varangian contingent, which had been joined by the almost legendary Norse hero

Harald Hardrada, returning from a pilgrimage to Jerusalem; its weakest a body of grumbling Lombards from Apulia who made no secret of their disgust at having been forced into Byzantine service. Landing in the late summer, at first it carried all before it. Courageously as the divided Saracens fought, they could do little to stem the tide. Messina fell almost at once and was followed, after heavy fighting, by Rometta, the key fortress commanding the pass linking Messina with the northern coastal road to Palermo. Of the next stage of the campaign we know little;[1] there seems however to have been a slow but steady advance on Syracuse, which fell to Maniakes in 1040.[2]

The demoralization of the Byzantine forces and their collapse after the victory of Syracuse were so sudden and so complete that one can readily understand the Saracens' contention that Allah had intervened on their behalf. Everything seemed to go wrong at once. So far as we can judge, the fault lay partly with Maniakes and partly with the Emperor's brother-in-law Stephen, for whom the general had never bothered to hide his contempt and upon whom, after some particularly crass piece of ineptitude on Stephen's part, he forgot himself so far as to launch a violent attack, casting doubts on his masculinity and accusing him of being nothing but a purveyor of pleasures for his brother-in-law. Stephen – for whom, in view of his assailant's size alone, the experience must have been alarming in the extreme – determined to have his revenge, and sent an urgent message to Constantinople accusing Maniakes of treason. The general was immediately summoned to the capital where, without being given any opportunity to answer the charges against him, he was flung unceremoniously into prison. He was succeeded in his command by Stephen – with results that could have been foreseen – and then, on Stephen's death soon afterwards, by a eunuch named Basil, who proved very little better. The army had by this time lost its momentum and its morale; and the retreat began.

And still more trouble was to come. For some years dissatisfaction

---

1 One of the few clues remaining is the abbey church of S. Maria di Maniace near Maletto, built on the site of one of Maniakes's victories by the local Greek population soon after the battle, then restored and enlarged by Count Roger I towards the end of the century. This was the church around which, in 1173, Queen Margaret of Navarre was to found the large and richly-endowed Benedictine abbey of Maniace, last of the great Norman foundations in Sicily. Later it was to form part of the Brontë estate, bestowed by Ferdinand IV on Lord Nelson in 1799.

2 The so-called Castello Maniace which still stands in Syracuse today is in fact nothing of the sort, having been erected by Frederick II almost exactly 200 years after the Byzantine capture of the city.

had been growing in Apulia, where the Lombard separatists had had little difficulty – particularly after the imperial press-gangs had begun their forcible recruiting – in working up the local populations against their Byzantine masters. Already in 1038 several leading officials had been murdered; in 1039 the situation was near flash-point; and in 1040 the signal was given for revolt. The *catapan* was assassinated, and all the local militias along the coast rose up in a mutiny which the depleted garrisons were totally unable to contain. The army was urgently summoned from Sicily to deal with the situation; and within a few months the entire island – with the single exception of Messina – was once again in Saracen hands. It was as if the great expedition had never been.

By the time the news of the disaster reached Constantinople, it was clear that the Emperor was dying. No longer capable of dealing with affairs of state, he spent his days in ever more desperate attempts to appease the divine anger which had reduced him, while still in his twenties, to a hideously bloated travesty of what he had been only a few years before when his beauty had won him the heart of an Empress. Messengers were sent to every corner of the Empire with orders to pay two pieces of gold to every parish priest and one to every monk in return for their prayers for his recovery; meanwhile he himself passed more and more time in Thessalonica, spreadeagled over the tomb of his beloved St Demetrius as he implored his intercession.

Government of the Empire was now in the capable hands of John the Orphanotrophus. The pages of certain chroniclers – Scylitzes and Zonaras among them – are full of stories of his iniquities. For Psellus, better placed to know the truth, John was neither unjust nor corrupt in matters that did not affect his family; he was, however, obsessed by the idea of founding a Paphlagonian dynasty, and in this one respect would stoop to anything that might further his ends. His brother Michael would die within a year or so, leaving no issue; how was he to ensure the succession of another member of his family? Already in 1037 he had made a determined bid for the Patriarchal throne, claiming that the present incumbent, Alexis of the Studium, had been uncanonically elected; but old Alexis had been too clever for him. If his election had indeed been uncanonical, he pointed out, every single one of the ecclesiastical appointments he had made in the past eleven years was null and void – as, incidentally, would be the coronations of the last three Emperors. John's support, such as it had been, fell away at once and no more was heard of the matter.

The question remained: who was to be Michael's successor? Of his and John's three brothers one, Nicetas, was already dead; the other two – eunuchs like John himself – were disqualified. His brother-in-law Stephen, to everyone's relief, was dead. One possibility only remained: Stephen's son Michael, generally known by the nickname of *Calaphates*, 'the caulker', after his father's early profession. It was not a particularly pleasing prospect: although the boy – the exact date of his birth is unknown, but he was not yet out of his teens – was agreeable enough to meet, those who knew him well had already found him to be a snake in the grass: a compulsive liar and inveterate schemer, whose apparent friendliness all too often concealed his true intentions. The mind of the Orphanotrophus, however, was made up. He had little difficulty in persuading the Emperor, while Zoe was in no position to refuse; and soon afterwards, at a high Mass in the Church of St Mary at Blachernae, his nephew's succession was assured. The old Empress, enthroned at the side of her pathetic young husband, declared her formal adoption of Michael the Caulker as her son, sitting him down – symbolically if somewhat ridiculously – upon her lap. The Emperor then feebly proclaimed him Caesar, and the youth – of whom the majority of the vast assembly had never even heard and whom they were now seeing for the first time – proceeded to the age-old ceremony of his consecration.

The new Caesar might have been unknown; but everyone recognized John the Orphanotrophus standing beside the thrones, and none could mistake his expression of satisfaction and triumph. Nor could they guess how soon he would regret the disaster he had unconsciously brought upon the Empire, his family and himself.

There is no need for us to investigate in any close detail the reasons for the revolt which broke out in Bulgaria in the summer of 1040. The severity of Byzantine taxation seems to have been largely to blame. Basil II had wisely allowed his Bulgar subjects to pay, as they always had, in kind; John the Orphanotrophus insisted on cash, thereby imposing a far heavier burden. The Bulgars had been angered, too, when on the death of the Slav Bishop of Ochrid in 1037 a Greek named Leo, the *chartophylax* of St Sophia, was appointed in his place. Three years later they took up arms, under the leadership of one Peter Deljan, who seems to have been the bastard grandson of Tsar Samuel and who was joined a few weeks later by his cousin Alusian, rescued from semi-captivity in Constantinople. The two quickly drove the Byzantines from western

Bulgaria and then, like Symeon and Samuel before them, invaded northern Greece. By the end of the year they had stormed Dyrrachium – thus giving them an outlet on the Adriatic – and penetrated as far south as the Gulf of Lepanto, whence they now pressed eastwards to lay siege to Thebes.

At this point an astonishing thing happened. The Emperor Michael, speaking from his Palace in Thessalonica, suddenly announced his intention of leading his army in person against the enemy. He was by now semi-paralysed, his monstrously swollen legs having been attacked by gangrene; the slightest movement was an agony. In vain did those around him – including his surviving brothers – implore him to renounce the idea; he refused to listen. It was bad enough, he pointed out, that his reign had seen no increase of the imperial dominions; he was at least determined that it should not witness any diminution. As Psellus puts it:

His first battle – in which he was victorious – was against members of his own intimate circle, before he ever came to grips with the barbarians; and the first trophy of the war was set up to commemorate his triumph over his own kinsmen and his associates – and himself. Bodily weakness was more than compensated for by strength of purpose, and in this strength he committed his cause to God.

But this, Psellus makes clear, was not an empty gesture. There were no vain heroics, nor any question of a mortally sick man riding out in search of a glorious death on the battlefield. The campaign was meticulously planned, and its specific targets carefully chosen, before the dying *basileus* led his army across the frontier to war.

Camp was pitched in a suitable spot when the expedition arrived in enemy territory. A council was held, and after it the Emperor decided to engage the Bulgars – an extraordinary plan, about which even his commanders who were there with him had contrary opinions. Nor is this surprising, for during the night his doctors had to be sent for and he nearly died. Yet at daybreak he immediately rose – some power apparently giving him new strength – mounted his horse, sat firm in the saddle, and managed the animal with skilful use of the bridle. Then, an object of wonder to all who saw him, he rode to the rear and formed up the various divisions of his army into one coherent force.

It would be pleasant indeed to be able to attribute the defeat of the Bulgar insurgents to the courage of the Emperor. In fact Alusian's men brought it on themselves by their lack of discipline, laying siege to Thessalonica and then falling into such disorder as virtually to invite the defenders to emerge from the city and destroy them. By this time too a serious quarrel had broken out between the two leaders, Deljan being quick to accuse Alusian of incompetence and even treachery. Alusian responded by setting a trap for his cousin and then removing his eyes and nose with a carving knife; soon afterwards, realizing that the insurrection no longer had any hope of success, he sent a secret message to the Emperor offering surrender in return for safe conduct back to Constantinople.

And so, early in 1041, Michael returned to his capital in triumph, followed by his army and a host of captives including the eyeless and noseless Deljan. Psellus, who was there, records the scene:

The entire population poured out of their houses to greet their Emperor. I myself saw him on this occasion, looking as if he were attending a funeral and swaying on his horse. The fingers that gripped his bridle were like those of a giant, for each of them was as thick as a man's arm – such were the effects of the disease from which he suffered. His face, too, preserved not a trace of its former beauty.

It was his last public appearance. As the year went on his condition grew steadily worse, until on 10 December, feeling the end to be near, he had himself carried to his own monastery of St Cosmas and St Damian. There he took off his imperial robes and diadem, donning in their place the robes of a simple monk. His brothers, John in particular, could not restrain their tears; only he remained happy and serene, confident that he had at last obtained the forgiveness for which he had so long striven. To the astonishment of all, the old Empress Zoe appeared at the monastery gate, having heard of her husband's condition and anxious to see him before he died; but Michael refused to receive her. (Before we condemn him for so unnecessary a snub to the old woman to whom he owed everything, we should remember that he had only a few hours to live, that he was in the last stages of exhaustion and that he knew Zoe a lot better than we do.) When the time came for Vespers, he called for a pair of sandals; hearing that those which were being made for him were not yet ready, he refused to wear the imperial purple buskins and hobbled barefoot into the chapel, supported by two of his fellow-monks. But the effort was too much for him. Gasping now for breath, he was carried back to his cell, where an hour or two later he died.

Of all those who occupied the Byzantine throne, few had risen from more lowly origins; few had attained power by more questionable methods; none, certainly, suffered a more agonizing end. And yet, had he lived, Michael might have proved a great Emperor. He might even have reversed the slow process of disintegration which had begun with the death of Basil II in 1025. He possessed wisdom, vision and – as he showed in that last astonishing Bulgarian expedition – almost super-human courage. He was a truly tragic figure; and, in the reigns that followed, there would be many who desperately regretted his loss.

17
The End of the Paphlagonians

[1041–2]

God is not unjust. I am guilty of grave crimes, and must now suffer the punishment that is my due.

The Emperor Michael V, shortly before his blinding

John the Orphanotrophus was deeply affected by the Emperor's death. Schemer and intriguer though he was, his love for Michael had been deep and genuine; and he kept vigil by the body for three days and three nights until its burial. His two other brothers behaved very differently. Determined as they were to establish their nephew firmly on the throne before any rival claimant could be put forward, they introduced him into the Palace almost before his predecessor had left it and would doubtless have pressed on with the coronation itself had they had the power to do so; fortunately they were obliged to await the return of the Orphanotrophus from his devotions. Psellus was actually in the Palace when he arrived, and describes the scene as an eye-witness:

When the brothers heard that John had crossed the threshold of the outer Palace, they approached him as if they were about to meet God Himself. The ceremonial was prepared beforehand: they gathered about him and smothered him with kisses, all kissing different parts of his body at once. Even his nephew stretched out his right hand towards him, as if there were some virtue to be gained from his very touch.

At the family conference that followed, John insisted on one point above all others: that nothing must be done without the consent, real or apparent, of the Empress. She alone, as niece of Basil II, represented the legitimate succession; her support was essential if Michael Calaphates were to be accepted as the new *basileus*. And so to Zoe they went,

Michael flinging himself at the feet of his adoptive mother and all four of them arguing that only through him could she regain the power that was her birthright. He would, they promised, be Emperor only in name; she herself would take over the reins of government – unless she preferred to rule through him, in which case he would still serve as her puppet-Emperor and mouthpiece. In either event he would continue to be her slave, ready at every moment to do her bidding. Old, weak, gullible, not particularly intelligent and with no one to advise her, Zoe was – as they had foreseen – easily persuaded. And so, with her blessing, Michael V proceeded to his consecration.

The Roman Empire of the East had now been in existence for a little more than 700 years, during which the throne had been occupied by fifty-five different sovereigns. Some had acquired it by heredity, others – like Michael IV – by marriage. Yet others – Nicephorus Phocas, for example, or John Tzimisces – had seized it, more or less by force; but they had done so as victorious generals, and had been acclaimed by their men according to a tradition older than Byzantium itself, going back as it did to the time of Augustus. It can thus safely be said that no Emperor in the whole history of Byzantium had less title to the throne than Michael Calaphates. The uncle had at least been the husband of the Empress; the nephew was not even her lover. His birth was lowly, his military record non-existent. He possessed no particular qualities of character or intelligence to recommend him beyond the lowliest of his subjects. The unpleasant young man who was now acclaimed as God's Vice-Gerent on Earth and Equal of the Apostles owed his elevation to two things only: to the machinations of a corrupt and self-seeking minister, and to the weakness of a foolish old woman.

During the first weeks of his reign he maintained an appropriate – if somewhat sickening – humility, addressing Zoe as 'my mistress, my sovereign' and the Orphanotrophus as 'my lord and master', even giving him a throne to sit on next to his own. But this preliminary phase did not last long, and a few weeks later John – who was no stranger to Michael's duplicity – was not surprised to discover that his nephew's attitude towards him was beginning to change dramatically the moment his back was turned. Soon, too, he made another discovery, more worrying still: that his own brother Constantine, for whom he had secured the position of Grand Domestic, was doing everything he could to encourage Michael's hostility to him.

Constantine, it appears, had long been jealous of his brother's success and had determined to destroy him as soon as he could safely do so; and to this end, from the moment that Michael had been created Caesar, he had assiduously cultivated the young man's friendship. So successful had he been that Michael on his accession had raised him to the rank of *nobilissimus* and now kept him permanently at his side; while Constantine, his position now assured, dropped even the pretence of civility towards the Orphanotrophus and openly insulted him whenever the opportunity arose. After one particularly violent altercation between them during a dinner with the Emperor, John rose angrily from the table and strode out of the Palace, going not to his own residence but to one of his country estates: a sign of displeasure which, he imagined, would soon bring Michael to his senses. Sure enough, a letter soon arrived bearing the imperial seal. It reproached him for his excessive pride, but asked him to return – in order, John assumed, to discuss certain secret government business. He therefore complied at once, expecting to be received by a suitably contrite nephew; but when he reached the Palace it was only to find that the Emperor had gone off to watch a performance at the theatre, leaving no message. Furious, he turned on his heel and went straight back to his estate.

Psellus, who tells this story, leaves us in no doubt that the Orphanotrophus had seriously underestimated the degree of the Emperor's hostility towards him. After this incident, he did so no longer. At last he saw, all too clearly, that the whole plan to raise his nephew to the throne had been a disastrous mistake; he saw, too, that unless he now directed all his energy and ingenuity to the task of over-throwing him, he must himself be overthrown. Unfortunately for him, Michael and Constantine had reached the same conclusion. They may have lacked his intelligence; they had, on the other hand, the whole power of government behind them. Some days later a vessel flying the imperial standard appeared at the landing-stage of John's estate – it was presumably somewhere along the Bosphorus or the Marmara shore – with a summons to present himself at once at the Palace to explain his recent conduct. The Orphanotrophus must have had his misgivings, but decided none the less to obey. Even now, it seems, he believed that he could bring his nephew to see where his own best interests lay.

But he was given no chance to do so. As he approached the Great Palace the Emperor, watching from the topmost terrace, gave a pre-arranged signal. The boat swung about; then another, larger vessel came alongside, took John on board and carried him off to exile – probably in the distant monastery of Monobatae, though Psellus claims that it was suitable only for bandits. He never saw Constantinople again. Michael, after his anger had cooled, is said to have relented to the extent of allowing his former benefactor a few primitive comforts; but Michael was not John's only enemy, nor were exile and imprisonment to be his only punishments.

After the removal of John the Orphanotrophus, and with him the last restraining influence on his own behaviour, Michael Calaphates could finally put into effect the ideas which, ever since his accession, had been germinating in his mind. His first target was the court aristocracy. It is not hard to imagine the barely concealed contempt with which they had treated him from the moment of his coronation: imperial protocol would have been minutely observed, but they would not have allowed him to forget either the baseness of his origins or the manner of his elevation. Determined on revenge, he now set about their destruction – abusing them, threatening them, humiliating them, depriving them one after the other of their privileges until they trembled for their lives. He dismissed his imperial guard (by now a semi-permanent force of Varangian and Anglo-Saxon Vikings), replacing it with a company of 'Scythians' – probably Slavs, and eunuchs to a man – whose loyalty he ensured by disproportionate rewards and who were consequently ready to act on his every whim. Meanwhile, writes Psellus, he gave ever more liberty and licence to the masses, on the grounds that his authority must be based on the love of his people rather than on any pampered elite. Not surprisingly, the masses responded. When the Emperor rode through the streets, purple hangings were draped from the windows and rich carpets spread in his path. All too soon, drunk with this adulation, he began to see himself as universally beloved, the father of his people, his position secure: so secure that he now resolved to pass on to the next stage of his plan – the elimination of his adoptive mother, the Empress Zoe.

To be sure, she had done him no harm. Indeed it was to her, almost as much as to his uncle, that he owed his elevation. But that alone was reason enough for him to treat her as he had treated John, since his character never allowed him to forgive those who done him a service. To him, moreover, Zoe represented everything he hated most: the old aristocracy, the Macedonian line, the hidebound and ossified traditions of the Byzantine court. It infuriated him to see her given precedence

Alabaster paten, with enamel of Christ: eleventh century

(*Above*) The Emperor Leo VI (886–912) prostrated before Christ: *c.*920, lunette mosaic over the Imperial Door, St Sophia, Istanbul

(*Opposite*) The Emperor Alexander (912–13): contemporary mosaic, north gallery, St Sophia, Istanbul

Jewelled and enamelled reliquary cover, once the property
of Constantine VII Porphyrogenitus, c.950

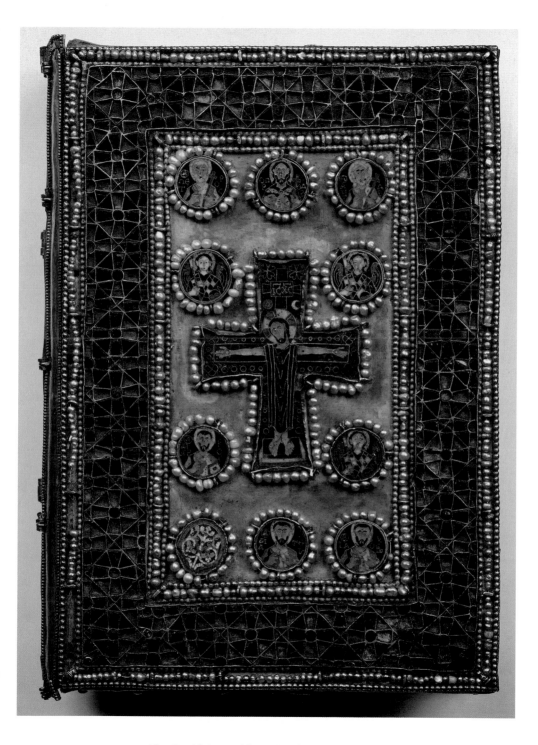

The Crucifixion: gold, pearl and cloisonné-enamel,
book cover, ninth or early tenth century

(*Top*) Chalice of the Patriarchs: sardonyx, silver-gilt,
and gold cloisonné-enamel, glass, tenth century

(*Bottom*) Chalice of the Emperor Romanus: sardonyx,
silver-gilt, gold cloisonné-enamel, glass, tenth century

Illuminations from the *Chronicle of Manasses*, c.1345

(*Top*) Basil II at Cimbalongus, 1014

(*Bottom*) Blinded Bulgar prisoners return to King Samuel, who dies of sorrow

Christ enthroned, between the Emperor Constantine IX
Monomachus (1042–55) and the Empress Zoe: contemporary
mosaic, south gallery, St Sophia, Istanbul

over him in church and court ceremonial, her name read out before his own in official proclamations. She was a constant reminder of his own miserable background, and of the humiliation he had felt in making those grovelling assurances with which he had gained her approval for his coronation. Did he also believe, as Glycas and Scylitzes maintain and as he himself later claimed to believe, that she had been responsible for the death of his predecessor and was already plotting his own? Perhaps he did: unbalanced as he undoubtedly was, he might have been persuaded of anything. The question must remain unanswered – but in any event hardly matters, for his mind was already made up. It was not enough that Zoe was old, and living in relative obscurity; into exile she must go.

The old Empress had already suffered hardship enough at the hands of her two husbands, but this was nothing compared with the treatment she now received at the hands of her adoptive son. For the third time she was confined to the *gynaeceum* she detested, cut off from the imperial treasury that was rightfully hers and obliged to exist on the most meagre of allowances; in the past, however, she had always received the outward respect due to her rank. This time no attempt was made to conceal the fact that she was being held prisoner. Even her rare public appearances – usually on the great Feasts of the Church – were forbidden. Her ladies and serving-women were removed; she was now consigned to the care of ill-educated and brutal warders appointed by Michael himself.

Yet even this did not satisfy him. On the Sunday after Easter, 18 April 1042, soldiers burst into the *gynaeceum* and arrested the luckless Zoe on a charge of attempted regicide. The tribunal that followed, at which several false witnesses gave the testimony they had been paid to give and the Empress was not even permitted to speak in her own defence, was a shameless travesty. Her hair was cut off and taken straight to the Emperor as he had commanded; she herself was then hustled down to a waiting ship and borne away that very night to a convent on the Marmara island of Prinkipo. Psellus writes affectingly of her grief as she tearfully called upon the spirit of her uncle, Basil II, imploring his protection. By the time of her arrival, however, she was quiet and seemingly resigned to her fate. She had, it seems, feared a worse one.

The next morning the Emperor called a meeting of the Senate. Whether its members believed his account of Zoe's repeated efforts to murder him we shall never know; but they were fully aware of the consequences of any protest, and obediently signified their approval. A public proclamation was accordingly read out by the City Prefect in person, to a large crowd assembled in the Forum of Constantine. Once again Zoe was accused of having brought her punishment on herself by her repeated attempts to murder her co-Emperor. Michael, it was stressed, had taken the only action possible in the circumstances, and had dealt similarly with Patriarch Alexis, who had been her accomplice in her nefarious designs.

We should like to know more about the involvement of the Patriarch. Our Greek sources tell us tantalizingly little; it is left to the thirteenth-century Arab chronicler Ibn al-Athir – who clearly had access to other authorities now lost – to record that the Emperor had his own reasons for wanting to get rid of him and had tricked him into visiting a monastery a little way up the Bosphorus, where a detachment of his Scythian guard was lying in wait to kill him. Alexis, however, managed to escape and returned at once to Constantinople, where he had all the church bells rung to summon the people to rise in revolt. We can believe this story or not, as we wish; but a popular uprising is precisely what now took place. Scarcely had the Prefect finished his reading when a voice was heard from the crowd, calling for the overthrow of the blasphemer Michael and his replacement by Zoe, the rightful Empress. Immediately the crowd took up the cry, one section of it making straight for the Prefect, who narrowly escaped with his life.

For, strangely enough – she had after all done little enough to deserve it – the people of Constantinople had taken Zoe to their hearts. It was not simply that she was the daughter, granddaughter and great-grand-daughter of Emperors, and the niece of the greatest that Byzantium had ever known; there was also the fact of her age. She had been Empress since before most of them had been born; almost without being aware of it, she had become an institution. Everyone knew that she had voluntarily adopted young Michael, and that it was to her that he owed his elevation only four months before; the idea that she should immediately try to murder him was as ridiculous as Michael's treatment of her was contemptible. Psellus gives a vivid eye-witness description of the scene that followed:

Since there was no longer anyone to stop them – the revolt having spread through the entire population – they took up their positions ready for action. At first they formed small groups, as if divided into companies; later, a citizen army, they marched in one body to the attack. Every man was armed; one grasped an axe, another brandished a heavy broadsword, another a bow, another a spear; but the bulk of the mob, some with huge stones in the folds of their clothing and holding others ready in their hands, ran in general disorder. Someone had thrown open all the prisons to swell the number of insurgents.

I myself was standing in the outer porch of the Palace, dictating confidential despatches when suddenly our ears were assailed by a noise as of horses' hooves, and the hearts of most of us trembled at the sound. Then there arrived a messenger with the news that all the people were roused against the Emperor. They were gathered in one body; they were marching under one common standard, with one single purpose . . . I straightway mounted my horse, and going through the midst of the city I saw with my own eyes the sight which I can now hardly believe.

It was as if the whole multitude shared some superhuman inspiration. They seemed different from their former selves. There was more madness in their running, more strength in their hands, the flash in their eyes was more fiery and inspired, the muscles of their bodies more powerful . . .

It was decided first to attack the Emperor's family and to tear down their proud and luxurious mansions. With this object the mob advanced to the general assault, and all was razed to the ground. Of the buildings, some were covered over, others left open to the sky; roofs falling to the ground were covered with débris, foundations were revealed as if the very earth were throwing off its burden and hurling away the floors. Nor was this the work of strong young men alone; young girls and children of both sexes assisted in the destruction. Every building fell at the first assault, and the destroyers looted the contents with utter indifference. The objects were all put up for sale, without a thought for the noble mansions from which they had come.

One of the first houses to be destroyed was that of Constantine, the Emperor's uncle. Somehow he and a group of retainers had made their way through the mob to the Great Palace, where they found Michael alone, deserted by his guard, cowering in a corner. Their one chance of survival, they realized, was to bring Zoe back at once from exile, and a boat was hurriedly sent to fetch her. Meanwhile Constantine – who, unlike his pathetic nephew, was not lacking in courage – gathered what few loyal forces he could find and prepared to defend the building until her arrival. All that day they fought, firing volley after volley of arrows and bolts from the towers and upper windows. Many of the insurgents were killed, but for each that fell several more arrived to take his place. The defenders were well-nigh exhausted by the time the old Empress arrived.

She herself was in little better state. Despite his situation, she was still terrified of Michael Calaphates: she was certainly in no mood to crow over him and the fate that he had brought upon himself, if only because it seemed that she might very easily be obliged to share it. She therefore readily agreed to do whatever she was asked: in particular, to show herself to the people as their lawful ruler and once again to make common cause with her adopted son. Her coarse woollen habit was hastily removed and replaced with a robe of purple, while the imperial diadem was arranged in such a way as to cover, so far as possible, the few wisps that were all that remained of her hair after her forcible tonsuring. So arrayed, she and Michael advanced tremblingly to the *kathisma*, the imperial box of the Hippodrome, to which there was direct access from the Palace.

The insurgent leaders, however, would have none of them. Zoe by herself they might have accepted, but the presence of the Emperor at her side was enough to convince them that she was still effectively his prisoner; so far as they were concerned there could be no solution to the crisis while Michael remained on the throne. Then, suddenly, a new thought struck them: what about Theodora? It was now fifteen years since Zoe, in a fit of wholly unjustifiable jealousy, had had her younger unmarried sister immured in the convent of the Petrion. Theodora had never re-emerged, and was by now largely forgotten: Psellus even goes so far as to maintain that when Michael Calaphates succeeded he did not even know of her existence. But she was still very much alive and still technically an Empress, with as much claim to the throne as Zoe and without her obvious disadvantages. Therefore, since Zoe could no longer be trusted to reign alone, she and her sister must do so jointly. That same afternoon a party led by the Patrician Constantine Cabasilas – and including all the eunuchs who had previously served her father and had later been dismissed by Michael – was sent off to the Petrion with orders to bring Theodora back immediately to Constantinople.

They found their mission far from easy. Theodora showed a good deal more spirit than Zoe had done, refusing absolutely to listen to the pleas of her father's old friends and taking sanctuary in the convent chapel. But Cabasilas and his followers were equally determined. They pursued her to her place of refuge and after a furious struggle dragged her forcibly out into the street. There she too was obliged to change her monastic habit for an imperial robe, after which she was borne in triumph to St Sophia where the Patriarch was waiting. And so it was that, late in the evening of Monday 19 April, the furious old lady received – with the greatest possible reluctance – the crown of Byzantium, while a vast concourse of people of every rank and from every class of society cheered her to the echo. Michael Calaphates for his part was condemned as a usurper and declared deposed. As soon as the ceremony had come to an end the congregation left the Great Church, reassembled outside, and marched towards the Palace.

Michael's position was now desperate. For hours he and his uncle, high in the *kathisma*, had tried to make themselves heard above the angry tumult in the Hippodrome below, pushing the miserable Zoe in front of them, repeatedly prostrating themselves before her in vain attempts to persuade the crowd that she, not they, held the reins of power. But the shouting grew ever louder and when the mob began throwing stones, and even firing arrows, in their direction they had been forced to retreat once again into the Palace where, not long afterwards, the news was brought to them of Theodora's arrival and coronation. By now Michael thought only of escape, of taking a ship from the imperial harbour of the Bucoleon along to the great monastery of the Studium, in the Psamatia district where the land walls met the Marmara shore, and there claiming sanctuary. His uncle Constantine, however, forbade it. An Emperor, he insisted, could never take flight. He must conquer, or die fighting. He himself was determined to defend the Palace to the last man, and he expected to have his nephew at his side.

At this moment, by an extraordinary coincidence, there arrived at the Bucoleon the Empire's most distinguished general, Catacalon Cecaumenus, thanks to whose valour and determination in the previous year the city of Messina had been saved for the Empire when the rest of Sicily had fallen to the Saracens. It was hardly the homecoming that he had expected; Michael, however, seemed to derive some degree of encouragement from his sudden appearance and agreed to stand his ground. All that night the fighting continued; but the first streaks of dawn revealed that the Palace had been completely cut off by the rebels from the landward side. Moreover, they were now launching a three-pronged assault: one group attacking the *kathisma* from the Hippodrome, one the Chalkē Gate from the Augusteum and the third marching on what was known as the *Tsykanisterion*, a vast open arena established two centuries before by Basil I for the exercising of his horses.

Tuesday, 20 April 1042 was one of the bloodiest days that Constantinople had seen in all its history. The carnage was appalling –

especially that suffered by the insurgents, for the most part defenceless against the fully armed and mail-clad imperial troops. In that one day, we are credibly informed, and in the night that followed, over 3,000 perished. But in the end, inevitably, numbers prevailed. In the early hours of Wednesday morning the Palace fell, and the whole vast complex of buildings was overrun by a frenzied, furious mob, pillaging and looting wherever it went but always with one supreme objective in mind: to find the Emperor and to kill him.

No longer could there be any question of a last stand. Shortly before dawn Michael and Constantine, pausing only to disguise themselves in dirty, tattered clothes, together boarded the waiting ship, sailed along the coast to the Studium, submitted to immediate tonsure and were forthwith accepted as members of the monastic community. Zoe, meanwhile, left alone in the Palace to fend for herself as best she might, was soon found by the insurgents, who immediately raised her on to their shoulders and set her upon the imperial throne. With the departure of Michael and Constantine, her courage had in some measure returned. Gratified as she was by this sudden reversal of her fortunes, she was nevertheless outraged when informed of the arrival and subsequent coronation of Theodora, whom she had thought – and devoutly hoped – never to see again. Her first reaction was to order her immediate return to the convent that she should never have left; only when she heard the cheering outside St Sophia and was told that it was for her sister did she begin to understand. This lugubrious and unattractive elderly virgin, forgotten by all until a few hours before, had suddenly and inexplicably become the idol of the populace. Reluctantly – and, we may be sure, fairly ungraciously – Zoe agreed to the partnership. It was better to reign as joint Empress than not to reign at all.

The scene now shifts to the Studium, where the Emperor and his uncle had hoped to lose themselves in monkish obscurity. They had, however, underestimated the strength of the popular feeling against them. As soon as their place of refuge became known, the mob left the Hippodrome and surged westward along the Mesē, bellowing for their blood. Psellus followed, with a detachment of the imperial guard, and has left us a terrifying account of the events that followed:

We found the monastery already surrounded by huge crowds, many of whom were trying to smash down the building in their eagerness to get inside. We had appalling difficulty in forcing our way through the hysterical throng, all shouting abuse and threatening the miserable fugitives with unspeakable atrocities.

Until that moment I had had no strong personal feelings one way or the other, although I had deplored the abominable way in which the Empress had been treated; but when I arrived in the chapel and saw the two unfortunates – the Emperor on his knees, clutching the altar, the *nobilissimus* standing on his left, both of them scarcely recognizable in their sordid rags, their very faces transformed by mortal fear, I stood there dumbfounded and my eyes filled with tears.

Realizing from his expression that Psellus was not entirely ill-disposed towards them, the two men cautiously approached him. Constantine earnestly protested that he had neither helped nor encouraged his nephew in the plot against Zoe. He had not tried to restrain him only because he feared the consequences: had he had any real control, would his whole family have suffered mutilation as it did? Michael, on the other hand, made no attempt to justify his conduct. He was guilty, and now he was paying the price.

All that afternoon the two men cowered at the altar while the mob, conscious of the respect due to the holy sanctuary, held back. How long it might have continued to do so we shall never know, because at dusk there arrived the new City Prefect, a certain Campanarus, claiming that he had orders from the Empress Theodora herself to take charge of the fugitives and promising them safe conduct back to the Palace. Michael and Constantine refused: they did not believe his assurances – rightly, as it turned out – and clung still more firmly to the altar. But the Prefect was not disposed to waste any more time: he ordered his men to seize them, and they were dragged, shouting and struggling, from the building. Many of those present – Psellus included – sought further guarantees from Campanarus that the two would come to no harm in his custody; but public opinion was overwhelmingly against them. There was, it seems, a widespread fear throughout the city that Zoe – whose jealousy of her sister was known to be such that she would have infinitely preferred to have Michael as her co-ruler – would somehow intervene to reinstate him. It was a risk that simply could not be contemplated.

This fear was shared in full measure by Theodora herself. If Scylitzes is to be believed, she had given secret instructions to the Prefect that the Emperor and his uncle should be blinded without delay; and Campanarus for his part was determined to carry out his orders. The two men – still

301

surrounded by the mob, whose imprecations had now given way to mockery – were mounted on donkeys and borne along the Mesē towards the Palace. Psellus continues:

They had not gone far along the way when they were met by the executioner who had been commanded to carry out the blinding. Showing their instructions to the mob, his men there and then began to sharpen their irons. Meanwhile the victims saw the fate that lay in store for them and were struck dumb with terror. They would have nearly died on the spot had not one of the senators present consoled them in their misery and restored some courage to their hearts.

Despite these efforts the Emperor, overwhelmed by his misfortunes, moaned and wailed aloud, begging for help, calling upon God, the Church, and anything else that he could think of. His uncle, on the other hand, summoned all his strength and faced his destiny with courage. Seeing the executioners ready, he calmly approached them, offering himself as their first victim. As the crowd surged round him he turned to the senior officer present and said in a firm voice: 'Make these people stand back, and you will see how bravely I shall bear my fate.' When they tried to tie his hands he refused, saying, 'If I move, you will be free to bind me to a stake!' With these words he lay flat on the ground and remained motionless, without a cry, a groan, or any change of colour. His eyes were then put out, one after the other. The Emperor meanwhile, seeing the fate that was so soon to overtake him, beat the air with his hands, tore his face and filled the air with his lamentations.

The Nobilissimus, rising to his feet unaided, pointed to his bleeding sockets and, leaning for support on one of his close friends, spoke to all those who approached him with such astonishing calm, such superhuman courage, that one might have thought him almost indifferent to what had occurred. Then it was the turn of the *basileus*, who was now in such a condition that the executioner was obliged to bind him fast and to hold him down with considerable force, so furiously did he struggle. After he too had been blinded the insolence of the mob, so marked before, died away, and their fury was abated.

And so the reign of Michael V came to a close, and with it the Paphlagonian dynasty. Soon afterwards he was sent to the monastery of Eleimon on Chios, his uncle Constantine to another religious house on Samos. Whether the two of them lived out their full span in the darkness to which they had been consigned or whether, like John the Orphanotrophus, they eventually suffered a still more dreadful fate we do not know.

What are we to make of Michael? Professor Bury, doyen of British Byzantinists, suggests that he has been unfairly maligned, and that he was in fact an ambitious and far-sighted ruler who aimed at nothing less than a radical reform of the imperial administration. Since this could not conceivably be realized while Zoe and John remained in power, their removal from the scene was, he continues, entirely justified: John in particular was by the time of his dismissal universally detested. For the rest, Michael can be credited with the release from prison of his uncle's arch-enemy Constantine Dalassenus and of George Maniakes — whom he sent back to Italy as *catapan* — as well as with the appointment, as his chief minister, of Constantine Likhoudes, destined to become one of the greatest statesmen of his day.[1]

Now all this may be perfectly true so far as it goes. Michael may — though the point is far from being proven — have had good intentions and, whatever we may think of his treatment of his adoptive mother, his elimination of the Orphanotrophus was probably a necessary measure. There remains, however, the inescapable fact that he managed to get himself deposed by a popular insurrection after only four months and eleven days on the throne. Any would-be reformer, if he is to succeed in his task, must tread warily; above all he must take account of popular feeling and make every effort to carry the people with him. Michael did neither of these things. Praiseworthy as his long-term ideas may have been, his statesmanship was consistently deplorable; and for this reason alone he could never have made a good Emperor. The story of his last days is scarcely edifying, and his subjects emerge from it with little credit; but they were right to get rid of him, and we too can be glad to see him go.

---

1 Professor Bury's opinion, not mine.

18

Constantine Monomachus and
the Schism

[1042–55]

Upon Michael, neophyte and false Patriarch, brought only by mortal fear to
assume the monkish habit, and now for his abominable crimes notorious; upon
Leo, so-called Bishop of Ochrid; upon Constantine, chancellor of that same
Michael, who has publicly trampled the liturgy of the Latins beneath his feet;
and upon all those who follow them in their aforesaid errors and presumptions,
except that they repent, let there be Anathema Maranatha as upon the Simoniacs,
Valesians, Arians, Donatists, Nicolaitans, Severians, Pneumatomachi, Manicheans,
Nazarenes, as upon all heretics and finally upon the Devil and all his angels. Amen,
Amen, Amen.

Last paragraph of Cardinal
Humbert's Bull of Excommunication

When Michael V met his fate on Tuesday evening, 20 April 1042, the
Empress Theodora was still in St Sophia. She had by now been there for
well over twenty-four hours, steadfastly refusing to proceed to the
Palace until she received word from her sister. Only the following
morning did Zoe, swallowing her pride, send the long-awaited invitation.
On Theodora's arrival, before a large concourse of nobles and senators,
the two old ladies marked their reconciliation with a somewhat chilly
embrace and settled down, improbably enough, to govern the Roman
Empire. All members of the former Emperor's family, together with a
few of his most enthusiastic supporters, were banished; but the vast
majority of those in senior positions, both civil and military, were
confirmed in office. From the outset Zoe, as the elder of the two, was
accorded precedence. When they sat in state, her throne was placed
slightly in advance of that of Theodora, who had always been of a more
retiring disposition and who seemed perfectly content with her inferior
status. Psellus gives us a lively description of the pair:

Zoe was the quicker to understand ideas, but the slower to give them utterance. With Theodora it was just the reverse: she concealed her inmost thoughts, but once she had embarked on a conversation she would chatter away with an informed and lively tongue. Zoe was a woman of passionate interests, prepared with equal enthusiasm for life or death. In this she reminded me of the waves of the sea, now lifting a vessel on high, now plunging it down again. Such extremes were not to be found in Theodora: she had a calm disposition – one might almost say a dull one. Zoe was prodigal, the sort of woman who could dispose of a whole ocean of gold dust in a single day; the other counted her coins when she gave away money, partly no doubt because all her life her limited resources had prevented her from any reckless spending, but partly also because she was naturally more self-controlled . . .

In personal appearance there was a still greater divergence. The elder, though not particularly tall, was distinctly plump. She had large eyes set wide apart, with imposing eyebrows. Her nose was inclined to be aquiline, though not overmuch. She still had golden hair, and her whole body shone with the whiteness of her skin. There were few signs of age in her appearance . . . there were no wrinkles, her skin being everywhere smooth and taut. Theodora was taller and thinner. Her head was disproportionately small. She was, as I have said, readier with her tongue than Zoe, and quicker in her movements. There was nothing stern in her glance: on the contrary she was cheerful and smiling, eager to find any opportunity for talk.

How well did this unlikely tandem govern the Empire? There are two schools of thought. For Psellus, the pair were a near-disaster: he claims that they understood nothing of finance or politics, that they were unable to distinguish between serious affairs of state and 'the most futile distractions of the *gynaeceum*', and that Zoe exhausted the exchequer by her insane largesse. John Scylitzes tells a very different story. He points to the imperial decrees against the buying and selling of offices, the improvements to the civil and military administration and several admirable high appointments, including that of Constantine Cabasilas as commander-in-chief of the European armies and – still more important – of George Maniakes as *catapan* in Italy with the rank of *magister*, the highest in the nobility outside the imperial family itself.[1] Meanwhile a tribunal was appointed to inquire into the abuses of the previous reign: the Nobilissimus Constantine was dragged from his monk's cell for searching interrogation, and ultimately revealed – by what means of persuasion

---

1 Scylitzes is almost certainly wrong here. We know that Maniakes returned to Italy as *catapan* at the end of April 1042, i.e., only a few days after the fall of Michael Calaphates; his appointment must therefore have been due to Michael rather than to Zoe.

we do not know – the existence of a secret hiding-place in his Palace in which were found 5,300 pounds of gold missing from the treasury.

Whatever the truth of the matter, one thing was certain: the joint regime lacked that fundamental stability without which it could never enjoy the confidence of the people. As the weeks passed and the two sisters' mutual dislike became ever more apparent, officials and senators were inevitably obliged to side with one or the other; the government thus began to show signs of a potentially dangerous polarization. Before long it was clear that it could not continue without a firm male hand at the helm. This, however, could be achieved in one way only: by an imperial marriage. Theodora, after well over half a century of virginity, refused absolutely to contemplate such a step; Zoe, on the other hand, asked nothing better. Although her previous attempts at matrimony had all been notably unsuccessful and third marriages were, as we have seen, viewed with horror by the Eastern Church, hope sprang eternal in her sixty-four-year-old breast and she immediately began to cast around for a suitable husband.

Her eye first fell on the distinguished and handsome Constantine Dalassenus – recently released from prison – who, it will be remembered, had in 1028 been the choice of her dying father until the civil bureaucracy had persuaded him to reconsider;[1] but when summoned to the court he shocked everyone by appearing in civilian clothes, and then adopted a manner so cold and haughty to the old Empress that she dismissed him at once. The next candidate was a certain Constantine Artoclines, a court official (also remarkably good-looking) whom she had always admired – so much, indeed, that there had been rumours of an amorous intrigue between them in the days of Romanus Argyrus, thirteen years before. Alas, he died in mysterious circumstances a few days before the wedding was due to take place – poisoned, it was said, by his own wife, who doubtless remembered the circumstances attending the marriage of Romanus and was anxious to avoid a repetition. In desperation, Zoe now turned to a third Constantine, a member of the ancient and noble family of Monomachus. He too was outstandingly attractive – always an important consideration with Zoe – and had acquired a formidable reputation as a ladies' man; he was also elegant, sophisticated and immensely rich. After the early death of his first wife he had married the niece of Romanus Argyrus, long before the latter's

1 See p. 269.

elevation to the throne; but only during Romanus's brief reign had he ever been properly accepted at court. In the days of Basil II and Constantine VIII there had been doubts about his loyalty, his father having once been implicated in a minor conspiracy; while Michael IV and John the Orphanotrophus, uneasy about his increasingly close relationship with Zoe, had banished him to Lesbos, where he had spent seven years in exile and whence he was now summoned.

Constantine Monomachus arrived in the capital in the second week of June. On the previous day he had been met at Damocrania on the Marmara where, in the Church of St Michael the Archangel, he had received the regalia and where an imperial vessel was waiting to carry him on the last stage of his journey. He was thus able to enter Constantinople in state, amid cheering crowds, and on 11 June he and Zoe were married in the chapel of the Nea. A slight cloud was cast over the proceedings by the absolute refusal of the Patriarch to officiate at what was, for both parties, a third marriage (one of the imperial chaplains fortunately proved more obliging), but by the following day he had overcome his scruples sufficiently to conduct the coronation service without protest.

The Emperor Constantine IX was more confident than Constantine VIII, more of a realist than Romanus Argyrus, healthier than Michael IV and less headstrong than Michael V. Politically, however, through sheer idleness and irresponsibility, he was to do the Empire more harm than the rest of them put together. By the time he died in 1055 the Normans of south Italy under their leader Robert Guiscard – the most dazzling military adventurer between Julius Caesar and Napoleon – were well on the way to eliminating once and for all the Byzantine presence in Apulia, Calabria and Sicily; the Seljuk Turks, now firmly established in Baghdad, were already beginning to contemplate their subsequent irruption into the Anatolian heartland; the Danube frontier had been broken by invading tribes from the steppes – Pechenegs, Cumans and Uz; the Eastern and Western Churches were effectively in schism; while within the Empire itself the nobility had made two near-successful attempts at revolt and the army had been allowed to decline until it was in a worse state than at any time in the past century. Constantine, meanwhile, scarcely seemed to notice. Unlike his predecessors in Zoe's bed, he made no attempt to check her wild prodigality; indeed, he spent even more than she did. Not since the days of Constantine VII had the capital seen such luxury and ostentation. The Porphyrogenitus, however, had used court ceremonial as a deliberate instrument of policy to increase his imperial prestige; Monomachus, by making no pretence of spending for anything other than his own pleasure, achieved precisely the contrary effect.

Zoe, for her part, proved equally tolerant towards her new husband. At last her interest in the physical aspects of marriage seems to have been on the wane: she certainly made no objection to his long-term association with the niece of his second wife, a lady of extraordinary charm who was the paternal granddaughter of old Bardas Sclerus, erstwhile rival of Basil II, and who had uncomplainingly shared her lover's seven long years of exile. When Monomachus had received his summons she had at first remained on Lesbos, obviously not wishing to compromise him and so prejudice his chances of the crown; knowing all too well the difficulties connected with third marriages, she seems not to have contemplated the possibility of his union with Zoe, the news of which had been a severe shock to her. Still greater, however, must have been her surprise when messengers arrived on the island with a letter from the old Empress, assuring her of her good will and encouraging her most warmly to return to the capital. There her initially modest dwelling was gradually transformed by the doting Constantine into a magnificent mansion while their affair, which was at first carried on with a seemly discretion, gradually became more and more open until finally the Emperor made a public admission. In the course of a most curious ceremony attended by the entire Senate, Monomachus and the Sclerina (as she is always called) were formally associated with one another by means of a contract known by the sycophantic senators as 'the loving-cup', after which she joined him and Zoe in an apparently happy *ménage à trois*. 'In appearance,' writes Psellus,

without being beautiful in the true sense of the word, she was so elegant, graceful and attractive that it was difficult indeed to criticize her. As for her character and temperament, she could beguile a heart of stone. Her manner of speech was delightful, unlike that of anyone else: rhythmic, subtle and harmonious. She possessed an exquisite voice, and her diction was as perfect as her tone was sweet. Everything she said had an inexpressible charm. She would often bewitch me by plying me with questions, in that gentle voice of hers, about the Greek myths, adding here and there little glosses that she had picked up from other experts on the subject. No woman was ever a better listener.

She endeared herself to the two Empresses by giving them everything that they most enjoyed. To Zoe she would make presents of gold, not to keep for herself but to give away, which was always the old lady's greatest pleasure. She would also provide her with sweet herbs and spices from the Indies, scented woods and unguents, tiny olives and sprigs of white laurel – in a word, all the ingredients necessary for her favourite pastime, the concoction of perfumes. To Theodora, on the other hand, she would present ancient coins and medals, of which that Empress possessed a large collection kept in specially-made cabinets of bronze.

Sadly, however, the warm feelings of the two old women towards their enchanting young benefactress were not shared by the people of Constantinople. Shocked and scandalized by the shamelessness of the affair, they soon made clear their displeasure. Scylitzes – though not Psellus – records how on 9 March 1044 an imperial procession in honour of the Holy Martyrs was interrupted by catcalls from the assembled crowd. 'Down with the Sclerina!' they shouted. 'Long live our beloved mothers,[1] Zoe and Theodora, whose very lives she threatens!' For a moment it appeared that the Emperor's own life was in danger; only after his wife and sister-in-law had shown themselves at the Palace windows did the mob disperse. The procession, meanwhile, was abandoned. Thenceforth Constantine seldom ventured out in public alone, being almost invariably accompanied by his wife on his right, his mistress on his left.

The accusation was certainly baseless. As the reader will by now be aware, there were many potential murderers at the Byzantine court, but the Sclerina was not one of them. Nor, so far as we can tell, was Constantine Monomachus. Weak, irresponsible and pleasure-loving he may have been, but there was no real evil in him. If, as was rumoured, he did indeed consider the possibility of somehow raising his mistress to the throne – and she was, after all, effectively there already – he could probably have done so by adopting her as his daughter and then simply declaring her co-Empress; Zoe's death would not have been necessary, Theodora's even less so. But the question is academic: it was not the Empresses who died, but the Sclerina herself. The date of her death is not recorded. All we are told is that she was attacked by some pulmonary disease, that she was unable to breathe and that the doctors were powerless to help her. The Emperor wept like a child, and buried her in the magnificent convent of St George at Manganes

---

1 In Greek, the familiar and affectionate Μάμαι (*Mamai*), literally 'Mums'; cf. 'the Queen Mum' in our own day.

(which he had had built next to her house, in order – it was said – to have an excuse for visiting her) alongside the grave that he had reserved for himself.

It is impossible not to feel sympathy for the Sclerina. She was clearly a woman of rare qualities, and her love for Constantine Monomachus was deep and true. But – although she herself cannot be blamed for it – her association with the Emperor had one disastrous consequence, which was to have a profound effect on the whole future of Byzantine Italy.

George Maniakes had, as we have seen, returned to the peninsula in April 1042. Since his recall to Constantinople two years before, the situation there had gone from bad to worse. In Sicily, Messina was the only city now remaining in Byzantine hands; on the mainland, the previous year had seen three major defeats at the hands of the Lombards and the Normans, who now possessed impregnable fortresses at Aversa and Melfi and were rapidly mopping up the whole of south Italy. The *catapan* landed with his army to find that, with the single exception of Trani, all Apulia north of a line drawn from Taranto to Brindisi was in open revolt. He wasted no time. The horrors of that summer were long remembered in the province – by those of its inhabitants who survived. Inexorably, pitilessly, Maniakes – assisted by a regiment of Varangians and the legendary Scandinavian warrior king Harald Hardrada – smashed his way from one insurgent town to the next in a fury of destruction, leaving a trail of smoking ruins and mutilated corpses in his wake. Men and women, monks and nuns, the aged and the children – none was spared: some were hanged, some beheaded; many (particularly the children) were buried alive. The rebels fought back, and for a while the two sides seemed fairly evenly matched; but then came the disaster. For the second time in two years, George Maniakes fell victim to palace intrigue.

His enemy on this occasion was the Sclerina's brother. The Anatolian estates of Romanus Sclerus bordered his own, and for eleven years already relations between the two had been poisoned by territorial disputes. Maniakes, as we already know, was a dangerous man to cross: some years before, in the course of a particularly violent altercation, he had laid hands on his neighbour and very nearly killed him. Romanus had sworn revenge; and now, finding himself through his sister a member of the Emperor's intimate circle and seeing his chance to even the score, he had little difficulty in persuading Constantine to recall Maniakes from Italy. Meanwhile, profiting by the latter's absence, he looted his house, laid waste his estate and as a final insult seduced his wife.

Maniakes received his letter of recall at the same time as the news of his other misfortunes. His rage was terrible to behold. When in September his successor arrived at Otranto he seized him, stuffed his ears, nose and mouth with horse dung and tortured him to death. The Patrician Tubakis, who had accompanied the luckless man from Constantinople, suffered a similar fate a week or two later. Maniakes, his anger still unabated, then had himself proclaimed Emperor by his men (who worshipped him) and led them back across the Adriatic – whose storms, according to an Apulian chronicler, he first tried to assuage by human sacrifice – with the intention of advancing along the Via Egnatia to Constantinople, gathering additional forces as he went. Marching on Thessalonica, he met and defeated an imperial army sent to intercept him at Ostrovo in Bulgaria but fell, mortally wounded, at the very moment of victory. His head was carried back to the capital and presented to the Emperor, who had it impaled on a spear and exhibited on the highest terrace of the Hippodrome. Later Monomachus staged a full-scale triumph, in which the rebel army – which had disintegrated on the death of its leader – was paraded round the arena, its men riding backwards on donkeys, their heads shaved and covered with ordure; but not even this humiliating display could conceal the fact that, but for a single well-aimed lance, Constantinople might well have fallen to Maniakes and found itself in the power of – if not necessarily the greatest – by far the most terrifying ruler in all its history.

George Maniakes was not the only threat to the throne of Constantine IX – nor even the greatest. An immense Russian fleet which appeared in the Bosphorus in the summer of 1043 was repulsed – thanks as always to Greek fire – without too much trouble; but four years later, in September 1047, there came a far more serious emergency. Once again, it took the form of a military uprising, this time on the part of the army in Thrace and Macedonia which had its headquarters at Adrianople. Its leader was the Emperor's second cousin, an aristocratic Armenian named Leo Tornices who had lived for a long time in the region and, says Psellus, 'reeked of Macedonian arrogance'. Constantine had long suspected him of subversion, and was additionally irritated by Leo's close friendship with his – Constantine's – younger sister Euprepia, who was perpetually singing the Armenian's praises and comparing him favourably with the Emperor himself. He therefore took every opportunity to abuse and humiliate the young man, at one moment having him forcibly tonsured and reduced to rags.

At last Tornices could bear it no longer. One night he slipped out of the city with a party of Macedonian supporters and made straight for Adrianople, delaying any pursuers by killing, at every stage of their journey, all the imperial post-horses. On arrival he deliberately started a rumour that the Emperor was dead, that Theodora was now mistress of the Empire and that she had chosen Leo as her co-ruler. The story spread like wildfire through the army. Leo was raised on a shield, robed in purple and proclaimed *basileus*; then, followed by several thousand cheering troops, he marched on Constantinople, the number of his followers constantly increasing as he approached the capital. On Friday, 25 September he pitched his camp beneath the walls and prepared for a siege.

He could hardly have arrived at a more opportune moment. For some years already the army had been suffering a rapid decline. The civil government, in its detestation of the military aristocracy, had systematically reduced the strength of the armed forces, encouraging those of the peasant rank and file who had not already fallen victim to the great landowners to buy their exemption from military service for an agreed payment in cash. At the same time they had removed the day-to-day government of each Theme from its *strategos* and entrusted it instead to a civil magistrate, destroying at a stroke much of the army's power and prestige. Apart from a handful of mercenaries on largely ceremonial duties, there were few soldiers in Constantinople or anywhere near it, while the army of the East – such as it was – was far away on the Iberian frontier, repelling invasions by the local barbarian tribes.

Nor was Constantine himself the man he had once been. At the time of his accession he was a regular winner of the pentathlon at the Games; now his feet were so swollen that he could hardly walk. His hands, too, which in his youth had been capable of crushing the hardest nuts – 'an arm gripped by him', writes Psellus, 'was painful for days' – had become misshapen and dislocated. He was in fact already far advanced in the arthritis which was to progress relentlessly for the next eight years until his death. Had he possessed the courage of Michael IV, it is possible that he might have taken a more active part in the defence of his capital; but heroism had never been part of his nature. All he could do was to prove to his enemies that, contrary to what they had been led to believe, he was still alive and in control. On 26 September he had himself carried to the Palace of Blachernae, at the northern extremity of the land walls; and there, in full imperial regalia, he installed himself at a high window looking out across the ramparts, the two old Empresses at his side. This inevitably exposed him to taunts and abuse from the besiegers – and before long to the attentions of a mounted archer, whose arrow missed him by an inch and struck one of his lieutenants. The others present hurriedly removed him from the window; but he was back there the following morning as if nothing had happened.

That day – it was Sunday, 27 September – Leo Tornices had Constantinople at his mercy. It is difficult to piece together exactly what occurred: it appears that under cover of darkness a corps of engineers had constructed and fortified an advance position outside the walls opposite Blachernae, from which they had hoped to inflict severe damage on Leo's men. They had, however, underestimated their opponents. The rebels did not hesitate. 'Like a swarm of hornets' they fell on this pathetic fortification, destroying it in a matter of minutes. Most of the unfortunate troops who manned it were cut down; few indeed managed to return alive. But this catastrophe was only the beginning. Seeing the massacre, those charged with the defence of the walls – mostly Saracen mercenaries, supplemented by a number of able-bodied civilians and convicts released from prison for the purpose – were seized by a sudden panic, deserted their posts and fled into the city, leaving (we are told) the gates open to the enemy.

What held Leo Tornices back from almost certain victory? For some of the chroniclers it was a miracle: Constantinople was always known to enjoy divine protection, and nothing else could have been expected. For others – Psellus included – it was simply a miscalculation. 'He was confidently awaiting our invitation to assume the throne: he assumed he would be led up to the Palace preceded by flaming torches, in a procession worthy of a sovereign.' Perhaps, too, he wanted to spare a city that he believed so soon to be his from the pillage which would certainly have followed. At all events he ordered his men to stay where they were, to shed no more blood and to pitch their tents for the night.

The mistake proved his undoing. The anticipated civic delegation never came. The people of Constantinople might not have been deeply enamoured of their Emperor, but they had no wish to see him overthrown by force, least of all by a Macedonian–Armenian of whom they knew nothing and suspected a good deal. They had had enough of rioting and violence. Within hours the panic had subsided, the gates were secured, the defenders were back at their posts. The city was saved. Disappointed and bewildered, Leo Tornices marched his prisoners to a point immediately below Blachernae. He had rehearsed them well:

They begged the people not to treat with contempt men of their own race and their own family, nor to be forced to watch while they themselves were pitiably hacked to pieces before their eyes, like victims at a sacrifice. They warned us not to tempt Providence by underestimating a sovereign such as the world had never before seen, as they knew from their own experience . . . Then, by way of contrast, they expatiated on the misdeeds of our own Emperor, describing how at the beginning of his reign he had raised high the hopes of the city, only to bring us down from the clouds to the edge of a precipice.

They were answered by a hail of projectiles, one of which narrowly missed Tornices himself. Then, and only then, did he realize that he had failed. The people did not want him after all. Encouraged by secret bribes from Constantine, his men began to desert him. In the first days of October he struck camp and moved away to the West. He was not immediately pursued: manpower in the capital was too short. Only when the army of the East, urgently summoned from distant Iberia, arrived in the city did Constantine give the order for his capture. By the time he was run to earth he had lost all his adherents save one – an old companion-in-arms named John Vatatzes. The two were brought back to Constantinople and, predictably, blinded.

Constantine Monomachus was fond of telling people that he led a charmed life. After the failure – by another almost incredible stroke of good fortune – of this second military insurrection in four years, there must have been many of his subjects who agreed with him.

For the progressive weakening of the Empire's military strength during his twelve-and-a-half-year reign, Constantine must take the lion's share of the responsibility. Had Basil II been on the throne, it is impossible to imagine that he would have permitted the Pecheneg tribes to cross the Danube in 1047 or thereabouts and to settle permanently in imperial territory. Over a century before, Constantine Porphyrogenitus had stressed the need to keep this most dangerous of barbarian races[1] under

---

1 See p. 164.

constant surveillance. His own policy had been to buy their alliance with lavish presents, using them to attack his enemies – Bulgars or Magyars – in the rear and so to prevent any southward advance on the part of the Russians. With Basil's conquest of Bulgaria, however, and the extension of the imperial frontier to the banks of the Danube, the situation had changed. There was no longer a buffer state between Byzantium and the nomad hordes; their incessant plundering raids were now directed not against the unfortunate Bulgars but against the Empire itself. Constantine Monomachus, unable to stem the tide, sought to turn it to his advantage by using the Pechenegs as mercenaries, particularly for the garrisons of the border strongholds. They proved, however, too untrustworthy: instead of keeping the peace they rapidly reduced the whole region to chaos. Before long he had no choice but to take up arms against them once more, but once more he was doomed to failure. After several humiliating defeats he returned to the old system of bribery. By now, however, the Pechenegs were not so easily bought off. Only by grants of valuable land and several high honorific titles could he obtain so much as a truce.

For the greatest tragedy of his entire reign – indeed, one of the most shattering disasters ever to have befallen Christendom – Constantine can, on the other hand, be largely absolved from blame. The religious schism between East and West had many causes, but imperial apathy was not among them. Indeed, Byzantine Emperors had traditionally favoured the concept of Roman supremacy against their own Church, if only because they were anxious to preserve the universality of their Empire and to maintain their claims to south Italy. Nevertheless, as readers of this history will be aware, the two Churches had been growing apart for centuries. Their slow but steady estrangement was in essence a reflection of the old rivalry between Latin and Greek, Rome and Byzantium. The Roman Pontificate was rapidly extending its effective authority across Europe, and as its power grew so too did its ambition and arrogance – tendencies which were viewed in Constantinople with resentment and not a little anxiety. There was also a fundamental difference in the approach of the two Churches to Christianity itself. The Byzantines, for whom their Emperor was Equal of the Apostles and matters of doctrine could be settled only by the Holy Ghost speaking through an Ecumenical Council, were scandalized by the presumption of the Pope – who was, in their view, merely *primus inter pares* among the Patriarchs – in formulating dogma and claiming both spiritual and temporal supremacy; while to the legalistic and disciplined minds of Rome the old Greek love of discussion and theological speculation was always repugnant, and occasionally shocking. Already two centuries before, matters had very nearly come to a head over Photius and the *Filioque*.[1] Fortunately, after the death of Pope Nicholas and thanks to the good will of his successors and of Photius himself, friendly relations had been outwardly restored; but the basic problems remained unsolved, the *Filioque* continued to gain adherents in the West and the Emperor maintained his claim to rule as God's Vice-Gerent on Earth. It was only a matter of time before the quarrel broke out again.

That it did so at this moment was largely the fault of the Patriarch of Constantinople, Michael Cerularius, who had succeeded old Alexis in 1043. From what we know of him, he does not appear as an attractive figure. After long service in the civil administration he had been involved in a conspiracy against Michael IV, and it was while serving a consequent sentence of exile that he had entered a monastery and decided – for he was consumed with ambition – on an ecclesiastical career. He was as unlike his distant predecessor Photius as can possibly be imagined. Where the latter had been the greatest scholar of his day, Cerularius was a mediocre theologian with only a sketchy knowledge of Church history; where Photius had been a highly cultivated man of intelligence and charm, Cerularius was rigid and narrow-minded: a bureaucrat through and through.[2] He was, however – as one might have expected – an able and efficient administrator; he possessed a will of iron; and – although it is not immediately easy to see why – he enjoyed considerable popularity in Constantinople.

If the Patriarch was the instrument of the new quarrel, its occasion was the alarming increase in the power of the Normans in south Italy. On 17 July 1053 Pope Leo IX, determined to eliminate these freebooting brigands once and for all, had attacked them with a large and heterogeneous army near the little town of Civitate; but he had suffered an ignominious defeat and had been held a virtual prisoner at Benevento for eight months, returning to Rome the following April only just in

---

1 See Chapter 6.

2 He seems, too, to have had in his character a streak of sheer vindictiveness, of which he gave an unpleasant demonstration in his treatment of his old enemy John the Orphanotrophus. Constantine on his accession had shown pity towards this now pathetic figure by transferring him from the dreadful Monobatae to his own former place of exile on Lesbos; one of the first acts of the new Patriarch, on the other hand, had been to have him blinded.

time to die. The Byzantine army had not turned up at Civitate – to the fury of the papalists, who understandably felt betrayed – but its leaders were every bit as apprehensive of the Norman menace as was the Pope himself, and it was plain enough to Argyrus, the Lombard-born commander of the imperial troops in the peninsula, that the only hope of saving the province for the Empire lay in an alliance with the Papacy. The Emperor, who admired and respected Argyrus, wholeheartedly agreed.

Cerularius, on the other hand, saw the issue in an exclusively ecclesiastical light and at once declared his bitter opposition. He disliked and distrusted the Latins; above all he hated the idea of papal supremacy, and he knew that such an alliance, even if it were to succeed in expelling the Normans, would effectively prevent the return of previously Norman-held territories to the jurisdiction of Constantinople. Even before Civitate he had struck his first blow: learning that the Normans, with papal approval, were enforcing Latin customs – in particular the use of unleavened bread for the Sacrament – on the Greek churches of south Italy, he had immediately ordered the Latin communities of Constantinople to adopt Greek usages, and when they objected he had closed them down. Next and more disastrous still, he had persuaded the head of the Bulgarian Church, Archbishop Leo of Ochrid, to write to the Orthodox Bishop John of Trani in Apulia a letter – to be passed on 'to all the bishops of the Franks, to the monks and people and to the most venerable Pope himself' – in which he violently condemned certain practices of the Roman Church as sinful and 'Judaistic'.

A copy of this letter, in a rough Latin translation, reached Pope Leo during his captivity at Benevento. Furious, he prepared a detailed reply – insultingly addressed 'to Michael of Constantinople and Leo of Ochrid, Bishops' – defending the Latin usages to which the Patriarch had objected and setting out all the arguments for papal supremacy; it was perhaps just as well that before it could be dispatched there arrived two more letters, one of which carried at its foot the huge purple scrawl of the Emperor himself. The text is lost, but is unlikely to have contained anything remarkable: Leo's surviving reply suggests that it expressed regrets for Civitate and made vague proposals for a further strengthening of the alliance. Far more surprising was the second letter which, apart from a few verbal infelicities, seemed to radiate conciliation and good will. It contained no reference to the disputed rites, it prayed for closer unity between the two Churches – and it was signed by Michael Cerularius, Patriarch of Constantinople.

It may have been the Emperor himself who persuaded the Patriarch to extend this obvious olive branch – though it is perhaps more likely to have been the Bishop of Trani, for whom the issue was far more immediate and who would have understood all too well how much was at stake. At any rate Cerularius seems to have made a genuine effort; Pope Leo would have been well advised to overlook the occasional little dig – he was addressed, for example, as 'brother' instead of 'father' – and to let the matter rest. But Leo was still angry and, very probably, already mortally ill; and his principal secretary, Cardinal Humbert of Mourmoutiers – who in the events that followed was to show himself not a jot less bigoted and waspish than the Patriarch himself – had no difficulty in persuading him to put his name to two more letters, and to approve the dispatch of an official legation to deliver them personally in Constantinople.

The first of these letters, to the Patriarch, addressed him as 'Archbishop', which was at least one degree politer than before; but it castigated him for his unpardonable presumption in even questioning the Latin usages, accused him of having pretensions to ecumenical authority (which was probably due to a mistake in the Latin translation of his letter) and finally suggested that his election had been uncanonical – a deliberate slur for which there was no justification whatever. The second letter was addressed to the Emperor and was, as we have seen, largely devoted to political affairs. It carried, however, a sting in the tail: the last paragraph contained a vehement protest against Cerularius's 'many and intolerable presumptions . . . in which if – as heaven forbid – he persists, he will in no wise retain our peaceful regard'. The Pope concluded with a commendation of the legates who would carry the two letters to Constantinople. He trusted that they would be given every assistance, and that they would find the Patriarch suitably repentant.

Leo was an able and intelligent man, but this time he had gravely miscalculated. Needing as he did all the help he could get against the Norman menace, he should have welcomed the opportunity of conciliation with the Orthodox Church; and had he been a little better informed about affairs in Constantinople he would have known that the Emperor – who was by now, like himself, a dying man – would never attempt to override the Patriarch, who was a far stronger character and had the whole weight of public opinion behind him. Still more unwise was his choice of legates on this particularly delicate mission: Humbert himself – narrow-minded, opinionated and rabidly anti-Greek – and two others,

Cardinal Frederick of Lorraine (later Pope Stephen IX) and Archbishop Peter of Amalfi, both of whom had fought at Civitate and bore a bitter grudge against the Byzantines for having let them down.

The three prelates arrived in Constantinople at the beginning of April 1054. From the outset, everything went wrong. Calling on the Patriarch, they immediately took offence at the manner in which they were received and stalked away in a huff, leaving the papal letter behind them. When Cerularius read it, it was his turn to fly into a fury. His worst suspicions were confirmed: forced against his better judgement to make a gesture of conciliation, he now found it flung back in his face. And worse was to follow: the legates, who had been welcomed by the Emperor with his usual courtesy, had been encouraged by their reception to publish, in Greek translation, the full text of the Pope's earlier, still undispatched, letter to the Patriarch and the Archbishop of Ochrid, together with a detailed memorandum on the usages in dispute.

To Michael Cerularius, this was the final insult. Here was a letter addressed to him, of whose very existence he had been unaware until copies were circulating all over the city. Meanwhile a closer examination of the second letter – which had at least, after a fashion, been delivered – revealed that the seals on it had been tampered with. If – as seemed all too clear – the legates had opened it, to whom might it not have been shown? For all he knew, it could even have been tampered with. These so-called legates, he decided, were not only discourteous; they were downright dishonest. He announced forthwith that he refused to accept their legatine authority or to receive from them any further communications.

A situation in which a fully accredited papal legation, cordially received by the Emperor, remained unrecognized and ignored by his Patriarch could obviously not continue for long; and it was lucky for Cerularius that a few weeks after its arrival there came the news that the Pope had died in Rome. Humbert and his colleagues had been Leo's personal representatives; his death consequently deprived them of all official standing. The Patriarch's satisfaction at this development can well be imagined; it must however have been somewhat mitigated by the absence of any obvious discomfiture on the part of the legates. Their proper course in the circumstances would have been to return at once to Rome; instead, they remained in Constantinople apparently unconcerned by what had happened, growing more arrogant and high-handed with every day that passed. The publication of the papal letter had provoked a firm riposte from a certain monk of the Studium named Nicetas Stethatus, in which he had criticized in particular the Latins' use of unleavened bread, their habit of fasting on the Sabbath and their attempts to impose celibacy on their clergy. Though not a particularly impressive document, it was couched in polite and respectful language; but it drew from Humbert, instead of a reasoned reply, a torrent of shrill, almost hysterical invective. Ranting on for page after page, describing Stethatus as 'pestiferous pimp' and 'disciple of the malignant Mahomet', suggesting that he must have emerged from a theatre or brothel rather than a monastery and finally pronouncing anathema upon him and all who shared in his 'perverse doctrine' – which, however, he made no attempt to refute – the cardinal can only have confirmed the average Byzantine in his opinion that the Church of Rome now consisted of little more than a bunch of crude barbarians with whom no argument, let alone agreement, could ever be possible.

Michael Cerularius, delighted to see his enemies not only shorn of their authority but making fools of themselves as well, continued to hold his peace. Even when the Emperor, now fearing with good reason for the future of the papal alliance on which he had set his heart, forced Stethatus to retract and apologize; even when Humbert went on to raise with Constantine the whole question of the *Filioque*, repudiation of which had by now become a cornerstone of Byzantine theology, no word issued from the Patriarchal Palace, no sign that the Orthodox authorities took any cognizance of the undignified wrangle which was now the talk of the city. At last – as Cerularius knew he would – Humbert lost the last shreds of his patience. At three o'clock in the afternoon of Saturday, 16 July 1054, in the presence of all the clergy assembled for the Eucharist, the three ex-legates of Rome, two cardinals and an archbishop, all in their full canonicals, strode into the Great Church of St Sophia and up to the high altar, on which they formally laid their solemn Bull of Excommunication. This done, they turned on their heel and marched from the building, pausing only to shake the dust symbolically from their feet. Two days later, having taken formal leave of the Emperor – who remained as courteous as ever and loaded them with presents – they left for Rome.

Even if we ignore the fact that the legates were without any papal authority and that the Bull itself was consequently invalid by all the standards of canon law, it remains an astonishing production. Sir Steven Runciman describes it thus:

Few important documents have been so full of demonstrable errors. It is indeed extraordinary that a man of Humbert's learning could have penned so lamentable a manifesto. It began by refusing to Cerularius, both personally and as Bishop of Constantinople, the title of Patriarch. It declared that there was nothing to be said against the citizens of the Empire or of Constantinople, but that all those who supported Cerularius were guilty of simony (which, as Humbert knew, was the dominant vice of his own Church), of encouraging castration (a practice that was also followed at Rome), of insisting on rebaptising Latins (which, at that time, was untrue), of allowing priests to marry (which was incorrect; a married man could become a priest but no one who was already ordained could marry), of baptising women in labour, even if they were dying (a good early Christian practice), of jettisoning the Mosaic Law (which was untrue), of refusing communion to men who had shaved their beards (which again was untrue, though the Greeks disapproved of shaven priests), and, finally, of omitting a clause in the Creed (which was the exact reverse of the truth). After such accusations, complaints about the closing of the Latin churches at Constantinople and of disobedience to the Papacy lost their effect.[1]

News of the excommunication spread like wildfire, and demonstrations in support of the Patriarch were held throughout the city. They were first directed principally against the Latins, but it was not long before the mob found a new target for its resentment: the Emperor himself, whose evident sympathy for the legates was rightly thought to have encouraged them in their excesses. Luckily for Constantine, he had a scapegoat ready to hand. Argyrus himself was in Italy, as yet unaware of what had happened and still working for the papal alliance; but those of his family who chanced to be in the capital were instantly arrested. This assuaged popular feeling to some extent, but it was only when the Bull had been publicly burnt and the three legates themselves formally anathematized that peace returned.

Such is the sequence of events, at Constantinople in the early summer of 1054, which resulted in the lasting separation of the Eastern and Western Churches. It is an unedifying story because, however inevitable the breach may have been, the events themselves should never – and need never – have occurred. More strength of will on the part of the dying Pope or the pleasure-loving Emperor, less bigotry on the part of the narrow-minded Patriarch or the pig-headed cardinal, and the situation could have been saved. The initial crisis arose in south Italy, the one crucial area in which a political understanding between Rome and

1 *The Eastern Schism.*

Constantinople was most vitally necessary. The fatal blow was struck by the disempowered legates of a dead Pope, representing a headless Church – since the new Pontiff had not yet been elected – and using an instrument at once uncanonical and inaccurate. Both the Latin and Greek excommunications were directed personally at the offending dignitaries rather than at the Churches for which they stood; both could later have been rescinded, and neither was at the time recognized as introducing a permanent schism. Technically indeed they did not do so, since twice in succeeding centuries – in the thirteenth at Lyons and in the fifteenth at Florence – was the Eastern Church to be compelled, for political reasons, to acknowledge the supremacy of Rome. But though a temporary bandage may cover an open wound it cannot heal it; and despite even the balm applied by the Ecumenical Council of 1965, the wound which was jointly inflicted nine centuries ago on the Christian Church by Cardinal Humbert and Patriarch Cerularius still bleeds today.

Despite the various disasters – political, spiritual and military – that marked the reign of Constantine Monomachus, life for the leisured classes in the capital must have been more agreeable than it had been for many years. The Emperor, for all his faults, possessed a sense of elegance and style that had been sadly lacking during the austere regime of Basil II and those of the ill-educated and boorish Paphlagonians who followed him. Not since the days of Constantine Porphyrogenitus had the court ceremonies been so magnificent, the entertainments so lavish. And if the *basileus* himself was no intellectual he was certainly not uncultured: he actively encouraged the arts and sciences and liked to surround himself with men of genuine learning. Of these the most remarkable was Michael Psellus: historian, politician, humanist, philosopher and by far the most distinguished classical scholar of his time. Moreover he was an orator of quite exceptional ability – at a period when that particular art was a good deal more important than it is today. The pity is that he should also have been self-seeking, sanctimonious, insufferably conceited – and, as we shall see, capable when the occasion demanded of the blackest perfidy.

Psellus's fellow-intellectuals in the inner circle around the Emperor were his oldest and most intimate friend, the lawyer John Xiphilinus of Trebizond, possessed of so prodigious a memory that he was said to carry the whole legal code of the Empire in his head; his old teacher, the poet and scholar John Mauropous; and the chief minister, Constantine

Likhoudes. It was to them that the cultural renaissance of the mid-eleventh century was chiefly due, they above all who were responsible for the revival in 1045 of the University of Constantinople. Their first concern was the Law School, which had sunk so low under Basil that by the accession of Monomachus there was not a single professor of jurisprudence remaining in the city. Now entirely reconstituted by Mauropous, it had at its head John Xiphilinus, who was given the resounding title of *nomophylax*, 'Guardian of the Law'. Courses at the new Faculty of Philosophy, entrusted to Psellus as 'Consul [*hypatus*] of Philosophers', opened with the ancient *trivium* of grammar, rhetoric and dialectic, continued with the *quadrivium* of arithmetic, geometry, astronomy and music and ended with philosophy itself, the ultimate synthesis of all knowledge.

Within a very few years, the university had become once again famous throughout Christendom and even beyond. For the past two centuries it had been the Arabs, rather than the Greeks, who dominated the intellectual world; the so-called wise men of Constantinople, they used to say, were not even mules – they were donkeys. Now, thanks to Psellus and his friends – and the enlightened patronage of Constantine Monomachus – Byzantium regained its old reputation and became once again a meeting-point for the scholars of Europe and Asia. As Psellus modestly wrote to Michael Cerularius:

The Celts and the Arabs are now our prisoners. From East and West alike my reputation brings them flocking to our city. The Nile may water the land of the Egyptians, but it is my golden words that nourish their spirit. Ask the Persians and the Ethiopians: they will tell you that they know me, that they admire me and seek me out. Only recently there arrived a Babylonian, impelled by an insurmountable desire to drink at the fountain of my eloquence.

All this must have done wonders for the Empire's international reputation, which had been steadily declining in the quarter-century since the death of Basil II; but the greatest benefit was to be felt at home. For years already, properly qualified judges and even trained civil servants had been in short supply. By the end of Constantine's reign the new university was producing a steady stream of highly educated young men on which the government could draw for its senior administrators. Their expertise would be more than ever necessary in the years to come.

Constantine IX never recovered his prestige after the departure of

Humbert and his friends. He continued to be suspected (with good reason) of pro-Latin sympathies, and his lame and grovelling excuses to the Patriarch – in which he tried to put the blame on everyone but himself – impressed nobody. But in any case he was by now a pathetic figure. Soon after his humiliation he retired to his monastery of Manganes, where his tomb, next to the Sclerina's, was already awaiting him. It was, perhaps, the most sumptuous foundation that even Constantinople had ever seen. Psellus writes:

The building was decorated throughout with golden stars, like the vault of heaven, but whereas heaven has its stars only at intervals, here the surface was entirely covered with gold, issuing forth from its centre in a never-ending stream. Surrounding it were other, smaller buildings, surrounded completely or in part by cloisters. The ground everywhere was levelled, and stretched further than the eye could see. Then came a second circle of buildings, larger than the first, with lawns covered with flowers . . . There were fountains which filled basins of water; gardens, some of them hanging, others sloping down to the level ground; and a bath that was beautiful beyond description.

In this bath the Emperor would lie for several hours every day, in an attempt to find some relief from his constant pain; but some time in the autumn of 1054, with the air already growing chill, he stayed in too long. Pleurisy resulted. At first he seemed to recover, but then his condition began rapidly to deteriorate. He lingered on until the new year; then, on 11 January 1055, he died.

19
Prelude to Catastrophe
[1055–9]

You would have thought that his entry into the capital had been some revelation of God Himself . . . I have taken part in many imperial processions and have assisted at ceremonies of a more religious character, but in all my life I have never seen such splendour. It was not merely the people of the City, nor the Senate, nor the host of farmers and merchants, that made up the happy throng; there were also students of the theological colleges, and dwellers on the mountain-tops, and hermits who had left their hermitages in the carved rock-tombs; the stylites too, whether they had slipped away from their rocks, or come down from their aerial perches, or exchanged the mountain heights for the level plains, all made the Emperor's procession into the City a most memorable sight.

Michael Psellus, on the entry of
Isaac I into Constantinople

Constantine IX died a widower. Three years after the Tornices revolt and four years before the schism, in 1050 on a precise date unknown, his wife Zoe had predeceased him. Surprisingly perhaps, he had been devastated. Admittedly he owed her a lot: not only his crown, but also his quasi-conjugal life with his mistress, which would have been impossible had the old Empress not looked kindly on it. On the other hand she was many years his senior, and the physical aspect of their own marriage – if indeed it had existed at all – had been of short duration and marked, so far as we can see, by a distinct lack of enthusiasm on both sides. To many people, therefore, his grief seemed somewhat overdone – particularly when he interpreted the growth of a small fungus on one of the columns supporting her tomb-canopy as a miraculous sign that she was now numbered with the angels.[1]

Be that as it may, on Constantine's death without legitimate issue the

---

1 A contemporary mosaic representation of Zoe and Constantine flanking the figure of Christ can be seen on the east wall of the south gallery of St Sophia, but all three heads have obviously been

imperial crown devolved once again on Theodora. Her imperial presence since being dragged from her monastery thirteen years before had been shadowy, to say the least; but now, refusing as always to contemplate the idea of marriage – however theoretical – she elected to govern on her own behalf. This she did, by all accounts, with remarkable efficiency: dispensing justice, promulgating laws, receiving ambassadors and stubbornly resisting repeated attempts by the Patriarch to take over the reins of government. One question, however, remained unanswered: who was to succeed her? She herself still showed little sign of age – both mentally and physically, she seemed in as good condition as she had ever been – but she was by now in her seventy-seventh year and could not last for ever. Clearly, she must appoint a successor; but she was superstitious and terrified of death, and could not be persuaded to turn her mind to the one problem whose urgency and importance increased with every day that passed.

It was still unresolved when, in the last days of August 1056, she was suddenly seized with intense abdominal pains. For once, poisoning was not suspected – the cause was probably acute appendicitis – but it soon became evident that the end was near. Anxiously, her counsellors conferred together – Psellus, who was with them, was shocked at the way 'they played fast and loose with the Empire, like men playing at dice' – to discuss the most suitable successor, whose name they would submit to the dying woman for her approval. Their choice finally fell on an elderly Patrician named Michael Bringas, who had formerly held the rank of *stratioticus*, a civil service post concerned with military administration.[1] 'He was,' sniffs Psellus, 'less qualified to rule than to be ruled and directed by others,' but this was seen by the cynics around the throne as being a distinct advantage: they asked nothing better than a cipher like Michael, who would be only too grateful for their guidance and through whom they could run the Empire as they liked.

By the time this decision was reached – it was about noon on 31 August

---

altered. The portrait of Zoe depicts a much younger woman, and may well date originally from the time of her marriage to Romanus Argyrus; but it was probably later defaced by Michael V after he exiled her, and would have been restored only after his death in 1042. The supposed portrait of Constantine is even more suspect, since it probably replaces one of Michael IV, which in turn replaced one of Romanus: no wonder the lettering above it is almost illegible.

1 Schlumberger seems to think that Michael had spent his entire active life in the army – surely a complete misreading. The new Emperor had, on the contrary, been chosen by the civil bureaucracy as being one of their own and detested everything military, as subsequent events were to show.

– the old Empress was sinking fast. She was no longer able to speak, but those closest to her insisted that they had distinctly seen her head nodding in consent. There was another brief delay while the Patriarch – refusing as always to be taken for granted – sought assurances that Michael had indeed been nominated by Theodora herself rather than her advisers; finally however he declared himself satisfied, and that same afternoon proceeded with the coronation. A few hours later the last representative of the Macedonian dynasty was dead, and Michael VI – known sometimes as 'Stratioticus' but more often simply as 'the Aged' – reigned supreme over the Roman Empire.

His reign began with a piece of high comedy when the following morning a certain Theodosius, a cousin or nephew of Constantine Monomachus who had apparently expected to succeed to the throne as of right, attempted an impromptu *coup d'état* and actually managed to storm the main prison, liberating all the prisoners who naturally flocked to his banner. All went well until he reached the Palace; but there, when he found himself confronted with the Varangian guard and a detachment of sailors from the imperial fleet, his courage suddenly evaporated. Turning back, he headed for St Sophia, thinking – on what grounds it is hard to understand – to enlist the support of the Patriarch; he had, however, sorely misjudged his man. Just as he was about to enter the church, the doors were slammed in his face. His followers were by now rapidly drifting away, and before long there remained of the rebel force only Theodosius and his son, cowering in the outer narthex, too frightened even to run away. They were lucky to escape with their eyes; but nobody seems to have taken them seriously enough to blind them. They were exiled to Pergamum, having succeeded only in increasing the new Emperor's popularity and strengthening his position on the throne.

Michael VI was a collateral descendant of that Joseph Bringas who had been chief minister under Romanus II and Theophano;[1] but he showed tragically little of the political acumen of his forebear. Wise government in mid-eleventh-century Byzantium consisted above all in striking a prudent balance between the civil administration and the military aristocracy: Michael simply indulged the one and victimized the other. In the spring of 1057 – during the annual Holy Week ceremony at which the Emperor traditionally distributed largesse to those who were thought

---

1 See Chapter 11.

to have been particularly meritorious during the past year – the entire Senate, together with all the senior magistrates and civil servants, were astonished to receive huge bonuses and automatic promotion, some of them by two or even three ranks. Then came the turn of the army. Psellus, once again an eye-witness, describes what took place:

The men who presented themselves were noble warriors, men of fine reputation. After bowing to him and making the usual reverences, they were told to stand to one side. At this point he should have taken them aside individually and begun with some words of gratitude. Instead, he first berated them all *en bloc* and next ordered the two chiefs – Isaac Comnenus and Catacalon Cecaumenus to stand forth. He then publicly turned on Isaac with a torrent of abuse, accusing him of having all but lost Antioch, corrupted his army, shown no signs of leadership and embezzled public money to satisfy his own personal greed. Isaac, who had expected praise and promotion, seemed stunned by the violence of this invective. Some of his fellow-generals attempted to defend him, but the Emperor forbade them to speak.

It was, by any standards, a deplorable exhibition. Certainly where the two generals were concerned, the Emperor had not the faintest grounds for his attack – which seems to have been the result, quite simply, of childish pique. For forty years he had been insulted and patronized by the military aristocracy; now at last he was in a position to tell them what he thought of them, and he did not mince his words. Nor, afterwards, did he express any regrets for what he had done. At a second interview, which followed at the generals' request a few days later, he had a perfect opportunity to apologize, or at least to show a modicum of good will. He did neither. And from that moment his downfall was assured.

The generals, outraged, determined to act. They had had enough of government by timid bureaucrats, by men who thought only of feathering their own nests while the army atrophied and the enemies of the Empire advanced from all sides; the time had come, they decided, to get rid of this long succession of weak, good-for-nothing Emperors and the epicene eunuchs who manipulated them, and to return to the old Roman tradition of the *imperator*, the Emperor-general who would put himself at the head of his troops and lead them to victory. But who was he to be? Isaac Comnenus was the obvious choice, but he persistently refused to put himself forward and retired instead to his estates in Paphlagonia. His colleagues, however, remained (at some risk to themselves) in the capital to take soundings, and were soon much encouraged to discover that they had an unexpected ally, perhaps the most valuable non-military supporter for whom they could possibly have hoped: Michael Cerularius, Patriarch of Constantinople – who, instead of closing the doors of St Sophia as he had on the ridiculous Theodosius in the previous year, now opened them secretly to the conspirators.

That same night, in the darkness of the Great Church, the military leaders of Byzantium met in conclave to discuss the overthrow of Michael Stratioticus and to decide on his successor. In view of the obvious unwillingness of Isaac Comnenus to be considered, they first selected that other victim of the old Emperor's wrath, Catacalon Cecaumenus, who had the additional advantage of being a considerably younger man; but he shook his head. Isaac, he maintained, was the only possible choice. With his commanding presence and formidable personality he stood head and shoulders above the others. If formally approached with a unanimous demand from his colleagues, how could he possibly refuse the call? And so it was that on 8 June 1057, on his Paphlagonian estate, Isaac Comnenus allowed himself to be proclaimed Emperor of the Romans. A month later he was joined by Catacalon, marching from his native Colonea at the head of no less than eight battalions that he had picked up on the way: five Byzantine, plus three more composed of foreign auxiliaries – Varangian, Frankish and Norman.

The movement led by Isaac Comnenus against Michael Stratioticus was no mere insurrection. It had nothing in common with the revolts of military adventurers like George Maniakes or Leo Tornices, however formidable these may have been. This was a full-scale civil war, in which virtually the whole of the army of Asia was marching against the Emperor, supported by vast numbers of Byzantines from all social classes and walks of life. Isaac, moreover, proclaimed by his soldiers and raised on a shield according to the old imperial tradition, had a far more legitimate claim to the throne than Michael; he came not as a pretender but as one who, in the eyes of his followers as well as in his own, was already the rightful *basileus*. Already, too, taxes were being collected in his name. Not surprisingly, there was little resistance as he and Catacalon advanced westward on Constantinople; at every stop, more and more of the local citizens, civil and military alike, flocked to his standard – so many that at moments chaos seemed to threaten. Fortunately Isaac possessed quite remarkable gifts, both of organization and of command. One look from him, we are told, was enough to silence opposition; strong men trembled at his frown. There and then he introduced a programme of rigid training. Every recruit was carefully examined: those of uncertain ability or spirit were given tasks behind the lines, while those of proved courage and obedience were formed into new companies and regiments. Every unit had its designated place in the camp or on the march, every man his place in the unit. Thanks to the tax collections, the soldiers were paid promptly and in full.

Michael Stratioticus, as far as we can tell, had suspected nothing until he received the news of the proclamation of his rival. He had then taken the only action open to him by calling on the army in Europe to come to his aid, supplemented by such few small detachments from Asia as had remained loyal. As a force, it was hardly impressive. Like Isaac's army, it contained a large proportion of foreign mercenaries, many of whom were soon to find themselves fighting their own compatriots. It was put under the supreme authority of Theodore, Domestic of the Schools, formerly one of Theodora's eunuchs who had been raised to the rank of *proedrus*; its far more experienced second-in-command, the *magister* Aaron, was a member of a princely Bulgarian family – who, however, unfortunately happened to be Isaac Comnenus's brother-in-law, Isaac having married his sister Catherine some years previously.

Arriving in Constantinople at the beginning of August, Theodore and Aaron immediately crossed to Asia and established their headquarters in Nicomedia. It was a disastrous mistake. Had they continued to Nicaea, whose tremendous walls commanded the only road round the Marmara, Isaac – who had no ships – would have been hard put to advance any further; instead, the city surrendered to him without a struggle, providing him with an ideal forward base for operations against the capital.

For a few weeks the two armies remained encamped within some five miles of each other, between Nicomedia and Nicaea, while the soldiers from each side, meeting unofficially on foraging expeditions, attempted – on the whole unsuccessfully – to persuade their reluctant enemies to transfer their allegiance. Then at last, on 20 August, battle was joined. It was not the rout that might have been expected. Theodore and Aaron fought bravely, there were heavy casualties on both sides and Isaac Comnenus himself, who had somehow got separated from his army, was set on by four huge Russian mercenaries and narrowly escaped with his life. But the ultimate outcome was inevitable, and the defeated army of Michael

Stratioticus fled in disorder back to Constantinople, where its two generals tendered to their master their formal resignations.

For the old Emperor the only hope now lay in diplomacy. By astute negotiations perhaps something might still be saved. A day or two later a delegation consisting of Michael Psellus and two colleagues that he had personally chosen – the former chief minister Constantine Likhoudes and the *proedrus* Theodore Alopus – set off for the camp of Isaac Comnenus. Their proposal was simple enough: that Isaac should come in peace to Constantinople, where he would immediately be crowned Caesar, on the further understanding that he would succeed to the throne on Michael's death. The three ambassadors arrived on 25 August, and were received informally: almost too informally, Psellus thought, since the general had at first limited himself to offering them refreshments and inquiring politely whether they had had a comfortable journey. On the following day, however, their reception was very different:

The sight that met our eyes was astonishing. First, our ears were deafened by the acclamations of the army. Their voices were not all raised at once: the front rank acclaimed him first, then the second took up the cry, then the third, and so on. Then, after the last rank had shouted, there was one great united roar which hit us like a thunderclap.

The Emperor [i.e. Isaac] was seated on a couch crowned with two head-rests, raised on a high platform and overlaid with gold, with a stool at its foot. A magnificent robe gave him an air of high distinction. He held his head up proudly and puffed out his chest – an effort that turned his cheeks deep red – while a far-away look in his eyes suggested that he was sunk in profoundest thought . . . Around him were circles upon circles of warriors. The nearest and most important comprised the highest ranks of the nobility, men who rivalled the stately grandeur of the Ancient Heroes . . . In the second circle were their lieutenants and the front-rank fighters, surrounding whom again were the light-armed troops without armour, and behind them all the forces which had joined him from the barbarian nations. There were Italians, and Scyths from the Taurus, men of fearful aspect in outlandish garb, glaring fiercely about them. Some had plucked their eyebrows and had covered themselves in war-paint, while others preserved their natural colour . . . Finally there were the warriors armed with long spears and carrying their single-edged battle-axes on their shoulders.

Psellus then put forward his master's proposal in a speech which, according to his own description of it, would have done credit to Demosthenes himself. At first, he tells us, there were the inevitable protests from the assembled soldiery; but as he continued they gradually became quiet, and by the time he reached his peroration it was clear that his arguments had prevailed. Isaac then took him aside and told him that he would be perfectly content with the title of Caesar, on the understanding that the Emperor would appoint no other successor, would recognize the honours that he, Isaac, had bestowed on his principal associates and would grant him the power to make certain civil and military appointments and promotions. 'Tonight,' he concluded, 'you will dine with me. Tomorrow you will carry my message to your master.'

The relief of the Emperor Michael when he heard this news can well be imagined. He sent Psellus straight back to the camp to say that he gladly accepted all his rival's conditions; he would receive him in Constantinople like a son and load him with all the honours and privileges he wanted. Isaac, equally delighted, immediately began to prepare his departure. That same evening, however, there arrived a messenger from the capital: a *coup d'état* by certain members of the Senate, aided and abetted by the Patriarch, had forcibly deposed Michael and obliged him to take refuge in St Sophia. At first both Isaac and Psellus were inclined to discount this as a rumour; but finally, when other messengers appeared with the same tidings supported now with an increasing amount of circumstantial detail, they allowed themselves to be convinced. Psellus frankly confesses that he got no sleep that night: as a spokesman for a deposed Emperor who had done his utmost to keep Isaac from the throne, he felt he could expect no mercy. But the general greeted him the next morning with his usual cordiality and even asked his advice on the art of government. On 1 September 1057, accompanied by thousands of Constantinopolitans who had sailed across the Marmara to greet him, Isaac I Comnenus entered his capital in triumph.

Michael the Aged had enjoyed one year of power. To his successor's eternal credit, he suffered no blinding, no exile. Abdication was enough. He died soon afterwards, a private citizen.

It is hardly surpring that Isaac Comnenus should have elected to be represented on his coins holding in his right hand a drawn sword. He assumed the throne of Byzantium with one object only in mind: to recover for the Empire, in the shortest possible time, the greatness it had known half a century before. Psellus tells us that he settled down to work on the very same evening that he entered the Palace, before he had taken a bath or even changed his clothes. His object was a complete

military reform, and he pursued it with military efficiency and ruthless-
ness. This is not to say that he imposed martial law, or appointed his
fellow-generals to all key positions in the State; on the contrary, no one
understood better than he the dangers of leaving too many victorious
soldiers idle in a rich and populous city, and one of his first preoccupations was to pay off his men and send them back to their homes to await
his further summons. Nor did he instantly dismiss all the civil bureaucrats
and senators from their posts. He did however ensure that the army
should once again receive the financial support that Zoe and her family
had so long withheld, and rapidly restored the firm military rule in
which, as Basil II had conclusively proved, lay the only lasting hope of
imperial security.

But all this needed money; and to make good the immense damage
that the Empire had suffered in recent years Isaac had no hesitation in
resorting to radical measures. Horrified to see how the immense reserves
that Basil had accumulated had been frittered away by his successors
(largely on gifts and sweeteners for their supporters and luxuries for
themselves) he immediately embarked on a programme of large-scale
territorial confiscation. The old legally-held estates were untouched – he
had no wish to reduce the power of his own aristocratic class – but vast
tracts of land which had been recently conferred on favourites and time-
servers were seized without compensation. The victims, provided that
they were individuals and laymen, might protest as vociferously as they
liked; they had no redress, and they knew it.

When, on the other hand, Isaac turned his attention towards Church
property, he must have known that he was inviting trouble. Michael
Cerularius, who had been working steadily ever since his accession to
build up his own position, was by now almost as powerful as the *basileus*
himself, and probably a good deal more popular. The Patriarch believed
– with good reason – that he had been substantially responsible for
Michael's overthrow; Isaac, he maintained, owed him his throne, and he
expected some recognition of the fact. The Emperor for his part was
perfectly prepared to be accommodating in areas in which imperial
interests were not, as he saw it, directly threatened. He willingly handed
over the administration of St Sophia – formerly an imperial responsibility
– to the Church, and agreed not to trespass on the Patriarch's ecclesiastical preserves, while Cerularius gave a similar undertaking with regard to
secular affairs of state. The difficulty was to know exactly where the line
was to be drawn between them; and on this subject in particular the

Patriarch had his own very definite ideas, in the forcible expression of which he did not scruple to cite the Donation of Constantine,[1] to threaten Isaac with deposition and – if John Scylitzes is to be believed – even at one point to don the Emperor's purple boots.

This, for Isaac, was going too far. While Cerularius remained in Constantinople his popularity was so great that he could not be touched; but when on 8 November 1058 he left the capital to visit a monastery some distance beyond the walls he was seized by the imperial guards and carried off into exile. Even then, however, he refused absolutely to resign the patriarchal throne; the Emperor had no choice but to arrange for a formal sentence of deposition. The necessary synod was held, prudently, in a provincial city; as might have been expected, its proceedings turned into something suspiciously resembling a show trial. The case for the prosecution – drawn up, to nobody's surprise, by Psellus – accused the Patriarch of every kind of heresy, blasphemy and vice. The inflexible Patriarch would, we can be sure, have put up a spirited defence; but he was by now an old man and the strain was too much for him. He died, of rage and a broken heart, before sentence was passed.

Isaac Comnenus seemed at first to have emerged victorious; but it soon became apparent that the battle was far from over. The local populace, who had barely contained their fury at the arrest of their beloved Patriarch, now chose to see him as a martyr: rioting followed, and although order was restored, the Emperor never regained his earlier popularity. Thus, little more than a year after his accession, he found the Church, the bureaucratic aristocracy and the people of Constantinople ranged implacably against him. Only the soldiers remained behind him to a man; thanks to them he successfully defended the eastern frontiers, beat off a determined attack by the Magyars and even held the dreaded Pechenegs firmly at bay. Psellus gives us an unforgettable description of this formidable tribe:

They are more difficult to fight and harder to subdue than any other people . . . They wear no breastplates, greaves or helmets, and carry no shields or swords. Their only weapon and sole means of defence is the spear . . . They build no protective palisades or ditches around their camps. In one dense mass, encouraged by sheer desperation, they shout their thunderous war-cries and hurl themselves pell-mell upon their adversaries and push them back, pressing

---

1 The theory according to which Constantine the Great had deliberately left his imperial crown to the Church for it to bestow on whomsoever it might select as temporal Emperor of the Romans. See *Byzantium: The Early Centuries*, p. 379.

against them in solid blocks, like towers, then pursuing them and slaying them without mercy. If on the other hand the opposing force withstands their assault, they turn about and seek safety in flight. But there is no order in their retreat ... They all disperse at the same moment; then later in some strange manner they reunite, one descending from a mountain, another emerging from a ravine, another from a river, all from different places of refuge. When they are thirsty and find water, either from springs or in running streams, they fling themselves down into it and gulp it up; if there is no water, each man dismounts from his horse, opens its veins with a knife, and drinks the blood ... After that they cut up the fattest of the horses, set fire to whatever wood they find ready to hand and, having slightly warmed the chopped limbs of the horse there on the spot, they gorge themselves on the meat, blood and all. The repast over, they hurry back to their primitive huts, where they lurk like snakes in the deep gullies and precipitous cliffs which constitute their home.

This time, he tells us, the sight of Isaac's army, with its unbroken line of shields, filled the Pechenegs with such terror that they abandoned their usual practice of trying to crush the enemy by sheer weight of numbers. Instead, they attacked in isolated groups and when these made no impression dispersed, announcing simply that they would give battle in three days' time. On the third day Isaac accepted the challenge and marched out to find them; but there were none to be seen. He contented himself by plundering and destroying their camp and then returned to the capital laden with booty and trophies.

Isaac Comnenus astonished all with whom he came in contact by his seemingly superhuman energy. Whether working in the Palace or on campaign, he seemed to need scarcely any sleep or even rest. His only recreation was the chase, into which he flung himself with the same tireless determination that he showed in every other field of activity; and it was while he was out hunting towards the end of 1059 that he contracted the fever that was to bring about his early death. At first he dismissed it as being of no importance, but his condition worsened and after a few days he took ship to Blachernae. Soon it was clear that he had not long to live; he was determined, however, to return to the Great Palace before he died. 'Here,' writes Psellus,

he demonstrated that he had lost none of his former courage. He left his chamber refusing the offer of any arm on which to lean. It was typical of the man's independent spirit. Like some towering cypress violently shaken by gusts of wind, he tottered as he advanced, and his hands trembled; but he walked unaided. In this condition he mounted his horse, but how he fared on the ride I do not know for I hurried on by the other road in order to arrive before him. When he reached the Palace I could see that he was extremely agitated and in a state of utter collapse. All his family sat around him, lamenting. They would willingly have died with him, had they been able.

It was at this point that the dying Emperor expressed a wish to enter the Church. His wife Catherine – daughter of the Bulgarian John Vladislav – made vigorous objection, but he refused to change his mind and insisted there and then on nominating his successor. His only son having died in his early youth, there remained his daughter Maria, his brother John and five nephews; his choice however, fell on none of these. Instead he sent for Constantine Ducas, the most aristocratic of that group of intellectuals who had been responsible for reviving the university a few years before, and solemnly entrusted him with the Empire. Then he had himself carried to the monastery of the Studium, where he adopted the monk's habit and where, a few days later, he died.

Such, at least, is Psellus's version of events. Other chroniclers tell somewhat different stories, according to which Isaac abdicated not on his deathbed but voluntarily – though perhaps during a fit of depression – simply because the political problems became too much for him. The exact truth is, as so often, impossible to establish; it can only be said that the theory of a voluntary abdication hardly accords with the character of Isaac as we know it; and that Psellus's account, supported as it is by a wealth of circumstantial detail, seems to have the ring of authenticity. In any case, there is a more important question to be asked: why did Isaac not choose a soldier like himself to succeed him on the throne, a man whom he could trust to continue those policies which (at least so far as the army was concerned) had already proved their effectiveness, instead of a hopelessly impractical and woolly-minded bureaucrat who – as he must have known – would undo all that he had done and simply bring back the bad old days of Constantine IX?

Once again, it is not difficult to see behind the whole story the hand of Psellus. A return of the bureaucratic party to power had been unthinkable two years before; now, thanks to the unpopularity of Isaac Comnenus and the death of Michael Cerularius, it was once again a possibility. Constantine Ducas was one of his oldest and closest friends – he describes him in his history as a paragon among men – who, he disingenuously informs us, possessed an additional advantage:

Others may speak of his many splendid successes, but for me there is one overriding consideration: the fact that this man, as admirable in reality as he was in appearance, should place more confidence in my judgement than in the scheming of my rivals. Whether he had discerned more evidence of wisdom in my opinions than in those of the others, or whether it was because he admired my character, I cannot tell; but so greatly was he attached to me, so much did he love me more than the rest, that he listened intently to every word that I uttered, depended on me absolutely for spiritual advice and entrusted his most precious possessions to my personal care.

Psellus cannot possibly have had the same power over Isaac Comnenus as he did over Constantine Ducas; but he possessed extraordinary powers of persuasion and it was he – we can be virtually sure – who somehow convinced the dying (or, if we prefer, simply depressed) Emperor that Constantine must be his successor. If this hypothesis is correct, it can only be said that his burden of guilt must be heavy indeed; for there is no Emperor in the whole history of the later Roman Empire whose accession had more disastrous consequences. Had Isaac Comnenus kept his health and energy, had he reigned for twenty years instead of two, he would have built up the strength of the army to the level it had known under Basil II. It would then, almost certainly, have been more than a match for the enemy that was already gathering its forces along the eastern frontier; Isaac would have been able to bequeath his Empire, undefeated and undiminished, directly to his nephew Alexius; and the third volume of this history would have had a very different – and far happier – story to tell. But it was not to be. Isaac's tragically premature death, and his inexplicable choice of successor, rendered inevitable the first of the two great catastrophes that were ultimately to bring about the downfall of Byzantium.

20

Manzikert

[1059–71]

Here one could see a dreadful sight: those celebrated Roman regiments who had brought both East and West under their sway, consisting now of only a handful of men – and men, moreover, bowed down with poverty and ill-health, no longer even fully armed. Instead of swords and other weapons they held, as the Bible has it, only pikes and scythes. And this was not even in time of peace. Yet because it was so long since any Emperor had fought here they lacked war horses and equipment of every kind. And since they were considered weak and cowardly and of no serious use they had received no subsistence money, nor their customary allowance to buy grain. Their very standards rang dully when struck, and looked dirty and as if blackened by smoke; and there were few to care for them. All this caused great sadness in the hearts of those who saw them, when they thought upon the condition from which the Roman armies had come, and that to which they had fallen.

John Scylitzes

Within weeks of Isaac's death it had become clear to all with eyes to see that his brief reign had constituted only a momentary pause in the imperial decline. This had begun immediately on the death of Basil II in 1025, with the accession of his hopeless, hedonist brother; it had continued all through the long, unedifying reigns of Zoe, her husbands, her sister and her adoptive son; and now, under Constantine X Ducas – arguably the most disastrous ruler ever to don the purple buskins – it reached its nadir. Not that there was anything evil or malevolent about Constantine. He was, as we have seen, the close friend, former pupil and to a certain extent the creature of Michael Psellus, on whose advice Isaac had named him his successor; he was a scholar and an intellectual, and – by Byzantine standards, which would certainly not be ours – a superb orator. Finally, he was a scion of one of the oldest and richest families of the military aristocracy. Had he but remained true to his background, had he continued Isaac's work for the eight years that he was to reign,

338

building up the army in preparation for the challenge that so obviously lay ahead, the situation might even at this late stage have been saved. But Constantine X was not one of nature's soldiers. He preferred the ease and comforts of Constantinople, spending his time in learned discussions and the drafting of interminable dissertations on the finer points of law. And the price that the Empire paid for him was heavy indeed.

Once again the bureaucracy was all-powerful, operating on a scale unmatched anywhere else (with the possible exception of China) for several centuries; for it has to be remembered that the Byzantine Empire, absolute monarchy though it might be, ran its economy on distinctly socialist lines. Capitalism was allowed, but rigidly controlled at every stage; production, labour, consumption, foreign trade, public welfare and even the movement of population were all firmly in the hands of the State. The consequence was a vast army of civil servants, taking its orders theoretically from the Emperor – though effectively, more often than not, from Psellus and his friends – and inspired, so far as one can see, by one overriding principle: to curb – if not actually to destroy – the power of the army. In the past seventeen years, they might have argued, the Empire had experienced three military insurrections: two had been quelled more by luck than anything else, the third had succeeded. It followed that the army must be humbled, and reduced to a proper state of subordination. It must be starved of funds, the authority of the generals must be limited, the former peasant-soldiers – many of whom had followed government advice and bought their exemption from military service – must be progressively replaced by foreign mercenaries.

What Constantine X and his government of intellectuals could never apparently understand was, first, that these were the very measures most likely to provoke further *coups*; second, that mercenaries were by their very nature unreliable, being loyal to their paymasters only for as long as they received their pay, or until someone else offered them more; third, and most important of all, that the enemy – the most formidable enemy that Byzantium had seen since the appearance of the Saracens 400 years before – was at the gates.

That enemy was a people who, being relatively new arrivals on the scene, have so far received only a passing mention in this book. The Seljuk Turks first appear as a distinctive tribe in the latter half of the tenth century in Transoxania, that region of Central Asia which lies between the rivers Oxus and Jaxartes south-east of the Aral Sea, where they quickly adopted the prevailing faith of Islam. At this time they were still entirely nomadic and leading a life of brigandage: fighting with neighbouring tribes, pillaging and plundering wherever the opportunity arose, finding amid the constant warfare of the local princes plenty of employment for their tough little war ponies, their swords and above all their bows, which they could string in the saddle; shooting as easily to the rear as to the front, they seldom wasted an arrow. By 1045, under their leader Tughrul Bey, they had spread across Persia; ten years later they were to make themselves masters of Baghdad, establishing a protectorate over the moribund Abbasid Caliphate and proclaiming Tughrul 'Sultan and King of East and West'.

The Caliphate, however, had never been their ultimate objective. Still less had the Byzantine Empire, whose existence had always been accepted by the rulers of Islam. This history has already recorded raids and incursions aplenty, in both directions across the frontier; but the idea of annihilating Byzantium would have struck the Seljuk Sultans as completely unrealistic, even ridiculous. The final goal on which their attention was fixed was Fatimid Egypt, whose Empire now extended across Palestine and Syria as far as Aleppo. As orthodox Sunni Muslims, blazing with all the fervour of recent converts, they detested these Shi'ite upstarts, who represented in their eyes not only unspeakable heresy but – since they had actually dared to set up a rival Caliphate in Cairo – a rupture in the fundamental unity of Islam. They knew that the Fatimids would not rest until they had taken Baghdad; and they were determined to destroy them before they had a chance to do so. First, however, there were certain matters to be settled nearer home; and the most important of these was Armenia.

From 1045 onwards, according to the agreement that John Smbat, King of Ani, had made with Basil II nearly twenty years before,[1] the larger part of Armenia was in Byzantine hands. Its annexation after John's death had been virtually the only diplomatic success of Constantine Monomachus; at the time he had made much of it, but it would have been better if he had left it alone – particularly since his subsequent policy, and that of Constantine Ducas, towards Armenia could hardly have been more short-sighted. The Empire's reason for

1 See p. 264.

acquiring this great mile-high mountain barrier on its north-eastern frontier can only have been strategic; yet one of Constantine's first acts after its acquisition had been to institute a fierce religious persecution of the staunchly monophysite Armenians, the surest possible way of turning them against him. His second successor Constantine X, while maintaining the persecution, was to go still further in idiocy. Armenia maintained a local militia of some 50,000 men, for the maintenance of which certain imperial taxes were remitted; in his constant search for new sources of money the Emperor ordered the taxes reimposed and the militia disbanded.

Thus it was that Byzantium lost an invaluable buffer state and gained instead, not an Armenian bulwark as it had hoped, but what might a century ago have been called an Armenian Question – a disaffected and discordant minority within the Empire which created more problems than it solved. The Armenian princes, left to themselves, would have put up as stiff a resistance to the Muslim invaders as they always had; now, demoralized and resentful, they found themselves wondering whether even conquest by the Turks would prove appreciably worse than their present subjection to the Greeks.

Tughrul Bey was not slow to turn this vastly improved situation to his advantage. His first attack on Vaspurakan as early as 1046 was a failure: the Byzantine Governor deliberately left a bait in the form of an undefended camp and ambushed the Turks as they were plundering it. Two years later, however, his unruly half-brother Ibrahim Inal took advantage of the temporary removal of Byzantine troops at the time of Leo Tornices's revolt and overran the city of Ardzen. The Armenian historian Matthew of Edessa speaks of 150,000 massacred, and goes on to describe 'the sons taken into slavery, the infants smashed without mercy against the rocks, the venerable old men abased in public squares, the gentle-born virgins dishonoured and carried off'; Matthew doubtless exaggerates, but the Seljuk sack of a wealthy city cannot have been a pleasant sight.[1] Thenceforth the raids continued almost annually. At one point Constantine Monomachus, obliged to withdraw troops from the East in order to deal with a more immediate threat from the Balkan Pechenegs, concluded a truce with Tughrul, but it did not last long: in 1054 the Seljuk Sultan personally led an expedition which ravaged

---

1 The survivors are said to have escaped to the neighbouring city of Theodosiopolis, which they renamed after their old home, Ardzen er-Rum (Ardzen of the Romans) – a name which over the years was corrupted into the modern Erzurum.

northern and central Armenia and the plain of Erzurum, pressing on to within some fifty miles of Trebizond itself. Although his entry into Baghdad in 1055 provided a brief interval of relief, the old pattern was resumed all too soon; now, too, the sufferings of the local populations were increased by the activities of the Turkomans – Turks who, though outwardly Islamicized, had never abandoned their nomadic habits, refused to accept the authority of the Sultan and cheerfully continued the brigand life of their ancestors.

Tughrul died in 1063, and was succeeded – after a good deal of family strife – by his nephew Alp Arslan, the son of his brother and co-ruler Chagri. Alp Arslan's moustaches were said to have been so long that they had to be tied behind his back when he went hunting; apart from that, the chroniclers tell us little about his personal appearance. As to his character, their accounts differ. Matthew of Edessa predictably calls him a drinker of blood, and Aristakes considers him one of the forces of Antichrist; in the opinion of Michael the Syrian, on the other hand, he ruled justly and well. The Arab historian Ibn al-Adim tells a story which suggests that he did not invariably observe the Prophet's strictures against the drinking of wine, but this failing was not unusual among Muslim princes of his day; all that we know of him for certain is that he was a superb commander in the field. At the time of his accession he was about thirty-three. Early the following year, 1064, he led a huge expedition against Armenia and besieged its capital, Ani.

No traveller visiting what remains of Ani today can fail to catch his breath in sheer astonishment at the splendour of the site: the towering walls, still partially standing, the rolling plain beyond it from which rise the ruins of some of the most magnificent churches of their time (Matthew of Edessa claims that there were a thousand and one of them) and – invisible until one is at the very brink – the sudden chasm formed by the river nowadays known as the Arpa Cay and one of its tributaries, thanks to which the city enjoyed one of the strongest defensive positions of any in the region. This was, however, of little use against the Seljuks. Unlike many of its neighbours Ani put up a show of resistance, holding out for twenty-five days before it surrendered. At the last moment its inhabitants are said to have sent out all their loveliest maidens and most handsome young men in an attempt to avoid a sack; but Alp Arslan was, as usual, merciless. The Arab historian Sibt ibn al-Gawzi quotes a purported eye-witness of what took place:

The army entered the city, massacred its inhabitants, pillaged and burned it; leaving it in ruins and taking prisoner all those who remained alive ... The dead bodies were so many that they blocked all the streets; one could not go anywhere without stepping over them. And the number of prisoners was not less than 50,000 souls. I was determined to enter the city and see the destruction with my own eyes. I tried to find a street in which I would not have to walk over the corpses; but that was impossible.

Even the Armenian historians admit that the fall of Ani was largely due to the low morale of its inhabitants; there seems, too, to have been little love lost between the local population and the Byzantine officials. Be that as it may, the city constituted the only serious interruption to the Seljuks' progress. From there they were able to advance deep into the centre of Anatolia, where the state of the Byzantine defences by that time can be judged from the fact that in 1067 they penetrated as far as the Cappadocian Caesarea, which was subjected to another merciless sack, and to within a hundred miles of Ancyra (Ankara) before withdrawing. More shameful still, scarcely a sword was lifted against them.

That same year saw the death of Constantine X. Even on his deathbed he had done his best to perpetuate his catastrophic policies, obliging his young wife Eudocia to swear that she would not remarry and demanding from all those around him written commitments that they would recognize only a member of his own family as his successor. In this the dying Emperor was almost certainly abetted by his brother, the Caesar John Ducas, and by Psellus himself, who must have known that he would get short shrift if a member of the military aristocracy should come to power: he had already once – to his deep disgust – been exiled to a monastery and was determined not to repeat the experience. But by this time the fate of Caesarea was known and alarm was widespread throughout Constantinople. Even among the civil bureaucracy there were many who saw that the Empire could be saved only by a radical change of policy. The problem was that, short of a *coup d'état*, the only way to ensure the kind of Emperor that was required was for Eudocia to marry him – the one thing that she had sworn not to do.

The Empress herself was perfectly willing to take another husband if she could be freed from her oath, but for this she needed a dispensation from both the Patriarch and the Senate. Unfortunately, since the former was Psellus's old friend John Xiphilinus – with him virtually a founder member of the new bureaucratic party – while the latter was almost entirely composed of Constantine's appointees, her chances appeared slim. Eudocia, however, was nothing if not resourceful. Aided by one of the Palace eunuchs, she put it about that she was seriously considering marriage to the Patriarch's brother, a rather dashing man-about-town; and Xiphilinus, who knew that his brother had always enjoyed considerable success with women, believed the story. He therefore summoned the Senators one by one, explaining to each in turn the iniquity of the oath that Constantine had forced on his widow. It was, he told them, unlawful and unjust, an attempt by one man to gratify his own personal vanity without thought for the good of the State. This latter, he continued, could be achieved only by the Empress's remarriage to some nobleman of distinction who would then, through her, inherit the imperial crown. Certain of the Senators agreed wholeheartedly, others needed persuasion of one kind or another; but eventually all gave their consent. Now at last Eudocia could announce her true intention: she would marry, not the Patriarch's brother, but a man who seemed, more than anyone else, to epitomize the Anatolian military aristocracy. His name was Romanus Diogenes.

The Emperor Romanus IV, who was probably married and certainly crowned on 1 January 1068, came of an old and distinguished military family with vast estates in Cappadocia. Still only in his early middle age, he had already served as Governor of Sardica in which capacity he had won several victories over the Pecheneg invaders; while in Bulgaria, however, he had been accused of conspiracy against the throne. The sentence of death pronounced on him after his return to the capital was subsequently commuted to one of exile, but this too was lifted on the death of Constantine X; Romanus was released and brought before the Empress, who is said to have wept when she saw him. The significance of her emotion is uncertain; we can hardly attribute it to love at first sight, although Romanus – according to Michael Attaleiates, who served with him in the field and knew him well – was quite exceptionally good-looking, with broad shoulders and bright, flashing eyes.[1] In any event, tears or no tears, the primary reason for the marriage was unquestionably one of policy: to raise a soldier to the throne and thus to save the State. Eudocia's earlier inclination had been towards the other leading general of the day, a certain Nicephorus Botaneiates, of whom we shall be

---

1 Attaleiates also implies that Eudocia anyway disliked sex; but since her only experience of it had been with her first husband this – from what we know of him – is not altogether surprising. Somehow, in any case, she had contrived to bear him three sons.

hearing more in due course; as a result of this single audience, however, she changed her mind. Romanus, who had left for Cappadocia immediately afterwards, had not even reached his home before he was summoned to return; the marriage and coronation followed a few days later.

It is impossible not to feel sorry for Romanus Diogenes. Although an arrogant man with a strong sense of his own importance, he was also an able and hard-working administrator and a brave soldier; and he fully recognized the gravity of the Seljuk menace. Already once he had risked his life to overthrow an Emperor whom he believed to be leading the Empire to its destruction; now that he found himself to be that Emperor's successor, he set to with spirit and determination to restore imperial fortunes – and it was not his fault that he failed. Wherever he looked, whatever he tried, the dice were loaded against him. In Constantinople, he had to contend with Psellus – who loathed him – and the Ducas family, who bitterly resented his rise to power and were resolved, sooner or later, to bring about his destruction. In the field, he found a hopelessly demoralized army composed largely of vacillating mercenaries, ill-fed, ill-equipped and frequently on the point of mutiny. Both 1068 and 1069 saw him leading military expeditions to the East, and it is a remarkable tribute to his powers of leadership that he achieved some degree of success – particularly in Syria, where he captured Hieropolis (the modern Mambij) and appreciably strengthened the Byzantine position; but the account of those expeditions by Attaleiates, who accompanied him as a member of his military tribunal, makes almost unbearably depressing reading. The Emperor's personal courage, his determination not to be defeated by conditions and circumstances that would have driven most generals to despair, shines out like a beacon in the darkness; for the rest, we have a seldom-interrupted saga of frustration and disorganization, of cowardice and chaos.

Fighting in the East continued through the first half of 1070, and was followed by a truce. This campaign was not, however, under Romanus's personal command. Every time that he left the capital there was a risk that his enemies – Psellus, the Ducas and their followers – might attempt a *coup*, and internal tensions during that year were such as to rule out any prolonged absence from Constantinople. In fact, his enforced stay had one major advantage: it enabled him to devote his energies to improving the lot of the army, settling arrears of pay, procuring new equipment, instituting training programmes and generally making good at least some of the damage wrought by Constantine IX and X and their predecessors. It also gave him time to recruit new forces. The experience of the past two years had shown him that the existing army of the East, even when in top fighting form, would never be sufficient to inflict on the Seljuk hordes a defeat decisive enough to ensure the safety of Armenia and, through Armenia, of Anatolia. The truce he had recently concluded with Alp Arslan was being continually broken by the raiding Turkomans and was, so far as he was concerned, a dead letter; he was therefore already planning a campaign for 1071 in which he would be able to throw some 60,000 to 70,000 men[1] into the fray.

That expedition crossed the Bosphorus in the second week of March 1071, and immediately headed eastward. Once again, Michael Attaleiates was present; and his version of the events of that summer, while it leaves a tantalizing number of points unexplained and questions unanswered, remains by far the most detailed and trustworthy account that has come down to us. As always, he makes no secret of his admiration for the Emperor; he notes, however, that after the army had gone some 200 miles Romanus's demeanour seemed to change:

He became a stranger to his own army, setting up his own separate camp and arranging for more ostentatious accommodation. When the army crossed the river Halys, for example, he did not cross over at the same time but remained behind and spent some days at a fortress which had recently been built at his command. Soon afterwards he issued an order to separate his private possessions from those of the army.

Scylitzes, whose narrative for this period clearly derives from Attaleiates, suggests that Romanus had been perturbed by various supposed portents, among them the sudden breakage of the central pole of his tent and an unexplained fire in which he lost much of his personal equipment, together with several of his best horses and mules. It may well be so – this was a superstitious age and the Byzantines were even more credulous than most; there seems little doubt, at any rate, that to his natural arrogance the Emperor now added several other faults which threatened to become liabilities in the days to come: remoteness, ill

---

1 Such figures as these are, as always, highly conjectural. Byzantine sources give no information, Muslim ones range from 200,000 to 600,000 and Matthew of Edessa claims, grotesquely, 1 million. Most modern historians seem to agree that the estimate given above is the most probable, though the true number could have been as high as 100,000.

temper, impatience with advice and a streak of cruelty which we have not seen before.[1]

Strangely enough, while the immense Byzantine army was marching across Anatolia, Alp Arslan was heading in a completely different direction. Being totally unable to control the Turkoman raiders and having frequently disclaimed all responsibility for their activities, he believed the truce of the previous year to be still in force; he had therefore decided that the moment had come to fulfil his long-cherished ambition of destroying the Fatimid Caliphate. Late in 1070 he left his headquarters at Khurasan, captured the Armenian fortresses of Manzikert and Archesh, then marched south-west to Amida and on to Edessa where, towards the end of March, he drew up his army beneath the walls. Scarcely had he begun the siege when he received a message from the Emperor proposing a renewal of the truce and the exchange of Manzikert and Archesh for Hieropolis in Syria, which he had captured three years before. He accepted and, leaving Edessa untaken, continued his march. Six weeks later he was besieging Aleppo when there arrived another envoy from Romanus, now in Armenia, repeating the offer but this time presenting it in distinctly threatening terms.

If Romanus had received Alp Arslan's previous acceptance of his offer, he had played the Sultan false. Even if he had not, he was now in a position of strength and putting forward what amounted to an ultimatum. Seeing at once that he had no choice but to abandon his Fatimid expedition, Alp Arslan turned about and made straight back for his homeland. Such was his haste that he failed to take adequate precautions in recrossing the Euphrates: many of his horses and mules were carried away by the current and drowned. But this hardly mattered to him. He knew that he would anyway have to raise a very much larger army before he could meet the Emperor on his own terms. Sending his vizier Nizam al-Mulk ahead to raise troops in Azerbaijan, he himself headed for Khoi (now Khvoi), between Lake Van and Lake Urmia, picking up some ten thousand Kurdish cavalry *en route*; there he was joined by his new army and set off in search of his foe.

---

1 At one point of the campaign a Byzantine soldier accused of stealing a donkey from a local inhabitant and brought before the Emperor was sentenced to have his nose severed – a punishment that had fortunately gone out of fashion in the eighth century. It was when Romanus upheld this sentence even after the poor man had invoked the intercession of the victory-bringing icon of the Holy Virgin of Blachernae (which was always carried by the *basileus* into battle) that Attaleiates reports his first presentiment of the divine vengeance that would follow.

Romanus had meanwhile encamped near Erzurum, where he had split his army into two. The greater part he dispatched under the command of his general Joseph Tarchaniotes to Khelat (now Ahlat), a strongly defended Seljuk-held fortress a few miles from the northern shore of Lake Van, while he himself – together with his other principal commander, Nicephorus Bryennius – set off with the remainder for the little fortress-town of Manzikert, which he believed would offer no serious resistance. He was, as it turned out, perfectly right: the garrison gave in without a struggle. Tarchaniotes, on the other hand, was less fortunate. We do not know precisely what happened. Later Muslim historians refer to a pitched battle in which Alp Arslan scored a decisive victory, but there is no mention of such an engagement in any Byzantine source – the most trustworthy, Attaleiates, simply reporting that the news of the Sultan's arrival with his new army was in itself sufficient to send 'the scoundrel' Tarchaniotes into headlong flight, his men after him. They never stopped until they reached Melitene on the Euphrates, and did not reappear again during the whole campaign.

But it cannot, surely, have been as simple as that. Joseph Tarchaniotes was a highly respected general, in command of a force of 30,000 to 40,000 – larger, very probably, than the entire Seljuk army. If we reject the Muslim version – that he was soundly beaten in the field – we are left with various other possibilities, all in varying degrees improbable: that he was angry with Romanus, whom he had strongly advised not to split the army, and determined to prove him wrong whatever the cost; that Alp Arslan had taken his army by surprise, and that since it had no opportunity to regroup a general *sauve-qui-peut* was the only answer; or – most intriguing of all – that Tarchaniotes was a traitor, a tool of the Ducas, who had actually set out from Constantinople with the deliberate intention of abandoning his Emperor when the moment came. If such a theory seems at present far-fetched, it may seem less so by the end of this chapter; and it would also go a long way to explain another mystery – why it was that no word of what had happened was sent to Romanus, only thirty miles away at Manzikert. But however much we may speculate about the cause of the rout, its consequence is all too clear: that by the time the Emperor finally met the Seljuks on the field of battle, more than half his army had deserted him.

Romanus Diogenes had captured the fortress of Manzikert; he did not have long, however, to savour his triumph. On the very next day some of his men, out on a foraging expedition, were set upon by mounted Seljuk bowmen and suffered heavy casualties. The Emperor, assuming that he had to deal with nothing more serious than a small band of marauders, sent out a small detachment of troops under Bryennius – and flew into a fury when he received, an hour or two later, an appeal for reinforcements. After some hesitation he dispatched a rather larger force under an impulsive Armenian named Basilacius; they tried to pursue the bowmen, but were trapped by them and quickly surrounded. Basilacius himself was captured, but few of those who followed him escaped with their lives. Bryennius, riding out once again – this time with the entire right wing of the army behind him – in an attempt to rescue his rescuers, found himself confronted with what must have been a considerable proportion of the entire Seljuk army. He and his men retreated in good order to the camp, but not before he had received no less than three wounds, two from arrows in the back and one, in the chest, from a lance. Fortunately all three proved to be superficial, and he was able to continue the campaign.

That night there was no moon – and little sleep for the Byzantine army. The Seljuks kept up an unremitting pressure, loosing hail after hail of arrows and generally causing so much tumult and confusion in the darkness that again and again they were thought to have broken down the defences and overrun the camp. It was a pleasant surprise to everyone the next morning to find that the palisades had held – but a most unpleasant shock to learn that a large contingent of Uz mercenaries had defected to the Seljuks; there were several other Turkic units in the army, any or all of which might at any moment follow their example. In such circumstances, and with half his army – including one of his best generals – vanished without trace, one might have expected the Emperor to welcome the delegation that arrived a day or two later. It came, officially, from the Caliph in Baghdad (though in fact it was obviously sent by Alp Arslan in the hopes that it might fare better than one from himself) and it proposed a truce.

Why, we may ask, did the Sultan want one? Almost certainly because he was far from sure of victory. We know that shortly before going into battle he spoke of possible martyrdom in the field; he dressed himself in white in order, as he explained, that his garment might also serve as his shroud; and he enforced oaths from those around him that his son Malik-Shah should succeed him in the event of his death. In the past the Seljuks had always relied upon their skill in irregular warfare – the warfare of raids, ambushes and surprise attacks. They disliked pitched battles, which they avoided whenever possible; and recent Byzantine humiliations notwithstanding, they still retained a healthy respect for the imperial army.[1] Besides, was there, from the Sultan's point of view, any real reason to fight? The one serious difference of political opinion concerned Armenia, which had considerable strategic value for both him and Romanus. If only the two of them could agree on a mutually acceptable division of Armenian territory, both armies could remain intact – and Alp Arslan could turn his attention back to what really interested him: the Fatimids.

But the Emperor's determination remained firm. This was, he knew, his only chance of freeing his Empire once and for all from the Turkish menace. Alp Arslan was only a few miles away with his full army; he himself, despite the disaster of Khelat, still commanded a force which, even if not quite its equal in size, was certainly larger than he was ever likely to muster again. Finally, if he were to return to Constantinople without having so much as engaged the Seljuks on the field, what chance would he have of keeping his throne – or indeed his life – against the intrigues of the Ducas? He dismissed the embassy with the minimum of courtesy and prepared for battle.

It is a curious and somehow frustrating fact that neither the date nor the location of one of the most decisive battles of the world can be universally agreed. Muslim historians are unanimous that it took place on a Friday, and the month was indubitably August; but scholars still argue whether it was fought on the 5th, 12th, 19th or 26th. Most European historians seem to have opted for the 19th, but in doing so they have ignored an important clue: the fact that according to Michael Attaleiates – who was there – the second or third night before the battle was moonless (*aselenos*). Now in August 1071 the full moon was on the 13th (Julian calendar), which means that the nights would still have been bright on the 16th and 17th; they would have been far darker on the 23rd and 24th, when the moon would have been visible only as a thin crescent, an hour or two before dawn. Leaving aside the possibility that Attaleiates simply meant that the sky was overcast – something extremely improbable in that place and season – we cannot but conclude that it was

---

1 But this raises another question: if the Seljuks had indeed defeated the Byzantines in pitched battle at Khelat, would the Sultan not have been rather more optimistic? The more one thinks about it, the more one comes to suspect that that battle never took place.

on Friday, 26 August that the fate of the Byzantine Empire was settled.[1]

As to the location, we know that the battle was fought on fairly level steppe, within a mile or two of the fortress of Manzikert (now marked by the modern Turkish town of Malazgirt). The chronicler Nicephorus Bryennius, grandson and namesake of Romanus's general and another valuable source, adds that in the closing stages the Byzantines ran into ambushes, which suggests – since steppes by their very nature afford few hiding-places – that there must also have been rougher, hillier country close by. Now Armenia is a mountainous country, but there is indeed just such a steppe, some three or four miles across, extending for perhaps ten miles on a south-west–north-east axis immediately to the south and east of the town. Beyond it a line of foothills, cut through with gullies and ravines – ideal ambush country – soon gives way once more to the mountains. Somewhere in those forty-odd square miles the two armies drew up opposite each other, early that Friday afternoon, and battle was joined.

Or was it? The fact of the matter is that Manzikert, for all its historical significance, was until its very final stages hardly a battle at all. Romanus had formed up his army according to the traditional army manuals, in one long line several ranks deep, with the cavalry on the flanks. He himself took the centre, with Bryennius on the left and, on the right, a Cappadocian general named Alyattes. Behind was a substantial rearguard composed, we are told, of the 'levies of the nobility' – in fact the private armies of the great landowners – under the command, somewhat surprisingly, of Andronicus Ducas, son of Caesar John Ducas and nephew of the late Emperor. This young man seems to have made little secret of his contempt for Romanus, and the wonder is that the latter should have ever allowed him to participate in the campaign at all. Presumably he thought it safer to have him under his eye as a potential hostage rather than to leave him to stir up trouble in Constantinople; if so, it was the gravest mistake of his life.

All through the afternoon the imperial army advanced across the steppe, but instead of coming forward to meet them the Seljuks steadily withdrew in a wide crescent, leaving the initiative to their mounted archers who galloped up and down on the Byzantine flanks, showering

---

1 For this information, as for much else in this chapter, I am indebted to the late Alfred Friendly, whose book *The Dreadful Day: The Battle of Manzikert, 1071* has proved invaluable.

them with arrows. The infuriated cavalry would then break line and pursue them into the foothills – straight, it need hardly be said, into the carefully prepared ambushes; but for the increasingly frustrated Emperor in the centre there remained, where the enemy should have been, an empty void. On and on he rode, apparently convinced that if he continued as far as the mountains he could somehow force his antagonists to turn and fight; then, suddenly, he noticed that the sun was fast declining and that he had left his camp virtually undefended. There was no point in further pursuit – if, indeed, he was actually pursuing anyone. He ordered the imperial standards to be reversed – the recognized signal for turning back – and wheeled his horse.

This was the moment for which Alp Arslan had been waiting. From his observation post in the hills above he had watched Romanus's every move; now and now only, he gave the order for the attack. As his men poured down on to the steppe the Byzantine line broke in confusion; some of the mercenary units, seeing the reversed standards and not understanding their true significance, assumed that the Emperor had been killed and took to their heels. Meanwhile the Seljuks cut across immediately behind the broken line, separating it from the rearguard. At this point that rearguard should have justified its existence by moving forward, squeezing the enemy between it and the forward line and preventing its escape. Instead, Andronicus Ducas deliberately spread the word among his troops that the Emperor was defeated and the battle lost. He and they thereupon fled from the field and, as the panic spread, more and more contingents followed them. Only the troops on the left wing, seeing the Emperor in difficulties, rode to his rescue; but the Seljuks bore down upon them swiftly from the rear and they too had to flee.

Romanus stood his ground, his personal guard around him, calling in vain on his troops to rally. But the chaos and confusion were too great. As Attaleiates describes it:

Outside the camp all were in flight, shouting incoherently and riding about in disorder; no one could say what was happening. Some maintained that the Emperor was still fighting with what was left of his army, and that the barbarians had been put to flight. Others claimed that he had been killed or captured. Everyone had something different to report . . .

It was like an earthquake: the shouting, the sweat, the swift rushes of fear, the clouds of dust, and not least the hordes of Turks riding all around us. Depending on his speed, resolution and strength, each man sought safety in flight. The enemy followed in pursuit, killing some, capturing others and trampling yet others under their horses' hooves. It was a tragic sight, beyond any mourning or lamenting. What indeed could be more pitiable than to see the entire imperial army in flight, defeated and pursued by cruel and inhuman barbarians; the Emperor defenceless and surrounded by more of the same; the imperial tents, symbols of military might and sovereignty, taken over by men of such a kind; the whole Roman state overturned – and knowing that the Empire itself was on the verge of collapse?

Who survived? Effectively, those who took flight in time. We cannot blame the Armenians for doing so; they had little love at the best of times for the Greeks, who had conquered their country and were even now persecuting their families for the faith that they had always upheld. To the mercenaries we need feel less sympathetic; admittedly they had no emotional loyalty to the Empire, and they understandably resented the Emperor's discrimination against them, together with his unconcealed preference for his native troops. But they were under contract, their wages had been paid, and – though their conduct was probably no worse than that of other soldiers of fortune the world over – they might have shown a little more spirit than in fact they did. The only real villains were the 'levies of the nobility' who formed the rearguard, and their commander Andronicus Ducas. Their shameful flight was probably due to treachery rather than cowardice, and was not a jot the more excusable for that.

There was another survivor too: Romanus Diogenes himself. Left almost alone, he had refused to flee; he fought like a lion to the end. Only when his horse was killed under him and a wound in his hand made it no longer possible for him to hold his sword did he allow himself to be taken prisoner. His captors must have known who he was, but they gave him no special treatment. All night he lay among the wounded and dying. Only the following morning was he brought before the Sultan, dressed as a common soldier, and in chains.

Few chroniclers of the period, Greek or Islamic, have been able to resist giving an account of the interview that took place between the victorious Sultan and the defeated Emperor on the morning after the battle. What is surprising, however, is not the number of these accounts but their similarity. At first, we are told, Alp Arslan refused to believe that the exhausted captive who was flung at his feet was indeed the Emperor of the Romans; only when he had been formally identified by former Turkish envoys and by his fellow-prisoner Basilacius did the Sultan rise from his throne and, ordering Romanus to kiss the ground before him, plant his foot on his victim's neck.

It was a symbolic gesture, nothing more. He then immediately helped Romanus to his feet, bade him sit down at his side and assured him that he would be treated with all the respect due to his rank. For the next week the Emperor remained a guest in the Turkish camp, eating at the Sultan's table; never once did Alp Arslan show him anything but friendliness and courtesy – although he frequently condemned the faithlessness of those who had deserted him in his hour of need and, we are told, occasionally permitted himself a few gentle criticisms of Byzantine generalship. All this was, of course, in the highest tradition of Islamic chivalry; we are inevitably reminded of the similar stories told of Saladin a century later. But it was also sound policy on the part of the Sultan: how much better, after all, that Romanus should return safely to Constantinople and resume the throne than that it should be taken over by some inexperienced and headstrong young man of whom he would know nothing and who would think only of revenge.

Considering the circumstances, the peace terms were both merciful and moderate. The Sultan demanded no extensive territories – not even Armenia, to which he believed that he possessed at least as much right as did the Empire. All he asked was the surrender of Manzikert, Antioch, Edessa and Hieropolis, together with one of the Emperor's daughters as a bride for one of his own sons. There remained the question of a ransom. Alp Arslan first suggested that 10 million gold pieces might be appropriate; but when Romanus objected that since the fitting out of his great expedition the imperial treasury simply did not possess such a sum, the Sultan willingly reduced his demand to a million and a half, with a further 360,000 in annual tribute. He also took the point that the Emperor should return to Constantinople at the earliest possible moment; there was otherwise a very real danger that he might be dethroned in his absence, in which case his successor would be highly unlikely to recognize the validity of the agreement that had just been made. It was thus only a week after the battle that Romanus set out on his homeward journey; Alp Arslan rode with him on the first stage, and for the remainder granted him an escort of two Emirs and a hundred Mamelukes. He had left his capital as an Emperor; as an Emperor he would return.

Or so, at least, he hoped. His feelings were not however shared in Constantinople, where the news of the defeat had come as the second

shattering blow in this most catastrophic of years. The previous April –
just a month after Romanus had left for the East – the Normans under
Robert Guiscard had captured Bari. Since the days of Justinian Bari had
been capital of Byzantine Apulia and headquarters of the imperial army:
the largest, wealthiest and best defended of all the Greek cities of the
peninsula. By the time the siege had begun, it had also been the only one
still remaining under imperial control. The Bariots had resisted valiantly,
for no less than thirty-two months; but surrounded as they were by an
impenetrable blockade by land and sea, they finally had no choice but to
surrender. It was the end, after more than five centuries, of Byzantine
Italy.

The reports from Bari had, however, at least been clear; from
Manzikert, they were hopelessly confused, creating at the court of
Constantinople an atmosphere of uncertainty and indecision. On one
point only was everyone – with the possible exception of the Empress
herself – in unanimous agreement: that even if Romanus were alive and at
liberty he was now defeated and disgraced; there could be no question of
his being allowed to continue as *basileus*. But who was to take his place?
Some called for Eudocia to resume the supreme power that she had
wielded before her marriage; others favoured Michael, her son by
Constantine X – perhaps as a co-ruler with his younger brothers
Andronicus and Constantine; yet others saw in the Caesar John Ducas
(who now hurriedly returned from Bithynia, whither Romanus had
exiled him before his departure) the best hope for the Empire in this
moment of crisis. In the event, it was John who acted – though not,
ostensibly, on his own behalf. There can be no doubt that he coveted
the throne; on the other hand his own faction was not large enough to
give a direct attempt upon it any real hope of success. Fortunately his
nephew Michael was a weak-willed youth, with whom – once his
mother were out of the way – John could do as he liked. Fortunately
too he had the Varangian guard behind him. While the rest were still
debating what was best to be done, he divided it into two groups. One,
under the command of his recently-returned son Andronicus, charged
through the Palace proclaiming Michael Emperor; with the other he
marched straight to the Empress's apartments and arrested her.

It was all over quite quickly. The terrified Eudocia was exiled to a
church she had founded at the mouth of the Hellespont, where she was
shortly afterwards tonsured and compelled to take the veil. A similar
sentence was passed on Anna Dalassena, sister-in-law of the late Emperor

Isaac Comnenus, as a warning to the only other family in the capital from whom trouble might be expected.[1] Michael VII Ducas was crowned with due ceremony by the Patriarch in St Sophia. It remained only to deal with Romanus Diogenes.

Romanus's movements after his departure from the Seljuk camp are hard indeed to trace: our authorities are few, and tend more often than not to contradict each other. All that we can deduce with any certainty is that he somehow managed to gather together what remained of his once-great army, with the intention of marching on the capital. John Ducas was, however, ready for him. There seem to have been two battles: one near Dokeia (Tokat) against a force commanded by the Caesar's youngest son Constantine, and one near Adana in Cilicia in which Romanus found himself confronted with the general who had betrayed him at Manzikert, Andronicus Ducas. In both he was defeated. After the second he finally gave himself up to Andronicus, agreeing to renounce all claims to the throne and to retire to a monastery, and receiving in return a guarantee from the new Emperor – endorsed by the Archbishops of Chalcedon, Heraclea and Colonea – that no harm would come to him.

It could perhaps be argued that the decision of Andronicus to mount the ex-Emperor on a mule and to parade him in his degradation the 500-odd miles from Adana to Cotiaeum – the modern Kütahya – was not actually harmful, though it seems a curious interpretation of the terms of his undertaking. In the light of what happened afterwards, however, the question seems academic. Referring to the archbishops, Scylitzes writes:

Although they wished to help him, they were weak and impotent when cruel and harsh men took him and pitilessly, mercilessly, put out his eyes. Carried forth on a cheap beast of burden like a decaying corpse, his eyes gouged out and his face and head alive with worms, he lived on a few days in pain with a foul stench all about him until he gave up the ghost, being buried on the island of Proti where he had built a monastery.

He was given a rich burial by his wife, the Empress Eudocia, leaving memories of trials and misfortunes too terrible to be told. But in all his

---

1 Nicephorus Bryennius records that she was made the victim of a show trial, in which forged letters were produced to implicate her in a conspiracy to restore Romanus. Her action in suddenly producing from the folds of her gown an icon of Christ, and bidding those present behold the true judge of the proceedings, was applauded as a splendid theatrical gesture – but cut, we are told, no ice.

misfortunes he uttered no curse or blasphemy, continuing always to give thanks to God and bearing courageously whatever befell him.

Michael Psellus, who always detested Romanus and never loses an opportunity to denigrate him, predictably attempts to justify the blinding:

I am reluctant to describe a deed that should never have taken place; and yet, if I may alter my words slightly [*sic*], it was a deed that should unquestionably have taken place. On the one hand the scruples of religion, allied to a natural unwillingness to inflict pain, would forbid it; on the other, the political situation and the sudden changes of both parties made it absolutely necessary ... since the more enthusiastic element in the imperial council[1] feared that Diogenes might succeed in his conspiracies and once again cause the Emperor embarrassment.

Nor was that his last insult. A few days before his death in the summer of 1072, Romanus received a letter from his old enemy. It was couched in the friendliest terms, and congratulated him on his good fortune in losing his eyes – a sure sign that the Almighty had found him worthy of a higher light. As he lay in his final agony, the thought must have given him profound comfort.

The battle of Manzikert was the greatest disaster suffered by the Empire of Byzantium in the seven and a half centuries of its existence. The humiliation was bad enough, the performance of the imperial army having been characterized by a combination of treachery, panic and ignominious flight; the fate of the Emperor, too, was unparalleled since the capture of Valerian by the Persian King Shapur I in AD 260, before Constantinople was even thought of. The real tragedy, however, lay not in the battle itself but in its appalling epilogue. Had Romanus Diogenes been permitted to retain his throne, all would have been well: he would have observed the terms of the treaty he had made with his captors, and Alp Arslan – who (let it never be forgotten) had no intention of making outright war on the Empire, far less of conquering it – would have resumed his expedition against Fatimid Egypt. Even had Romanus been succeeded by an Emperor worthy of the name, the damage could easily have been contained: a Nicephorus Phocas or a John Tzimisces – let alone a Basil II – would have restored the status quo in a matter of months, and the Seljuks did not begin any systematic move into Anatolia

---

1 I.e., Caesar John Ducas. Psellus goes on to say that he gave the order for the blinding without consulting the Emperor Michael.

until the summer of 1073 – two years after the battle. By then they can hardly be blamed for doing so. Michael VII's refusal to accept the obligations of the treaty signed with Romanus gave them a legitimate motive for their action, while the chaos that reigned within the Empire and the collapse of the old defensive system based on military holdings ensured that they met with no resistance.

Thus it came about that tens of thousands of Turkoman tribesmen swarmed into Anatolia from the north-east, and that by 1080 or thereabouts the Seljuk Sultan Malik-Shah[1] controlled a broad tongue of territory covering perhaps 30,000 square miles and extending deep into the heartland: an area which, in recognition of its former history as part of the Roman Empire, he named the Sultanate of Rum. The Empire still retained western Asia Minor and its former Mediterranean and Black Sea coasts; but it had lost, at a single stroke, the source of a considerable portion of its grain and more than half its manpower. And it had done so not because of the superior fighting power of the Seljuk Turks, but as the result of its own inefficiency and short-sightedness. The battle through which it had suffered that loss had been directed against an unwilling enemy; it need never have been fought and could easily have been won. Even after defeat, its long-term consequences might have been avoided by judicious diplomacy. But those in power in Constantinople, led by Caesar John Ducas and inspired by the odious Michael Psellus, systematically refused to take the steps that were so obviously necessary. Blinkered by their own smug intellectualism and obsessive personal ambition, they made every mistake, threw away every opportunity offered to them. In doing so they martyred a courageous and upright man who, though no genius, was worth more than all of them put together and could, with their loyalty and support, have saved the situation; and they dealt the Byzantine Empire a blow from which it would never recover.

The reign of Michael VII continued as disastrously as it had begun. The year after Manzikert saw a serious uprising in Bulgaria as a result of which a certain Constantine Bodin, son of Prince Michael of Zeta,[2] had

---

1 The son of Alp Arslan who had been physically attacked by one of his junior commanders and had died of his wounds on 24 November 1072 at the age of forty-one.

2 Formerly known as Dioclea and theoretically a semi-independent principality within the Empire, Zeta had broken away in about 1035 and had refused to recognize Byzantine overlordship – the first Slav state in the Balkans to do so after the death of Basil II.

been crowned Tsar in the city of Prizren. Thanks largely to the efforts of Nicephorus Bryennius the Empire eventually managed to reimpose control, but at a heavy cost; it was clear that further outbreaks could not be long delayed. Meanwhile Rome was steadily extending its influence beyond the Adriatic, in the lands over which Basil II had formerly claimed suzerainty. In 1075 the legates of Pope Gregory VII crowned a vassal named Demetrius Zvonimir King of Croatia, and in 1077 there came a further blow for Byzantium when Michael of Zeta also received a papal coronation. As the imperial hold weakened, the Pechenegs and Hungarians became increasingly troublesome. Thus, within half a century of Basil's death, his whole magnificent achievement in the Balkans was already crumbling away.

At home the situation was very little better. Inflation was rising, to the point where a gold *nomisma* would no longer buy a whole measure of wheat, but only three-quarters. Before long the Emperor became known as Michael Parapinaces, or 'Minus-a-quarter', a nickname which stuck with him until his death. Weak and feckless as always, he also allowed himself to fall under the influence of a sinister new arrival on the political scene, the eunuch Nicephoritzes, who took over the effective government of the Empire, cast aside Psellus and the Caesar John and rapidly became the same sort of power in the capital that John the Orphanotrophus had been forty years before. Determined still further to strengthen the centralized bureaucracy of the State, he went further than any of his predecessors by turning the corn trade into a government monopoly, building a vast official granary at the port of Rhaedestum on the Marmara at which all corn shipped to the capital was to be stored until resale. The attempt, predictably enough, proved yet another disaster. The landed proprietors in those areas of Anatolia still in imperial control sustained heavy losses, while the urban consumers found that Nicephoritzes was less interested in ensuring adequate supplies than in increasing state revenues by screwing up the price of bread. This in turn led to a general increase in prices and a further twist of the inflationary spiral.

Then there were the military insurrections. The first of these was inspired by the leader of the Norman mercenaries, a soldier of fortune named Roussel of Bailleul. His fighting record was not unblemished, since he had been involved with Joseph Tarchaniotes in the mysterious events at Khelat; somehow, however, he had charmed his way back into imperial favour – it sometimes seemed that anyone who had

betrayed Romanus Diogenes was by definition a friend of his successor
– and had later been sent with a mixed force of Norman and Frankish
cavalry against Seljuk marauders in Anatolia. Once deep in Turkish-
controlled territory he had yet again betrayed his trust and, with 300 loyal
followers, had set up a self-declared independent Norman state on the
south Italian pattern. Had Michael VII and his advisers thought for a
moment, they would surely have realized that, compared with the
Turkish tide that threatened to engulf them, Roussel was little more
than a mild irritant; instead, so determined were they to liquidate him
that they turned to the Seljuks for aid, offering them in return the
formal cession of territories that they already held and thus immeasurably
strengthening their hold on Asia Minor. Even then Roussel managed to
escape; only when an army was sent out from Constantinople under the
command of the ablest of the Empire's younger generals, Alexius
Comnenus, was he hunted down and brought back in chains to the
capital.

But Alexius Comnenus could not be everywhere at once and, owing
to the neglect of the army during the previous half-century, experienced
generals were in short supply; thus it was that, a year or two later, when
the Empire was faced with two new and far more serious insurrections,
one in the East and one in the West, Roussel was suddenly released from
his captivity and found himself fighting at Alexius's side against the two
new pretenders to the imperial throne. The first of these was Nicephorus
Bryennius who, having fought with distinction at Manzikert, had been
installed as Governor (*dux*) of Dyrrachium, where he had been principally
responsible for putting down the Slav revolt of 1072. No longer
prepared to accept the incompetence of Michael Parapinaces and his
government – and having learnt that the eunuch Nicephoritzes had
listed him for assassination – he raised the standard of revolt in
November 1077 and marched to his native city of Adrianople, where he
was acclaimed *basileus*. A week later he and his army were beneath the
walls of Constantinople.

His insurrection might well have succeeded had it not been for
another, almost simultaneous, rising in the East. Its leader was the
strategos of the Anatolikon Theme, Nicephorus Botaneiates. He has made
one previous, passing appearance in this story as a prospective husband
for the Empress Eudocia, before the arrival of Romanus Diogenes
banished the idea from her mind. Presumably because he had doubts
about his loyalty, Romanus had deliberately excluded Botaneiates from

the Manzikert expedition; the general had returned to his extensive estates in Anatolia, where he had received his present appointment soon after Michael's accession; but now he too – probably, like Bryennius, for the highest motives – took up arms against the Emperor.

Of the two rival claimants, Bryennius was first in the field; Botaneiates was, however, of far nobler birth, being a kinsman of the Phocas and thus a member of the old military aristocracy; he was also the stronger, particularly since he had managed to suborn the Seljuk forces hired by Michael to oppose him. Neither made a direct attack on Constantinople, knowing full well from secret contacts within the capital that popular discontent over rising prices would soon bring matters to a head – which, in March 1078, it did. Riots broke out in every corner of the city. Many government buildings were burnt to the ground, among them Nicephoritzes's new granary. The eunuch himself was seized by the mob and tortured to death. The miserable Michael, lucky to escape with his life, quickly abdicated and withdrew to the Studium, and on 24 March Nicephorus Botaneiates entered Constantinople in triumph. His rival Bryennius was captured and blinded.

It was an inauspicious start to the new reign. Botaneiates had been a competent general, but he knew nothing of politics or statesmanship; besides, he was getting old – he was already well into his seventies – and his bid for the throne, successful as it had been, had used up much of his remaining strength. Utterly incapable of coping with the crisis he had inherited, he could do little but preside, helpless, over the further disintegration of the Empire, during which one revolt followed another and the State drifted further and further into anarchy. The old party of the civil bureaucracy had collapsed with the murder of Nicephoritzes, and with it the authority of the Senate; all that was left to the Byzantines was to pray that of the several military commanders now struggling for power, one might establish himself above the rest; and that that man might prove himself a leader capable of putting an end to the chaos.

Three years later – in the nick of time – their prayer was answered; and answered more completely than anyone could have dared to hope. The pathetic old Botaneiates abdicated in his turn in favour of an aristocratic young general who, coming to the throne on Easter Day 1081, was to reign for the next thirty-seven years, giving the Empire the stability that it so desperately needed and governing it with a firm and steady hand. That general was Alexius Comnenus, nephew of Isaac I and father of the celebrated Anna Comnena, who was to make him the subject of one of the most wholly enjoyable of all medieval biographies. Not even Alexius could undo the damage done by the battle of Manzikert; that, alas, was past repair. But he could, and did, restore to Byzantium its reputation and its good name among nations, thus preparing it to play its part in the great drama that was to begin to unfold even before the end of that turbulent century: the Crusades.

List of Emperors

1042–55	Constantine IX Monomachus	1046–56	Henry III
1055–6	Theodora		
1056–7	Michael VI		
1057–9	Isaac I Comnenus		
1059–67	Constantine X Ducas		
1068–71	Romanus IV Diogenes		
1071–8	Michael VII Ducas		
1078–81	Nicephorus III Botaneiates		
1081–1118	Alexius I Comnenus	1084–1105	Henry IV

List of Muslim Sultans

List of Patriarchs

784–806	Tarasius	970–4	Basil the Scamandrian
806–15	Nicephorus I	974–9	Antony III of the Stu-
815–21	Theodotus Cassiteras		dium
821–37	Antony I Cassimatas	979–91	Nicholas II
837–43	John the Grammarian		Chrysoberges
843–7	Methodius I		
847–58	Ignatius		
858–67	Photius		
867–77	Ignatius (again)	996–8	Sisinnius II
877–86	Photius (again)	1001–19	Sergius II
886–93	Stephen I	1019–25	Eustatius
893–901	Antony II Cauleas	1025–43	Alexis of the Studium
901–7	Nicholas I Mysticus	1043–58	Michael I Cerularius
907–12	Euthymius I	1059–63	Constantine III
912–25	Nicholas I Mysticus		Likhoudes
	(again)	1064–75	John VIII Xiphilinus
925–7	Stephen II	1075–81	Cosmas I
927–31	Tryphonlus	1081–4	Eustratius Garidas
931–56	Theophylact	1084–1111	Nicholas III the
956–70	Polyeuctus		Grammarian

List of Popes

795–816	Leo III	963–5	Leo VIII
816–17	Stephen IV (V)	964–6	Benedict V
817–24	Paschal I	965–72	John XIII
824–7	Eugenius II	973–4	Benedict VI
827	Valentine	[974, 984–5	Boniface VII]
827–44	Gregory IV		
[844	John]	974–83	Benedict VII
844–7	Sergius II	983–4	John XIV
847–55	Leo IV	985–96	John XV
855–8	Benedict III	996–9	Gregory V
[855	Anastasius]	[997–8	John XVI]
858–67	Nicholas I	999–1003	Silvester II
867–72	Hadrian II	1003	John XVII
872–82	John VIII	1004–9	John XVIII
882–4	Marinus I	1009–12	Sergius IV
884–5	Hadrian III	1012–24	Benedict VIII
885–91	Stephen V (VI)	[1012	Gregory]
891–6	Formosus	1024–32	John XIX
896	Boniface VI	1032–44	Benedict IX
896–7	Stephen VI (VII)	1045–6	Gregory VI
897	Romanus	1046–7	Clement II
897	Theodore II	1047–8	Benedict IX
898–900	John IX	1048	Damasus II
900–3	Benedict IV	1049–54	Leo IX
903	Leo V	1055–7	Victor II
[903–4	Christopher]	1057–8	Stephen IX (X)
904–11	Sergius III	[1058–9	Benedict X]
911–13	Anastasius III	1059–61	Nicholas II
913–14	Lando	1061–73	Alexander II
914–28	John X	[1061–72	Honorius II]
928	Leo VI	1073–85	Gregory VII

928–31   Stephen VII (VIII)   [1080, ⎫
931–5   John XI   1084– ⎬ Clement III]
936–9   Leo VII   1100   ⎭
939–42   Stephen VIII (IX)   1086–7   Victor III
942–6   Marinus II   1088–99 Urban II
946–55   Agapetus II   1099–1118 Paschal II
955–64   John XII

Bibliography

I. Original Sources

COLLECTIONS OF SOURCES

Byzantion. Revue Internationale des Etudes Byzantines. Paris and Liège 1924–9; Paris and Brussels 1930; Brussels etc. 1931– . (B.)

Corpus Scriptorum Ecclesiasticorum Latinorum. 57 vols. Vienna 1866– (incomplete). (C.S.E.L.)

Corpus Scriptorum Historiae Byzantinae. Bonn 1828– (incomplete). (C.S.H.B.)

COUSIN, L. *Histoire de Constantinople.* Fr. trans. 8 vols. Paris 1685. (C.H.C.)

DE BOOR, C. (Ed.) *Opuscula Historica.* Leipzig 1880. (B.O.H.)

HOARE, F. R. *The Western Fathers.* Eng. trans. London 1954. (H.W.F.)

MAI, Cardinal A. (Ed.) *Novae Patrum Bibliothecae.* 10 vols. Rome 1844–1905. (M.N.P.B.)

MIGNE, J. P. *Patrologia Graeca.* 161 vols. Paris 1857–66. (M.P.G.)

— *Patrologia Latina.* 221 vols. Paris 1844–55. (M.P.L.)

Monumenta Germaniae Historica. Eds. G. H. Pertz, T. Mommsen *et al.* Hanover 1826– (in progress). (M.G.H.)

MULLER, C. I. T. *Fragmenta Historicorum Graecorum.* 5 vols. Paris 1841–83. (M.F.H.G.)

MURATORI, L. A. *Rerum Italicarum Scriptores.* 25 vols. Milan 1723–51. (M.R.I.S.)

Nicene and Post-Nicene Fathers, Library of the. 2nd ser. 14 vols. with trans. Oxford 1890–1900. (N.P.N.F.)

Revue des Etudes Grecques. Paris 1888– . (R.E.G.)

Revue Historique. (R.H.)

369

INDIVIDUAL SOURCES

ARISTAKES, of Lastivert. *History of Armenia*. Fr. trans. by M. Canard and Haig Berberian. *Editions de Byzantion*, Brussels 1973.

ATTALEIATES, Michael. *Historia*. C.S.H.B., Vol. 50. Partial Fr. trans. by H. Grégoire, *Byzantinische Zeitschrift*, Vol. 28 (1958), and E. Janssens, *Annuaire de l'Institut de Philologie et d'Histoire Orientales et Slaves*, Vol. 20, 1968–72.

BRYENNIUS, Nicephorus. *Histories*. C.S.H.B., Vol. 26. Fr. trans. by H. Grégoire. B., Vol. 23, 1953.

CECAUMENUS, *Strategicon*. Ed. W. Wassiliewsky and V. Jernstedt. St Petersburg 1896.

CEDRENUS, Georgius. *Compendium Historiarum*. C.S.H.B.; M.P.G., Vols. 121–2.

— *Synopsis Historiarum* (containing John Scylitzes and Scylitzes Continuatus). C.S.H.B.; M.P.G., Vols. 121–2.

CONSTANTINE VII PORPHYROGENITUS. *De Administrando Imperio*. Gk text with Eng. trans. by R. J. H. Jenkins. Washington, DC 1969.

— Commentary, by R. J. H. Jenkins, London 1962.

— *De Ceremoniis Aulae Byzantinae*. Ed. and Ger. trans. by J. J. Reiske. C.S.H.B.

—*Narratio de Imagine Edessena*. M.P.G., Vol. 113.

GENESIUS, Joseph. *Regna*. Ed. C. Lachmann. C.S.H.B.

GLYCAS, M. *Chronicon*. Ed. I. Bekker. C.S.H.B.

IGNATIUS, Diaconus. *Vita Nicephori Patriarchae*. B.O.H.

LEO, Diaconus. *Historia*. C.S.H.B.; M.P.G., Vol. 117.

LEO, Grammaticus. *Chronographia*. Ed. I. Bekker. C.S.H.B.; M.P.G., Vol. 108.

Liber Pontificalis. De Gestis Romanorum Pontificum. Text, intro. and comm. by L. Duchesne. 2 vols. Paris 1886–92 (reprint, Paris 1955).

LIUDPRAND, Bishop of Cremona. *Opera*. Ed. I. Bekker. Hanover 1915. Eng. trans. by F. A. Wright, London 1930.

MANASSES, Constantine. *Compendium Chronicum*. C.S.H.B.; M.P.G., Vol. 127.

MATTHEW, of Edessa. *Chronicle*. Fr. trans. by E. Dulaurier. Paris 1858.

MICHAEL, Monk of the Studium. *Vita etc. S. Theodori abb. mon. Studii*. M.N.P.B., Vol. 6.

MICHAEL, the Syrian. *Chronicle*. Ed. with Fr. trans. by J. B. Chabot. Paris 1905–6.

NESTOR. *Chronique dite de Nestor*. Ed. and Fr. trans. by L. Léger. Paris 1884.

NICHOLAS I, Pope. *Epistolae*. M.P.L., Vol. 119.

NICHOLAS MYSTICUS, Patriarch. *Epistolae*. M.P.G., Vol. 111.

PAUL, Diaconus. *Historia Langobardorum*. M.G.H. Scriptores, Vols. 2, 12. Eng. trans. by W. C. Foulke, Philadelphia 1905.

PETER DAMIAN, St. *Opuscula*. M.P.L., Vol. 145.

PHOTIUS, Patriarch of Constantinople. *Epistolae*. M.P.G., Vol. 102.

— *Homilies. The Homilies of Photius*. Eng. trans., intro. and comm. by C. Mango. Harvard 1958.

PSELLUS, Michael. *Chronographia*. Eng. trans. by E. R. A. Sewter, 1953. Fr. trans. by E. Renauld. 2 vols. Paris 1926.

SCRIPTOR INCERTUS. *De Leone Armenio*. C.S.H.B.

SCYLITZES, John. See CEDRENUS.

SIMEON, Magister, or Metaphrastes. *Chronicon*. M.P.G., Vols. 109, 113–16.

— *Vita Theodori Grapti*. M.P.G., Vol. 116.

SIMEON LOGOTHETES. Survives in various forms, incl. Leo, Grammaticus, *q.v.*

THEODORE, of the Studium, St. *Epistolae*. M.P.G., Vol. 99.

THEODOSIUS, Melitenus. *Chronicon*. Ed. G. L. F. Tafel. Munich 1859.

THEOPHANES, St (called Isaacius). *Chronographia*. Ed. C. de Boor. 2 vols. Leipzig 1883 (reprinted Hildesheim 1963). Also in M.P.G., Vols. 108–9.

THEOPHANES Continuatus. *Chronographia*. Ed. I. Bekker. C.S.H.B.; M.P.G., Vol. 109.

Vita Ignatii Patriarchae. M.P.G., Vol. 105.

Vita Nicholai Papae. M.P.L., Vol. 119.

Vita Sancti Euthymii. Ed. with Eng. trans. by P. Karlin-Hayter. B., Vols. 25–7, 1955–7.

YAHYA, of Antioch. *History*. Partial Fr. trans. by M. Canard, in Vasiliev, A. A., *Byzance et les Arabes* (*q.v.*), II, ii.

ZONARAS, Joannes. *Annales*. Ed. L. Dindorf, 6 vols. Leipzig 1868–75. Also in M.P.G., Vols. 134–5.

II. Modern Works

ADONTZ, N. *L'Age et l'Origine de l'Empereur Basile I.* B., Vols. 8–9, 1933–4.

ALEXANDER, P. J. *The Patriarch Nicephorus of Constantinople.* Oxford 1958.

ALMEDINGEN, E. M. *Charlemagne.* London 1968.

BAYNES, N. H. *Byzantine Studies and Other Essays.* London 1955.

The Blue Guide to Istanbul. Ed. J. Freely. 2nd ed. London and New York 1987.

The Blue Guide to Turkey (The Aegean and Mediterranean Coasts). Ed. B. McDonagh. London and New York 1989.

BRÉHIER, L. *La Querelle des Images.* Paris 1904.

BURY, J. B. *The Imperial Administrative System in the Ninth Century.* British Academy, Supplemental Papers, 1911.

— *A History of the Later Roman Empire, 802–867.* London 1912.

Cambridge Medieval History. Esp. Vol. IV, *The Byzantine Empire, 717–1453.* New edition, ed. J. M. Hussey. 2 vols. Cambridge 1966–7.

CAHEN, C. *La Campagne de Manzikert d'après les Sources Musselmanes.* B., Vol. 9, 1934.

— *La Première Pénétration Turque en Asie-Mineur.* B., Vol. 18, 1948.

— *Pre-Ottoman Turkey.* Trans. J. Jones-Williams, New York 1968.

CANARD, M. 'La Campagne Arménienne du Sultan Salguqide [*sic*], Alp Arslan et la Prise d'Ani en 1064'. *Revue des Etudes Arméniennes*, II, Paris 1965.

COBHAM, C. D. *The Patriarchs of Constantinople.* Cambridge 1911.

DELEHAYE, H. *Les Saints Stylites.* Brussels and Paris 1923.

Dictionnaire d'Histoire et de Géographie Ecclésiastiques. Eds. A. Baudrillart, R. Aubert and others. Paris 1912–   (in progress).

Dictionnaire de Théologie Catholique. 15 vols. in 30. Paris 1909–50 (with supplements).

DIEHL, C. *Figures Byzantines.* 1st ser., Paris 1906; 2nd ser., Paris 1913.

— *Histoire de l'Empire Byzantin.* Paris 1918.

— *Choses et Gens de Byzance.* Paris 1926.

DVORNIK, F. *The Photian Schism: History and Legend.* Cambridge 1948.

EBERSOLT, J. *Le Grand Palais de Constantinople et le Livre des Cérémonies.* Paris 1910.

Enciclopedia Italiana. 36 vols. 1929–39 (with later appendices).

Encyclopaedia Britannica. 11th ed. 29 vols. Cambridge 1910–11.

— 15th ed. 30 vols. University of Chicago 1974.

Encyclopaedia of Islam. 4 vols. Leiden, London 1913–34. (New edition in progress, 1960– .)

FINLAY, G. *History of Greece, 146 BC to AD 1864*. New ed. Ed. H. F. Tozer. 8 vols. 1877.

FLICHE, A. and MARTIN, V. *Histoire de l'Eglise, depuis les Origines jusqu'à nos Jours*. Paris 1934.

FRENCH, R. M. *The Eastern Orthodox Church*. London and New York 1951.

FRIENDLY, A. *The Dreadful Day: The Battle of Manzikert, 1071*. London 1981.

FULLER, J. F. C. *The Decisive Battles of the Western World*. Vol. 1. London 1954.

GARDNER, A. *Theodore of Studium, his Life and Times*. London 1905.

GFRORER, A. F. *Byzantinische Geschichten*. Ed. J. B. Weiss. 3 vols. Graz 1872–7.

GIBBON, E. *The History of the Decline and Fall of the Roman Empire*. 7 vols. Ed. J. B. Bury. London 1896.

GIUSTINIANI, H. *The History of Chios*. Cambridge 1943.

GRÉGOIRE, H. *Etudes sur le 9ᵉ. Siècle*. B., Vol. 8. 1933.

— *Etudes sur l'Epopée Byzantine*. R.E.G., Vol. 46. 1933.

GROSVENOR, E. A. *Constantinople*. 2 vols. Boston 1895.

GRUMEL, V. *La Chronologie*. (Vol. I of *Traité des Etudes Byzantines*, ed. P. Lemerle. Paris 1958.)

HARNACK, T. G. A. *History of Dogma*. Eng. trans. London 1899.

HAUSSIG, H. W. *History of Byzantine Civilisation*. Trans. J. M. Hussey. London 1971.

HEFELE, C. J. von. *Histoire des Conciles d'après les Documents Originaux*. Fr. trans. from Ger. by H. Leclercq. 5 vols. in 10. Paris 1907–13.

HILL, Sir George. *A History of Cyprus*. 3 vols. Cambridge 1913.

HITTI, P. K. *History of the Arabs*. 3rd ed. New York 1951.

JANIN, R. *Constantinople Byzantine*. Paris 1950.

JENKINS, R. *Byzantium: The Imperial Centuries, AD 610–1071*. London 1966.

— *The Byzantine Empire on the Eve of the Crusades*. London 1953.

KARLIN-HAYTER, P. 'The Emperor Alexander's Bad Name'. *Speculum*, Vol. 44. 1969.

LETHABY, W. R. and SWAINSON, H. *The Church of Sancta Sophia, Constantinople: a Study of Byzantine Building*. London 1894.

MAINSTONE, R. J. *Hagia Sophia: Architecture, Structure and Liturgy of Justinian's Great Church*. London 1988.

MANGO, C. *The Homilies of Photius, Patriarch of Constantinople*. Eng. trans., intro. and comm. Harvard 1958.

— *The Mosaics of St Sophia at Istanbul*. Washington (Dumbarton Oaks) 1962.

MANN, H. K. *The Lives of the Popes in the Middle Ages*. 18 vols. London 1902–32.

MARIN, E. *Les Moines de Constantinople*. Paris 1897.

MARTIN, E. J. *A History of the Iconoclastic Controversy*. London 1930.

MINNS, E. H. 'St Cyril Really Knew Hebrew'. In *Mélanges Publiés en l'Honneur de M. Paul Boyer*, Paris 1925. (London Library Pamphlets, Vol. 2859.)

NEANDER, A. *General History of the Christian Religion and Church*. 9 vols. Eng. trans. London 1876.

New Catholic Encyclopedia. Washington, DC 1967.

NORWICH, J. J. *The Normans in the South*. London 1967.

— *A History of Venice: Vol. I, The Rise to Empire*. London 1977.

— *Byzantium: The Early Centuries*. London 1988.

OBOLENSKY, D. *The Byzantine Commonwealth*. London 1971.

OCKLEY, S. *History of the Saracens*. 4th ed. London 1847.

OIKONOMIDES, N. 'Leo VI and the Narthex Mosaic at St Sophia'. *Dumbarton Oaks Papers*, Vol. 30. 1976.

OMAN, C. W. C. *The Byzantine Empire*. London 1897.

OSTROGORSKY, G. *History of the Byzantine State*. Trans. J. Hussey. 2nd ed. Oxford 1968.

RAMBAUD, A. *L'Empire Grec au Dixième Siècle: Constantin Porphyrogénète*. Paris 1870.

RAMSAY, Sir William. *The Historical Geography of Asia Minor*. R.G.S. Supplementary Papers, Vol. IV. 1890.

RUNCIMAN, Sir Steven. *A History of the First Bulgarian Empire*. London 1930.

— *The Eastern Schism: A Study of the Papacy and the Eastern Churches during the 11th and 12th Centuries*. Oxford 1955.

— *The Emperor Romanus Lecapenus and his Reign*. 2nd ed. Cambridge 1963.

SCHLUMBERGER, G. *Un Empereur Byzantin au Dixième Siècle: Nicéphore Phocas*. Paris 1890.

— *L'Epopée Byzantine à la fin du Dixième Siècle*. Vol. I. Paris 1896.

BIBLIOGRAPHY

SEGAL, J. B. *Edessa, 'The Blessed City'*. Oxford 1970.

SMITH, W. and WACE, H. *Dictionary of Christian Biography*. 4 vols. London 1877–87.

SUMNER-BOYD, H. and FREELY, J. *Strolling through Istanbul*. Istanbul 1972.

SWIFT, E. A. *Hagia Sophia*. New York 1940.

TOYNBEE, A. *Constantine Porphyrogenitus and his World*. London 1973.

VAN DER MEER, F. *Atlas of Western Civilisation*. Trans. T. A. Birrell. Amsterdam 1954.

— and MOHRMANN, C. *Atlas of the Early Christian World*. Trans. M. F. Hedlund and H. H. Rowley. London 1958.

VASILIEV, A. A. *Byzance et les Arabes*. Fr. ed. prepared by H. Grégoire and M. Canard. Vol. I: *La Dynastie d'Amorium, 820–867*. Brussels 1935. Vol. II: *La Dynastie Macédonienne, 867–959*. Brussels 1950.

— *History of the Byzantine Empire, 324–1453*. Madison, Wisconsin 1952.

VOGT, A. *Basile Ier et la Civilisation Byzantine à la Fin du Onzième Siècle*. Paris 1908.

— 'La Jeunesse de Léon VI le Sage.' *Revue Historique*, Vol. clxxiv. 1934.

VRYONIS, S. *Byzantium and Europe*. London 1967.

— *The Decline of Medieval Hellenism in Asia Minor and the Process of Islamization from the Seventh through the Fifteenth Century*. Los Angeles, 1971

WHELER BUSH, R. *St Athanasias: His Life and Times*. London 1888.

Index